From Mr. Leo Helmreich and
Mark Helmreich;

To: Mr. and Mrs. Yaakov Gross;

With best wishes for health,
happiness, and success.

William B. Helmreich

The World of the Yeshiva

An Intimate Portrait of Orthodox Jewry

The World of the Yeshiva

An Intimate Portrait of Orthodox Jewry

William B. Helmreich

THE FREE PRESS
A Division of Macmillan Publishing Co., Inc.
NEW YORK

Collier Macmillan Publishers
LONDON

The Free Press
A Division of Macmillan Publishing Co., Inc.
866 Third Avenue, New York, N.Y. 10022

Collier Macmillan Canada, Inc.

Printed in the United States of America

printing number

1   2   3   4   5   6   7   8   9   10

Library of Congress Cataloging in Publication Data

Helmreich, William B.
    The world of the yeshiva.

    Bibliography: p.
    Includes index.
    1. Rabbinical seminaries—United States. 2. Orthodox
Judaism—United States. 3. Judaism—Study and teaching
(Higher)—United States. I. Title.
BM75.H44   296′.07′1173   81-67440
ISBN 0-02-914640-2   AACR2

To
Leo and Sally Helmreich
and
Harry and Dorothy Gewirtz

Contents

Preface

It is not your duty to complete the task,
but you are not free to desist from it.

Sayings of the Fathers 2:21

IT IS 10:15 P.M. and the station is almost deserted. At the far end of the platform, a tall, thin, sallow man in his mid-twenties stands alone, a somewhat battered yet sturdy suitcase at his side. He is wearing a dark jacket and pants with an open-necked white shirt. As the train pulls in he closes the book he has been reading and lightly kisses its cover. Adjusting his black hat, he enters the first car and quickly finds a seat in an unoccupied compartment.

Again opening his book, a Hebrew commentary on the Bible, he thinks briefly about his destination, New York City. It is a week before Passover and he is returning home to be with his family for the holiday. He has not seen them in almost six months although he lives but a few hours away from them. How will they react, he wonders, when he tells them that he wants to wait one more year before looking for a job? "Seven years is enough," his father had written him. "It's time to think about a career." But for Eliezer looking for a job can wait. He has, after all, far more important things on his mind.

Eliezer is an Orthodox Jew, a member of that segment of the Jewish community which views the 613 commandments of the Torah, or Old Testament, as divinely inspired laws to be followed completely and without question. According to most estimates, there are approximately 500,000 Jews in America today who identify themselves as Orthodox. Many came here from Europe in the aftermath of World War II determined to rebuild their way of life and in the last forty years they have established a network of synagogues, schools, and other organizations that has made them a powerful force in American Jewish life.

ix

Moreover, the way of life followed by the Orthodox has become increasingly attractive in recent years to thousands of previously unaffiliated young Jews who are becoming religiously observant as a way of giving direction and purpose to their lives.

Eliezer, however, is far more than simply a part of this community. He is a member of a most remarkable and unique institution whose members constitute an elite of sorts. He is one of thousands of young Orthodox Jews who have given up everything in life so that they might study day and night in a post–high school, or advanced yeshiva, a religious institution whose history goes back literally thousands of years. Here he wakes up every morning at the crack of dawn and, after saying his morning prayers, begins a day of intensive study of the Talmud, a 63-volume work dealing with Jewish laws, traditions, and history. As he pores over the ancient texts, the outside world and its concerns seem far away. He is not interested in the things that are important to most Americans of his age. For him what matters most is reaching a certain level of holiness through deep understanding and knowledge of the teachings of the faith.

While the central activities of the ''yeshiva'' (from the Hebrew root verb ''to sit'') are intellectual, those who walk through its doors do far more than study. They lead a life so different from that prevailing in the larger society as to be scarcely imaginable. Although no gates slam shut, no iron bars exist, and no guards stand watch, those who become members of the yeshiva community join a world within the world, a closed society governed by special rules that has its own value system. This is especially true of those yeshivas where most of the students live on the grounds of the institution. Activities such as attending movies, social dating, trips to the beach, and so on are rigidly proscribed and contact with those who are not Orthodox Jews is severely limited.

That yeshivas have been in existence for centuries would probably be enough to justify a careful examination of them. After all, how many social institutions can lay claim to having survived for 2,000 years? Even more fascinating, is that they have not only survived but are flourishing and growing more numerous year by year. Moreover, this phenomenon is occurring in a society where opportunities for Jews are virtually unlimited.

It was not always so. Until World War II, advanced yeshivas were few in number. Even among the strictly observant the idea of studying in such institutions beyond high school or even elementary school found little acceptance. Parents sent their children to a lower level yeshiva so that they might acquire the basics of the religion and absorb other aspects of Jewish culture. They did not, as a rule, see any need to do more. Those who did attend the handful of advanced yeshivas that existed then were either extremely motivated or came from homes where the tradition of talmudic study had somehow been preserved intact from the Eastern European communities in which it had originated.

The outbreak of World War II had a lasting impact on the development of Jewish education in America. With it, a thousand-year-old culture that had existed in Europe came to an abrupt and tragic end for its Jewish communities. Millions of Jews were slaughtered, especially in Eastern Europe, the home of the advanced yeshivas, and only those fortunate enough to have left in time, or lucky enough to have survived the Holocaust, remained. Among this group were the leaders of numerous European yeshivas, most of which were in Lithuania, who came to the United States and founded institutions or academies of higher learning modeled after their European predecessors.

These leaders, or *rosh yeshivas,* as they are commonly known, were successful beyond their wildest dreams. Supported by a large number of devout immigrants who arrived in the postwar period, they went about rebuilding their institutions with a strength and energy that was remarkable for a community which had so recently undergone tremendous suffering at the hands of the Nazis. New yeshiva day schools were begun to meet the needs of this population, and the number of such institutions quadrupled in just a few years. Although this book is concerned almost solely with the advanced yeshivas, this was an important development for them too because the lower level yeshivas taught the basics of Judaism, thereby preparing youngsters for more serious study when they became older.

Today, thirty-five years later, advanced, "Lithuanian-style" yeshivas are solidly entrenched in America. There are between fifty and sixty such institutions, of which about twenty might be called "major" schools in terms of either numbers of students or the institution's influence in the community. The other yeshivas tend to be smaller; some have as few as ten or fifteen students. Nevertheless, if they have a teacher, or *rebbe,* with a classroom, and a program of study, they are legitimate, functioning yeshivas. The combined enrollment of these schools is estimated at about 5,000 students.

Generally speaking, an advanced yeshiva, or *yeshiva gedola,* is a school with an intensive program of Talmud study whose student body consists largely of young men who have graduated from high school and are seventeen years of age or older. A number of such yeshivas have preparatory high schools attached to them. In such cases there may be a few precocious individuals who are permitted to enter the *yeshiva gedola* for advanced studies while still seniors or juniors in the secular division of the high school. At the high school level, the religious studies division is known as the *mesivta;* at the post–high school level it is called the *beis medrash.* The *beis medrash* is also the term for the large room in which the students prepare for class or review their teachers' lectures.

The yeshiva is not merely an institution where Orthodox rabbis are ordained. In fact, many students who enroll do not become practicing rabbis or, for that matter, teachers in religious schools. They are more likely to enter accounting, law, business, or other secular fields. This is entirely consistent with the goals of the yeshiva since its primary purpose is to produce pious and God-fearing individuals who are well versed in the laws and customs of the Jewish faith.

Structurally and administratively, yeshivas resemble universities in many ways. They have ''campuses'' that include libraries, study halls, cafeterias, classrooms, administrative offices, and, in many instances, dormitories. There are professors of Talmud, known as *rebbes,* a ''president'' known as the *rosh yeshiva,* a dean of men, called a *mashgiach,* and, of course, students. The yeshiva is a federally accredited institution of higher learning and is therefore eligible for various types of government aid such as Work-Study and Basic Education Opportunity Grants (BEOG). Unlike most universities, students do not take a specific number of courses leading to a degree. Rather, they study Talmud in the yeshiva to acquire knowledge for its own sake and to fulfill what they view as a heavenly mandate to delve into the Torah. The Talmud, which is an elaboration of the laws of the Torah, is regarded by Orthodox Jews as part of the Oral Tradition given to Moses by God on Mount Sinai.

Written primarily in Aramaic, the complexities and intricacies of the Talmud are such that achieving complete mastery over it is almost impossible for most students. Instead, those in the yeshiva devote their time to mastering as much as possible while recognizing their limitations. There is no fixed number of years that one spends in a yeshiva. Some stay only a year or two while others remain for ten or more. The decision on how long depends on many factors including the person's ability, desire, and financial means.

In the yeshiva's eyes, length of stay is not as important as what happens to the individual *after* he leaves. If he devotes his life to

talmudic study, even on a part-time basis, then the institution feels it
has succeeded in its efforts to instill in him a love for and commitment
to learning. In fact, there are today thousands of persons in the United
States who study Talmud for one, two, even three or four hours daily
while holding down full-time jobs. It is how they choose to spend most
of their spare time. They generally study together with others, perhaps
during their lunch hour at the office, or at 7:00 A.M. before leaving
their home, immediately after they have finished saying their morning
prayers.

Those who attend such yeshivas frequently come from homes
where the parents are themselves observant Jews. Their decision to
enroll in an advanced yeshiva is essentially a voluntary one, though
they have no doubt been strongly influenced by their upbringing. The
majority have gone to elementary and high school yeshivas, though occasionally students without such backgrounds manage to adapt to the
highly demanding program.

Why are thousands of youths of college age willing to spend the
most active years of their lives absorbed in the study of codes of law that
appear irrelevant even to many of their coreligionists? How can we account for the vitality of these institutions, and what can they tell us
about the survival of the Jewish people and the resurgence of Orthodoxy in particular? More fundamentally, what does their existence
in the last quarter of the twentieth century tell about how religion can
survive in an essentially secular society? These are some of the questions that this book attempts to answer.

To date, hardly anything has been written about life inside these
schools. We know very little about how those who attend think, what
are the things that matter to them, the dreams and hopes they share,
and the disappointments and frustrations they experience. How, for
example, do its members deal with temptation and religious doubts?
What happens to those who do not fit into the yeshiva's mold? What
about those who, unable to adjust to the rigors of yeshiva life, defect
completely from it? Our lack of knowledge about the yeshivas is certainly not due to the unimportance of the subject. Not only do they
transmit Jewish knowledge and traditions at the highest levels, but virtually all Orthodox and quite a few Conservative rabbis have been
trained in them. In addition, most of the thousands of teachers at the
secondary and day school yeshiva levels, as well as at the afternoon
Hebrew schools, have studied in advanced yeshivas. Since the beginnings of the yeshivas in this country, perhaps tens of thousands of

young men have gone to them, and they have been profoundly affected by the years spent in them.

The lack of available information on this important influence in Jewish life may be due in part to the formidable difficulties of gaining entry into the world of the yeshiva. In this regard, I benefited greatly from the fact that I had attended such yeshivas as a youth and was therefore familiar with talmudic study and fluent in both Hebrew and Yiddish. At the same time I have used the tools of my trade as a sociologist to evaluate the yeshiva. Looked at from this perspective the yeshiva emerges as a place that, while it is special in many ways, also has many things in common with universities, seminaries of other faiths, corporations, foundations, and organizations in general. It has a certain structure, a set of both general and specific goals, a hierarchy of leaders and followers who play a variety of roles in the functioning of the institution. It is concerned with questions of status, norms, values, class, and other areas of interest to sociologists. The yeshiva must deal with those who do not wish to conform to its expectations, and it must adequately reward those who do. On another level, it must raise funds from both insiders and outsiders to insure its survival. These and other questions of a similar nature are a major part of this book. That I belonged to this community made my job both easier and harder. Although a full explanation of how the project was carried out appears at the end of the book, a brief description at this point may be useful to the reader.

Four different approaches were combined in this study. The first was direct observation. I enrolled as a student in a major yeshiva that had students who lived on the premises as well as day students. I attended classes and also studied with a "learning partner" for about four hours at a time, six days a week, in the spring of 1974 and again in the spring of 1975. In addition, I interacted with the students socially in a variety of settings.

From 1976 until 1980, in-depth interviews were conducted with 179 members and leaders of the yeshiva community, ranging from present and former students to faculty, administrators, and key community leaders. Especially valuable were the interviews and discussions with the heads of almost every major yeshiva, such as Rabbi Moshe Feinstein of Mesivta Tifereth Jerusalem, Rabbi Shneur Kotler of the Beth Medrash Govoha Yeshiva, and Rabbi Joseph B. Soloveitchik of Yeshiva University. Most of the interviews were taped. Together, they provide a portrait of a community that could not have been obtained through observation alone.

The third approach was statistical. A lengthy and detailed questionnaire was sent to 878 alumni of one of the largest yeshivas in the United States.* More than half of those queried responded, a very high proportion for a mail survey. The 78 items included questions regarding religious practices, political preferences, and socioeconomic level, and a series of questions about how the alumnus viewed his experiences in the yeshiva. This is, to my knowledge, the first time that such a large group of Orthodox Jews has been systematically surveyed with respect to these and many other questions. Although a full analysis of the results will take years, a sizeable portion of the data appear in this book.

Finally, written material from a wide variety of sources was analyzed and applied to the present study wherever appropriate. This included hundreds of books and articles as well as unpublished documents ranging from sociological theory to popular articles in the mass media. A list of almost 200 works on yeshivas, brought together for the first time, appears in a special bibliography at the end of the book.

This book is intended for both the scholar and the general reader interested in the topic. I have therefore tried to keep the use of sociological jargon to a minimum. Footnotes appear in the back, and the statistical information is presented in a way that should be comprehensible to both lay and professional people.

In most cases real names have been used. In my view, this is very important both for historical accuracy and because it lends greater weight and validity to the material itself. Those few persons who requested anonymity have been given pseudonyms and are identified as such by an asterisk next to the name. All places and names of institutions are real except where otherwise noted.

* At the request of its leaders, this yeshiva is not identified but is referred to as the Beth David Yeshiva throughout this book.

Acknowledgments

THIS WORK TOOK MORE THAN seven years to complete. Many helped along the way, and in the process of acknowledging my debts I will probably inadvertantly leave out some names. I hope these people understand and forgive.

I would like, first of all, to express my gratitude to the various yeshiva heads who allowed me to speak with them. They are listed here in alphabetical order: Rabbi Shmuel Berenbaum (Mirrer Yeshiva), Rabbi Moshe Feinstein (Mesivta Tifereth Jerusalem), Rabbi Mordechai Gifter (Telshe Yeshiva), Rabbi Yitzchok Hutner* (Chaim Berlin Yeshiva), Rabbi Shraga Moshe Kalmanowitz (Mirrer Yeshiva), Rabbi Yaakov Kamenecki (Mesivta Torah Vodaath), Rabbi Shneur Kotler (Beth Medrash Govoha), Rabbi Henoch Leibowitz (Rabbinical Seminary of America), Rabbi Yaakov Perlow (Yeshiva Rabbi Samson Rafael Hirsch), Rabbi Yaakov Ruderman (Ner Israel Rabbinical College), Rabbi Aharon Schechter (Chaim Berlin Yeshiva), Rabbi Gedalia Schorr* (Mesivta Torah Vodaath), Rabbi Joseph B. Soloveitchik (Yeshiva University), Rabbi Elya Svei (Talmudical Academy of Philadelphia), and Rabbi Yaakov Weinberg (Ner Israel Rabbinical College). Rabbi Kotler spent many hours with me and introduced me to various members of the yeshiva community. In the hierarchical world of the yeshiva his support was crucial, and I am deeply indebted to him. Taken together, the interviews with these leaders greatly expanded my understanding of the larger issues in this study.

A number of people read and evaluated the manuscript in its entirety. Among them I am most grateful to Dr. Marvin Schick, who wrote more than thirty pages of single-spaced typewritten observa-

---

* Deceased.

tions, all of them informative, many of them critical. His knowledge of the subject is encyclopedic; every researcher should be blessed with such readers. I was also fortunate in having the insight and evaluation of my father, Leo Helmreich, Professors Sid Z. Leiman and Lawrence Grossman, Rabbi Nosson Scherman, and Dr. Joseph Kaminetsky, all of whom meticulously reviewed the manuscript and made countless suggestions that proved invaluable. My colleagues Joseph Bensman, William McCord, and Bernard Rosenberg were equally helpful. Their reputation as first-rate sociologists is richly deserved, and I benefited enormously from their knowledge, experience, and analytical talents.

Many individuals read portions of the manuscript, discussed various aspects pertaining to the community with me, and/or opened doors that might otherwise have remained closed. They are, alphabetically: Dr. Moshe Bernstein, Dr. William Brickman, Rabbi Zevulun Charlop, Rabbi Robert Fierstein, Dr. Bernard Fryshman, Rabbi Abba Zalka Gewirtz, Rabbi Aaron Gewirtz, Dr. John Goering, Rabbi Bernard Goldenberg, Dr. Eli Goldschmidt, Dr. Irving Greenberg, Sam Hartstein, Professor Irving Louis Horowitz, Rabbi Yaakov Jacobs, Nathan Kalt, Professor David Kranzler, Professor Seymour Lachman, Rabbi Norman Lamm, Dr. Bernard Lander, Jeffrey and Chava Miller, Rabbi Herman Neuberger, Rabbi Shrage Neuberger, Rabbi Yaakov Neuberger, Dr. Simon Noveck, Rabbi Betzalel Ostrow, Rabbi Aaron Rothkoff, Dr. Allan Rudolf, Rabbi Morris Samuel, Rabbi Moshe Sherer, Dr. Solomon Skaist, Rabbi Jacob Slotnick, Howard Spierer, Rabbi Pinchas Stolper, Rabbi Mordechai Tendler, Professor Mervin Verbit, Rabbi Yaakov Weisberg, Rabbi Nisson Wolpin, and Rabbi Pinchas Yurowitz. While I have only mentioned their names here, their contributions to this study were significant and are truly appreciated.

I want to give special thanks to Professors Simon Herman, Solomon Poll, Israel Rubin, and Marshall Sklare both for their substantive reactions to my work and helpful comments and for their encouragement and support. My colleague Philip Leonhard-Spark deserves a great deal of credit for his input into the quantitative portion of this project and for suggesting how it might best be applied to the yeshiva community. Zippy Helmreich, Marc Silverman, Leah Moses, and Julius Vorchheimer did excellent jobs as interviewers and research assistants. They were dedicated and sincere as well as insightful and genuinely interested in the research process.

Several foundations gave funds that allowed me to devote all my energies to writing and thinking. I would like first to express my appreciation to the Spencer Foundation, especially H. Thomas James and Marion M. Faldet, who believed in the importance of the subject. In addition, I am profoundly grateful to the American Jewish Committee, in particular Irving Levine, and to the Memorial Foundation for Jewish Culture, mainly Dr. Jerry Hochbaum. Other small grants for which I am duly thankful came from the National Endowment for the Humanities and the City University Research Foundation. Finally, City College of New York granted me a sabbatical leave to pursue my work.

An environment conducive to intellectual thinking is crucial if one's research is to bear fruit. The Sociology Department at City College was for me just the setting I needed. My colleagues, many of them individuals with national reputations, gave willingly of their time, and shared their expertise with me. In addition, they showed by example that true collegiality in the academic sense is not merely social interaction but intense commitment to the market place of ideas. I want therefore to thank them collectively for providing me with an intellectual haven these past eight years.

Librarians are among the least appreciated resources in academia, especially when compared to the magnitude of their contributions to many projects. I was fortunate in having guidance and assistance from numerous such individuals in the libraries of Yeshiva University, Jewish Theological Seminary, YIVO, and City College. My thanks to the people there and especially to Dr. Shmuel Klein at Yeshiva, an old classmate and friend.

I was fortunate to have two editors at The Free Press who demonstrated sensitivity to the material and an ability to apply their considerable skills to a difficult subject. Gladys Topkis was both friend and critic. She read the manuscript very carefully and tremendously improved it. Joyce Seltzer, who took over in the later stages, continued to have faith in the merits of the book and gave me both moral and substantive support. George A. Rowland guided the book most capably through the various production stages.

Of all the people involved in this project, none played a more important role than my wife, Helaine. Besides the usual indispensable functions of empathy, sensitivity, and a willingness to listen, she was, as always, a full partner in the intellectual process. She not only read and reread the manuscript but she provided me with literally hundreds of ideas and suggestions. In truth, words could not fully express my debt to her except, perhaps, to say that no one could ask for more.

CHAPTER 1

From Jacob's Tents to America's Cities

THOUSANDS OF YEARS AGO, when the Jews were a small, semi-nomadic people wandering from place to place in the Land of Canaan, the idea of Jewish learning had already taken root. According to later rabbinic tradition the Bible was known to the patriarchs Abraham, Isaac, and Jacob prior to the revelation at Mount Sinai. Their training took place in the *yeshivas** of their day, known as the "study houses of Shem and Ever."[1] Jacob in particular came to be associated with love of learning. According to the talmudic sage Rabbi Hanina, Jacob sent his son Judah to Egypt for the purpose of building a house of study so that when Jacob arrived there he would be able to pass his last years on earth in the service of God.[2]

Though little is known about these institutions, the importance of education and study is stressed throughout the Torah (Written and Oral Law). It is perhaps most succinctly stated in the *shema,* one of the holiest Jewish prayers, recited several times a day by observant Jews:

> And these words, which I command thee this day, shall be upon thy heart; and thou shalt teach them diligently unto thy children, and shalt talk of them when thou sittest in thy

---

* Throughout this book *yeshiva* refers to an advanced or post–high school institution, unless otherwise noted.

1

house, and when thou walkest by the way, and when thou
liest down, and when thou risest up.

Deuteronomy 6:6-7

This exhortation was presented by Moses in the name of
God to the Israelites,[3] and in it we can already discern the direction taken in later times by Jewish scholarship: the commandment to learn was of divine origin, as was knowledge itself. The
laws could be interpreted and expanded upon but not changed;
they could be questioned but not challenged.

Beginnings of the Portable Homeland

With the destruction of the Second Temple by the Romans
in 70 C.E., the Jewish nation ceased to exist as an independent
political entity. In the absence of a land and with their temple in
ruins, the Jews desperately needed a religious symbol on which
to pin their hopes. Aware of this need, the sage Rabbi Johanan
ben Zakkai established an academy, or yeshiva, at Yavneh, west
of the now-fallen Jerusalem. Gathering around him the most
noted scholars in the country, he moved swiftly to assert the authority of his center. The policy-making body of the community
known as the Sanhedrin was transferred to Yavneh, and new
laws were promulgated there to make it clear to all that, although
the Jews no longer retained physical control of their country,
they would survive through the "portable homeland" of their
holy books and the thought and vision of their sages.[4] At the
same time, new centers of scholarship began to emerge in neighboring Babylonia, which was to remain a focal point of Jewish
learning for the next ten centuries.

The central activity occurring in these yeshivas was the
study and elaboration of the Five Books of Moses or Torah (also
known as Written Law). The process had already begun in
earnest a century earlier when the *Tannaim* (meaning those who
study and pass on their knowledge), led by Rabbi Judah haNasi,
had begun compiling and arranging the laws of the Torah in a
systematic fashion. Known as the Mishna, this work was completed in 240 C.E. Together with the *Gemora,* which is the analysis
and interpretation of the Mishna by the sages of those times, this
body of work became known as the Talmud (also referred to as
Oral Law). In its written form, which has been preserved vir-

tually intact for centuries, the Talmud constitutes the bulk of what is studied in advanced yeshivas today.

Throughout the long history of the Jewish people since those days, their fortunes have varied considerably from country to country. There were periods of great suffering as well as times of peace and prosperity. Whatever their situation, learning remained an important part of their culture. As a result, yeshivas functioned at various times in a wide range of countries where Jews resided, including France, Germany, Spain, Poland, North Africa, and Egypt. How they fared in these countries is a separate topic. In terms of understanding the modern yeshiva in America, however, we need to begin with the eighteenth century in Eastern Europe, where the prototypes of today's yeshiva emerged.

Hasidim and Misnagdim

At this point in Jewish history, two men emerged who were to profoundly influence its development for centuries. One was born in Poland, the other in Lithuania; both were deeply religious but one emphasized the emotions, the other the intellect. The first, born in Podolia, a province of Poland, was Israel Baal Shem Tov (1700–1760), founder of Hasidism. Hasidism espoused the philosophy that it was possible to achieve closeness to God through prayer, song, and joy, in addition to learning. Until then study of the Bible and Talmud had been regarded as the primary way of reaching this goal. For the majority of Ukrainian and Polish Jews, educated only in the basics of the religion, the possibility of attaining a high level of spirituality through this method seized and held their imaginations. Hasidism, while it did not disregard the importance of the Torah and *halacha* (Jewish law), argued that God was everywhere and that simple prayers, if sincerely offered, were enough to become a partner in the creation process itself. It also advanced the notion that all God's creations contained a certain beauty, and that one could therefore enjoy the good things in life (within reason) provided one was constantly aware that God made them possible. Structurally, it was a fundamentalist movement, appealing to the emotions, particularly through the charismatic leaders, who emerged as Hasidism gained in popularity.[5]

The second individual is of greater interest to us here because his philosophy and work were crucial to the growth and rebirth of the yeshivas in Eastern Europe. Elijah ben Solomon Zalman was born in Selets, Lithuania, in 1720. As a child he was a prodigy; he mastered the Bible at age six and most of the Talmud by the time he was thirteen years old. Though offered rabbinical posts on many occasions, he always declined out of fear that such a position would give him less time for Torah study. As the years passed his reputation grew, and he became acknowledged as the intellectual giant of eighteenth-century Jewry. The honorary title "*gaon*," last used in Babylonian times, was conferred upon him, indicative of the great esteem in which he was held by his contemporaries.

Due, perhaps, to having studied on his own, the "Vilna Gaon" developed a philosophy and approach to learning and to life in general that was in many ways unique. Arguing that everything, past, present, and future, could be found in the Torah, he urged Jews to intensify their study of it, and vigorously opposed all efforts to dilute it. Though committed to the notion of Torah's supremacy, the Vilna Gaon familiarized himself with secular subjects, because he felt that all knowledge was holy and that it could therefore serve as an aid in comprehending the Written and Oral Law. Besides persuading his students to translate various secular works such as Euclid's *Geometry* into Hebrew, he wrote treatises on various topics himself. The author or originator of more than seventy known works, the Vilna Gaon's major contribution was in the area of *halacha*. His explication of numerous laws in Judaism, which had until then appeared in only partial form throughout the Talmud, and his approach to so doing, were emulated by generations of scholars who followed him.[6]

The Vilna Gaon spent much of his time engaged in solitary study. So as not to be disturbed, he was in the habit of shutting the windows of his room during the day, relying for light on a candle. Nevertheless, he emerged from his isolation to combat the Hasidic movement, which he regarded as an insidious threat to the faith itself. In his opinion, the Hasidic emphasis upon prayer and emotion denigrated and devalued the importance of the Torah. It meant that there were alternate methods of achieving closeness to God. Moreover, the Hasidic emphasis on the holy qualities of the *rebbe* or *tzaddik*, especially his ability to intercede with God on behalf of the common man, were considered blasphemous by the Vilna Gaon, who felt that all men, created as they were in God's image, could communicate directly with their Maker. The story is told of a Rabbi Leib who observed to the Hasidic master Rabbi Dov Baer of Mezritch: "I did not go to the *maggid* (storyteller) in order to hear Torah from him, but to see how he unlaces his felt shoes and how he laces them up again."[7] To Elijah Gaon, such hero worship was beneath contempt. Under his influence, the Jewish community in Vilna moved twice within a span of twenty-five years to excommunicate the Hasidim, an act that was accompanied by a public burning of their works.

The vehemence and bitterness of the Vilna Gaon's attacks against the Hasidic movement may seem excessively severe to some, but to Rabbi Elijah and his disciples, the Hasidic movement posed a threat of great magnitude precisely because it located itself within Judaism while holding to a diametrically opposed view of how such faith might most effectively be practiced. The Vilna Gaon sought to uplift and glorify the people by raising the level of learning to new heights. To accomplish this, it was necessary to dignify learning itself and exhort people to study constantly. Any other path was not worthy of serious consideration. The Hasidim, on the other hand, wanted to turn religion into a vehicle wherein all could find true fulfillment, and to them this meant accepting novel approaches to it. Their stress on the emotional and the spiritual gave many a sense of satisfaction that they had not previously experienced. Thus, while the *Misnagdim* (as those opposed to the Hasidim were called) tried to make the common man into an uncommon scholar, the Hasidim tried to reshape the tradition into a mold that could be apprehended by the common man.[8]

It would be simplistic and even untrue, to an extent, to depict the Hasidic movement as one that appealed to the uneducated masses resentful of the rabbis and learned men who looked down upon them. To begin with, as the historian Jacob Katz has pointed out, Hasidism developed against a backdrop of serious economic dislocations. These dislocations weakened the community and its institutions, adversely affecting the quality of leadership and the yeshivas themselves, which had seriously declined by the mid-eighteenth century. Consequently, the community was eager for new leaders with new ideas.[9] Second, the supporters of the Hasidim included many well-to-do merchants and townspeople who lived in southern Poland, where the movement was strongest. Lithuania, where the *Misnagdim* were most powerful, was a much poorer region with many adherents whose lifestyle did not compare to that of their coreligionists in the South. Finally, the conflict was at its roots an ideological one, and religious ideologies, if strongly held, often transcend socioeconomic groupings.[10]

By the beginning of the nineteenth century, the conflict that had raged between Hasidim and *Misnagdim* began to wane in the face of a new threat to the faith as a whole—namely, the Haskala, or "Jewish Enlightenment." Different as their perspectives on religion were, both the Hasidim and *Misnagdim* were observant, sent their children to *cheder* (elementary school) and yeshiva, and had little to do with the society around them. The leaders of the Haskala urged greater participation in Russian and Polish culture, including the establishment of secular studies as part of the Jewish school curriculum. They called for an easing of control over Jewish life by the rabbinate and attempted to change the character of Jewish life in a wide range of areas. Having seen how the Haskala had been accompanied by assimilationist trends in Germany, where it had begun earlier, both Hasidim and *Misnagdim* saw a need to tone down their internal fighting.

The Modern Yeshiva Emerges

The philosophical concepts and approach articulated by the Vilna Gaon had a lasting impact on his students. The most famous of these was Reb Chaim Volozhiner, who had studied under the Gaon in Vilna as part of a small circle of disciples. In 1802 he founded the most famous yeshiva ever to exist in Lithuania. Located in the tiny town of Volozhin, not far from Vilna, it became a model for all the yeshivas founded in Lithuania in the nineteenth century. The motivation to establish it there, rather than in a larger community, was probably to enable the yeshiva to function independently of the community and to allow the student, or *bochur,* to pursue his studies in an atmosphere free from outside distractions. Though we are speaking of an institution founded 180 years ago, its effect on modern-day yeshivas was in many ways seminal.

Determined to raise the prestige of the yeshiva and, therefore, Torah, to new heights, Reb Chaim resolved to convert the yeshiva into an institution not dependent upon the already strained resources of the local community. Thus, he set up a network of emissaries who collected money throughout Europe (and later the United States). In this manner the coffers of the yeshiva's treasury grew along with the pride of thousands of Jews who, though they might not be learned, could at least derive satisfaction from the knowledge of having contributed to the spread of learning. Reb Chaim supported indigent students from yeshiva funds and made efforts to house all students on the grounds of the yeshiva instead of in private homes.

The idea of *Torah lishmo*—study for its own sake or, more precisely, for a higher spiritual purpose—became the central feature of the yeshivas' philosophy, both at Volozhin and in the scores of yeshivas that were set up as the years passed. One did not study to become a "rabbi." The guiding motive was to attain knowledge as an end in itself, not spiritual ecstasy or the acquisition of practical skills.[11] Inspired by his leadership, challenged by the high standards he set, students from all parts of the world vied for acceptance at Reb Chaim's yeshiva, known as the Etz Chaim Yeshiva. Once they were there, the requirements were informal. No formal examinations were given; instead, the heads of the yeshiva would engage the students in conversations about their work. The young men, or *bochorim,* studied in pairs, or *chavrusas,* sometimes engaging older students to help them. Since most *bochorim* depended on the yeshiva for income, they had to make do with "bread and tea for breakfast and supper, bread and some warm dish for luncheon, and meat once a week—on the Sabbath."[12] These were meager rations, no doubt, but in the rarefied atmosphere of the yeshiva, where the sounds of learning could be heard in the *beis medrash* (house of study) literally twenty-four hours a day, nourishment was for the soul—the body would take care of itself.

In 1854, Rabbi Naftali Zevi Judah Berlin became head of the Volozhin Yeshiva. Under his aegis, the yeshiva reached its greatest heights, at times enrolling as many as 400 students. A rigorous program of instruction was devised, with daily classes and regular examinations. Thus, the institution began to resemble today's advanced yeshivas more and more.[13] One of the most popular lecturers at the yeshiva was Rabbi Chaim Soloveichik. A man of unusual brilliance, he developed an analytical method of studying Talmud that became widely used in yeshivas everywhere.[14]

Volozhin's yeshiva was the best known of these institutions, but there were other important schools as well. The yeshiva at Mir, founded in 1815, also achieved great renown. Other well-known yeshivas were founded during the nineteenth century in Minsk, Radin, Telshe, Slabodka, Slutsk, Lomza, Eyshishok, Kamenetz, and Nevardok.[15]

The period inaugurated by the yeshiva at Volozhin marks an important development in the history of yeshivas. Quite a few became international institutions, drawing their student bodies and financial support from outside the local communities. Volo-zhin was the first yeshiva to send out *meshullachim* (fund-raisers) to other communities. Beginning in the nineteenth century, ye-shivas also became more or less independent institutions, places where students lived as well as studied, and on a full-time basis. They were not generally schools made up of small groups of in-dividuals attracted to one great scholar, who studied in a *beis med-rash* that served also as a synagogue. Moreover, the requirements gradually became formalized, with students advancing from class to class after giving evidence of a certain level of scholar-ship. These are general characteristics, of course, and there were considerable variations in emphasis and procedure from yeshiva to yeshiva.

In addition to these prototypical yeshivas, there were many smaller yeshivas in Lithuania–Poland about which far less is known. Moreover, the majority of young men, especially in Poland, received their knowledge of Torah in the local syna-gogues of the communities in which they grew up, often turning to older men in the community for help in their studies. The role of the larger yeshivas was central, for they served as an elite to be emulated. In so doing, they created a community where learning was prized, even by those who lacked the ability or means to study in the larger yeshivas. Thus, these smaller yeshivas and synagogue study groups flourished because they existed in an en-vironment permeated by the spirit of learning.

Poetry, Novels, and Emancipation

The growth of the Haskala posed a serious threat to the ye-shivas. Brought about, in large part, by a general process of en-lightenment that had been occurring throughout Europe since the end of the eighteenth century, the Haskala gained impetus in Russia with the ascent to the throne of the liberal Czar Alexander

II. Writing in Yiddish for the masses and in Hebrew for the intellectuals, the *maskilim*, as those who joined the Haskala were called, produced prodigious amounts of literature. Opposed to assimilation, they tried to engender pride in the ancient Jewish heritage through their writings. They talked about the Jews as a nation, ushering in a period that was to culminate in the full-fledged development of Zionism. They wrote poetry and novels, often using biblical events to buttress themes which dealt essentially with contemporary life. Parallel to these efforts, they urged their brethren to become conversant with Russian culture and ideals, to "emancipate" themselves from old ways of thinking and what they saw as rigid patterns of behavior.

As it swept through the Jewish communities of Eastern Europe, the Haskala penetrated the walls of the yeshiva too. Though the reading of Haskala literature was strictly forbidden, many students did so anyway, albeit clandestinely.[16] Many yeshiva *bochorim* in their adult years became well-known *maskilim*. The inroads made by the Haskala compelled the yeshivas to adapt to the movement's considerable influence in the larger community. While some *maskilim* strongly opposed the yeshiva, others were not so certain. Their ambiguity was perhaps best captured by the famous Hebrew poet Chaim Nahman Bialik in his poem, *Hamatmid* (The Diligent Student):

> . . .Like thieves in attics and cellars gathered
> Our sons have studied the forbidden Torah,
> And glories inextinguishably bright
> Have issued from these cellars, while from attics
> A people's saints and leaders have come down.
> Dear to the Torah is the life of sorrow,
> And in the chastity of poverty
> The people and its sons have kept the faith.[17]
> . . .And now when in my memory rise those voices,
> Those dying lamentations in the night,
> The heart in me cries out: Lord of the World!
> To what end is this mighty sacrifice?[18]

Rabbi Israel Salanter and the *Mussar* Movement

Reacting, in some measure, to the inroads made by the Haskala, a new movement came into being called *mussar*, or ethics. Founded by Rabbi Israel Salanter, it was to have a decided impact on the yeshiva. Rabbi Salanter was concerned that, without ethical behavior and spiritual warmth, study of the Talmud would become motivated by vanity and that adherence to the laws would turn into an unfeeling, mechanical process. The *mussar* movement's overall goal was a spiritual uplifting of man in his relations with God and with his fellow man. In order for man to improve himself, he had to recognize that the achievement of ethical human relations was a lifelong goal, a task that was by definition completed only when one left this world. The movement developed guidelines by which individuals might enhance themselves. These included the reading of ethical works on a daily basis with intensity. Such study was generally done to the accompaniment of various melodies. The constant repetition of ethical principles was required so that they could become ingrained in the lives of those who learned them. Moreover, it was crucial that one study ethics together with others.

Although Rabbi Salanter at first intended to propagate his movement directly to local communities, he quickly found that he would have greater success by focusing on the yeshivas, whose students were more receptive to his teachings. Apparently, it was easier to instill values in those who were younger and therefore less affected by outside influences. By appealing to the yeshivas, however, Salanter restricted himself to a somewhat exclusive group, and the movement became directed toward a relatively small number of people, as opposed to Hasidism, which attempted to reach people from every walk of life. The movement was not initially welcomed with open arms. While *mussar,* unlike Hasidism, never challenged the Lithuanian belief in the centrality of talmudic study, it seemed to many to be elevating *mussar* above the Torah. Its most prominent opponent was probably Rabbi Yitzchok Elchonon Spektor, who vigorously opposed its inclusion in the yeshiva curriculum.[19]

In the end, however, the movement prevailed, gaining adherents even among those who had formerly declared themselves to be its implacable foes, and *mussar* became a separate topic of study in almost all the Lithuanian yeshivas.[20] The responsibility for inculcating the ideals of *mussar* usually rested on the shoulders of the *mashgiach,* or supervisor of the yeshiva. Among his duties were those of counseling students, disciplining them, giving a *shmuess* or talk aimed at the spiritual uplifting of the budding scholar, and the various administrative tasks of running a yeshiva. A good *mashgiach* was supposed to be sensitive to each student, and to know, often intuitively, how best to approach each individual: when to be stern and when to be kind, when to cajole and when to scold. The overall goal of the supervisor was to help in the development of the complete human being, aiding the young man in the successful integration of mind, body, and soul.

One of the most famous supervisors was Rabbi Note Hirsch Finkel of the Slabodka Yeshiva (founded 1882) where, under his guidance, *mussar* became firmly entrenched.[21] Rabbi Finkel lived as he preached, accepting no salary from the yeshiva, existing on the meager income derived from a small store run by him and his wife. He was greatly respected and loved by his students, who affectionately referred to him as "Der Alter fun Slabodka" (The Old One from Slabodka).[22] As we shall see later, the study of *mussar* has become part of the curriculum in today's yeshivas.

One major yeshiva which resisted the *mussar* movement was the school founded in Telshe (also known as Telz) in 1875. Ethics were studied in the institution but, unlike the *mussar* yeshivas, it was not seen as a separate subject by its leaders. One leader was reported to have said: "People are under the impression that Mussar should be studied with the heart and *Gemora* with the head, but I say that Mussar must be studied with the head, too, *Gemora* also with the heart."[23] At the center of the Telshe Yeshiva's program of study were classes devoted primarily to discussions of *halacha* (law). This approach is still employed today in the Telshe Yeshiva, now located in Wickliffe, a suburb of Cleveland, Ohio.

Volozhin Is Closed, but the Yeshivas Continue to Grow

In 1892 the yeshiva of Volozhin, the institution which had trained so many of the brightest scholars, closed its doors rather than accede to the Russian government's demands that secular studies and the Hebrew language be taught there.[24] While to some this might seem an innocuous request, since the yeshiva itself would have been permitted to continue teaching Talmud, the leaders of the yeshiva saw the demand as the first step in a deliberate campaign to destroy the institution. Rather than permit this to happen, they disbanded the yeshiva. Though there was criticism of this decision by many who looked upon Volozhin as a cultural institution and symbol of intellectual greatness, subsequent events justified the closing of the yeshiva. This did not lead to a diminution of learning. The faculty and students simply joined or founded new institutions in other towns throughout Lithuania. Volozhin itself became the home of a reconstituted version of the yeshiva, and remained in existence until the outbreak of World War II.

The creation of yeshivas in Lithuania eventually began to affect the Hasidic movement, which also began founding yeshivas, though they did not do so on a large scale until the period between the two world wars. An exception to this was the Lubavitcher movement, which in 1897 established the Tomchei Temimim Yeshiva in Lubavitch. Within a few years of its founding, branches of the institution were set up in numerous other cities. The main center in Lubavitch had a student body of several hundred. Though the program of study resembled the Lithuanian yeshivas, considerable emphasis was also placed upon Hasidic philosophy and the works of the movement's founder, Rabbi Shneur Zalman of Ladi.[25]

By the beginning of the twentieth century, East European Jewry had already gone through a prolonged period of exposure to outside influences. While the departure of about 2 million Jews for America had not caused the yeshivas to decline significantly, the effect on those left behind was profound. Increased contact with Jews in other parts of the world accelerated the modernization process in the regions where the yeshivas were located. True, most of the Orthodox Jews who formed the constituency of the yeshivas preferred not to leave, calling the United States "The *Trefene Medina*" (The non-kosher country), but they could not avoid being influenced by developments in America. Contact between the Orthodox communities that had sprung up elsewhere, especially in the United States, and the yeshivas, in Lithuania and Poland, became a matter of necessity as socioeconomic conditions worsened after the October Revolution in Russia. These "bad times" caused the yeshivas to turn to Americans for funds to keep the yeshivas going. Some leaders in the yeshiva world, most notably Rabbi Naftali Zevi Judah Berlin of Volozhin, also gave support, or at least encouragement, to the growing fascination with Zionism on the part of the masses. In addition, hundreds of thousands of Jews were attracted to socialism under the banner of the Jewish *Bund* (Alliance) while at the same time assimilationism became a fact of life in many Jewish communities.

One man who responded to the times was Rabbi Isaac Jacob Reines. Though a graduate of the Volozhin Yeshiva, he felt there was a need for a modern yeshiva that offered both religious and secular studies. Only such institutions could, in his opinion, dull the effects of various movements and trends that were threatening the fabric of Jewish religious life. The yeshiva must offer an alternative that was relevant to the times, yet firmly rooted in Jewish tradition. It was difficult to ignore the appeal of this approach; for Reines could not be characterized as a *maskil,* or secularist, who simply wanted to destroy the yeshiva. Students flocked to his new institution, which was established in Lida in 1905. Reines did not confine his efforts to the yeshiva, which was disbanded in the wake of World War I. He was also one of the founders and the first head of Mizrachi, a movement of religious Zionism. Most of the other yeshiva leaders were quite opposed to his yeshiva. In their opinion a strict separation had to be maintained between the secular and the religious spheres of Judaism. Their attitudes foreshadowed a conflict that continues to exist in the present between the modern and the traditional or right-wing Orthodox communities.[26]

The leaders of the yeshivas realized that in order to save their way of life they would have to unite and develop strong and centralized organizations at all levels. This meant basically organizing Jewish education so that it would become widely available, not simply the province of an elite minority. At the highest levels, this meant that the quality of learning would suffer somewhat as admission became easier; but this lowering of standards was deemed a necessary price of survival. Elementary school education became more formalized, and the yeshiva high school emerged to prepare youngsters for the advanced yeshivas. Secular studies were begun at the lower levels. A system of religious schools for girls, the Beth Jacob schools, was also created. A key element in these developments was the founding in 1912 of the Agudath Israel organization, which played a major role in spreading education through its school system, known as *Horeb,* a system that had close to 50,000 pupils on the eve of World War II. A more liberal school system was the *Tarbut,* which numbered about 45,000 students at its height during the interwar period. Unlike the Agudah schools, which eschewed the use of Hebrew as a language of instruction, the *Tarbut* schools not only preferred Hebrew to Yiddish but stressed Zionism as well.[27]

While the focus of this chapter is to trace the history of yeshivas to their transplantation from Eastern Europe onto American soil, any discussion of them would be inadequate without at least a mention of the Hungarian yeshivas. Though they did not, except in the case of the Hasidic community (a separate topic altogether), reestablish themselves in the United States to any great degree, they were very important in the life of Central European Jewry, producing many noted scholars. The best known of these yeshivas was established early in the nineteenth century by Rabbi Moses Sofer (the *Hatam Sofer*) in Pressburg. In the years that followed, many others were started in Hungary that were similar to the Pressburg Yeshiva.[28] Moreover, a yeshiva was begun in Frankfurt, Germany, by Rabbi Solomon Breuer, who had received his training in Pressburg.[29] In any event, the history of yeshivas in Hungary, and how they differed from their Lithuanian counterparts, has been well covered in a fine work by Armin Friedman, whose discussion spans life in the Hungarian yeshivas between 1848 and 1948.[30]

Between the Two World Wars

The outbreak of World War I resulted in the temporary closing of the yeshivas in Russia and in Lithuania, which at the time had approximately 10,000 young men studying in about thirty yeshivas. After the war ended, the Soviet regime made life very difficult for those who wanted to pursue a religious way of life, and the Russian yeshivas were therefore relocated in newly independent Lithuania and in Poland, which had also achieved complete independence by then. Although many scholars had perished during the war, there still remained charismatic leaders in the yeshiva community who now undertook the difficult task of restoring the yeshivas.

Besides the Chofetz Chaim (Rabbi Israel Meir haCohen), who became one of the cofounders of the *Vaad haYeshivoth,* a group organized to raise funds for the yeshivas, various other figures emerged to meet the challenge of the times. One of the most gifted scholars was Rabbi Chaim Ozer Grodzensky, who as a child prodigy had so impressed those who met him with his talmudic knowledge that at age fifteen he was admitted to the Volozhin Yeshiva, where he belonged to the inner circle of those who studied with Rabbi Chaim Soloveichik. A man who opposed both Zionism and secular education, Rabbi Grodzensky played a pivotal role in all the important Orthodox organizations created during the interwar years.[31]

One of the greatest educators of the era was Rabbi ("Reb") Elchonon Wasserman. His yeshiva in Baranowicz welcomed the many Hasidic students who came to study with him. By this time a number of Hasidic groups, especially the Radomsker Hasidim, had built yeshivas in Poland. While many Hasidim were reluctant to place their children in the alien Lithuanian environment, Reb Elchonon's receptiveness to them encouraged more and more Hasidic parents to do so. At the yeshiva, substantial efforts were made to synthesize the religious outlooks of *mussar* and Hasidism.[32] Yet another prominent *rosh yeshiva* was Rabbi Isser Zalman Meltzer. Like many, he learned the *"Litvishe derech,"* or Lithuanian way of Talmud study, at the Volozhin Yeshiva under Rabbi Soloveichik. After heading the yeshiva at Slutsk, Russia, he emigrated to Israel in 1925, and became head of the Etz Chaim Yeshiva in Jerusalem.[33]

Of the organizations created to help yeshivas between the wars, none was more effective than the Agudath Israel. A two-day conference in 1912 in Kattowicz, attended by over 600 leaders, proclaimed the following goal: "the solution of *all problems* facing the Jewish people in the spirit of Torah." In line with its stated purpose, the Agudah quickly became involved in a wide range of secular as well as religious activities. In what was a first for the Orthodox community, it became a recognized political party in the Polish government and was represented in the *Sejm* (Polish Parliament) between 1919 and 1939, when Poland was invaded by Germany.

Through the establishment of its schools at the primary and secondary levels, Agudath Israel played a fundamental role, organizing the schools and obtaining government recognition for them. It accomplished this by raising pedagogical standards and by arranging for secular studies to be taught in the schools. In 1937, the Agudah-controlled schools in Poland and Lithuania had a combined enrollment of 71,000 boys and 35,586 girls, impressive figures for an organization with such a short history.[34]

At the level of the higher yeshivas, Agudah's involvement was significant. At the outset, it explicitly committed itself to the concept that rabbinical authority not only was unquestionable, but that active steps were necessary to maintain its supremacy in the community. To this end, it created the *Mo'etzet Gedolei Torah* (Council of Torah Sages), made up of many of the most important rabbinical leaders, and invested them with final authority in all matters undertaken by the organization. These sages included local rabbis, heads of yeshivas, and Hasidic leaders. Insofar as the advanced yeshivas were concerned, it became in effect their political arm, fighting for their interests in many areas. This involvement has grown through the years. Today, the Agudath Israel in the United States is the most important agency for the yeshivas in their contact with the external world.[35]

The period between the two wars was one in which the yeshivas demonstrated vitality and strength. Partly because the major waves of Jewish immigration to this country from Europe occurred before World War II, historians have paid relatively little attention to European Jewish cultural and social life in the years between the two wars. This lack of attention is also true of Jews who became Bundists, nationalists, and assimilationists, but it is especially applicable to the Orthodox community, which gained greater influence in the community at large during this time than it had enjoyed for hundreds of years. Much of its growth and influence can be attributed to the high level of organization achieved in those years. Advances in communications and the burgeoning communities in the United States facilitated the fund-raising process essential to the well-being of the yeshivas. Moreover, the expansion that these developments made possible had a salutary effect of its own. Their graduates carried the philosophy of the yeshiva with them wherever they lived, and in so doing enhanced the already sizeable reputations of the various *rosh yeshivas*. In a community where most Jews, educated or not, now recognized the value of such education, if not for themselves, then for their young, these bearers of the tradition were both respected and admired.

Since the yeshivas were now far less dependent upon the local communities, their power base rivaled and often exceeded that of the local rabbis who nominally led the communities.[36]

How the increased influence of the yeshivas would have affected the structure and general life of the community[37] had they continued to grow can only be speculated upon. The outbreak of World War II permanently altered the nature of these institutions as rabbis and students died by the thousands and those able to escape, mostly via Vilna, Lithuania, eventually made their way to Israel and the United States. One of the most productive eras in Jewish scholarship and leadership had ended in the flames of Hitler's holocaust against the Jews. But the flight of the survivors and their determination to preserve their heritage meant that the long and ancient history of the yeshiva would continue in still another country.

CHAPTER 2

An Ancient Tradition in a New Land

The Beginnings of Jewish Education in America

The earliest beginnings of Jewish education in America were quite modest, and gave no indication that the United States was destined to become one of the greatest centers of talmudic scholarship in the world. The first yeshiva at the elementary school level was established in the 1750s. Known as the Minchat Areb Yeshiva, it was founded by members of the Shearith Israel Congregation who wished to give their young both a general education and an appreciation of the faith. During the nineteenth century similar schools were begun, and in 1886 Etz Chaim, the first such school for Eastern European immigrants, was started.[1] It was not until 1896, however, that yeshivas at the advanced level made their first appearance on the American scene. In that year the Rabbi Isaac Elchanan Theological Seminary (RIETS) was set up on New York City's Lower East Side by a group of men interested in providing some form of education for Jewish youth that went beyond the basic level.[2]

To understand fully the significance of this undertaking, it is necessary to consider the environment from which it emerged. Between 1881 and 1914, approximately 2 million Jews made their way to the United States from Eastern Europe. Most of these immigrants arrived impoverished. Many had spent their

18

last pennies for the trip and their most pressing problem was securing employment. They soon learned that this meant working on the Sabbath. Whereas in the Eastern European *shtetl* (small town) working on the Day of Rest would have brought condemnation, the American community, with its weak Orthodox leadership, could exercise little influence. The leaders of these groups of Americanized Jews of Sephardic (from Spain and Portugal) and German origin also displayed a condescending attitude toward their Russian and Polish brethren. Besides, their brand of Orthodoxy was alien to that which the Eastern European immigrant had known in the old country. Finally, the spread of socialism, Marxism, secularism, and anarchism in Russia and Poland meant that many immigrants arrived with antireligious beliefs and attitudes. As a result, community norms promoting observance of the laws were virtually nonexistent. The situation was exacerbated by the fact that many of those who came were no longer strictly orthodox either prior to or shortly after emigration. Their very arrival was a likely indicator of their views, for America had been roundly condemned by European religious leaders, who saw it as a spiritual wasteland, a place where adherence to ''Torah law'' was extremely difficult, if not impossible.

The social context within which the immigrant attempted to carve out a living space for himself and his family was also at variance with traditional religious values and practices. The Lower East Side, where most Jews first settled, was a haven for crime of all sorts, including prostitution, gambling, and juvenile delinquency. Family values were rapidly eroded as children saw their parents forced to accept unsuitable work, for long hours, at little pay. Faced with hardship and deprivation, many abandoned their religion, hoping that acculturation to the dominant society would make their lot easier. The bitterness with which many viewed their tradition and their disrespect for it is captured in the following announcement of a ball to be held by Jewish anarchists in 1890 in Brooklyn:

Grand Yom Kippur Ball
With theatre
Arranged with the consent of all new rabbis of Liberty
Koll Nydre Night and Day
In the year 5651, after the invention of the Jewish idols,

and 1890, after the birth of the false Messiah. . . .
The Koll Nydre will be offered by John Most.
Music, Dancing, buffet, "Marseillaise," and other hymns
against Satan.[3]

While the anarchists did not represent the prevailing mode
of thinking in the Jewish community, they did have a constituency of sorts and the mere fact that such an advertisement was
even posted said much about the impotence of Orthodox
Judaism in those days.

The differences between the old and the new homeland were
aptly stated by one observer close to the Lower East Side scene:

> In a simple Jewish community in Russia, where the *chaider*
> [Jewish elementary school] is the only school, where the
> government is hostile and the Jews therefore thrown back
> upon their own customs, the boy loves his religion, he loves
> his parents, his highest ambition is to be a great scholar—to
> know the Bible in all its glorious meaning, to know the
> Talmudical comments upon it, and to serve God. . . . But in
> America, at the beginning—from his playmates in the
> streets, from his older brother or sister, he picks up a little
> English, a little American slang, hears older boys boast of
> prizefighter Bernstein, and vaguely to feel that there is a
> strange and fascinating life on the street . . . he may even
> begin to black boots, gamble in pennies, and be filled with a
> "wild surmise" about American dollars. . . . [In public
> school] He achieves a growing comprehension and sym-
> pathy with the independent, free rather skeptical spirit of the
> American boy . . . and tends to prefer Sherlock Holmes to
> Abraham as a hero.[4]

Small wonder, then, that Jewish education should have
been low on the new arrivals' list of priorities.

Yeshiva University: Emergence and Growth

It is against this backdrop that we must consider the
establishment of the Rabbi Isaac Elchanan Theological
Seminary. Little is known about the specific motivations of those
who attended, since neither these individuals nor the institution
itself left many records of those early years. The yeshiva's charter

identified the school as a place where Talmud and the language of the land would be taught.[5]

The first *rebbes* were of Lithuanian origin and training and the school met in the apartment of one of the teachers, Rabbi Moses Matlin, who had studied in the yeshiva of Kovno, Lithuania. From the outset, the yeshiva was committed to the idea of *Torah lishmo,* viewing ordination as of only secondary importance. Eventually, though, rabbinic ordination and secular studies became two of the most basic features of the yeshiva.

The students included those born and raised here, whose parents were involved in the yeshiva's early development, as well as recent immigrants, quite a few of whom were about to receive or had already received ordination in the European yeshivas. The students ranged generally between sixteen and twenty-one years of age. H. Bramson, President of RIETS in 1900, envisioned the school as a place where educators and rabbis would be trained who could relate to the American environment and the particular demands it made on new citizens. Still, most of the students in the early days did not enter these fields. Of the eleven students attending the school in 1901, only two became Hebrew teachers and one a rabbi. Akiva Matlin, Rabbi Matlin's son, even went to the University of Tennessee Medical School.

The early years of the twentieth century were a time of growth and expansion for RIETS. Separate divisions were begun for older and younger students, a small building was purchased, and the newly formed Union of Orthodox Rabbis (*Agudas haRabbonim*) threw its full support behind the yeshiva. In a sense, the yeshiva served as a place where European immigrants could make the transition to American culture without serious dislocation. Notwithstanding their European training, many of the students wanted secular studies to become part of the RIETS curriculum. After several student strikes over the issues, the school's program was redesigned to include the knowledge the students felt was necessary for future American rabbis. In addition to a secular program and secular subjects, training was also given in Jewish culture and history.[6]

In 1915 Etz Chaim Yeshiva merged with the Rabbi Isaac Elchanan Theological Seminary, with Etz Chaim assuming responsibility for training at the elementary and high school levels, offering both religious and secular classes. RIETS became solely

an advanced yeshiva, charged with preparing students for ordination. The selection of Dr. Bernard Revel, a man well trained
in both talmudic and secular scholarship, to serve as head of the
institution, reflected the board's view that the American student
needed to be well versed in both. [7]

Under Dr. Revel's direction the yeshiva expanded its program. Students in RIETS were required to take courses in Jewish history, Bible, and Hebrew. Besides recognizing the need for
such training in a general sense the leaders of the school were
faced with a changing student body. In the earlier period, those
who attended RIETS were mostly immigrants. By 1915, however, World War I had all but ended immigration, and the board
realized that it would have to develop a more rounded program
that would be attractive to American-born students. [8] The school
continued to expand, opening a high school called Talmudical
Academy in 1916 and absorbing the Mizrachi–run Hebrew
Teachers' Institute in 1921. On March 29, 1928, Yeshiva College was established as a four-year liberal arts school. It was the
first such institution under Orthodox Jewish auspices. Using his
considerable personal charm and persuasiveness, Dr. Revel succeeded in convincing key members of the Orthodox community
that instruction in the liberal arts and sciences would enable
young Jewish men to realize the best of both worlds.

There is no doubt that Yeshiva College's orientation was toward combining secular with religious studies. While Dr. Revel
realized his dream of secular and religious studies under one
roof, there was much opposition to it from various elements in
the Orthodox community. Many of its members had been
brought up in a European environment which viewed with deep
suspicion all efforts at secularization. To them, secular education
beyond elementary school was associated with irreligiosity. They
wished to see Yeshiva as a place where the supremacy of Torah
was both unchallenged and undiluted. In 1932, the following
anonymous placard was distributed in Orthodox synagogues
throughout the east coast:

> We Jews of New York discovered that in the Yeshiva Rabbi
> Isaac Elchanan . . . there is a nest of atheism and Apikursus
> (denial of God). Therefore we do warn and announce, that
> you should not send your children or the children of your ac-
> quaintances into this Yeshiva until you will find out what is

going on in the Yeshiva, who is responsible for the terrible situation, and how it is to be remedied.[9]

Such tensions were even more pronounced in the school itself, where the *rosh yeshivas* (those teaching in RIETS) made plain their opposition to secular influences which they felt would alter the character of the institution. In the 1930s, when the Depression created financial hardship for those employed at Yeshiva, the protests grew more vociferous as the *rosh yeshivas* became suspicious that funds that might have gone to RIETS were being diverted to the college and the Teacher's Institute.[10]

Imbued with the idea that the yeshiva should represent the highest standards of excellence in all areas, Dr. Revel naturally sought to attract the best minds of the Lithuanian yeshivas to give classes at RIETS. One who was successfully recruited in 1922 was Rabbi Solomon Polachek, a brilliant disciple of the famed European sage, Rabbi Chaim Soloveichik. Having taught in the yeshivas of Bialystok and Lida, schools which included some secular subjects as part of their curriculum, he had the combination of openness to new ideas and respect for traditional ways that Dr. Revel was seeking. In 1929, Rabbi Moshe Soloveichik accepted an invitation to teach at Yeshiva. Almost immediately upon his arrival, Rabbi Soloveichik gained the respect and admiration of his students as a brilliant and demanding teacher. Other well-known scholars who taught at Yeshiva for varying lengths of time or gave guest lectures there included rabbis Shimon Shkop, Avrohom Bloch, Aharon Kotler, and Boruch Ber Leibowitz.

In more than a few instances, visiting rabbis invited promising students to study at the European yeshivas. This helped create a feeling of closeness between the American and European yeshiva communities. Nevertheless, despite these contacts, many in Europe were opposed to emigration to America, not only because of concern about the state of Orthodoxy there, but also because of a desire to maintain the strength of the European yeshivas. The following remarks by Rabbi Yerucham Levovitz of the famed Mirrer Yeshiva, aimed at a *rosh yeshiva* about to depart for America, were typical:

Under no circumstances may one forsake a *makom Torah* [place where Torah is studied] without clear permission

from heaven. . . . Furthermore, we are afraid that your decision . . . will destroy several yeshivas, as it will become a
light matter in their eyes to pack up and leave for America. [11]

Despite the presence of prominent scholars in RIETS, men
whose abilities were acknowledged by all who moved within the
orbit of talmudic learning, opposition to Yeshiva's philosophy
was constant. Sometimes it was rancorous. When the famed
head of the yeshiva in Baranowicz, Rabbi Elchonon Wasserman,
visited the United States, he praised the more traditional institution, Mesivta Torah Vodaath, and condemned Yeshiva College.
He refused, despite personal pleas by Dr. Revel, to set foot in the
building. Rabbi Wasserman's view was that although philosophy
had been studied in the past by *gedolim* (giants in scholarship)
such as the Vilna Gaon, in these times there were no individuals
of sufficient stature to study such subjects without risking their
faith.

The Hebrew Theological College and the Orthodox Rabbinical Seminary

The second major yeshiva founded in America was not a
traditional yeshiva. Established in 1922 as a rabbinical seminary,
the Hebrew Theological College (HTC) of Chicago was the out-
growth of a high school set up at the turn of the century. Chicago
had witnessed the arrival of about 250,000 Jews in the early part
of the twentieth century, and there was a need for a local institution to provide advanced training for committed Jews. Like
Yeshiva College, the HTC offered secular studies and courses in
Bible and Hebrew literature, taught by trained teachers as well
as rabbis. Owing in part to its location and its pedagogical approach, it did not, as a rule, attract scholars of the same caliber as
those in some of the other yeshivas. Nonetheless, it had a highly
qualified faculty and was successful in training a large number of
young men for the rabbinate. [12]

Today's advanced yeshivas incorporate, in varying degrees,
the teaching of ethics in the spirit of the *mussar* movement
founded by Rabbi Yisroel Salanter in the nineteenth century.
Surprisingly, the founding of the first *mussar* yeshiva in this country, and the first yeshiva patterned almost completely after those

in Europe, has received little attention. Called the Beis Medrash leRabbonim (Orthodox Rabbinical Seminary), it was set up in New Haven by Rabbi Yehuda Levenberg, who had come to America after an illustrious career as a student in the yeshiva of Slabodka. In 1917 he accepted a position as Chief Rabbi of New Haven, and shortly thereafter realized his dream of setting up a yeshiva where Torah would be studied for its own sake. Unlike Yeshiva College or the Hebrew Theological College, no secular studies were offered. The reputation of the yeshiva grew rapidly among talmudic scholars immigrating to the United States. It ordained people but many, after the European style, learned there *lishmo.* Prominent figures who taught there at various times included Rabbi Moshe Feinstein, today one of the greatest rabbinical authorities in the world, Rabbi Yaakov Ruderman, presently head of Ner Israel Rabbinical College, Dr. Samuel Belkin, former President of Yeshiva University, [13] and many other well-known rabbis and leaders in a variety of Jewish organizations. [14]

Most of its students had come directly from Europe and were past high school age. An exception to this rule was Rabbi Solomon Skaist who, at age seventeen, was the youngest student in the yeshiva. Born and raised in Baltimore, Maryland, where his father was a *shochet* (ritual slaughterer), he arrived in New Haven in 1928 not long before the Depression. At a time when men were selling apples on the street, barely eking out a living, students, who in the best of times depended on the community's generosity, were especially hard hit. Rabbi Skaist's description aptly sums up the situation:

> It was just like a European yeshiva. You learned all day and night and the community helped us exist. But when the Depression hit, things got very tough. Every morning a fellow in the yeshiva would get up at 6:30 A.M. and go from butcher to butcher with a paper bag. And they would throw in scraps of meat. Some of the bakers gave us old bread and every Friday before *Shabbos* [Sabbath] some women would come around and donate a couple of chickens. I remember one Rosh Hashanah when all we had was a little *challa* [bread] and two tomatoes and that was it. [15]

Lured by the promise of a good position in a large synagogue and the opportunity to build a larger school, Rabbi Levenberg moved the yeshiva to Cleveland in 1930. Many of the thirty or so *bochorim* did not want to leave New Haven but a number went along to Cleveland. Unfortunately, the move was not successful. The synagogue turned out to be heavily in debt. Despite Rabbi Levenberg's great oratorical skills, he was unable to change its fortunes. Though the yeshiva had what was in those times quite a few students, around forty-five or so, there were disagreements within the school and by the late 1930s the yeshiva had closed.[16]

Torah Vodaath, Chofetz Chaim, and Mesivta Tifereth Jerusalem

The passage of certain laws in the United States further restricted immigration in 1921 and 1924, turning what had been only a trickle of immigrant scholars into almost nothing. It was in this climate that yet a fourth school, Mesivta Torah Vodaath,* decided to form a high school in 1926. Torah Vodaath had been founded as an elementary school in 1917 by a group of people who instituted a modern educational approach that included teaching all subjects in Hebrew. In 1921 Rabbi Shraga Feivel Mendlowitz, a man destined to play one of the most important roles in the development of yeshivas, became principal of the elementary school and reorganized it along more traditional lines. Religious studies were taught in Yiddish and Talmud was taught in a manner similar to the mode of instruction in the Hungarian yeshivas which Rabbi Mendlowitz had attended as a youth. Charismatic, imaginative, and endowed with tremendous energy, he soon proved to be an outstanding administrator and educator. Well versed in traditional learning and Hasidic philosophy, as well as in Hebrew grammar, Jewish history, and philosophy, he was able to develop a program satisfactory to both the more modern and traditional elements involved with the institution. As a result of the esteem in which he was held, he was able to establish a *mesivta,* or high school, five years later.[17]

Dr. Bernard Revel, who headed the Talmudical Academy high school at the time, was not happy about this development.

* Although called "*Mesivta,*" the Hebrew word for high school, both this school and others, such as Mesivta Tifereth Jerusalem, had post–high school (*beis medrash*) divisions. This is simply the way they are popularly referred to among those in the community.

There were far fewer families to draw upon for students than to-day, and he felt that the new high school might weaken his own institution. In addition to pronouncements opposing the new ye-shiva from the *Agudas haRabbonim,* which was closely affiliated with RIETS, strenuous efforts were made by school officials to dissuade students from going there. The following incident high-lights such attempts and demonstrates the depth of concern that existed while at the same time indicating the difficulties facing Rabbi Mendlowitz in persuading parents to send their children to the *mesivta:*

> I went to Torah Vodaas* for elementary school and then to Yitzchak Elchanan [RIETS] for high school. I was there for 2 ½ years when Rabbi Mendlowitz asked me to come back to Torah Vodaas along with about 8 or 9 of my friends. We were all in RIETS. At that time you learned *Gemora* [Talmud] until 3:00 P.M. and then English. Rav Mendlo-witz wanted to break this tradition and have us go to high school at night and learn all day. Then Dr. Revel and Dr. Safir, he was the principal, called us in and they said: "What do you want to leave for? There's no need for a new yeshiva in New York. Torah Vodaas won't last. Stay with us." And they tried to induce us to remain. You know, to offer a young boy five dollars a month in those days was a lot of money. Dr. Revel also said: "we have the Meitsheter Illui [Rabbi Shlomo Polachek] here." Little did they know that he used to come to us [at Torah Vodaath] once a month. I think he wanted to leave Y.U. but the Agudas haRabbonim prevailed upon him not to.
>
> But we left and went to Eastern District High School at night. Go to school at night? You can't imagine what a dis-grace this was for our parents. Only immigrants and the very poor did that. But we went because we wanted to learn and Rav Mendlowitz gave us that feeling. He was the most unique personality in the last 100 years.[18]

In essence, Torah Vodaath was a local school then, attrac-ting mostly children from the Williamsburg, Brooklyn area in which it was situated.[19] A relatively new Orthodox community had begun to grow there shortly after World War I, and the com-munity sent many of its children there.[20] In an effort to raise the prestige of the school, Rabbi Dovid Leibowitz, a well-known

---

*In conversation, Torah Vodaa*th* is almost always called Torah Vodaa*s*.

scholar, was invited to become head of the newly formed *beis medrash,* which was made up primarily of the first graduating high school class, in 1929. Rabbi Leibowitz had studied in the renowned yeshivas of Slabodka and Radin, and he brought to the yeshiva high levels of scholarship accompanied by the Lithuanian emphasis on *mussar.* It was a difficult decision for him to leave Europe, where he had been offered a position at the yeshiva in Warsaw, but, after consulting with the Chofetz Chaim, who instructed him to spread Torah in America, he decided his future lay here.[21]

After a short stay at the yeshiva, during which time he greatly enhanced its reputation, Rabbi Leibowitz left and started his own yeshiva in 1933. His departure was brought about by conflicts between him and Rabbi Mendlowitz. According to former students of that era, the two men differed in philosophy, personality, outlook, and style.[22] Called the Chofetz Chaim Yeshiva, or Rabbinical Seminary of America,* and housed in a four-story building on Bedford Avenue, the yeshiva attracted students from as far away as Pittsburgh, Rochester, Washington, D.C., and Bangor, Maine. The yeshiva developed an approach to talmudic study that reflected that of its Lithuanian *rosh yeshiva.* The Talmud was to be studied carefully and deliberately, with all points subject to rational and searching analysis. Covering ground was not that important—understanding clearly was. A *mussar shmuess* (talk on ethics) was given once a week, and the *bochorim* were required to study ethics on their own as well. In addition, emphasis was placed upon training individuals to go out into the community. Reb Dovid's philosophy is best summed up by his son, Rabbi Henoch Leibowitz, presently *rosh yeshiva* of the Chofetz Chaim Yeshiva:

> My father made the effort to implant Torah in his students in a way that will not just give them emotional inspiration which passes and fades and is not long-lasting, but an inspiration that comes as a result of many, many years of Torah study. As a result, one is imbued with the beauty and profundity and the *mussar* aspect which is very much stressed in the yeshiva, as my father learned in Slabodka. This feeling contributes greatly to that which the students get . . . that

* Throughout this book, "Chofetz Chaim Yeshiva" refers to the institution located in Queens, N.Y., not one by the same name that is situated in Manhattan.

its moral values and teachings, as derived from Torah directly, can exert a tremendous impact to those one comes in contact with.[23]

The impression made on many of his students was deep and long lasting. Hundreds entered the rabbinate and Jewish education, motivated by his dedication and high standards. As one former student put it:

> "*Rebbe*" emphasized understanding things clearly. In learning he would not allow us to quote authority unless we were ready to defend it logically. He never tried to impress us with what he knew. Rather his aim was always to get us to understand on our own.[24]

About two years after Rabbi Leibowitz' departure from Torah Vodaath, Rabbi Shlomo Heiman became head of Torah Vodaath. He remained there until his death in 1944. During these years, with Rabbi Heiman serving as *rosh yeshiva* and Rabbi Mendlowitz (he preferred, out of modesty, to be called "Mr.") as administrator, Torah Vodaath entered a period of significant growth and expansion.

Rabbi Heiman had been head of the well-known yeshiva in Baranowicz, Poland, prior to his arrival, and he attempted to maintain the standards of the yeshiva at a very high level. His goal was to elevate the American yeshiva *bochur* to the point where he was a serious student of the Talmud, not simply a young man acquiring a basic education. One of his students recalled:

> Rav Heiman gave you a feeling for love of learning that penetrated into your very body and soul. He considered his first twenty or thirty students, as twenty or thirty yeshivas. What he meant was if each individual was a potential yeshiva one had to be very careful with how something was explained. He always tried to show how maybe what you were saying was the right answer but he never allowed it to compromise his search for truth.

At Mendlowitz' urging, the yeshiva had adopted as a primary goal the training of *baalei batim* (laymen), men who, though they would not enter the field of Jewish education, would become scholars, not dilettantes, and who would study *Gemora* on their own as adults serving also as role models for their own children.

Under the joint guidance of rabbis Heiman and Mendlowitz, an entire generation of such individuals was trained. Many entered the rabbinate and Jewish education but an even greater number became lay leaders of the Jewish community, professionals in other areas, and businessmen.

In the meantime, yet another yeshiva opened its doors on the Lower East Side. Many associate the establishment of Mesivta Tifereth Jerusalem's (MTJ) advanced division with the appointment of Rabbi Moshe Feinstein as its head in 1938. In reality, MTJ was already in operation as an advanced yeshiva by the early 1930s under the leadership of Rabbi Joseph Adler. Many of the students attended City College of New York three evenings a week while pursuing their religious studies during the day. Often, people came with their friends to study at a particular yeshiva. Rabbi Morris Charner described his decision to enroll in MTJ as follows:

> I grew up in Newark and there was no yeshiva there at the time. So in 1932 my mother, who was a very religious woman, began a campaign to persuade Mesivta Tifereth Jerusalem to open up a dormitory for out of town boys so they could come to the yeshiva and after two years she was successful. Besides me, there was a whole contingent of about ten boys from Newark.[25]

MTJ was not a major yeshiva in the thirties. When asked why he chose the school over Yeshiva College, Rabbi David Singer of Boro Park, Brooklyn, responded:

> My father was a very Orthodox man. I wouldn't go to Yeshiva College. But there was another reason too. Many of the *bochorim* who came had no money and the yeshiva didn't charge too much. If you couldn't pay, they let you get away with it. The conditions were not too good either since it was a poor yeshiva. In one room we had 20 guys. People brought their own butter and cream cheese. You would get a roll with a knife stuck in it. That was supposed to be the butter, but they never opened it. Once in a while I had an egg for breakfast. We were always called into the office and asked if we knew any rich people right before they went on a campaign giving out calendars.[26]

Did Rabbi Singer mean that Yeshiva College was not an Orthodox yeshiva? Not at all. It was simply that then, as today, there were those families for whom a yeshiva that had secular and religious studies in one building was not good enough.

It is important to understand that Orthodoxy was not the ascendant pattern of religious identification during this period. Many Jews who were not disaffiliated entirely from the faith had aligned themselves with either Conservative or Reform Judaism. During the twenties and thirties, there was a decided shift on the part of the Eastern European community toward the Conservative movement as they sought to establish a prestigious counterpart to the Reform temples of the German Jews who preceded them.[27] Most often this took place in the areas of second settlement, but observant Orthodox Jews were certainly not a majority on the Lower East Side, the area of first settlement, either. The strains of maintaining an Orthodox way of life, in an open society characterized by high mobility and powerful trends encouraging secular values, often proved too difficult for a community in transition.[28]

Thus, most parents did not elect to send their children to yeshivas. Orthodox leaders today often feel that many American Jews of that time were not only unwilling to sacrifice opportunity for the sake of tradition, but had an unduly pessimistic view of the problems standing in the way of Orthodoxy. Often, these Jews were themselves somewhat observant. Addressing himself to this issue, Rabbi Moshe Feinstein, who is probably the foremost *halachic* (legal) authority alive today, and whose decisions are crucial for hundreds of thousands of Jews, said:

> Even though they themselves were kosher Jews and withstood many temptations; yet by harping to their children about the difficulty of keeping the Torah, they created a great negative temptation in the eyes of their children, who were unable to understand it. Those fathers misled a whole generation from Judaism. That was the counsel of the *yeitzer horo* [evil spirit] and it was successful.[29]

According to Rabbi Yitzchok Hutner,* who came here in the 1930s and later headed Yeshiva Rabbi Chaim Berlin:

> It was like a *midbar* [desert]. We had so much to do. We had to convince Jewish parents that it wasn't so terrible if the child didn't go to a public elementary school. The parents

* Deceased.

were only afraid of the truant officer. They taught nothing in these schools! Nothing! They taught that two plus two equals four. It took them eight years to teach what you could learn in one. For our Jewish children it was a joke. And so we built and developed our own schools. And they didn't lose anything from not going to public schools.[30]

Even among those who considered themselves strictly Orthodox, yeshiva education beyond elementary, and especially high school, was often considered a luxury. Comparing the past to the present, Rabbi Moshe Sherer, President of Agudath Israel of America, stated:

When I was a youngster, it was very possible for someone to be an Orthodox Jew without continuing . . . past elementary school yeshiva. . . . Today it is unthinkable that one can really be an Orthodox Jew unless he at least graduated yeshiva high school.[31]

Clearly, attending yeshiva in no way constituted a movement of the masses. This being the case, was this era an important one in the long history of yeshivas? The answer is yes—especially in terms of the effect of its graduates upon the shape and direction subsequently taken by American Jewry in the years that followed. Those that went through the yeshiva system constituted an elite of sorts. Besides setting a standard to which others might aspire and respect, they became bearers of the culture in whatever occupations they entered, whatever communities they lived in, and among all who had contact with them. More directly, they developed an entire generation of communal and lay leaders whose influence stretched far beyond the confines of Orthodoxy. These individuals formed the nucleus of those who staffed the elementary school yeshivas that were beginning to appear throughout the country. Between 1938 and 1946, the number of such schools in the United States grew from 14 to 84 and the number of students increased from about 4,000 to 17,500.[32]

Ner Israel Rabbinical College and Yeshiva Rabbi Chaim Berlin

Two yeshivas that arose in the 1930s deserve special mention. Ner Israel Rabbinical College (also known as Ner Israel

Yeshiva and Ner Yisroel Yeshiva) was founded in 1933 in Balti-more, Maryland, by Rabbi Yaakov Ruderman, who is still its *rosh yeshiva*. After receiving his training in Slabodka, he came to the United States and affiliated himself with Rabbi Levenberg's yeshiva, by then in Cleveland. After teaching there for some time, he left for Baltimore to found his own institution. Rabbi Ruderman described the skepticism that greeted his efforts to re-create a yeshiva modeled after those in Lithuania:

> When I first came to Baltimore in the early thirties, many non-observant Jews didn't know what a yeshiva was. They [the Jewish community] didn't believe it could be built. After all, people came here to learn English, not to attend a yeshiva.[33]

At first the yeshiva barely survived. The minutes of the first ladies' auxiliary include an entry thanking one woman for hav-ing donated six herring to the yeshiva.[34] Adding to the difficulties was the location of the yeshiva in a city where support for the idea of Jewish learning was not nearly so great as it was in New York or Chicago. Nonetheless, aided by about thirty Orthodox families, the first fifteen or so students stayed on and became the nucleus for what eventually became one of the largest and most successful yeshivas in America. The yeshiva was one of the few that began with an advanced division, adding a high school later.

In assessing the general contribution of yeshivas such as Ner Israel, it is important to take into account the population they served. Though Orthodox Jews in the United States restricted themselves, for the most part, to the heavily populated areas, a good number migrated to parts of the country where there were only small Orthodox communities. More often than not, their choice was bounded by economic necessity. A kosher butcher or the rabbi of a synagogue might be the only such individual for hundreds of miles. Interested as these Jews were in transmitting their own religious values to their offspring, they were eager to support institutions that made it unnecessary for them to send their children to New York City, though, of course, quite a few did. For such people yeshivas in Cleveland, Baltimore, and Chicago served a vital function as regional centers for dispersed communities.[35]

The Yeshiva Rabbi Chaim Berlin is the oldest such institu-tion in Brooklyn, having opened an elementary school in

Brownsville in 1906. It was not until 1939, though, that it became an advanced yeshiva. In that year, one of the most brilliant and dynamic figures ever to head an American yeshiva was appointed as its *rosh yeshiva*. To the extent that successful movements often have great leadership, Rabbi Hutner exemplified this requirement, and a portrait of this individual is important both in terms of understanding the role of the *rosh yeshiva* in a yeshiva and in terms of comprehending how such leaders affect their followers.[36]

Born in 1907, Rabbi Hutner studied in the Slabodka Yeshiva and later on in Hebron, Palestine, when the Slabodka Yeshiva inaugurated a branch there. Following a massacre of Jewish residents of Hebron in 1929, he returned to Europe and studied at the University of Berlin, an unusual move for a man steeped in the Lithuanian talmudic tradition. He arrived in America in 1935, engaging first in private scholarship and holding a post on the faculty of the Rabbi Jacob Joseph School (this school did not at the time have an advanced division) before accepting an invitation to head Chaim Berlin.[37]

From the start, Rabbi Hutner established an extremely close relationship with his students. Most of them were American-born or -raised, and often their exposure to him was their first contact with a European–trained scholar of high stature. According to a number of students from those days, Rabbi Hutner had a flair for the dramatic. The following comments were typical of this view:

> I came to the yeshiva as a young fellow from out of town and I still remember from a quarter of a century ago what it was like to hear a *mussar shmuess* from him. We met in a room in the yeshiva and it was very crowded with about 50 or 60 guys in the room and a path would have to be made for him. But it was so narrow that it took a miracle on the order of the splitting of the Red Sea to make room for him.

A student who attended in the early 1940s when the *bochorim* had their weekly ethics talk in the *rosh yeshiva*'s home described this in strikingly similar terms:

> We would go in the late afternoon and then, as darkness fell over the room, he would emerge from another room, looking like he had just been in a holy place. And he would sit down, his eyes covered by his hands, never seeming to look at anyone, speaking slowly, dramatically.

Those who attended the yeshiva, even if they did not become part of the inner circle that quickly sprang up around him, felt his interest and concern for their welfare in many ways:

> My roommate had recently become engaged. So I asked him: "Did you tell the *rosh yeshiva*?" And he looked at me, shocked, and said: "Why don't you ask me if I told my father? What do you think?"
>
> When we went over to his house on Purim, each person got a *shalach monos* [a gift given on the holiday of Purim] and he addressed you by your first name.

There were on the average only about fifty to seventy students in the yeshiva in the early years, so perhaps such personal attention is not so striking to the outsider. What was important to the student, however, was that a man whom they knew to be a great *talmid chochom* (scholar) took such an interest in them.

Perhaps no other yeshiva was so completely dominated by one individual. Even the school board was subservient to him. It is said that as an independently wealthy man he did not, as was the case with other *rosh yeshivas,* depend upon the board members for his livelihood. On one occasion, hearing that members of the school board were dissatisfied with a particular policy, he threatened to start a new yeshiva and take every student with him. The lay leaders backed down. Rabbi Hutner's powerful personality may have been responsible for a certain *esprit de corps* and, in some cases, elitism on the part of many students in the yeshiva who let it be known to those attending other yeshivas that their institution was in a class by itself. Called "Chaim Berlin *shtick*" by its detractors, it gave those in the school a feeling of unity and self-confidence. One individual who attended the yeshiva analyzed it in the following manner:

> I think that it had a very important and positive effect on the fellows, though I did not belong to the "in group." I went to college and, while permitted, college was looked down upon. With some exceptions, the top fellows didn't go. The strength of Rav Hutner's personality—my feet trembled whenever I spoke to him—drew us all in. It enabled you to resist your more modern parents who often wanted you to go to college. He built up your ego and made you feel you were great.

It is difficult to say to what extent, if any, Rabbi Hutner cultivated such an image, and precisely what he had in mind when and if he did so. Although he was interviewed, he chose not to speak on this topic. What can be said, however, is that a large number of important scholars and Jewish community leaders were produced by the yeshiva, and all with whom I spoke cited Rabbi Hutner as the central influence in shaping their outlook on life. In truth, virtually all heads of yeshivas strongly affect the lives of those who attend their institutions. This is simply one of the better attested examples of the phenomenon.[38]

Rabbi Shraga Feivel Mendlowitz: Leader and Visionary

Mention has been made of Rabbi Mendlowitz in terms of his contributions to the growth of Yeshiva Torah Vodaath. His major role was that of visionary, a man who foresaw with remarkable prescience the need to develop Jewish education on a national scale. To realize this goal, it would be necessary to train an entire "army" of young men committed to this objective. With this in mind, Rabbi Mendlowitz established an institute in Spring Valley, New York, called Esh Dat, literally "Fire of Faith," where students were to be trained so that not only would they know Talmud, but they would also have the skills necessary to transmit it to others and the motivation to build schools throughout the United States. For a variety of reasons, Esh Dat did not survive as a training institute and was eventually replaced by a major advanced yeshiva, Beis Medrash Elyon. Nevertheless, many who fell under his influence went into Jewish education imbued with his spirit and ideals. His crowning achievement, in the view of many, was the creation in 1944 of Torah Umesorah (National Society for Hebrew Day Schools), an organization which today numbers more than 500 day schools throughout the United States and Canada.[39]

To comprehend fully the range and scope of Rabbi Mendlowitz' endeavors, we might point out some of the many things he tried to do but was unable to accomplish in his lifetime. He hoped to create a federation of yeshivas which would consolidate all fund-raising efforts so that the various yeshivas would not compete for often scarce funds, instead pooling their resources and sharing equally in the benefits of such efforts. He also suggested, at one point, that upon receiving ordination graduates of the yeshivas be required to do a two-year internship in a small town in a part of the country where they were needed. Moreover, he wanted to have the yeshiva pay individuals to travel through rural America, tutoring young Jewish boys and girls who lived in villages and on farms.[40] It was innovative thinking of this sort, combined with selflessness and humility, that made Rabbi Mendlowitz a "giant of the spirit." Finally, he was gifted with an ability to remember the little things that often tell more about a man's character than those that take place in the public arena. Rabbi Elias Schwartz, a former student, recalls such an incident:

> One year during the Depression, Rabbi Mendlowitz called me down to his office and said: "Here's $50.00 for *Pesach* [Passover]: go buy yourself a suit and some other things." So I said, "Rabbi, you never gave me money in the past, so why now?" "In the past you didn't need it. This year your father's not working and you need it." You have to consider that I was one of hundreds of students.[41]

The War Years: RIETS, Lakewood, Telshe, and Mirrer Yeshiva

Perhaps more than any other issue, the outbreak of World War II unified the entire Jewish community. After Poland was invaded by Germany in 1939, scholars from the various yeshivas of Europe began desperately searching for a place of refuge. Many went to Vilna, Lithuania, where some of them were able to secure permission to travel to the United States and Palestine through Russia and Japan.[42] The arrangements were often complex, involving delicate negotiations and maneuvers at various levels of government, both in this country and in Europe. Yeshiva College played a crucial role in making the arrangements for the arrival of many prominent individuals in the yeshiva world.[43]

The year 1941 was marked by several developments which were to have a profound impact upon the future of advanced yeshivas in America. At RIETS, Rabbi Joseph B. Soloveitchik was elevated to the post of *rosh yeshiva,* succeeding his father, who had died that year. Also, during that year the leaders of an important European yeshiva, the Telshe Yeshiva, came to this country and reestablished the school in Cleveland. Finally, Rabbi Aharon

Kotler, head of the yeshiva in Kletsk, Poland, was among a group of scholars who arrived here. He was destined to transform higher Jewish learning in America.

Rabbi Soloveitchik came to the United States in 1932 at the age of twenty-nine with a reputation for having mastered both religious and secular studies. Born into a distinguished rabbinical family, he had studied with his grandfather, the famed Reb Chaim Brisker Soloveichik, and with his father Rabbi Moshe Soloveichik. In addition, he held a doctorate in philosophy from the University of Berlin.[44]

Under his leadership, Yeshiva's reputation was greatly enhanced, and hundreds of American–trained rabbis made him their mentor in all matters spiritual and religious. While he is condemned by many in the "yeshiva community"* for his "modern" views, thousands regard him as the foremost personality in the Orthodox community. Among the organizations he has led or strongly affected are the Rabbinical Council of America and the Religious Zionists of America, and even those who feel his views are too radical do not dispute his vast knowledge of talmudic law and erudition. An accomplished speaker and outstanding teacher, his published work has focused primarily on the unique relationship between the Jew and Jewish law.[45] Insofar as the other rosh yeshivas are concerned, "the Rav," as he is popularly known, has rarely participated in their deliberations, nor has he been accepted as part of their circle. Nevertheless, the often angry denunciations of his liberal attitudes by those in the rest of the yeshiva community are in themselves an indication of how much a part of their world he really is. Within Yeshiva University, he does not impose his views or philosophy on the other rabbis who teach there. There are, in fact, rabbis within RIETS who are either more liberal or more conservative than "the Rav," whose own positions on a variety of issues often fall into one or the other camp.

The Telshe Yeshiva lay directly in the path of the German Army as it marched through Poland and western Russia. Thus,

---

* By "yeshiva community" or "yeshiva world" we mean students, parents of students, alumni, institutional faculty, administrators, community leaders, and all those who support the yeshiva and consider themselves a part of it, at least in a general sense. It can be noted that there exists a definite perception of a distinct group of this sort among members of the community that is reflected in both their interaction among themselves and with others as well as in their own writings.

it became clear early in the war that the yeshiva would have to be transferred to a safer location. In 1940 rabbis Elya Meir Bloch and Chaim Mordechai Katz set out on a long and arduous journey through Siberia and Japan, finally arriving in Seattle. On October 28, 1941, the reborn yeshiva opened its doors in Cleveland, having been invited there by a group of Orthodox Jews interested in seeing an advanced institution of high caliber become part of their community.*[46]

At this point, rabbis Katz and Bloch tackled the problems of obtaining visas and asylum for other surviving members of the Telshe Yeshiva community. (The Nazis had massacred most of the Jews in Telshe shortly after the two *rosh yeshivas* had departed on their mission.) Earlier, in 1940, they had appealed to Dr. Bernard Revel to aid them in rescuing various scholars, and he had responded by bringing as many as possible to this country. Since Yeshiva was recognized as a legitimate institution of higher learning by the U.S. government, it found itself pressured by numerous European yeshivas, but Dr. Revel, having studied in Telshe as a youth, had a special place in his heart for the yeshiva.[47]

Meanwhile, the Telshe Yeshiva turned to the task of rebuilding so that the traditions that had sustained it in Europe would take root on American soil. There had been a "*Telzer derech,*" or characteristic way of learning, since the early years of the yeshiva in the 1880s. It was characterized most by an analytical approach which, through dialectical reasoning, focused on a clear comprehension of Jewish law. It did not consider *mussar* as a separate area, but as an integral part of the *halacha* (law). Organizationally, the school was probably the first in Eastern Europe to have separate classes based on one's talmudic knowledge. It also created a preparatory school for the higher yeshiva and two elementary schools. It was known for having a strict, disciplinary approach toward the students. Its leaders both commanded and demanded respect. This view of how a yeshiva should be run was brought to America and to this very day is a hallmark of the institution. In addition, various songs, prayers, styles of lecture, study schedules, and even seating arrangements were preserved intact whenever possible.[48] All this served to instill in those af-

* Unless otherwise indicated, all references to the Telshe Yeshiva in the United States refer to the institution located in Cleveland, not the branch in Chicago.

filiated with the yeshiva a feeling that they were part of a long and still unbroken chain of Jewish history, carriers of a noble and ancient tradition.

An understanding of the yeshiva movement in America is impossible without dwelling to some degree on the history and development of the Beth Medrash Govoha, established in April, 1943 in Lakewood, New Jersey. This institution is known as the "Harvard" of yeshivas, and its impact on the community has been enormous. The man responsible for this was "Reb" Aharon Kotler.

Reb Aharon was born in 1892 into a distinguished rabbinical family. After private study with his father, he entered the yeshiva of Rabbi Sender Shapiro at the age of ten. One year after his *bar mitzvah* (confirmation), he was admitted to the renowned yeshiva in Slabodka, where he was soon recognized as an exceptionally brilliant young man. He married the daughter of Rabbi Isser Zalman Meltzer and became assistant to him in his yeshiva at Slutsk, relocated to Kletsk, Poland, following World War I. In 1921 Rabbi Kotler became head of the yeshiva, a post he held for twenty years.

In 1935 Rabbi Kotler visited the United States, where he lectured and met with prominent members of the Orthodox community, including Rabbi Mendlowitz of Torah Vodaath, to whom he outlined the type of yeshiva that he felt was needed to insure the growth of talmudic scholarship in America. It was, in his view, to be an institution located away from the urban centers and devoted entirely to learning for its own sake, not ordination, as was most often the case with the yeshivas in the United States at the time. As a result of this visit, he was known to many leaders in this country not only by reputation, but personally, before he settled in the United States. One of those he met was Irving Bunim, a leader and philanthropist in the Jewish community. Because of his position in the European community, Reb Aharon was one of a small group of individuals given special visas and asylum in the United States by President Roosevelt. But funds were needed for transportation and support of Rabbi Kotler and other refugees. One of the main obstacles to such support was the lack of awareness in the Jewish community of both the desperation and the urgency confronting European Jewry. Bunim and others raced against time to persuade as many people as possible to become actively involved. One event described by

Bunim indicates both the difficulty of these efforts and the drastic measures that were occasionally taken to convert others to the cause of saving Jewish lives:

> IB: During the war he [Rabbi Kotler] was stuck in Russia. I knew about him so I helped get him out. One *Shabbos* noon I was sitting and having lunch when Rabbi Boruch Kaplan [a founder of the Orthodox Beth Jacob schools] and Rabbi Sender Linchner [a son-in-law of Rabbi Mendlowitz] came over in a cab. Rabbi Feinstein, Rabbi Heiman, and Rabbi Mendlowitz sent them to me in a cab on *Shabbos* to go and raise money for that purpose. I think it was 1940. So we went to Flatbush in a cab. They wanted to lynch me there in Flatbush [for violating the Sabbath by traveling in an automobile], but with the rabbis there we convinced them. This is how we raised the money. Then we took it to the Joint Distribution Committee and they made the arrangements.
>
> WH: Why did you feel it was necessary to go on the Sabbath?
>
> IB: For two reasons. First, we needed the money immediately and second, the idea was to create a commotion . . . so they shouldn't sleep on it.[49]

After an arduous journey through Russia, Rabbi Kotler arrived in San Francisco and then traveled by train to New York City. From the moment of his arrival, he was driven by two primary goals: saving other Jews from the clutches of death in Europe and raising the level of Jewish learning in America. Although, in the beginning he worked mostly on the first goal, he did not at any point lay aside the other. Reb Aharon helped the important organization called the *Vaad Hatzala* (Rescue Committee) and was heavily involved in Holocaust–related matters. Still, he found time to give private classes, mostly on weekends, to scholars who were now beginning to come from the great institutions of Eastern Europe.[50] An effort was made to establish a *beis medrash* in White Plains, New York, under the nominal leadership of Rabbi Hillel Bishco, a man whose primary efforts both in Europe and here were devoted to fund-raising, but who was familiar with Lithuanian scholarship. The students had asked Rabbi Kotler to head their group, but he had declined citing the need to continue his rescue efforts. Later, they attempted to persuade other scholars of stature, but for a variety of reasons these men had also turned down the offer. Finally, in desperation, they returned to Reb Aharon and begged him to reconsider, promising that there would be no financial responsibilities.[51] He would simply "say a *shiur*" (give a class). Rabbi Kotler agreed, and in this manner the yeshiva was founded.[52]

There was, of course, still the problem of finding a permanent home for the yeshiva. In accordance with Rabbi Kotler's wishes, it had to be in a small place away from any distractions from learning. In Irving Bunim's words:

> What was needed was a small city without nightclubs, without entertainment. Lakewood was an ideal place because, although it was small, it was a tourist area and near New York; so people would hear about it. So we bought a house together with a lot, for $15,000. I came to Rabbi Kotler with three people—Sam Kaufman, David Shapiro, and Israel Farber. All we had was $5,000—so I personally signed a note for the other $10,000.[53]

Bunim was well versed in Jewish laws and customs; others, while not always knowledgeable in Talmud, gave money because they believed in the importance of Jewish survival.

Another key figure during this time was Rabbi Nissan Waxman, rabbi of Lakewood's Jewish community, who knew Reb Aharon from Europe. Recalling those years, Rabbi Waxman described his efforts to convince Rabbi Kotler to reestablish his yeshiva in the resort town:

> At first, he was reluctant to the idea, claiming that it was a place where people came for pleasure and vanity and did not fit for a spiritual center. However, I persuaded him and persevered, and visited him five times until he was convinced.[54]

From a nucleus of fourteen young men, the Lakewood Yeshiva grew to the point where, with close to 850 students, it is the largest and most prestigious such institution in America, attracting men of college age and older from every corner of the globe.[55]

The role of Reb Aharon in the development of "Lakewood" was, of course, crucial. He embodied the yeshiva in all its aspects. He was a man endowed with many of the qualities essential to the fulfillment of the task he chose for himself. He had dramatic presence, was brilliant, selfless, and incredibly hardworking. Uncompromising in his principles, he won people over to his cause by the sincerity and force of his convictions. As his daughter and long-time personal secretary, Mrs. Sarah Kotler-Schwartzman, put it:

> The late Dr. Abraham Joshua Heschel [well-known theologian and professor at the Jewish Theological Seminary] once challenged me in 1966: "There is no question that your father wrought a revolution in this country. But I never got a satisfactory answer when I asked people close to him. What was the source of his power to influence American Jewish youth? With what personal resources did he do it?" Although a definitive answer may be beyond my immediate capacity, I responded: "Spiritual leadership is successful in proportion to the degree of truthfulness and dedication. Father's devotion to truth was his quintessential quality. He believed absolutely in the truth of the Torah and his own philosophy and his personal sense of mission, responsibility, and selfless dedication were passionate and total."[56]

Eyes blazing, talking very fast, Rabbi Kotler gave his listeners the feeling that they were going to share in a project that would profoundly affect the nature of Jewish education in this country. His view was that the Torah should be studied because it was God's revealed truth, not because it provided a possibility of employment as a rabbi or yeshiva teacher. In his daughter's words:

> Father often used to challenge *baalei batim*. On one such occasion at an emergency fund-raising meeting, he put it in approximately these words: "I don't want you to misunderstand me; I don't want to mislead you. There is a need for *rosh yeshivas* in this country and elsewhere and Lakewood will produce them. There is a need for effective teachers and for the right kind of rabbis and Lakewood will produce these too. There is a need for *baalei-batim-talmidei chachomim* (laymen-scholars) and Lakewood will send them forth. However, the raison d'être of Lakewood is '*limud haTorah lishmo*'—to learn Torah for its own value. It is with this understanding, and for this purpose, that I am asking for your support."[57]

It was not easy to explain and popularize this approach to talmudic education in the United States for the Orthodox community was quite Americanized. Even the right-wing yeshivas such as Torah Vodaath had adopted to some extent the utilitarian view that Talmud study would be oriented toward producing rabbis and teachers. While well aware of the tradition of European yeshivas, they had accommodated themselves in certain areas to life in America and the values of the new American Orthodox communities. Although they would be understandably reluctant to acknowledge this publicly, quite a few rabbis who hold or held Conservative and/or Reform pulpits today received their training and/or ordination from the right-wing yeshivas such as Telshe, Ner Israel, Torah Vodaath, and Chaim Berlin, as well as from the more liberal RIETS. This was especially true during and before World War II. One Reform rabbi in the New York area who received his training at the Telshe Yeshiva in the early 1940s explained: "America was different then insofar as the yeshivas were concerned. Orthodoxy wasn't that strong and they couldn't just throw out people who didn't do what they liked. Many of the students weren't that religious even when they were there."

The problems facing Reb Aharon with respect to education in this country were articulated to me in an interview with his son, Rabbi Shneur Kotler, the present head of the yeshiva:

> The main difficulty was that the level of learning wasn't that high and our desire was to develop a generation of *gedolei Torah* [giants in Torah knowledge] who were American-trained products.
>
> The second obstacle was that my father, may he rest in peace, felt that there should be *Torah lishmo* [for a higher, spiritual purpose] and that all practical benefits would come from it anyway. He felt that *Torah lishmo* tremendously raises the general level of the Jewish community. The problem was that this was against the spirit in the country. People asked: What's the *tachlis* [purpose] of studying Torah? What can be gained from it? This was the attitude. It was hard to explain that sometimes the most lasting things seem to come out from things which seem to have no purpose.[58]

Yet, aided by a cadre of people whose loyalty was total and unquestioning, Rabbi Kotler's dream eventually became the central approach to Talmud study in the yeshiva world.

Like Rabbi Mendlowitz, Reb Aharon paid attention to every detail of ethical life. On one occasion he ran after a beggar in Jerusalem and pressed some coins into his hand, explaining that he recognized the man as one who had approached him several years earlier for alms at a time when he had none to give.[59] On the highway, Rabbi Kotler would make a point of passing through a manned rather than an automatic toll booth, saying: "It's not *kovod habriyos* (respectful of humanity) to pass up a man for a machine."[60] These stories served to underscore the importance to Reb Aharon of making his every act consonant with his religious beliefs.

Rabbi Kotler's achievements for Orthodox Jewry were not limited to rescuing Holocaust victims and establishing a world-famous yeshiva. He was also chairman of the rabbinical board of Torah Umesorah, the nationwide day school organization, and the leader of Chinuch Atzmai, the Agudah–run school system in Israel. A leader by acclamation of thousands of strictly observant Jews around the world, Rabbi Kotler was seen as their supreme authority. In particular, his insistence that Orthodox rabbis should not belong to rabbinical bodies whose members included Conservative and Reform rabbis marked a turning point in the split between the modern and right-wing communities. This view was directed largely at the Synagogue Council of America, which has members from all three groups. Between 1945 and his death in 1962, no major decision of any sort was made without his advice.

The Postwar Period: A Time of Unparalleled Growth

With the Allied victory over the Nazis in 1945 a new era began for the yeshiva world. Between 1947 and 1951 almost 120,000 Jews arrived in the United States. Of these, slightly more than half entered under the Displaced Persons Act of 1949. Among them were thousands of Orthodox Jews. Many had long regarded America as a wasteland of religious life. Were it not for the catastrophe that befell them, these Jews would never have emigrated to American shores. Their decision, forced upon them by circumstances, was destined to change American Jewish life.

While there are studies of the more recent Israeli and Russian Jewish migrations to the United States, plus several works on the Hasidic communities, there is no study focusing on the history of the post–World War II immigrant generation in general and certainly none on the Orthodox community as a whole during this period, one which also saw the arrival of thousands of Hungarian Jews in the wake of the 1956 Hungarian

Revolution.[61] This is unfortunate because it is a group whose impact has been considerable, especially on Jewish education. Largely because of their influence, the growth of Hebrew day schools since World War II has been phenomenal, particularly when one considers the assimilationist tendencies of other ethnic groups in this country. In 1944 there were 39 day schools in the United States. By 1978 the number had grown to 463, including 313 elementary schools and 150 high schools.[62] At the higher levels, between 50 and 60 Lithuanian-style yeshivas and 40 to 50 Hasidic institutions emerged in the last thirty-five years. Most are in or near large American cities, with the majority located in the New York metropolitan area. There are, however, quite a few important schools in other cities, including Lakewood, Cleveland, and Baltimore.

With the rise in population among the Orthodox, the yeshiva movement became more of a mass movement with thousands attending where previously only hundreds had done so. The figures presented in the following chart not only indicate the situation in the mid-sixties, but also demonstrate the steady and significant growth that has occurred since then.

Numerous yeshivas were established in the decades following the war. Among the most important were Mirrer Yeshiva, Beth haTalmud Rabbinical College, and the Talmudical Academy of Philadelphia. In addition, Yeshiva Rabbi Jacob Joseph, whose elementary school had opened its doors in 1899, developed into an important advanced yeshiva in the late 1940s and early 1950s.[63]

The death of thousands upon thousands of yeshiva leaders and students during the Nazi era represented an intellectual and spiritual loss to the Orthodox community that is incalculable. Yet those who came to America to rebuild the yeshivas were a priceless asset to those interested in reinvigorating Orthodox Judaism. They brought with them not only knowledge, memories, and experiences, but a *Weltanschauung* that challenged and ultimately overcame the prevailing trend toward compromise with secular American values that existed in the Orthodox camp. Although their uncompromising positions often polarized the community, they succeeded in raising the level of debate concerning its future to one that had not been present before.

A hint of future polarization concerning secular studies (see

Chapter 9, pp. 219–238) came in a fascinating development that occurred in 1946 and that is almost unknown today, even among those long active in yeshiva circles. In that year, a petition was submitted to the Regents of the University of the State of New York requesting a charter for a new institution to be known as the American Hebrew Theological University. The proposed college was to be formed by the merger of Yeshiva Torah Vodaath and Yeshiva Rabbi Chaim Berlin. Its Board of Trustees included Rabbi Shraga Feivel Mendlowitz, Rabbi Yitzchok Hutner, and other prominent scholars and educators.[64] According to the charter application, the school would offer a basic liberal arts program "equal to that of other junior colleges chartered by the Regents."[65] While credits were to be given for Hebrew studies, there was to be a full complement of secular courses such as psychology, chemistry, mathematics, and so on, according to Rabbi Harold Leiman, then principal of Chaim Berlin's high school and the originator of the idea.[66] The petition also proposed to establish the following graduate schools, for which a B.A. would be required for admission:

1. School of Theology—a two-year course of study and research in Jewish theology leading to the D.Th. degree and a three-year course of study leading to the Ph.D. that would involve an original research project.
2. School of Social Studies—a two-year course of intensive study in methods of social research, Jewish community problems, and community organization leading to the M.A. degree.
3. School of Administration—a two-year intensive course of study in educational research, organization, administration, and supervision of Jewish educational institution(s) (leading to the M.S. degree).[67]

According to Rabbi Leiman, who went to Albany to obtain the charter and who prepared the catalogue, regular college courses were to be offered by qualified instructors who were Orthodox Jews. Explaining the motives behind the idea, Rabbi Leiman stated:

RL: We at Torah Vodaas were confronted with the problem of people leaving the yeshiva altogether to go to Brooklyn College. There they had teachers who ridiculed religion. Therefore we wanted to establish a college right in the yeshiva so that the boys

Advanced Yeshivas in America*

Name	Location	Year Founded	Enrollment	
			1963–1964	1977
Rabbinical Seminary of America (Yeshiva Rabbi Israel Meir Hacohen)	Queens, N.Y.	1933	85	238
Rabbi Chaim Berlin Yeshiva	Brooklyn, N.Y.	1939	200	273
Yeshiva University (RIETS only)	New York, N.Y.	1896	465	569
Yeshiva Torah Vodaath	Brooklyn, N.Y.	1926	240	660
Ner Israel Rabbinical College	Baltimore, Md.	1933	200	303
Rabbinical College of Telshe	Cleveland, Ohio	1941	199	282
Beth Medrash Govoha of America	Lakewood, N.J.	1943	220	655
Central Yeshiva Beth Joseph Rabbinical Seminary	Brooklyn, N.Y.	1941	32	60

Yeshiva Chofetz Chaim of Radun	New York, N.Y.	1944	73	118
Mirrer Yeshiva	Brooklyn, N.Y.	1946	230	415
Beth haTalmud Rabbinical College	Brooklyn, N.Y.	1949	125	94
Talmudical Academy of Philadelphia	Philadelphia, Pa.	1953	50	92
Kamenitzer Yeshiva of Boro Park	Brooklyn, N.Y.	1960	70	95
TOTAL:			2,189	3,854

* This is only a sampling of yeshivas based largely on availability. The earlier figures are taken from Charles S. Liebman, "Orthodoxy in American Jewish Life," in Morris Fine and Milton Himmelfarb (eds.), *American Jewish Yearbook*, vol. 69 (Philadelphia: Jewish Publication Society, 1965) *Appendix*, and the current figures may be found in Arthur Podolsky and Carolyn R. Smith, *Education Directory, Colleges and Universities* (Washington D.C.: National Center for Education Statistics, U.S. Department of Health, Education, and Welfare, 1977–78). Although the data are from different secondary sources, the primary sources, with but one or two exceptions, are the yeshivas themselves. Other sources believe that the figures may be somewhat high, but this could not be confirmed. Hasidic yeshivas are not included here. The *Education Directory*, however, lists numerous Hasidic institutions whose students total 4,033. Taken together with a total listing of 5,548 young men attending Lithuanian yeshivas, there were 9,581 advanced students in the United States in 1977.

would not waste time going to Brooklyn and be exposed to contrary philosophies.

WH: How could this have been contemplated when various European rabbinical authorities such as Rabbi Elchonon Wasserman and Rabbi Boruch Ber Leibowitz had stated that secular college studies were forbidden?

RL: It was done because we faced a serious problem and we approved it because of the circumstances of the day.[68]

Although Rabbi Leiman disavowed any attempt at competing with Yeshiva University, quite a few students from Brooklyn attended the Manhattan school. It can only be speculated how many would have enrolled in the new university since, despite plans drawn up by an architect, a detailed curriculum, and considerable involvement by attorneys (as evidenced by correspondence), the school never actually opened.

Torah Vodaath and Chaim Berlin were granted a provisional charter on July 18, 1946. Almost a year later, on June 20, 1947, the application was withdrawn and the American Hebrew Theological University died without ever having gotten off the ground.[69] The circumstances surrounding the withdrawal are shrouded in mystery. Members of the board with whom I spoke were uncertain as to precisely what had happened. Some claimed the idea was not a serious one. Rabbi Leiman, however, attributed the decision to abandon the project to a long discussion between Rabbi Mendlowitz and Rabbi Kotler in which the latter expressed his strong opposition to the idea.

Up to now, we have identified the yeshiva as an institution that has existed for thousands of years. Although in many respects modern yeshivas differ from their Babylonian predecessors, the similarities far outweigh the differences in importance. At all times in their history, yeshivas were places where the Torah was studied. Even in Babylonia there were classes, *rosh yeshivas,* full-time and part-time students. Most importantly, the subjects studied in today's yeshivas are based on the discussions that took place in these ancient academies in the aftermath of the destruction of the Second Temple.

The scholars who arrived from Europe have maintained this continuity. While one can speak of the transplantation of various specific institutions, of greater importance is that the institution *of* the yeshiva, in the sociological and historical sense, was brought over and preserved. Thus the Mirrer Yeshiva brings over a tradition, not simply a school. Scholars from Mir become teachers in such American yeshivas as Yeshiva University's RIETS division and Ner Israel Rabbinical College, passing on the intellectual and philosophical approach learned in the European institutions to hundreds of students, many of whom have become the *rebbes* and administrators of the contemporary American yeshiva as it has evolved over the past several decades. At this point, we are ready to examine the contemporary yeshiva from a sociological perspective.

CHAPTER 3

The Yeshiva Today

ADVANCED LITHUANIAN YESHIVAS appeal to a clearly identifiable segment of the Orthodox community. To understand the world of the yeshiva, it is important to distinguish among the various groupings of observant Orthodox Jews* which, altogether, number about 250,000 to 300,000 persons in the United States.[1] Broadly speaking, there are three types of Orthodox Jews, which range along a continuum from strict observance and interpretation of the Written and Oral Law of the Bible to one that is quite liberal. These are not hard and fast categories, and they are presented here simply for the purpose of clarifying distinctions often made by the Orthodox community itself.

The Community: The Ultra Orthodox, the Modern Orthodox, and the Strictly Orthodox

The most prominent of the Ultra Orthodox sects are the Lubavitcher, headquartered in the Crown Heights section of

---

* There are probably 250,000 Jews who identify themselves as Orthodox, i.e., in terms of synagogue affiliation or philosophically, but who do not observe rituals associated with the group, such as eating kosher food. Throughout this book, Orthodox Jews means those who are observant, unless otherwise specified.

Brooklyn, New York, and the Satmarer, located primarily in Williamsburg, Brooklyn, but also, of late, in Boro Park, Brooklyn. Other important sects with substantial communities in Brooklyn and Israel are Ger, Bobov, Belz, Tzelem, Stolin, and Papa, all of whom, as is customary among Hasidic groups, derive their names from the European towns in which they originated. With the exception of the Lubavitcher, whose dress and demeanor are somewhat more modern, the Ultra Orthodox are characterized by a distinctive garb and physical appearance that includes long black coats, large black hats, and full beards, all of which make them noticeable to even the most casual observer. They do not as a rule attend secular college* and most are engaged in trades or business. Their social interaction with outsiders is minimal. The various sects are extremely loyal to their leaders or "rebbes," consulting them whenever possible on both religious and secular matters. In addition to rigid adherence to the laws of the Torah, they have added many customs unique to their own respective groups.

At the other end of the continuum are the Modern Orthodox. They participate fully in the larger society. Many are professionals: doctors, lawyers, accountants, professors, and the like. They are observant in that they eat kosher food, abstain from work on the Sabbath, pray every day, and celebrate Jewish holidays as prescribed by Jewish law. At the same time, they maintain a delicate balance between the outside world and their own community, which at times results in a watering down of various observances. They may sometimes eat certain dairy foods in a nonkosher restaurant, fail to recite a blessing while lunching with a gentile or even Jewish business client, not wear a yarmulke (skullcap), and be generally liberal in their interpretation of the gray areas in Jewish law.

The Modern Orthodox tend to send their children to coed, ideologically liberal yeshivas at both the elementary and high school levels, and attend synagogues which have a more modern and formal service—that is, more English in the service, sermons by the rabbi, and so on. They swim in a pool together with members of the opposite sex, often attend movies, plays, and other entertainments, and, in increasing numbers, live in the suburbs of

---

* Throughout this book, "college" refers to a secular institution, unless otherwise noted.

the central city.[2] The women do not as a rule cover their hair except in synagogue, and parents place a good deal of importance on securing a good secular as well as religious education for their children. They do not, by and large, send their children to the types of yeshivas under discussion here, choosing instead a secular college, with some continuing Hebrew studies in the evening at whatever institution will accommodate them. There are special yeshivas for those who wish to study Talmud on a limited basis. Among those Modern Orthodox parents who do enroll their children in advanced yeshivas, Yeshiva University or the Hebrew Theological College is usually their first choice, though a small number have enrolled in the more traditional yeshivas.

The third group, which I have arbitrarily labeled the "Strictly Orthodox," falls somewhere between the Ultra Orthodox and the Modern Orthodox. They are the least studied of the three groups, although they number in the tens of thousands, if one is to judge from current enrollment, yeshiva alumni lists, membership in various organizations, and visits to the communities in which they live.[3] It is from this group that the advanced yeshivas under discussion here draw most of their students, faculty, and administrators.

The Strictly Orthodox are probably just as religiously observant as the Ultra Orthodox, though less noticeably so. Their women generally keep their hair covered at all times when in public, and they are far more careful than the Modern Orthodox in what food they will eat outside the home and what types of plays or movies they will see—that is, only those films with a "G" rating, or none at all. Unlike the Modern Orthodox, they do not participate in mixed swimming or mixed dancing. In the street and at work, the men are likely to keep their heads covered, wearing either a hat or a simple black skullcap (as opposed to the knitted yarmulke often worn by the Modern Orthodox Jew). Their children are likely to attend more Orthodox yeshivas, usually all-boys or all-girls schools, and many prefer synagogues whose services are reminiscent of their experiences in the yeshivas they attended. On the other hand, many are highly educated with most, unlike the Hasidim, having gone to college. They are also clustered in the professions, although, because of their greater degree of observance, their choices are somewhat more limited than those of their Modern Orthodox counterparts. Of late, they seem to be interacting more with the Ultra Orthodox.

Since we are speaking of a continuum rather than of totally separate categories, it is to be expected that there will be crossing over and a blurring of distinctions among all three groups as well as differing interpretations of what constitutes Strictly or Modern Orthodox and who is a centrist and who an extremist. Not all children of the Modern Orthodox attend coed yeshivas, and not all children of the Strictly Orthodox go to all-boys or all-girls yeshivas. Some Strictly Orthodox males will, under certain circumstances, appear in public with their heads uncovered or see certain films while others will not. Moreover, there are Ultra Orthodox who go to secular colleges and there are Strictly Orthodox who do not and whose behavior is really Hasidic. A highly complex system of norms exists within these subcommunities that establishes the category to which an individual is assigned by others, and criteria for making that decision vary greatly from individual to individual. A good many persons have been reared with involvement in more than one community. Still, there are certain schools, groups, and neighborhoods that are either predominantly Modern or Strictly Orthodox. For example, the elementary school Ohr Yisroel in Queens, New York, is supported by the Strictly Orthodox, the Yeshiva Dov Revel in Queens by the Modern Orthodox, and the Yeshiva Tifereth Moshe of Queens, by both groups, though the Strictly Orthodox may be more numerous. New Rochelle, New York, is known as a Modern Orthodox or "Young Israel" community and certain parts of Monsey, New York, are considered Strictly Orthodox or "yeshiva" communities. Each group has its own vacation resorts and social gathering places, with the result that they continue to evolve in different directions while retaining numerous common features.

The Advanced Yeshiva: Some General Remarks

Another area in need of early clarification concerns the nature of the specific yeshivas themselves. While the Hasidim have developed their own yeshivas in America at all levels, the focus of this study is upon the Lithuanian-style institutions since it is they who represent the intellectual tradition of the yeshiva in its purest form.[4]

The Lithuanian-style yeshivas differ in various ways from each other, but their similarities in important areas are sufficiently great to justify considering them as one community. The major similarities among the Lithuanian yeshivas are as follows:

1. All such institutions have programs in which the students spend most of their time in talmudic study. Subjects such as ethics and Bible are also taught.

2. All yeshivas have one or more of the following goals—to transmit the tradition at the highest levels, to train rabbis and teachers, and to bring other Jews closer to the Jewish faith.

3. The hierarchy in all yeshivas is similar with the *rosh yeshiva* at the head of the institution.

4. Most yeshivas have European antecedents in that the faculty members are European or the entire school has been transferred to this country from Europe. Certainly their philosophical approach originated there, for the most part.

5. Leaders and members of the yeshivas, with the possible exception of the more modern Yeshiva University and the Hebrew Theological College, tend to move in the same social circles, sharing a common system of norms and values.

Naturally, within a large system encompassing various schools of thought and different methods for achieving objectives, there are significant differences. Nevertheless, the abovementioned characteristics are central to all such institutions, and in this sense those who attend yeshivas can be viewed as belonging to a single community. Two indications of this are the ease with which young men are able to transfer from one yeshiva to another and the common points of interest that manifest themselves when members or graduates of yeshivas come together for various purposes or reside in the same community.

Yeshiva University is viewed by many in the other major yeshivas as not being part of the community because it not only permits secular education but maintains a college on its campus that is a required part of study for all undergraduates. It does, however, possess the essential criteria that define a yeshiva, although it is the most liberal of such institutions. Since it has been roundly attacked for its philosophy and approach by the other yeshivas, it is important to explain briefly why it falls within the category of *yeshiva gedolas* (advanced yeshivas) despite such criticism. These observations apply only to the Rabbi Isaac Elchanan Theological Seminary (RIETS), the religious division, which has Talmud study as its main focus and which ordains candidates who have completed an approved course of study for the rabbinate. The other two religious divisions, Erna Michael College (EMC) and the James Striar School (JSS), concentrate respectively on training Hebrew teachers and providing students of limited background with a strong foundation in the basics of the faith.

The program of Talmud study in RIETS is as intensive as that of most other yeshivas. Students study, both on their own and in a classroom setting, from 9:00 A.M. to 3:00 P.M. plus several hours in the evening as schedules permit. Secular classes in the college are usually held between 3:00 P.M. and 10:00 P.M., with most students attending three or four nights a week. Also, RIETS has a full-time program for married students and has students who do not study for ordination but who, in the time-honored tradition, study for the sake of acquiring knowledge. The level of scholarship at RIETS is high. Faculty members publish their research in the most prestigious journals in the field. Moreover, the older *rebbes,* having received their training in the European yeshivas, are for the most part indistinguishable from their counterparts in the more traditional schools. The younger ones, American-born and -trained, are nonetheless quite conservative in their outlook and positions on religious issues, although their views do not enjoy the same institutional support that exists elsewhere. It is true that many RIETS graduates enter secular professions, such as law and accounting, but this is also true of graduates of the other yeshivas. What can be said is that more Orthodox *pulpit* rabbis have graduated from RIETS than from any other yeshiva, and that its program is more geared to the practical aspects of the rabbinate.

Today's RIETS student is far more likely to be religiously conservative in both his attitudes and lifestyle than, say, ten years ago (see pp. 233–236). Finally, it may be noted that no attempt is (or ever was) made to bring secular studies into talmudic discussions any more than at any other yeshiva. Still, because RIETS operates in an environment different from that prevailing in the other schools, the influence of these distinctions in shaping the students must be taken into account. Since the number of people in the yeshiva community who are not in the Yeshiva University orbit far exceeds those who are, the present book focuses primarily on them and their attitudes.

Throughout the discussion, reference will be made, where appropriate, to seminaries of other faiths. Great caution must be used in generalizing from such examples. The yeshiva has not been sufficiently studied to allow for comparisons that are anything more than tentative. More importantly, there are often vast differences between seminaries of the various faiths. Both Christian and Jewish seminaries train clergymen and teachers, encourage a spiritual way of life and concern for one's fellow man, and initiate their students into a way of life that generally discourages contact with the outside world. On the other hand, yeshivas do not have as their sole avowed goal training for the ministry and religious teaching, as is the case with Protestant and Catholic seminaries. As we shall see, many yeshiva students do not enter religiously oriented fields. Further, Catholic clergy take a vow of celibacy; rabbis are expected to marry. Finally, the emphasis in the yeshiva is on intellectual *and* spiritual development, while the Christian seminaries place greater stress on the latter.

The Physical Features

When the Polish Yeshiva Chachmei Lublin opened its doors in 1930, it was probably the most modern and best-equipped yeshiva in Poland. Founded by Rabbi Meir Shapira, it had comfortable living facilities for the students, large lecture halls, a huge auditorium, and a 40,000-volume library.[5] Students from every part of Eastern Europe vied for admission to the prestigious institution, whose high standards included a requirement that each prospective student be capable of reciting by heart two hundred folio pages of the Talmud.

Today the terms "comfortable," "spacious," and "well-equipped" could easily be applied to at least some, if not many, of the advanced yeshivas in this country. Although they generally began as modest-looking institutions, they have evolved in recent years to the point where some can even boast of having a "campus" rather than being simply a collection of buildings. True, the majority are still struggling, but the trend of growth and expansion is clear. More and more yeshivas are remodeling and building to accommodate ever increasing numbers of students, who in turn reflect the yeshivas' growing financial base.

Like secular colleges, yeshivas vary considerably in the quality of their facilities and surroundings. Ner Israel Rabbinical College in Baltimore is located in a suburban section of the city amid sixty-six acres of wooded, gently rolling hills. The red brick buildings are both up to date and well designed. By contrast, the Rabbinical Seminary of America (popularly known as the Chofetz Chaim Yeshiva) must make do with a single three-story building, which, while adequate, is certainly not luxurious by any stretch of the imagination. Moreover, although Chofetz Chaim is in a pleasant, tree-lined neighborhood of one-family homes, its location, in Queens, New York City, means that its students are very much a part of the big city. This factor is of some concern to the administration, which has in the past explored the possibility of moving elsewhere.[6] Regardless of size or location, however, yeshivas tend to have certain similar features essential to their functioning. Let us take a closer look at them and assess their nature and importance.

The Beis Medrash

This multipurpose room is the most important component of any yeshiva. It is the place where yeshiva students spend most of their day studying the Talmud and related works. The *beis medrash* at the Chofetz Chaim Yeshiva is typical. Located on the ground floor of the building, it is a large, brightly lit, high-ceilinged room about sixty feet long and perhaps thirty feet wide. Most of the available space is taken up by wooden tables with metal folding legs at which the students sit on wooden or metal folding chairs, usually about four to a table. Pairs of young men and occasionally three students are assigned to work together at understanding and explicating the arguments and points made in the *Gemora*. These study groups, known as *chavrusas*, are the accepted pattern of Talmud study.[7] Usually, books are strewn about the tables in a manner suggesting that they are in constant use. This is because, as the students study the basic text, they often find it necessary either to examine commentaries or to look up references in the Bible or other volumes of the Talmud. In addition, each student has notes on the class lectures presented by his teacher or *rebbe*. Atop each table, one generally finds one or more cardboard boxes containing *seforim* (religious books).

The back wall of the *beis medrash* is lined with bookcases containing numerous sets of the entire Talmud and the Pentateuch, plus hundreds of other books dealing with aspects of Jewish law. That most are in almost constant use is attested by their well-worn covers and often dog-eared pages. Those who expect to find the quiet *ambiance* of a university library in the *beis medrash* are likely to be disappointed. It is a noisy room dominated by the sound of loud voices as the students argue back and forth over this and that point. Through the clamor one can occasionally catch the distinctive singsong of a student engaged in solitary study as he reads the ancient Aramaic text of the *Gemora*.[8] Despite the noise no one complains, and most newcomers soon find themselves able to concentrate. Although the majority study at their tables, a number of students can be seen standing at lightweight wooden lecterns (*shtenders*), hunched over the *Gemora*, while gently swaying back and forth, absorbed in thought. Others pace up and down the aisles between the tables, heads down, repeating aloud to themselves various points. One can also see students standing in various parts of the room, gesticulating, talking in animated tones, and even occasionally banging their fists down on a nearby table or *shtender* as they seek to persuade one another of the merits of their arguments. Many become so preoccupied with their studies that they are oblivious to everything around them including persons trying to pass. Since single-minded dedication to Talmud study is the most important value in the community, such involvement is highly regarded by others.

The *beis medrash* is used for other activities as well as study, most notably prayer. All three daily services are said in the *beis medrash,* converted to a synagogue for the purpose. Students may be joined at such services by Orthodox Jews of the community, who like the style of service or find the location convenient. Adult members of the surrounding Orthodox community can sometimes be seen engaged in study in the *beis medrash,* especially during the evening hours. The services do not differ greatly from those in most Orthodox synagogues except that there is almost no talking, even at those points in the services where brief conversations are socially acceptable.[9] The fervor with which the prayers are said approaches that sometimes found in Hasidic small synagogues (*shtibls*), especially when the first line of the *shema* prayer "Hear O Israel, the Lord is our God, the Lord is one" is said in unison.[10]

In some yeshivas the *beis medrash* is the place where talks on ethics (*mussar shmuessim*) are given, generally once a week. These talks are attended by the entire student body. Guest lecturers from other institutions or organizations sometimes speak in the *beis medrash*, which is almost always the largest room in the building. Though in a few cases students from the high school may study in the *beis medrash* this is highly unusual. Most yeshivas have a separate study room for *mesivta* students.

Finally, the *beis medrash* serves as a social gathering point. Although it is considered a holy place for study and prayer, still there are quiet periods during the day when very little study occurs, such as immediately after the morning service, around 8:30 A.M., when most of the students go to the dining hall for breakfast, until about 9:30, when the official schedule calls for study to begin. Another social occasion may be when most students are in classes or late at night when very few persons are in the *beis medrash*. During these periods, people may talk about matters unrelated to Torah study. Often, there is a fine line between what may or may not be done in the *beis medrash*. It may be acceptable to discuss something having to do with a college course during a slack period. On the other hand, reading or even opening a secular book in the *beis medrash* is frowned upon.

With all these functions, the *beis medrash* is the center of activity in the yeshiva. The average student spends at least ten hours a day there. It is here that the interested and knowledgeable observer can acquire a sense of what a particular yeshiva is all about by noting, for example, the students' characteristic attire, their intensity in study, the hours when the *beis medrash* is filled to capacity, and the general appearance of the room. For insiders, many subtle cues abound, ranging from the degree of interest displayed by the students toward a stranger to how empty the *beis medrash* is at, say, 9:00 P.M., a time when college classes are being held elsewhere.

The Dormitory

Most of the major yeshivas and even some of the smaller ones have residence halls which house both students who live in other parts of the city and those who come from "out of town," and these are a very important component of the yeshiva. Given the rigorous schedule and the institution's desire to have the student totally involved in his studies, there is often a requirement that even those within commuting distance live at the yeshiva.

Specific rules regarding when one may go home vary. All yeshivas have vacation periods, usually during the Succoth (early fall) and Passover (spring) holidays, as well as for part of the summer. Some yeshivas permit students to go home on weekends and others do not. Some yeshivas feel it is important for the young man to experience a *Shabbos* in the yeshiva with his peers. On the other hand, they recognize that some individuals may wish to spend the Sabbath with their families. To mediate between these two needs, a few yeshivas require students to stay in the yeshiva for certain weekends and allow them to return home for others. These weekends are often referred to as an "out-*Shabbos*" or "in-*Shabbos*" by the *bochorim*. Several yeshivas, such as the Chaim Berlin Yeshiva in Brooklyn, occasionally place students who live far away and seldom go home with local families for the Sabbath so that they need not spend all of their time in an institutional setting.

In the 1950s and early 1960s living facilities at most yeshivas were notoriously inadequate—overcrowded and poorly maintained. Today the situation is quite different, largely because of the improved financial state of the yeshivas. At Beth Medrash Govoha in Lakewood, I received permission to take a self-conducted tour of the residence halls. There was no time for the yeshiva to spruce up the rooms and inform the residents that I was coming. It was midday and most of the students were away. As I entered, I was struck by how well kept the buildings were. They were modern in both design and decor, well lit, and spotlessly clean. Glancing through the doorway of an open room I saw four neatly made-up beds, two sinks, plenty of closet space, two desks, and a few bookcases. Yeshivas such as Telshe in Cleveland and Ner Israel in Baltimore can boast similar living conditions; but there are still some yeshivas where dormitory rooms house up to six students, with little closet space and doubledecker beds. In such institutions the students tended, when questioned about their feelings on the matter, to vacillate between complaints and assertions that physical comfort was unimportant.

Regardless of the prevailing conditions, dormitory living has a significant effect on the young men. One student at the Mirrer Yeshiva in Brooklyn described it as follows:

> When you're thrown into a *seviva* [environment] with a lot of fellas you learn to deal with people. If you watch you can pick up *meilos* [good qualities] from certain people. At home you depend on your parents and you're spoiled by them. My roommates [laughter] would never spoil me.[11]

An older student in the yeshiva usually serves as the dormitory counselor and is nominally in charge of the day-to-day affairs in the residence hall. Some yeshivas have a counselor only for the high school dormitory while others have one at the advanced level too. How these individuals are viewed by the other students depends on their personalities as well as on how they carry out their responsibilities. A description of the counselor's role as well as his powers appears in the following account prepared by a large New York City yeshiva:

> The dormitory is supervised by a member of the faculty, assisted by a graduate student, who is responsible for the welfare of the dormitory students and the proper upkeep of the rooms. Students are responsible for the cleanliness and upkeep of their own rooms and are required to report needed repairs to the Director of Maintenance. The dormitory supervisor makes *periodic sudden inspections* [italics added] of the rooms.[12]

At some yeshivas there is not enough room in the dormitory to accommodate everyone. In such cases students, most often older and more responsible individuals, live in apartments in buildings that are sometimes owned by the yeshivas.

Other Facilities

Every yeshiva has a Judaica library. These collections range in size from that of Torah Vodaath, with 20,000 volumes, to those of small institutions with less than a thousand books. While it is obviously an important part of the school, the library is used primarily for research, not for study. Those books that are in constant use are generally available in open shelves along the walls of the *beis medrash*. Talmudic or biblical works (*seforim*) are an integral part of the yeshiva *bochur's* world, and many students begin building a private library while still in their teens. Still, there are many rare or expensive works out of their financial reach, and it is here that a well-stocked yeshiva library fulfills an important function by making such books readily available. In addition, libraries contain books on Jewish philosophy, history, various editions of the Talmud, responsa literature, and relevant periodicals.

Most yeshivas also have dining halls, administration offices, and classrooms. Some institutions have faculty housing on the yeshiva grounds. Almost all have recreational facilities, but these vary greatly in quality, and are in any case underused since the students have so little free time. Nevertheless, a few students can usually be found playing basketball or baseball on a Friday afternoon, when there are usually no classes, or for a short time before dinner or during the lunch break. One or two yeshivas, recognizing the importance of exercise, have even made arrangements with local YMHAs for use of the facilities once a week. Sports and exercise are, however, a relatively unimportant part of student life. Except for the summer, when a good number of students attend camps, some of which are owned and run by the yeshivas, there is no organized sports program.

The Hierarchy

The yeshiva is a complex organization with numerous officials playing a role in its operation. There is no single pattern, but Figure 3-1 describes the principal components of a typical yeshiva. Many of the smaller yeshivas are one-man operations; some of the larger ones have divisions, in addition to the ones enumerated in the chart. Despite the high degree of structure suggested by the chart, the existence of boards of trustees and written constitutions, many yeshivas operate in a rather disorganized fashion. Nevertheless, the arrangements presented here are necessary for a better understanding of some of the more important parts of the institution.[13]

Figure 3-1

Structure of the Yeshiva

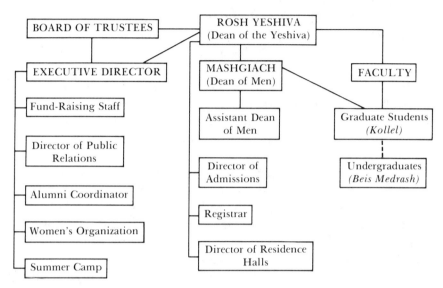

Note: The dotted line between "graduate students" and "undergraduates" indicates that this is not a formal line of authority. Nevertheless, it is an important part of the hierarchical structure.

The Rosh Yeshiva

The *rosh yeshiva* often, though not always, derives authority from his reputation as a *talmid chochom* (scholar). The description of his abilities by others in this area can take on charismatic overtones. He may be portrayed as a genius who knew all 63 volumes of the Talmud at, say, the age of fifteen. Typical is the story told of the European scholar, Rabbi Chaim Ozer Grodzensky. When asked to deliver a *drasha* (sermon) at his bar mitzvah celebration, he suggested that instead the guests ask him to recite from memory any page of the commentaries on a large section of the Code of Jewish Law, a Herculean feat in terms of the amount and depth of the material. Several guests took him up on his offer, and he successfully cited page after page verbatim, without any errors.[14] In another instance, Rabbi Raphael Boruch Sorotzkin, former head of the Telshe Yeshiva, is cited as having traveled, during World War II, by Trans-Siberian Railroad through all of Russia, studying Talmud the entire time, despite the atmosphere of grave crisis which prevailed then. This capacity of intense involvement reportedly stemmed from his grandfather, Rabbi Laizer Gordon, also a *rosh yeshiva,* who was said to have literally "vaulted" through the open window of a *beis medrash* in his enthusiasm to take part in a talmudic discussion he had overheard.[15] Thus, we see that it is not only erudition but dedication to study that counts. Moreover, these stories, many of which appear in the *Jewish Observer,* a monthly magazine published by the Agudath Israel organization and probably the most widely read journal of its kind in the yeshiva world, play an important part in establishing such attributes as basic legitimations to a *rosh yeshiva.*

The two central features of the Lithuanian tradition are that of talmudic knowledge and *mussar,* and virtuosity in these areas is expected of those selected to be *rosh yeshivas.* The *rosh yeshiva* frequently serves as a role model for the students, and his efforts to portray Torah knowledge as superior to all other areas of scholarship can sometimes have unfortunate consequences. In his acceptance of this position, the student may come to regard other subjects of study as "not serious" only to discover later that his views were based on misinformation. The following comments by a university professor who had attended a yeshiva in his youth indicate the role of the *rosh yeshiva* in the development of such attitudes and how they are internalized by the student:

> The rumor about Rabbi Gifter [presently *rosh yeshiva* at the Telshe Yeshiva] was after he returned to America from Europe he went to a college and the professor said to him: "You know everything we have to teach. You might as well just leave." This went over only because none of us had any idea of what was going on in college. You see, at Telz [Telshe], none of us went to college. There was this feeling that if you're smart, if you know how to speak well and can use fancy language, then there's nothing to learn. We didn't know any better. But let's face it; history, philosophy, and science—you can't just know it *intuitively.* You have to acquire the information.

Yeshiva authorities sometimes acknowledge that they minimize the value of secular learning because they feel that until he reaches a certain level of maturity the student may be unduly influenced by such exposure and turn away from the teachings of the faith. They argue that as adults the former *bochorim* recognize the motivations behind such actions.

Another source of influence for the *rosh yeshiva* is his *yichus,* or family lineage. Often, upon the death of a *rosh yeshiva* the mantle of leadership is passed on to his son or, less frequently, his son-in-law. This is a highly sensitive topic in the yeshiva world because, officially, only criteria of merit are used in determining who succeeds a *rosh yeshiva.* Yet everyone is aware that certain families are in positions of power in the various yeshivas. There are quite a few heads of different yeshivas who are related to one another. The practice is generally accepted for the following reasons: First, the yeshiva is not a democracy. Leaders are held in awe and reverence by most members of the community, and challenging authority is unthinkable to them. Furthermore, quite a few people in the community believe in the efficacy of such a selection process, pointing to the existence of certain prominent rabbinical families such as Soloveitchik, Bloch, and others as proof of its validity. Third, selection of a son as successor provides a sense of continuity when a dominant personality passes away. Finally, such decisions are often made at the request of the *rosh yeshiva* himself, who not only may wish to install his progeny as the new head but who may also want to avoid a divisive battle between competing candidates which might weaken the institution as a whole. Sometimes the son-in-law is preferred over the son because, as one individual familiar with the yeshiva scene put it: "The son-in-law is chosen as a grown man when you know his capabilities whereas the son is chosen at birth and he isn't always that capable."

Yichus is, however, a mixed blessing. It does not always eliminate conflict; in fact, it often increases it. Interviews with students in numerous yeshivas revealed a considerable degree of bitterness over this issue, with the complaint frequently voiced that those related to the *rosh yeshiva* were likely to get better jobs both within and outside the institution as a result of their family's influence. Just how often this occurs is not known, but when it does both the quality of the school as well as faculty and student morale, suffer. Moreover, the yeshiva is often a less open institution in general when *yichus* prevails because those in charge may receive support from faculty and administrators for policies that are based on family loyalty rather than on the best interests of the yeshiva. Of course, nepotism exists in many types of private organizations, including colleges, business enterprises, hospitals, and so on. In a place such as the yeshiva, however, with its emphasis on morally proper behavior, it may be more noticeable and of greater concern to those involved.

From the early stages of the yeshiva's development as a formal institution in Babylonia, the *rosh yeshiva* has headed the institution. A twentieth-century scholar thus anointed does not as a result step into a vacuum. A certain aura of authority already surrounds his position, whose legitimacy is centuries old. As a result, the *rosh yeshiva* can command unquestioning obedience, especially in areas where religious values, attitudes, and practices are concerned. In fact, his views are eagerly sought on such matters. A term commonly used in the yeshiva world to refer to the collective (and, on occasion, individual leader's) viewpoint of the leading *rosh yeshivas* and other religious authorities is called *daas Torah,* or the opinion of Torah leaders. When these authorities express potentially controversial positions, they are freely discussed by adherents but almost never openly challenged. Rabbi Moshe Feinstein expressed this view when he said:

> Those who maintained: "What do they (the *talmidei chachamim*) know about politics? This is a field where we are better versed"—groups that set their policies in such a manner cannot be considered as being in the Torah camp.
>
> One might well say that ignoring the advice of the *talmid chacham* is far worse than transgressing a *lav* (negative command) clearly expressed in the Torah. Whereas one may violate a command because he finds himself too weak to resist the insistent attractions of that which is wrong, at least he realizes that his action is wrong. By contrast, when one does not heed the advice of a *talmid chacham,* he denies the superior wisdom of the Torah personality. This is a far more serious breach.[16]

This statement is significant on at least two counts. First, it demonstrates the degree of authority exercised by the *rosh yeshivas,* especially since it bears the imprint of the foremost leader of the yeshiva community. Moreover, it indicates that the *rosh yeshivas* view their domain as extending beyond spiritual matters and into the political arena. Rabbi Nosson Scherman, a prominent educator and leader in the yeshiva community, elaborated on this theme when asked about Rabbi Feinstein's remarks concerning political decisions:

> At the 1977 Agudah Convention people were expecting Rav Moshe [Feinstein] to give a defense of the Agudah's position in support of the Begin government. And he said, in effect: "I don't have to explain to you. We are the ones who have the responsibility for making the decision and we have to decide." After seeking intelligent input, they must make the key decisions and we should have enough confidence in them to accept their judgement.[17]

Thus we see that the charismatic traits, intellectual abilities, and family lineage possessed by the *rosh yeshiva* are considerably buttressed by his title and the power of his office.

The concept of *daas Torah* is an important one requiring further elaboration. It starts with a given, namely, that the Torah is the blueprint of all creation, the key to man's understanding of his role and to the deciphering of events. It stands to reason, therefore, that the great man who is totally immersed in Torah is best able to discern the truth and define it in relation to material life and its challenges. His judgment is undiluted by extraneous values. More importantly, because of his spiritual greatness, he is granted a degree of divine guidance, particularly when his views affect the community. His judgment, whether instinctive or reasoned, is the product of a total "Torah personality." Stripped of its metaphysical dimension, *daas Torah* is akin to the confidence community members feel when speaking to a specialist as opposed to an informed generalist. Those who help forge the general view of *daas Torah* are not always *rosh yeshivas*. A good number of them are community leaders or independent scholars. Examples are Rabbi Shimon Schwab of New York, Rabbi Pinchas Teitz of Elizabeth, New Jersey, the Debriciner Rov of Brooklyn, and the Lubavitcher Rebbe.

In conventionally structured organizations, leaders are selected on the basis of clearly defined qualifications, and have powers and obligations that are clearly spelled out. Though some may argue that it is only done in a *pro forma* fashion, the *rosh yeshiva*'s rights and duties are identified in the written constitution which many yeshivas have drawn up, and these form yet another basis, at least in theory, for his authority.

Typically, the *rosh yeshiva*'s primary area of control is educational policy. The board of trustees cannot veto his policies, but are limited to an advisory capacity. Since the main business of any yeshiva is education, the *rosh yeshiva*'s preeminent position in this area inevitably broadens his authority in related matters as well. While the Board of Trustees appoints the *rosh yeshiva,* he himself is generally a voting member of the board and sometimes has two votes. Because of his understanding of the all-important educational system, the *rosh yeshiva* most often has control over the administrative and financial divisions of the yeshiva, and the executive director will ordinarily consult with him before making any important decisions. While the board of trustees may interview and even appoint lower-echelon officials in the institution, such appointments are often nullified if the *rosh yeshiva* opposes them. Faculty members are appointed by the *rosh yeshiva* and are directly responsible to him. Under ideal circumstances, the relationship between the board and the *rosh yeshiva* is one in which decisions are made by consensus and in consultation with the board. More often, however, an institution will be ruled either by a *rosh yeshiva* or by the board, with bitter struggles for power a distinct possibility. Nevertheless, of eight yeshiva constitutions examined, all invested the *rosh yeshiva* with final authority in any disputes that might arise among those who run the institution.

The *rosh yeshiva* in at least one institution is appointed for life, and quite a few have indeed served out their term of office until their deaths. Yet this is not always the case. Internal politics within an institution have, at times, resulted in a *rosh yeshiva*'s being forced out. In such instances, the departure is most often explained as retirement rather than dismissal. In other cases, a *rosh yeshiva* has left an institution because of an inability to get along with his peer in a situation where two *rosh yeshivas* have joint control. In such cases one individual may be very adept at fund-raising and public relations, while the other's strengths lie in talmudic scholarship and relating to the students. Although the table organization would seem to indicate that fund-raising and public relations are not within the province of the *rosh yeshiva,* he is often called upon to fill these roles.

The *rosh yeshiva* is the head of the institution, but he is far more than that. He is the embodiment of the yeshiva, and his name is often synonymous with the school. If a yeshiva achieves prominence, it is most often due to the reputation of its *rosh yeshiva*. The style, philosophy, and general approach of the yeshiva often grow out of the tone set by him and this in turn is often a result, not only of his training, but of his personality. This is a subtle quality difficult to encapsulate, but impossible not to consider. Within the yeshiva world there is a "Chofetz Chaim Yeshiva" type. He is a person dedicated to Jewish education, willing to reach out beyond his community, and careful in his ethical and moral conduct. The Telshe student is often highly intellectual, disciplined, and very meticulous in his approach to talmudic study. These are obviously gross generalizations, but they are recognized as reasonably accurate characteristics of the typical student at these yeshivas. When the *rosh yeshiva* presents a certain image to his students, he is in a sense telling them how he expects them to behave. He may do so in the way he responds to a question, in his greeting to a student, or in his dress.

The image he presents is important to outsiders as well. A financial contributor to a large yeshiva explained his impression of its *rosh yeshiva* as follows:

> He looks right. The way he dresses—long, black coat, neatly trimmed beard. And you can see by the way he carries himself that he's someone important, a man who commands respect.

The *rosh yeshiva* is frequently called upon to represent the yeshiva to persons unfamiliar with the institution. Parents attempting to make a choice between one or another yeshiva may judge the school in part by their impression of its head. Government officials with whom the yeshiva must deal are apt to form impressions based in some measure upon the *rosh yeshiva*'s personality and demeanor.

A more direct and manifest function of the *rosh yeshiva* is that of teacher. Almost all *rosh yeshivas* teach a class, invariably the most advanced in the school. Partly because of the difficulty of the material taught, partly because advanced students spend much more time on their studies, and also because of the press of the *rosh yeshiva*'s other responsibilities, his class usually meets once a week or even less often. Examinations are given in the *rosh yeshiva*'s class rarely, if at all, for the student is quite experienced and knowledgeable at this stage. While a student may spend one or two years with each teacher in a lower class, it is not unusual to find young men remaining in the *rosh yeshiva*'s class for five, six, or seven years.

Being admitted into the *rosh yeshiva*'s class is generally a sign of distinction, but it does present problems for some students who prefer to have close contact with their *rebbe,* or teacher. One young man stated:

> I never looked forward to getting into his *shiur.* Getting in his *shiur* meant not attending *shiur* because he only gave *shiur* once in a blue moon. Also my impression was there's no accountability, no tests or anything, no way to gauge your progress.

People who are uncomfortable with a lack of structure and the prospect of working independently find it a problem to deal with a setting where independent study is the mark of the accomplished scholar.

Character development is another function fulfilled by the *rosh yeshiva.* In some yeshivas the *rosh yeshiva* delivers a weekly *mussar shmuess,* in which he discusses general principles concerning ethics and morality. In other institutions this may be the domain of the *mashgiach* (dean of men), and in still others both the *mashgiach* and the *rosh yeshiva* present such lectures, which are attended by the entire student body. In the Lithuanian tradition, emphasis on proper behavior toward others is high and such topics are integrated into the classroom discussion as well. It should be remembered that large portions of the Talmud itself deal with this subject.

The *rosh yeshiva*'s involvement in this area is often of a highly personal nature. Many students look to the *rosh yeshiva* for advice and counsel in their personal affairs, in addition to consulting their own *rebbes* and other administrators. For example, a student may seek the *rosh yeshiva*'s advice on whether to marry a less Orthodox girl whose family can continue to support his full-time study, or someone who is more Orthodox but not from a wealthy family. Another may speak to the *rosh yeshiva* about his dissatisfaction with the progress he is making with his study partner. He may seek the *rosh yeshiva*'s opinion on whether it is permitted to take a girl he is dating (dating is permitted only for the express purpose of finding a marriage partner) to see a "G" rated movie. Since the *rosh yeshiva* is quite busy, the student will usually make an appointment to see him only if he feels he cannot get satisfaction from the various guidance counselors and unofficial advisers who make up part of the yeshiva hierarchy.

Frequently there are certain individuals, usually older students, whose job it is to screen students' requests to see the *rosh yeshiva* and determine whether the problem warrants his personal attention. An impression is often deliberately created that the *rosh yeshiva* is even busier than he actually is, to discourage students from coming to him with every minor problem. Naturally, in case of a genuine emergency the *rosh yeshiva* becomes accessible rather quickly. The degree to which the institution's head is available depends on numerous factors, such as his other duties, his personality, the size of the yeshiva, his health (quite a few are advanced in age and not well), and how he perceives his own role in this area.

Some *rosh yeshivas* try to make up for the impersonality of their school in various ways. At the Chofetz Chaim Yeshiva, Rabbi Henoch Leibowitz has instituted a practice of having Friday night dinner during the winter months with a different group of students each week, and having an open house on Sabbath day during which the students can avail themselves of his counsel and guidance in matters relating to personal faith. The *rosh yeshiva*'s activities in this area are especially important to students living away from home. He often becomes something of a father figure to the *bochorim*. One young man at a smaller yeshiva explained his reaction to his *rosh yeshiva* in the following manner:

> The *rosh yeshiva*'s personality and attitude and the rapport he establishes is really a great thing. It's an away from home place and he knows it so he invites you over to his house. Most people think he just asks you questions in learning— that this is all that's on his mind, but it's not true. He has a whole tableful of food set up, tells you to eat and sing and talks about the old neighborhood in Washington Heights where he came from.

Another student recounted an experience of a different nature in a Brooklyn yeshiva:

> My *rosh yeshiva* never talks to anyone except for his chosen few. Oh, he might come over two or three times a year to ask you how you're doing, but I can't bring myself to really talk to him. Partly it's because I'm too shy but partly it's because he's somewhat distant. Then again he *is* the *rosh yeshiva* and who am I?

These differing descriptions point up the difficulty of the *rosh yeshiva*'s various roles. He must give the appearance of a strong leader, concerned with major problems, a figure people can look up to. He cannot afford to be "a regular guy" because this will diminish the importance of his position thereby eroding the authority of the yeshiva. At the same time he must be warm, friendly, and approachable, making the students feel that they can confide in him. He must show that greatness in scholarship and a high level as a teacher cannot be reached without a parallel ascension in the area of morality. One of the most effective ways of demonstrating this is by showing the students that he does not forget or belittle their needs. This is especially hard to do when, as is often the case, he must spend a good deal of time away from the yeshiva raising funds for its maintenance. To combine such roles is no easy task and represents one of the dilemmas inherent in the position as it is defined by the yeshiva community at large.

In his capacity as fund-raiser the *rosh yeshiva* faces his greatest challenge. No function is of more immediate importance to the yeshiva's survival, yet none is less directly related to the lofty goals he presumably embodies. Without funding no yeshiva can survive, and it is a fact of life that a personal appeal or appearance by the *rosh yeshiva* lends urgency and significance to appeals for funds. Some individuals will give money only if the *rosh yeshiva* himself pays them a visit. Unfortunately, this prevents him from ministering to the needs of the students, teaching and guiding them.

It is ironic that many yeshiva graduates aspire to become *rosh yeshivas* rather than rabbis because a rabbi often has social and administrative duties that allow him little time to study Talmud. Yet the *rosh yeshiva* frequently finds himself equally hard pressed for time. One of the ways in which money is raised is through so-called parlor meetings, gatherings in the home of a prominent community member to which local contributors are invited. Generally, a *rosh yeshiva* or his representative will speak briefly about the yeshiva and its needs. Afterward, the donors will take the opportunity to chat personally with the *rosh yeshiva* over coffee and cake. Students of the yeshiva often resent this approach to fund-raising. One student at the Lakewood Yeshiva voiced his objections:

Reb Shneur [Kotler] has responsibilities that are enormous. But he gets *shlepped* [dragged] around in a way that is terri-

ble. The donors want him to come to them before they give
the money. This is a disgrace for the name of Torah. His
learning time is easily worth $100 an hour. They should pay
so that he *shouldn't* come to them if they really want to support Torah. This way he loses time from study and the whole
yeshiva that these people claim to be supporting does not
have the benefit of his presence.

Naturally, such problems are not the exclusive province of yeshivas. They are faced by college presidents, heads of private
agencies serving the poor, the handicapped, and others with
problems, all of whom must toady to people to remain solvent.

The yeshiva does not rely primarily on such avenues for its
financial survival. Tuition, appeals through the mail, advertisements in journals, and dinners are also employed. In addition,
various forms of federal assistance are made available to the yeshivas. In these instances, with the exception of making an occasional speech, the *rosh yeshiva* plays only a peripheral role, leaving
matters basically in the hands of his staff.

As the head of a very important institution in the Jewish
community, the *rosh yeshiva* exerts considerable influence outside
the yeshiva. Orthodox Jews see him not only as an educational
leader but as an important community leader and policy maker,
and he is often called upon to act in this capacity. Generally, the
rosh yeshivas act in concert on major issues. A number of them
belong to an Agudah–sponsored group known as the Moetzes
Gedolei Torah (Council of Torah Sages) which deals largely with
policy issues, such as support for the Israeli government, the response to missionary activity, and the participation of Orthodox
rabbis in groups that include Conservative and Reform rabbis.[18]

Another important group of leading *rosh yeshivas* is the Rabbinical Administrative Board, sponsored by Torah uMesorah
(National Society for Hebrew Day Schools). Generally, it focuses
less on broad policy matters than on educational issues, such as
whether a new school should be opened in a certain area, who
should be the head of it, and so on. Several *rosh yeshivas* belong to
both groups. In essence, however, the *rosh yeshivas* face many
problems of this sort regarding their own yeshivas that require
independent action and do not involve the other *rosh yeshivas* at
all.

We have noted that the *rosh yeshiva* will see students about
various problems confronting them. He may also see members of
the larger community. An ordinary Orthodox Jew who may

never have gone to the *rosh yeshiva*'s school may approach a man
like Rabbi Yaakov Ruderman of the Ner Israel Yeshiva or Rabbi
Shmuel Berenbaum of the Mirrer Yeshiva about a problem simply because of the esteem in which the leader is held. Thus an individual may ask the *rosh yeshiva* whether his son, who is a
talented singer, should be allowed to take private lessons leading
to a vocal career in this area, even though it may take a good deal
of time away from his high school studies in Talmud. He may
want to know whether he has a moral or legal obligation to move
out of a community that has limited opportunities for rearing his
children in a truly Orthodox environment even if he may tem-
porarily lose his means of livelihood. Sometimes a friend or student of the *rosh yeshiva* makes the introduction, and sometimes
not. While a grateful beneficiary of such counsel may make a
donation to the yeshiva, this is not a requirement.

No doubt, many of the difficulties confronting the *rosh yeshiva* have to do with the many functions he performs—community leader and policy maker, fund-raiser, adviser to students,
teacher. Each yeshiva head stresses those areas that he feels deserve the most attention and tends to downplay others—for
which he is usually criticized by those who fail to realize that the
position of the *rosh yeshiva* is actually several full-time jobs under
one heading.[19]

The Rosh Yeshiva and the Board of Trustees

Adding to the stresses and demands of heading a yeshiva are
certain problems inherent in the hierarchical structure of the yeshiva itself. According to the organizational chart presented
earlier (Figure 3–1), control over the yeshiva is shared between
the board of trustees and the *rosh yeshiva*. In practice, however,
there is considerable variation in the distribution of power; some
yeshivas are dominated by the board, others, perhaps most, by
the *rosh yeshiva,* and some fulfill the ideal of harmonious coexistence. Of all the areas of potential conflict in the yeshiva hierarchy, this is the most serious, since the location of these two
sources of authority at the top of the scale must, of necessity, affect all members of the organization. It is a fact of yeshiva life
that such conflicts occur, and that they have been responsible for
the breakup of more than one school.

On the one hand, the *rosh yeshiva* is viewed as the ultimate authority in the yeshiva in all areas. His special domain is education, in an institution whose sole purpose is education, and no yeshiva constitution spells out areas that are beyond his control. The board of trustees, on the other hand, has powers over finances, administration, hiring and firing of staff, overall policy, and long-range planning. Nevertheless, the *rosh yeshiva* also has authority in these areas and regularly exercises it. In most yeshivas, the *rosh yeshiva* is not only a member and/or chairman of the board, but the bylaws and regulations state that all decisions affecting the institution are to be made in consultation with him. One should not read too much into these constitutions, for there is often an informal understanding within the yeshiva as to who is in charge of various areas. Still, the vagueness with which jurisdiction is defined means that if things do not go smoothly in the yeshiva, conflict resolution becomes much more difficult.

Another problem is that the control the board has is threatened, in a fundamental sense, by the personal charisma of the *rosh yeshiva*. He cannot be compared to the principal of a school, who derives his power solely from the rights given him by the board. The *rosh yeshiva*'s charismatic authority, as we have noted, is essential to the well-being of the yeshiva, and the board knows it. To tamper with the esteem in which he is held by the students and the community at large is to jeopardize the entire structure. The voluntary nature of board membership exerts a different sort of pressure on those who sit on it. While prestige is a perquisite of such membership, most individuals define their participation in altruistic terms and may feel that giving of their valuable time, even if it is only four hours a month, should be both appreciated and translated into meaningful power and control. Often accustomed to positions of leadership in other spheres of their lives, they do not easily acclimate themselves to sharing power or being overruled by the *rosh yeshiva* whose salary they pay.

People bring differing needs and interests with them when they accept positions on such boards, and these may conflict with the goals of the institution.[20] Their priorities as laymen may not coincide with those of the institution's religious leaders. Although adherence to Orthodox beliefs and practices is a *sine qua non* for board membership in most cases, the average board member's greater contact with outsiders may result in a different view of the yeshiva's needs and goals than that of the more other-worldly *rosh yeshiva.*

Given the nature of the yeshiva hierarchy, both sides have formidable weapons at their disposal in the event of a power struggle. In some cases the board controls the purse strings, most notably the budget and the disbursement of funds, and has the power to appoint people to a variety of posts within the yeshiva. Although it cannot ordinarily discharge a *rosh yeshiva* without risking cries of blatant interference from the students and others sympathetic to him, it can make life very unpleasant for the institution's head and trigger his resignation. The former board chairman of one now-defunct yeshiva, asked why two of its *rosh yeshivas* had departed, replied: "They left because we [the board] wouldn't give them what they wanted. They should have kept out of politics."

Similarly, the *rosh yeshiva* has ways of marshalling support for his interests. He has a natural power base in the student body, and more than one *rosh yeshiva* has relied on such backing to have his way. Moreover, he can appeal to the community and alumni for support. He also has the traditional authority of his position, which allows him to invoke the label of "defender of the faith" in support of his positions. Finally, because he is often in daily contact with the institution, he can fight more effectively for his goals.

It must be remembered that the yeshiva is structured in such a way as to insure the centrality of the *rosh yeshiva*'s role. Any attempt to tamper with that has repercussions throughout the entire system, especially among the students. An examination of those yeshivas which have had problems reveals a pattern of heavy involvement on the part of the *baalei batim* (lay people, or board).[21] Where the *rosh yeshiva* controls all the affairs of the yeshiva, he may pay the price of becoming unavailable to students. Nevertheless, to the *rosh yeshiva* this may be preferable to board control. Shortly after Rabbi Dovid Leibowitz founded the Chofetz Chaim Yeshiva in 1933, he was approached by a group of *baalei batim* who said to him, in essence: "We want you to have the freedom to study in the yeshiva with the *bochorim* day and night. So you study and we'll run the yeshiva as far as money and the rest goes." When Rabbi Leibowitz insisted that a yeshiva cannot be run by *baalei batim,* but only by its head, several *baalei batim* refused to accept this arrangement and walked out of the meeting. Those who stayed allowed Rabbi Leibowitz a free hand in developing the institution.[22]

One yeshiva which has adopted a somewhat different system is Ner Israel Rabbinical College in Baltimore. There neither the *rosh yeshiva* nor the board is responsible for finances and administration; these all-important areas are in the hands of Rabbi Herman Neuberger, the executive director. Whereas in most other yeshivas the executive director exerts only nominal control in such matters, at Ner Israel Rabbi Neuberger is completely in charge. Under this arrangement an insider who is a full-time professional runs the yeshiva, allowing the *rosh yeshiva* to spend his time in scholarly activity, as befits his position. Unfortunately, there are not many men in the yeshiva world with Rabbi Neuberger's administrative abilities. He has the added advantage of being trusted completely by the *rosh yeshiva,* who is his brother-in-law. For most yeshivas, however, as long as lines of authority and power remain ambiguous and as long as there are competing interests and mixed motives among those who run the yeshiva, problems in administration will continue.

The Mashgiach

Most yeshivas have a *mashgiach* (supervisor, or dean of students), an innovation of the nineteenth-century Lithuanian yeshivas.[23] His main function is to assume responsibility for the moral and ethical growth of the students in the yeshiva. Usually an accomplished scholar, the *mashgiach* sometimes teaches one of the advanced classes in the school, most often the one directly below that of the *rosh yeshiva.* Although the *rosh yeshiva* may also deliver a *mussar shmuess,* this is actually the province of the *mashgiach,* who usually presents such a talk on *Shabbos* (Sabbath) between the afternoon and evening services. These talks are designed to instill in the young novitiate a desire to perfect his character and strengthen his faith in God.

Students in the modern yeshiva are subject to temptations which did not exist in Europe among earlier generations. They live in an open society which offers them numerous opportunities should they decide to leave the yeshiva. The *mashgiach*'s job is to help the student grow spiritually so that he can resist the call of lifestyles and careers at variance with the yeshiva's goals. To achieve this objective, he must successfully impart an approach to religion which integrates intellectual study with spiritual gratification. In order to gain the trust of the students he must project an image of approachability. *Bochorim* frequently look to the *mashgiach* for guidance in areas such as marriage, career choices, and problems in achieving a certain level in talmudic study. Questions of faith and personal problems are also brought to his attention.[24] In an environment where the intellect is strained to the utmost the *mashgiach*'s role is crucial. As one student put it:

> Unofficially, the *mashgiach* is the lightning rod of the yeshiva. He's there so that everybody should be able to get things out of their system. He listens and lets you spew it out on him. He prevents an explosion in the yeshiva. And it affects him so much he has ulcers and a nervous skin condition.

The *mashgiach* also acts as a sort of overseer, disciplining the students where necessary. If he feels a student will benefit from a tongue-lashing because, for example, he consistently comes late for the morning prayer service, he will administer one. Conversely, he will overlook infractions if he feels it is in the student's best interests. It is his job to make certain that students regularly attend services, arrive on time for the daily learning session in the *beis medrash,* and study while they are there. It is customary for him to walk around the *beis medrash* in the performance of his duties, and many an idle conversation has been cut short upon his approach. At the advanced level, it is not so much fear of punishment by the *mashgiach* but the embarrassment at having to be rebuked that promotes conformity to the discipline of the institution. Nevertheless, certain students require actual punishment. On rare occasions, students will be expelled from the yeshiva for serious infractions. How strict the supervisor is depends on the school's philosophy and the *mashgiach*'s own personality. Some supervisors conduct raids on the dormitory several times a year, confiscating radios, secular magazines, and other items considered inappropriate in a yeshiva. Some delegate such actions to subordinates, usually older students or dormitory supervisors, while others rely on exhortation and peer pressure to do the trick.

The *mashgiach*'s influence is probably greatest among students who are away from home; they will often come to him with problems that would otherwise be taken up within the family.

Because of his overall role and his personal involvement in the lives of the student body, many students are profoundly influenced by him, especially when he is a forceful and dynamic individual. In the questionnaire sent to yeshiva alumni, more than two-thirds of those who mentioned the influence of the administration and faculty on their personal growth and development singled out the *mashgiach* for special mention.

The *mashgiach*'s position in the yeshiva is an important one. Next to the *rosh yeshiva,* with whom he consults regularly, he is the most powerful member in the hierarchy. As a result, tensions sometimes develop between the *rosh yeshiva* and the *mashgiach* and, on occasion, a supervisor has been dismissed when the *rosh yeshiva* feels that his authority is being usurped or that his popularity among the *bochorim* is diminished by the presence of the *mashgiach.* Because of this situation and his general duties in the yeshiva, the role of the *mashgiach* is a highly delicate one, requiring great sensitivity and perceptiveness in addition to an ability to deal with the needs of a diverse student body.

The Registrar and Other Officials

The registrar is typical of a variety of administrative officials in the larger yeshivas, whose duties are quite specific and rather limited in scope and authority though they are essential to the smooth functioning of the yeshiva. In the smaller institutions, several positions are likely to be combined into one. It is the registrar's job to keep track of the students, maintaining a record of who enrolls, who leaves, and how long each stays. He is responsible for keeping accurate statistics and is in charge of administering federal loan programs. The registrar also handles matters such as helping foreign students become citizens, filling out medical insurance forms, and answering questions concerning students from agencies and organizations outside the yeshiva.

The larger yeshivas may also employ a director of field services for community-oriented programs and branch schools, a librarian, a director of professional studies, and so on. It should be stressed, however, that most yeshivas, even the larger ones, do not have a more complex administrative hierarchy than that which appears in the flow chart (Figure 3–1).

The Faculty

Within the yeshiva world, appointment to the faculty of an advanced yeshiva is in itself a badge of high achievement. There are relatively few positions in the field of Jewish education at this level. Most students, having spent many years in the yeshiva engaged in intensive talmudic study, want to teach advanced classes that allow them to utilize the full range of their knowledge rather than starting at a very basic level. Thus, those who teach at the *beis medrash* level are usually highly qualified.[25]

A look at the faculties of some of the major yeshivas reveals the following general profile: the average faculty member is likely to be European-born and in his mid- to late fifties. Those who are American-trained have usually done most of their studying at the yeshiva in which they presently teach. The trend is toward replacing the older faculty with younger men who are American-born and -educated.

Since faculty appointments are most often long term, the selection process is careful and thorough. Such appointments are generally made by the *rosh yeshiva* in consultation with the faculty. Criteria employed in determining appointment to the staff include scholarly background, experience and ability, recommendations from various sources, a demonstrated commitment to the institution's objectives, and family or other personal contacts. The candidate must also have a sensitivity to student needs and problems. The yeshiva community is relatively small and applicants are usually known to the yeshiva personally or by reputation. How the applicant is viewed by his peers, the quality of the yeshivas at which he studied, whatever works he may have published, and the level of distinction he has reached in the community at large are all taken into account. Quite a few yeshivas favor candidates from their own institutions, arguing that they can best transmit the school's philosophy and are more likely to be loyal to the yeshiva, thereby enhancing its stability. Clearly, such inbreeding means that faculty are less likely to be independent and outspoken. Nor are they likely to bring about changes in the yeshiva's philosophy, goals, and ways of doing things. Then again, the yeshiva is not especially interested in promoting diverse viewpoints. Independence is valued and encouraged only in the realm of scholarship, where it is considered essential to the learning process.

Being a teacher in a yeshiva is a difficult job. The pay is low, generally between $12,000 and $16,000 a year, the hours are long, and the fringe benefits are minimal. On the other hand, a yeshiva *rebbe* has considerable prestige in his community plus the opportunity to work full time at what he presumably likes— teaching, counseling, and research. Despite the similarities in responsibilities, his do not resemble those of the typical college professor. He is, as a rule, on duty Sunday through Thursday from 9:30 to about 6:30, plus one evening a week and a half day on Friday. During the average week, he delivers between three and five complex lectures, each lasting between one and a half and two hours. He often spends hours preparing his material, and is available throughout the day to students who need help understanding the finer points of the talmudic discussion and related commentaries that were taken up during the class. In addition, students will often discuss their own independent study of other portions of the Talmud with the *rebbe*. Faculty are required to supervise and evaluate the progress of their students on a regular basis, through both intensive consultation and formal testing in the classroom. Such tests are usually oral but on occasion consist of a written examination. College professors generally teach about eight or, at most, nine months out of the year; a *rebbe* teaches a full ten months. He is, however, free during the summer.

Another important function of the faculty is to be available to students for guidance. Although this is officially the *mashgiach*'s area of jurisdiction, students will often approach their own *rebbe*, with whom they have daily contact, for help in solving a personal problem before going to the *mashgiach*. Ultimately, this depends upon the individual's relationship with his *rebbe*. In the yeshiva, how a student gets along with his teacher is of far greater importance than in the average educational setting. This is not only because of the long hours and total involvement of the *rebbe* with his class, but also because the *rebbe* serves both as a pedagogue and as a role model. As might be expected, faculty differ in personality, and some may relate better to some students than to others. Some students seem to flourish under the stern disciplinarian who makes the *bochorim* work hard while others prefer a *rebbe* who is gentle, sympathetic, and lenient. The totality of the yeshiva environment and the fact that the young man has but one *rebbe* a year (sometimes he will be in the same class for two or three years) means that the *rebbe*'s role is a pivotal one. Although the majority adjust, whether or not the student has a rewarding relationship with the teacher can profoundly affect him. At the very least, it will make or break his year and may even precipitate his departure from the institution. To be sure, students can ask to be placed in another class, but this is no simple matter in an institution where everyone knows everyone else.

During the course of a year, the *bochur* will become familiar not only with the *rebbe* but with his family as well. *Rebbes* in a *yeshiva gedola* generally live within walking distance of the school since they spend so much of their time there. Their homes are usually open to the students, who will often drop by uninvited to seek advice or simply say hello. Even those *rebbes* who guard their privacy will at least invite students to their homes throughout the year, perhaps for a *Shabbos* meal. Whether the purpose is purely social or to resolve a problem, such contact over a long period of time results in the *rebbe*'s becoming an integral part of the young man's total experience at the yeshiva.

Faculty members are expected to engage in research in order to maintain a high level of scholarship that is reflected in the quality of instruction. Although they may publish original research in journals such as *Hapardes* and *Hadorom,* there is no pressure to publish externally; a few yeshivas ask their faculty to contribute papers that are disseminated within the yeshiva.

Those who teach in the yeshiva are not, as a rule, permitted to have outside employment, for their job is both demanding and strenuous. It is only during the summer that they are free. Even then, many stay around the yeshiva or, if the institution has a summer camp, combine vacation with the somewhat abbreviated teaching schedule that is part of the summer camp's program. Faculty also present lectures at meetings and convocations in the Orthodox community at large. It must be stressed that any activity involving Torah study is not seen as "work," and that the position of *rebbe* is far more than a "job." It is in his eyes an opportunity to fulfill the purpose for which man was created. As a result, while he may not like some of the bureaucratic functions that are part of his duties, he certainly does not view spending all day in the *beis medrash* as onerous nor does he see the lengthy academic year as an imposition. As we shall see, most yeshiva graduates continue studying for the rest of their lives. Often, after a full day of work at a secular job, they attend and give classes in the evening hours, a time when most other Americans relax by reading novels, watching television, going to the movies, and the like.

Like members of an academic department in a university, faculty meet regularly with their "chairman," the *rosh yeshiva*, to discuss the policy and administration of the school in areas relevant to their responsibilities. The *rosh yeshiva* is responsible for evaluating the performance of each teacher, generally by speaking with other faculty, administrators, and students. Ultimately, the effectiveness of a *rebbe* is judged by the enthusiasm for learning he generates in his students and the degree to which they master the intricacies of the Talmud. In the yeshiva the abilities of the various *rebbes* are a prime topic of discussion and are well known to all members.

Graduate Students

While they are not a formal part of the yeshiva hierarchy, graduate students (*kollel*) play an important role. By virtue of their greater experience in the yeshiva, they are often sought out by many younger students for advice on problems that they are reluctant to broach with a *rebbe* or *mashgiach*. Sometimes the problem may concern the *rebbe* himself, and in such an instance the *eltere bochur* (older student) provides a shoulder to cry on. On a more academic level, graduate students frequently serve as study partners for younger *bochorim* who may need help with some of the more difficult sections of the program of study. Finally, the *kollel* student functions as a role model for younger *bochorim*, who also obtain, through him, a clearer perspective on what the future holds for them.[26] The *beis medrash* (undergraduate) student is often called on to fulfill a similar role in yeshivas that have a *mesivta* division by acting as a sort of "big brother" to the high school student. In other instances, *beis medrash bochorim* may participate in community programs where they teach and counsel younger boys in the local community.

Undergraduates (Beis Medrash Students)

To some extent, the class a student is in affects his position in the hierarchy. Students in the *rosh yeshiva*'s class are often deferred to by those in the lower classes. Often their advice is sought on a variety of issues, some pertaining to the learning process.

In addition to class rank, there are various committees led and run by students, and those who play prominent roles may also be looked up to. For example, certain students are in charge of giving out various honors relating to the prayer service and the reading of the Torah; purchasing prayer books, renting the bus for a wedding or funeral, or making certain provisions are bought for use by the school during various religious holidays. A special committee of students exists in most institutions for the purpose of lending money to needy students at no interest. The funds come from other students who lend money to the committee. Those who serve on the committee derive a certain status from their involvement in a good cause.

The Executive Director and the Fund-Raising Staff

Yeshivas are not, by and large, wealthy institutions. At many, only a small minority of the students pay full tuition. They do not have endowments and generally operate at a deficit. The case of Torah Vodaath, which almost closed several years ago and was unable to pay its faculty their salaries for several months, is atypical but suggestive of the problems that face most yeshivas.

The executive director bears primary responsibility, at times in conjunction with the *rosh yeshiva,* for managing the yeshiva's fiscal affairs. He is also in charge of the school's promotional activities and supervises the office staff on a day-to-day basis, but his most important area is finances. He and his staff must insure that the institution remains solvent, and even in yeshivas where the *rosh yeshiva* retains control over such efforts, the expertise and experience of the executive director are often crucial factors in their success. Funding is obtained in a variety of ways. The following breakdown is typical:

Personal solicitations	25%
Student tuition	12
Government aid	27
Mass mailings	12
Other sources	24

Each yeshiva tends to have a few major contributors plus many small ones. The major donors are generally Orthodox businessmen who have a strong commitment to the institution's goals. They may or may not have attended the yeshiva; sometimes they have children enrolled in it. A few very large contributors give money to several yeshivas. In most cases such individuals are members of the board of trustees. Depending on how active an interest they take in the institution, they will be kept informed by the executive director regarding the finances of the school. Of the 59 members of the board at the Beth Medrash Govoha in 1977, all but four were in business of one sort or another. Predictably, given the residential patterns of Orthodox Jews in America, the majority were located in the New York area. The following conversation with the executive director of one of the largest yeshivas revealed some interesting insights into who gives and why:

WH: What is the level of religious observance among your contributors?

ED: That's an interesting question. Many of them are not Orthodox though most are. Those who aren't religious see it as a matter of survival. We say to them: "Look, you may not care about how religious your kids are. But don't you care about Jewish identity? Do you want your children to intermarry and assimilate? We train many of the people who will eventually pass on the tradition to your own children in the yeshivas and Talmud Torahs [afternoon Hebrew schools]. Without schools like ours there will be no one capable of teaching them." And this is not a ploy to get them to give. It's true and they know it. [27]

WH: What are some of the other reasons why people give money?

ED: Everyone has their own reasons. Many give because they want recognition. That's why you have to have annual dinners honoring people. But many give for idealistic reasons. More than one-third of our supporters do not want their names made public.

The much larger group of small donors is also crucial to the yeshiva. Years ago, especially in Europe, it was common for fund-raisers or "collectors" to travel from community to community soliciting funds while keeping a portion for themselves as commission. Quite a few *rosh yeshivas* opposed the practice, arguing that it was inappropriate for yeshiva funds to be used as commission payments. [28] Today this approach is less common;

collectors, or *meshullachim,* are generally full-time, salaried professionals. They crisscross the American continent searching out those who want to fulfill the *mitzva* (religious commandment) of charity. Most, especially the old-timers, collect with a certain flair and a distinctive style that are the result of many years of experience. They do not simply ask for money. They sit down and *shmuess* (chat) for a while, perhaps over a glass of tea, and when they finally get down to business they make it clear that the donor, not the collector, is privileged, for it is he who will receive the *mitzva* for giving.

Perhaps the dean of the *meshullachim* was Rabbi Chaim Nachman Kowalsky, who performed his services for Ner Israel Rabbinical College. Educated in European yeshivas, he came here in 1927 and collected door-to-door, for the most part, nearly $3 million over the last half century. He built up friendships that endured for decades. He once told a businessman in Milwaukee, Wisconsin: "I collected from your grandfather and G-d willing, I'll collect from your son as well."[29]

The average *meshullach* today is a clean-shaven young man with a college education, but the approach is still the same. Relying on contacts, mostly former classmates at the yeshiva, to lead him to potential donors, he travels around the country, often staying in the homes of local Orthodox Jews in whatever city he happens to be. He is always on the lookout for the big contribution, but knows that most will be small and that they do add up in the long run. He must be personable, intelligent, highly motivated, and willing to be away from his family for extended periods of time. Most important, perhaps, he must be able to accept the fact that many people, upon hearing his voice on the telephone, will display no great eagerness to see him. Some yeshivas also ask their own students to solicit donations, usually when they are home on vacation in their own communities.

Another important source of revenue is tuition. According to the self-studies prepared by the yeshivas, financial ability to pay plays no part in the admissions policy; many students receive full scholarships in keeping with the historically high regard of the Jewish community for education. Besides direct aid from the yeshiva, needy students can apply to the federal government for Basic and Supplemental Educational Opportunity Grants, College Work Study Programs, and National Direct Student Loans, since the yeshiva qualifies as an institution of higher learning.[30]

Years ago, in Eastern Europe, yeshivas, like the rest of the Orthodox community, often found themselves at the mercy of corrupt governments and venal officials interested only in milking those under their jurisdiction as much as possible. In such circumstances, it was often necessary to employ bribery and other means of subterfuge merely to survive. The governments in Poland and Russia were not benevolent masters, especially when it came to the Jews. Obviously, this is not the case here and yeshivas enjoy many benefits from the government, such as financial aid to students, that were unheard of in Europe. To many immigrant members of the Orthodox and yeshiva community, the workings of the American government came as a surprise. Aware of the need to reshape perceptions that were the outcome of centuries of oppression and prejudice, leaders in the Orthodox community have taken great pains to sensitize their people toward the moral issues involved. Because of their dress— that is, yarmulke or black hat, white shirt open at the neck—and religious practices, members of the yeshiva community, while not as noticeable as Hasidic Jews, are more visible than other segments of the Jewish community. Presumably, this is what Rabbi Moshe Feinstein had in mind when he wrote a letter on this topic that was distributed in 1977 to many Orthodox Jews by *Yosher,* an organization founded to raise the ethical behavior in the community. The letter said, in part:

> Behold . . . G-d . . . in His great mercy . . . brought us here where we established centers of Torah transplanted from Europe and new ones. . . . This *malchut shel chesed* (kindly government) . . . has established numerous programs to aid students.
>
> But certainly we are warned by G-d who commanded us so through his holy Torah to beware taking more than the government programs are established to grant. . . . For aside from its being prohibited as theft, there are also involved here severe prohibitions of false statements, lies and deceit; and also desecration of G-d's name, and disgrace of the Torah and its scholars. There is absolutely no basis for a permissive decision (in these matters). . . .
>
> Of course, heads of Yeshivot and principals, who are G-d fearing men, are not suspected of violating (such) prohibitions. . . . Nevertheless, we deem it appropriate to arouse concern as to this matter so that there be greater attention paid to the entire issue; . . . To all who are excep-

tionally careful (in these matters), may they be blessed with good . . . for it is well known and clear to everyone that Yeshiva students are the best of citizens in their personal qualities and good deeds.

That Rabbi Feinstein found it necessary to write such a letter indicates the existence of a problem. However, it is not one of numbers since only a small number of Orthodox Jews, relatively speaking, have been identified as participants in various unethical practices. Yet because they point with pride to their adherence to the laws of the Torah and claim theirs is a morally superior way of life, they sometimes make other groups uneasy to the point where the slightest abberation by Orthodox Jews is judged very harshly. Several years ago there was a scandal involving a federally supported school lunch program that included aid to yeshivas. Although only a few Orthodox Jews were implicated, the entire community was tarred with the same brush by many outside it—both Jews and non-Jews.

Mass mailings are another source of revenue. Yeshivas use lists garnered from synagogues and national organizations, but the core of their list is their own alumni. This presents a logistical problem because approximately 15 percent of the addresses become outdated each year, and many individuals leave no forwarding address. For purposes of the fund-raising mailings anyone who attended the yeshiva, even if only for a year, is considered an alumnus. According to the executive directors of five yeshivas, about one-third of their contributions come from alumni.

The fund-soliciting letter is generally accompanied by a Jewish calendar and one or more pamphlets containing lectures and writings of some of the more prominent *rebbes* in the institution. In at least one yeshiva, cassette recordings of the *mashgiach*'s *mussar shmuessim* are mailed to former students in the hope of inspiring them to make a contribution. While large numbers of alumni give to their alma mater, some cite their own negative experiences at the institution as the reason for declining to send in a donation. As one put it:

> You know, I am grateful to them for having given me a scholarship and all while I was there but, you know, they had this guy when I was there who was a real "yo-yo." When outsiders would tour the yeshiva he would come ahead of them to inspect the rooms; he was an administrator

there, and he would do it in a really nasty way. One time, I had left my hat on the bed and he threw it in the garbage can. This left me with a bitter taste. Please, please don't tell the yeshiva I said this because it would really embarrass me.

This individual believes his attitude is wrong, but his own feelings of hostility compel him to act in this fashion. In this case the person has a reputation for giving freely to other yeshivas and is not using his negative experiences as an excuse for not giving charity altogether.

Dinners, bazaars, parlor meetings, raffles and contests (first prize is usually a trip to Israel), and appeals in synagogues all come under the heading of "other sources" and they account for about 24 percent of the typical yeshiva's income. The annual dinner, where advertisements are sold for the "dinner journal," is an especially important source of revenue. There is considerable variation in this area; some of the more efficiently run yeshivas derive more than half their funds from it and others less than 10 percent. One relatively small New York City yeshiva reported a net gain of $250,000 from such a function. These events are usually arranged by alumni who contact former fellow students and urge them to come or otherwise participate. Gatherings like these not only supply needed funds to the yeshiva, but also reinforce the social bonds among those who have shared a common experience.

The larger yeshivas with several hundred students generally have a yearly budget of at least $750,000. Figure 3–2 shows how the pie is divided among the various needs facing one major yeshiva. It is based on actual figures given in a self-study of the yeshiva and prepared for a government accrediting agency.

The distributions for the other seven yeshivas whose budgets were examined were quite similar. These figures are for 1973; since then, according to the financial offices of several yeshivas, a greater portion of the budget has been allocated for the *kollel,* or postgraduate division, which has grown in popularity in recent years. At one yeshiva, the amount set aside for stipends to *kollel* students went from $45,810 in 1973 to $80,200 in 1974.

Summer Camp

This component of the yeshiva deserves special mention because it is far more than a place for fun and relaxation, though it

Figure 3-2

Distribution of a Major Yeshiva's Budget Funds

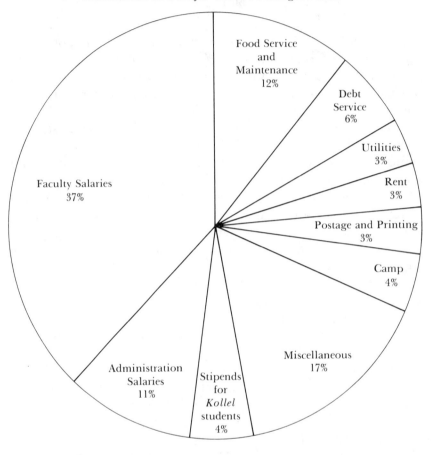

is that too. The camp is an extension of the school year, for all ye-shiva camps have an extensive program of study in addition to the usual program of baseball, swimming, hikes, and so on. At least half of each day is spent in Talmud study. Lured by the of-fer of free cottages for the summer in a country setting, *rebbes* from the yeshiva come up with their families and, in exchange for room and board, give lectures to the students in an informal atmosphere. Located, for the most part, in the Catskill Moun-tains, such camps were first established almost seventy years ago. Both students of the sponsoring yeshiva and young men from other yeshivas are usually eligible to enroll in the camp. Students pay for the camp at rates which compare favorably with those of private Orthodox Jewish camps. The significance of the camp is that, as a result of going there, the *bochur* remains within the yeshiva world for the entire year, thereby strengthening the socialization process which every yeshiva feels is essential for developing observant and knowledgeable Jews.[31]

It should be evident by now that the structure and organization of the typical yeshiva is highly complex, a far cry from the form taken by most yeshivas in Eastern Europe a century or even a half century ago. The existence of such a bureaucracy inevitably results in some degree of alienation on the part of many students. Except in the smaller yeshivas, the personal touch tends to be lost or at least diminished. Yeshivas are aware of this problem and have taken steps to deal with it by appointing guidance counselors, usually older students or administrators, but this is often not enough. In an institution where the *rosh yeshiva* so clearly dominates the scene the importance of other administrators, with the possible exception of the *rebbes* and the *mashgiach,* often pales into insignificance. When, because of the press of other obligations, the *rosh yeshiva* must be continually absent from the yeshiva, the student may feel that his needs are being neglected. If he is told that he must wait a month before he can see the *rosh yeshiva,* he may come to regard the yeshiva as an impersonal institution more interested in self-perpetuation than in serving those who attend it. Such a view was indeed expressed in many interviews and mailed questionnaire responses. Those who attended a yeshiva in the years when it was still small were more likely to cite the warmth and feelings of closeness that permeated the yeshiva in their open-ended responses to the question: "What did you like most about the yeshiva?" The dilemma posed by this condition is probably most acute in the area of character development, which is a cornerstone of the yeshiva's program. It is difficult to emphasize concern for the individual if top officials in the yeshiva hierarchy are often unavailable. Yet it should be stated that the yeshiva, compared to other educational institutions, is still a place where the individual receives a good deal of personal attention. Nevertheless, this may become something of a problem as the yeshivas, in their efforts to meet the needs of a growing Orthodox population, continue to increase in size. Whether this will lead to a trend favoring the smaller and less established yeshivas remains to be seen.

CHAPTER 4

In the Path
of the Lord:
Teachings
of the Faith

Rabbi Hananiah ben Akashya said: The Holy One, praised be He, wished to grant merit to the nation of Israel. He therefore gave them a complex *Torah* and many commandments, for it is written (*Isaiah* 42:21): "The Lord was pleased, for His righteousness' sake, to magnify His Law and make it glorious."[1]

It is this mandate that the yeshiva student accepts when he begins studying in the yeshiva and becomes a part of its community. In doing so, he asserts his commitment to the goals of intellectual scholarship and purification of the soul. Though others may regard his interests and beliefs as narrow and parochial, they are the central focus of his life, the embodiment of that for which man was created. His entry into the yeshiva sets into motion a process of learning which will come to dominate most of his waking hours and will define and determine the pattern of his existence. Every action of consequence he takes, every event in life that affects him, will be judged through the eyes of one who sees God's guiding hand everywhere.

Of course, these remarks apply to the ideal student. The majority are not entirely successful in attaining this high intellectual and spiritual plateau. Yet most students regard it as a goal worth striving for and do attempt to reach it. To provide the student with the means toward this objective, he is challenged to undertake a rigorous program of study. The yeshiva sees its mission, in part, as creating a cadre of people who will be the contemporary link in the long chain of tradition that began with the giving of the Torah to Moses on Mount Sinai. These young men are viewed as an elite group who will provide the leadership and set the standards of excellence necessary for the survival and well-being of the Jewish community.

A Typical Program

The day begins early, usually about 7:15 A.M., when the *bochur* is awakened by the cry, often said in Yiddish, "Wake up! Wake up to do the work of the Creator!"[2] The young man washes up, recites the prayer customarily said at this time, and leaves the residence hall for the *beis medrash,* to participate in the morning prayer service. The prayers are not said hurriedly, but with great care and precision. With no job or responsibilities, the student can afford to take his time to reflect on the words in the service.

The morning service is followed by breakfast and perhaps a short break to allow the student to take care of his personal needs. At about 9:30, the learning part of the day officially begins, though some people may be in the *beis medrash* even earlier. Until about noon, the students learn* together in preparation for the lecture to be given by the *rebbe.* Together with their learning partners, they struggle to understand and explicate the often difficult concepts in the Talmud, taking note of those that escape their comprehension with the intention of raising them in class. Similarly, they try to develop insights into the text that will both make the projected class discussion clearer and earn them the approval of the teacher and their classmates. The process of studying the text in advance of the lecture is called "making a *leining.*" At the appointed time, everyone goes into his respective classroom, where, for the next one and a half hours or so, he discusses and debates the assigned portion of the text

---

*In yeshiva parlance, the word "learn" almost always means study. To avoid confusion between quotes from students and rabbis and also to remain faithful to what is an important term in the community we will use it throughout, i.e., "He *learns* well" really means he studies well or, more generally, that he is a good student.

with the *rebbe* and the other students. Alternating between lecturing and a give-and-take discussion, the *rebbe* controls the tempo of the class.

After class, a short break is taken for lunch, perhaps followed by a half hour or so spent perusing various works of an ethical or philosophical nature. At about 3:00 P.M. the afternoon session begins. Students spend the next several hours in independent study, either reviewing the material covered in class or learning (studying) other portions of the Talmud. At those yeshivas where college attendance is permitted, those who go generally depart at about 4:30 P.M. The usual pattern in such schools is to allow the *bochur* to attend a secular institution two nights a week. Those who are not enrolled in college classes study until suppertime (usually between 6:00 and 7:00 P.M.) when they break for an hour before returning to the *beis medrash* for yet a third session of Talmud study, usually in a subject area of their own choosing. During the afternoon and evening sessions, students are encouraged to approach their teacher, if he is available, for help in understanding the lecture, or for anything else they might happen to be studying. As a rule, the *rebbe* is in the *beis medrash* for at least one of these two sessions. The 10:00 P.M. evening prayer service marks the conclusion of the formally required study period. After this, the young man is free to do whatever he pleases—read a book, get something to eat in the school canteen, or just relax with friends in his room or elsewhere on the yeshiva grounds. Quite a few of the students continue learning in the *beis medrash* until the wee hours of the morning, stopping only when overtaken by fatigue.

On Friday, most yeshivas have only a morning session devoted to independent study. Students have the afternoon off, both to relax and to prepare for the Sabbath. On the Sabbath itself, there are no classes given by the *rebbe*. After the Friday evening service the students enjoy a traditional meal of gefilte fish, chicken soup, roast chicken, and dessert. Songs honoring the holiday are sung between courses, and the atmosphere is festive. The rest of the evening is spent visiting with friends, looking through the Bible, usually the portion to be read on Sabbath morning, perhaps joining the *rebbe* at his house, or simply sleeping. The Sabbath morning service is the longest of the week, followed by lunch at noon with more singing. Generally, the students, as is the custom with most Orthodox Jews, sleep in the afternoon, rising at about 3:30 P.M. for the afternoon service. Supper (called "*Shalesheudes*"), the third meal of the Sabbath, is usually served about two hours before the Sabbath ends, followed by the weekly ethics lecture (*mussar shmuess*) given by the *mashgiach,* an often emotional discourse that is one of the highlights of yeshiva life.[3]

The policy with regard to Saturday night varies. Some yeshivas give their students the evening off but others have a *melave malka,* a program combining a party with refreshments, singing, dancing, and short presentations dealing with various aspects of the Talmud or Bible, or Prophets (*dvar Torah*), which often lasts until past midnight. Sunday is identical with the other days of the week with the same program of study sessions, lectures, and so on.

The academic year is generally divided into three periods, each of which is known as a *zman* (term). The first is the longest of the three, beginning after the Succoth holiday in October and ending in April, at Passover. The second commences about a week after the end of Passover and lasts until the Hebrew month of Ab (usually July). The third and final *zman* starts sometime in mid-August and lasts until Yom Kippur, generally in September. All told, the students have about nine weeks of vacation throughout the year, but a good portion of the student body continues learning even during these periods (the study of Torah must be engaged in every day).

Upon entry into the yeshiva, the student is placed in a class on the basis of prior level of accomplishment. Class size varies greatly, with some having only fifteen or twenty students while others, especially the *rosh yeshiva*'s class, have more than one hundred. Since students come from high schools where the programs vary considerably in quality, it is not axiomatic that all entering students will be placed in the first-year class. Under normal circumstances, the student steadily progresses through three or four classes, eventually gaining entry into the *rosh yeshiva*'s class. Sometimes boys remain in a class for two or three years, either because they have not progressed to a level justifying promotion or because they have developed a strong liking for a particular teacher. Sooner or later, however, everyone moves up. Promotion is not necessarily determined by examination, but may be suggested by the teacher on the basis of a general impression that the young man is "ready."

Looking at the program of study, it is difficult to imagine how people tolerate it without great hardship. Surely a comparable program of college study would be judged very demanding, to say the least. Although their level of intelligence is fairly high, many of those studying in yeshivas are not brilliant. Besides their intellectual talents, what enables them to handle the program is their high degree of preparation and the fact that they see themselves as carrying out a mission. From the time he started first grade (if he went to a yeshiva elementary school), the yeshiva student has been exposed to a "double program" of Jewish studies in the morning hours and secular subjects in the afternoon. In most yeshiva elementary schools whose graduates eventually attend the traditional advanced yeshivas, the day ends for students at around 6:00 P.M. as early as the sixth grade, and there is at least a half day of school on Sundays. Through the high school years, the day becomes still longer; most yeshivas conclude at around 6:30 P.M., including Sunday, and the majority require their students to learn two or more evenings a week. Thus, the entering *beis medrash* student is prepared psychologically for the long day that awaits him.

The student has a motivation beyond intellectual curiosity. He sees his obligation to study as a religious commandment. To the extent that human beings respond to positive reinforcement, the yeshiva *bochur* derives gratification from the approval of his *rebbe.* But, over and above that, the force that sustains him is often the spiritual strength he derives from the certainty that in studying the Torah he is carrying out God's will, a strength common to true believers of all faiths.

Mastering the Talmud

While there are intellectually oriented orders such as the Jesuits, more than a few Christian orders display apathy and even some condescension toward intellectualism, arguing that it can interfere with spiritual goals.[4] In the yeshiva, however, developing one's intellect is of great importance. This is true not only in theory but in practice as well, for if a student is not completely involved in the study of the Talmud it is easy to lose track of the arguments being presented with the result that it all becomes meaningless, boring, and frustrating. Emphasis in the yeshiva is not so much upon prayer and meditation or on ethical behavior toward one's fellow man. These are important aspects of yeshiva life as well as divine commandments, but the key element is fulfilling the obligation of Torah study.

This book does not pretend to be an intellectual treatise on the Talmud.[5] Nevertheless, if we are to fully understand the sociological characteristics of the yeshiva we must take into account what its members consider important and try to explain its role in their lives. The Talmud is based entirely on the Bible, also referred to as the Written Law. Anyone who undertakes talmudic study must be familiar with the Bible, for this is the basis for all discussions in the Talmud. Moreover, he needs to be familiar with the rules of logic and method that are unique to talmudic study; to study Talmud without a strong grounding in basic principles of Jewish law is like trying to run before one can crawl.

In order to provide a better understanding of the central activity of yeshiva life, I present here a verbatim excerpt from a typical lecture given (in English) to students in the second year of study at an advanced yeshiva. The selection, taken from the tractate (or volume) *Baba Kamma* 46a, is a moderately difficult one as such discussions go. Figure 4–1 is a reproduction of the actual text as it appears in its original form. In the center column, in larger type, is the main body of the work and on either side are the commentaries. The basic purpose here is to capture the flavor and spirit of the learning process, not so much its content; to see how the *rebbe* and his students interact on what can appropriately be described as an intellectual battlefield. The "battle" is a joint effort to arrive at a genuine understanding of the law by engaging in verbal jousting that seeks to introduce hidden meanings and to provide interpretations, often of a novel nature, to an often complex and intricate text. The format is that of questions and answers rather than a straight presentation of facts. This is crucial to the goal of developing independent and original thinking. The *rebbe* is not content with merely having the young man absorb information; he wants him to develop the capacity to think on his own, and his approach in the classroom reflects this desire.

According to the Talmud, there is no jealousy between a teacher and his student, and the setting in the classroom gives credence to this statement. While the *rebbe* possesses greater

Figure 4-1
Talmudic Text: *Baba Kamma* 46A

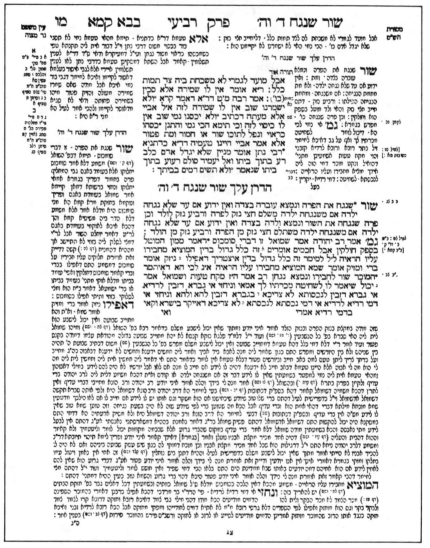

knowledge, he encourages the students to come up with new ideas and applications, bestowing lavish praise on those who do so. The excitement in the room is contagious and at times eight or nine members of the class will argue and yell at each other in a cacophony of sound that forces the *rebbe* to bang on his desk and shout for order. The selection below attempts to capture this atmosphere and to indicate why those in the yeshiva world find it such an exciting and challenging place:

> REBBE: Okay, who knows the Mishna *clor* [well]? Yechezkel, start saying. Just say the first part and then go to the *Gemora*.
>
> YECHEZKEL: If an ox gored a cow and they found its newly born calf nearby, what do you do? Do you say that the owner of the ox also has to pay for the dead calf even though we don't know for sure if the ox killed the cow when the fetus was still in it—or do we say that maybe she had already given birth before she was gored and it would have been a still-birth anyway?
>
> CHAIM: What about for the cow? Does the owner have to pay damages for her?
>
> REBBE: Of course he does! Are you sleeping? That's obvious. He [the owner] admits that. The question is on the calf. Where were you yesterday when we explained that? *Nu.* Go on, Yechezkel.
>
> DOVID: But where did this happen? On public property or private property?
>
> REBBE: Let's say it was public property. We don't need to overcomplicate matters here. It gets complicated enough as it is.
>
> YECHEZKEL: So the *halacha* [law] is that on the mother you pay half the value and on the child a quarter of the value.
>
> REUVAIN: Why should you pay half on the mother and only one-quarter on the calf?
>
> REBBE: Good question, Reuvain. Who knows the answer?
>
> YAAKOV: Maybe it's because the calf has no value at the time it's born?
>
> CHAIM: What are you talking about? Obviously it'll have value later on.
>
> YAAKOV: But we're not sure at this point what will happen to it.
>
> REBBE: C'mon, c'mon! We learned this already; what's the *klal* [principle] here? Dovid?
>
> DOVID: The *klal* is that in money matters you always split it down the middle when in doubt.
>
> REBBE: Right. At least *somebody* remembers what we learned. Now let's try to understand the whole thing a little better. What kind of ox are we talking about? We're talking about a *shor tam,* meaning an ox that didn't have the reputation as an ox that gores habitually, and the law in such a case is that the owner pays half.

Because you're not responsible to watch it that much. Now on the calf we don't know; so we say you split it down the middle. Now, let's look at the *Gemora*. Who does this Mishna go according to?

YECHIEL: [Rabbi] Sumchus.

REBBE: Right. Go on, Yechezkel. Say the *Gemora*.

YECHEZKEL: The *chachomim* [a group of sages with whom Sumchus was learning] say that this idea of splitting the money goes against a basic principle—that if you want to collect from someone you have to bring proof. So therefore in this case he wouldn't have to pay anything for this fetus because there's no proof the ox was responsible for its death.

YECHIEL: But how could a person *ever* be certain?

REBBE: That's not a question. You saw it happen. What's the difference? Okay. Yechezkel, go on with the *Gemora*.

YECHEZKEL: The *Gemora* asks: Why do the *chachomim* say this is a *klal "gadol"* ["major" principle] [that a claimant for damages must bring proof]? This is an extra word. Why don't they leave out "major"? What are they getting at? And the answer is: We need it to show you that even in a case where, let's say, it was your calf that I damaged but I'm not sure I did and you are, even in that case you can't collect anything.

DOVID: But why should that be? The guy didn't see it.

SIX OR SEVEN STUDENTS, ALL SHOUTING AT ONCE: That's why it's a *klal gadol!* That even when one is sure and the other isn't, it applies.

[*Dovid appears momentarily perplexed; perhaps he is taken aback by the vehemence of the opposition. Sensing his confusion, his learning partner, Ephraim, tries to explain it to him.*]

EPHRAIM: Look. Can you go to court in America and collect without witnesses as a rule? Just show up and say I know?

DOVID: But there's no one to really argue with him.

SEVERAL STUDENTS [INCLUDING EPHRAIM]: What's the difference?

DOVID: A big difference [*heatedly*]!

VARIOUS STUDENTS: No, there isn't!

DOVID: Yes there is! Let me explain it.

REBBE: Hold it! Hold it! Everybody quiet down. Let's go over the whole thing from the beginning again.

[*The teacher painstakingly explains the arguments, trying this time to make his points easier to follow by citing concrete examples such as the following one.*]

REBBE: Let's take a real-life situation. Suppose you rent me your bungalow in the Catskill Mountains, or I rent it from your parents. Then there's damage done to it and your parents say I did it. But I say, I'm not sure. Maybe it was a storm. According to the *chachomim, you* have to bring proof that I damaged it. You don't divide the money down the middle.

[*After he has explained the* Gemora, *the* rebbe *says:*]

REBBE: Okay. Let's go to the *Tosfos.** Nosson, say the *Tosfos.*

NOSSON: And if you'll say that we have a general principle that if a person has to swear and for some reason he can't, then the *din* [law] is he has to pay the full amount; and this is one of those cases because he's a *modeh bemiktsas* [has made a partial admission of guilt] . . .

REBBE: Hold it. How is he a *modeh bemiktsas* here? *Nu,* Pinchas?

PINCHAS: [*Startled because his mind has probably been wandering.*] Uh, he isn't because he pays on both.

REBBE: That makes no sense at all. The question is why is he paying only one-quarter on the calf? What's the matter with you? Maybe you're staying up too late. It's nice to sit in the *beis medrash* until 1:30 in the morning, but you have to be awake the next day too [*all this is said in a half-jesting tone, implying mild rebuke only*].

DOVID: He's a *modeh bemiktsas* because he admits on the cow.

REBBE: Okay. Now continue, Nosson.

NOSSON: So here he should have to pay the whole thing which in this case is half on the cow and half on the calf instead of a quarter. So *Tosfos* says that Shmuel [Rabbi Samuel] argues with this principle [in another tractate of the *Talmud, Shevuoth,* 46]. Now we come to another principle here. When a person who has to pay a *knas* [special penalty] admits his obligation to do so, then he doesn't have to swear. And this is a case of *knas,* not *mammon* [money matters alone]. But *rebbe—Why* is this a case of *knas*?

REBBE: Who knows the answer? [*pause*] Come on. Who wants to go on with the *Tosfos* and tell me what *Tosfos* is saying here? Betzalel! Do you know what's going on here? Yes? Okay. Start.

BETZALEL: Actually, this is based on an argument on why he should pay half. One person holds that really he should pay full damages because it's his responsibility, but God had pity on him so he only pays half. The other one says just the opposite. Really,

* *Tosfos* is the name given to a collective work of a number of commentaries on the Talmud itself, whose writings appear on one side of the folio pages.

he shouldn't pay anything because it's a quiet ox; because we believe that oxen do not generally do damage. But the Torah made a special penalty on him.

REBBE: Excellent, Betzalel! You know what's going on here. I only hope everyone else does too. Now to sum up: *Tosfos* gives two answers here as to why you don't have to pay the full amount which is actually half. First, because Shmuel argues with the principle that wherever you have to swear and you can't you then have to pay and second, you don't have to swear because this is a case of *knas* and not *mammon.*

BETZALEL: Wait a minute [*excitedly*]! If, as *Tosfos* says, we're speaking about *knas* he shouldn't have to pay anything because of the rule of *modeh biknas potur* [a person who admits to having to pay a special penalty doesn't have to pay].

REBBE: Aha! I see what's bothering you. Does everyone hear what Betzalel is asking [*Betzalel is beaming with pleasure because he knows he has asked a good question*]? Betzalel is being *mechaven* [discovering independently] to what the Maharam says—namely that the case here is actually with witnesses. Okay, we'll come back to that. Let's go on just a little further with the *Tosfos.*

[*Betzalel continues saying the* Tosfos *for a few minutes. When he reaches a certain point in the discussion, the* rebbe *stops him and says*:

REBBE: Okay. Let's look at the *Rambam* [Maimonides] who argues on what *Tosfos* is saying, on this third answer that *Tosfos* gives. Chaim, say the *Rambam.*

[*Chaim reads aloud and attempts to explain what Maimonides is saying on this particular portion of the* Tosfos *but he seems unable to do so. Displeased, the* rebbe *says in a somewhat sarcastic tone of voice*:]

REBBE: Chaim, this is how you read a *Rambam?* Did you prepare this?

CHAIM: I tried to, *rebbe.*

REBBE: I know you can do a lot better as you've done in the past. If this is the way you try you may soon be trying in Rabbi Mandel's class [the class immediately below this one].

After calling on another student who successfully negotiates the arguments and points made by the *Rambam,* the *rebbe* concludes the class, saying:

REBBE: This afternoon, or tomorrow morning, I want you to look at the *Rabad* and the *Rosh* [other commentaries] and try to fit them

into what *Tosfos* and the *Rambam* are saying. Then, if you have
time, look through the rest of the *Tosfos* and the next one.

The fact that the Talmud is treated as a living document is
indicated by the constant reference to the talmudic sages and the
commentaries in the present tense. As one *rosh yeshiva* said: "As
long as these works are being studied it is as if the sages themselves are alive for it is the wisdom of their teachings that was
dearest to their hearts." Relevance, however, is not the primary
consideration in Talmud study. The impetus for study stems
from the belief that God commanded the Jews to do so, and that
it is one of the most important obligations among the 613 commandments (*mitzvas*), regardless of its applicability to today's
times.[6] In fact, many of the laws discussed in the Talmud,
especially those pertaining to the holidays and personal observances, do have relevance and are relied upon by hundreds of
thousands of Jews as a guide to daily living. Even the legal concepts, which would seem not to apply in modern times, where
secular courts of law decide such matters, have been used by Orthodox Jews in Jewish courts, headed by rabbinical authorities
set up for that purpose. In Boston, for example, a local *beis din*
(court) is used by Orthodox Jews to settle landlord–tenant disputes and the like. In such cases, plaintiff and defendant agree in
advance to abide by the court's rulings. Also, Orthodox Jews
believe that when the Messiah comes and all the Jews return to
Israel, the ancient laws will once again be in force.

The above discussion dealt with only six or seven lines in the
text but took almost two hours. Moreover, the class spent
another three days elaborating and arguing various points regarding this brief segment of the Talmud! When one considers
that the Talmud comprises 63 volumes which total 5,800 folio
pages, not to mention thousands of pages of commentaries, it
becomes clear why he who undertakes such study is referred to as
plunging into "the sea of the Talmud." Small wonder, then,
that no more than a few dozen people in the world today are
thoroughly familiar with the entire Talmud.

It may be noted, parenthetically, that virtually all students
at times find the class discussion somewhat above their heads.
They welcome the opportunity later on in the day to review the
material with the stronger students. This is crucial, for if the student fails to grasp the material of the day, he will be unable to fol-

low the discussion in future classes and may have to wait several weeks before a new topic is considered.

The Content of the Talmud

The above-quoted discussion has, as its central focus, the Jewish legal system, a system marked by a strong relationship between law and ethics. Both civil and criminal law are covered in the Talmud and are based on the Torah. Although political, economic, and social considerations influenced the shape of the laws, such constructions could take place only if they were consistent with the Torah. Moreover, the laws and regulations were designed within a framework characterized by a concern for social justice and morality.

History, theology, medicine, jurisprudence, mathematics, marriage and divorce, biology, philosophy, geography—all these and more constitute the domain of the Talmud. Considering the long period of dispersion undergone by the Jews, such a work would have had to be invented to insure the survival of the community in exile. Fortunately, it was already in place in the form of its original source, the Torah itself. Besides guiding the Jew in his economic and social relationships with others, the Talmud heightened his sensitivity to moral and ethical issues, inasmuch as the community stressed the importance of Talmud study, holding its scholars and rabbis in esteem. In the eyes of the sages, ethical conduct was meaningful only if it was extended to all people in every situation. Thus, for example, the Talmud says the fine for a thief who stole a sheep should be less than that for a thief who stole a bull because, unlike a bull, the sheep might have to be carried at some point while being led to the market. Living in an environment where such values were stressed must surely have influenced the Jew's perceptions of his community and the larger society in which he operated.

Sometimes talmudic discussions center on the culture of a particular historical period, thus enlightening the student about the development of his people and how they functioned under different circumstances. The effect is to strengthen the student's identification with his culture and its history. As he becomes familiar with discussions on secular topics, the student of the Talmud comes to appreciate its broad range and level of sophistication. A long treatise on how the human body functions, an involved discussion on the workings of the solar system, the introduction of mathematical concepts into the text, all demonstrate that the Talmud's scope is far-reaching. One ought not, however, to assume that yeshivas are places where lengthy discussions on astronomy or medicine take place. These are usually mentioned only in passing. The primary focus is on the legal discussions of the type presented in the sample lecture above. Within such a context the discussion may involve areas such as personal and property damage, interest law, labor law, contractual law, trusts and wills, and real estate laws.

The Talmud can be understood at various levels. For the beginning student, it is enough of a challenge merely to understand the argument. At the advanced level, however, much more is required. To arrive at a clear understanding, it is generally necessary that one be knowledgeable in many areas of Jewish law. This is because the Talmud is not so much a systematic code of laws as a series of independent rulings on particular cases. In order to arrive at the general principles that apply in a new instance, it is often essential to marshal evidence from a large number of cases. The student of the Talmud often measures his progress by his ability to bring evidence to bear on a particular discussion from a variety of relevant sources presented in the text. As was apparent in the class discussion, a claimant must bring proof in refutation or support of his position. The ability to do so represents a sort of breakthrough for the student much as he achieved a breakthrough at an earlier point in time when he was able, for the first time, to read from the *Gemora* without having to ask someone to explain the meaning of the words. Such breakthroughs, often the result of strenuous efforts accompanied by much frustration, are among the chief sources of satisfaction for the yeshiva *bochur*.

Talmudic study in the yeshiva is, notwithstanding historical references to the times that appear within the talmudic text itself, basically ahistorical. Within the traditional yeshivas, lectures are rarely if ever given on life and culture during the talmudic period, and modern Jewish scholars have often criticized the yeshivas for this failing. The yeshivas' position is based, in large part, on their perception of the Talmud's origin. Basically, they reject the examination of the Talmud in light of the Greco-Roman culture in which it evolved since to credit outside factors with having influenced talmudic law would be to challenge the notion that it is based on divine law. Even those sympathetic to this position have noted that, in the absence of any discussion concerning history, the student often remains ignorant of basic facts such as when the earlier sages (known as *Tannaim*) lived and when the era of the later sages (*Amoraim*) began, and what pressures and influences affected the Jewish community in those days. Unfamiliar with even the order of conquest of Palestine ("Was it the Greeks first or the Romans?" more than one student asked me), there is a tendency to see the talmudic era in one-dimensional terms rather than as part of a complex and highly variegated Jewish community.

The Method of the Talmud

The Talmud employs a unique system of hermeneutical rules (hermeneutics is the science of biblical interpretation) in its efforts to understand and explicate the laws of the Bible. These rules number in the hundreds, but the most commonly used are the thirteen established by Rabbi Ishmael, a scholar who lived in the second century C.E. One example of such a rule is *kal vechomer,* which means an argument from a minor premise to a major premise. As a rather simple example of its application, we know that according to the Bible the Sabbath is the most important of all the holidays. It therefore can be inferred that if a certain task may not be performed on the festival of Succoth, it can most certainly not be performed on the Sabbath.

Another well-known rule is *gezera shava,* a procedure by which the meaning of a vague law or word is inferred from another passage containing the same word or words but presented clearly. Since many words can be interpreted in a variety of ways, it requires considerable expertise in the language and structure of the Bible to know just how to apply this rule. For instance, *gezera shava* can only be used if one is certain that the relevant words in the passages are there for that reason. To prevent misapplication of the rule, it is a basic requirement that one can advance a *gezera shava* only if he has acquired it from his teachers.

These and other rules are generally simple enough. The

challenge is in knowing how they are to be applied and in determining the interrelationships of the various principles.

The talmudic discussion cited earlier contains several examples of the Talmud's methodological approach. Cases from other parts of the *Gemora* are brought into play and used as models to see if they apply, in much the same way that a mathematician would employ a model. These models must be used in accordance with a variety of principles, several of which also appear in the discussion. It is believed that every word and letter in the Torah is there for a reason, and the sages therefore made efforts to account for them, though sometimes they were unsuccessful.

According to the tradition, "the Torah was received by Moses on Mount Sinai, who handed it down to Joshua and Joshua to the elders, and the elders to the prophets and the prophets handed it down to the Men of the Great Assembly."[7] Since the sages of the talmudic era are yet another link in this tradition, statements they make in the Talmud receive the same careful scrutiny. Broadly speaking, Orthodox Jews believe in a hierarchy of religious authority that is related to the giving of the Torah. The closer to that period one has lived, the greater the degree of holiness. Thus the words of a talmudic sage of, say, the third century, are taken more seriously than those of an eighteenth-century authority. The basis for this view is not so much rational as metaphysical.

The fact that each and every word in the Talmud has been carefully edited (by Rav Ashi and his students in the fourth and fifth centuries), and that exacting and precise logical methods are used in its study stands in marked contrast to the open and freewheeling discussion that is the norm in talmudic study. All arguments and queries must be satisfied before a conclusion is accepted. The Talmud is never content with "reasonable doubt." The answer must be absolutely correct to the best of the sages' ability.

One of the *rebbe*'s primary objectives in the classroom is to help the student both deepen and expand his levels of thinking. For this reason, a class will often focus on a small segment of the Talmud for weeks at a time. By treating the subject matter in such great depth, it is hoped that the student will become capable of independently applying the same method of analysis to other portions of the Talmud. Naturally, such capabilities take time to grow, and the student must therefore often consult with both older and more experienced students and faculty members as he studies. For this reason the entire yeshiva will usually focus on the same tractate (*masechta*) in a given year, so that the intricacies and implications of the issues are fresh in the minds of all.

At the same time, yeshivas must consider the need for the student to become familiar with the basic laws in a wide range of areas. Part of each day, usually the afternoon or evening session, is spent proceeding quickly through one or another portion of the Talmud. How much time to spend on an issue is often the subject of considerable controversy, as indicated in the following comments by Rabbi Mordechai Willig of Yeshiva University's RIETS division:

> I feel that a *shiur* should cover more in terms of both *Gemora* and classical *meforshim* [commentaries]. I think this can be done without sacrificing basic analysis but by avoiding undue *qveching* [pointless argumentation] and *ploidering* [discussing issues to the point of meaninglessness] which often reflects ignorance rather than profundity.[8]

There are different approaches to Talmud study, and the students are usually aware of the approaches favored by particular institutions. As a third-year student in the Telshe Yeshiva stated:

> In Telshe they tend to emphasize covering ground although they explain everything very carefully. In Philadelphia they stress how well you understand what you're talking about. They don't stress trying to finish as much as you could. In Chofetz Chaim [in Queens] they also emphasize understanding in great depth.[9]

The primary mode of study in the yeshiva is the *chavrusa,* or learning partner system. As the students examine the material they engage in an ongoing dialogue and debate. Each must defend his position while the other must challenge his partner's statements, even if they are only slightly inaccurate or incomplete. The relationship is analogous to the ''study group'' found in law schools. Under certain circumstances students will study by themselves—if they are especially interested in a certain area and cannot find a partner, but joint study is considered the best way to insure preciseness and clarity of thought even at the highest levels when the student is no longer in a class as such.

The introduction I received to my own *chavrusa* when I joined the yeshiva that I observed underscores the adjustment process that is sometimes required. Before meeting him, the *rebbe,* who was responsible for bringing individuals together in this manner, cautioned me:

> Aharon has a great deal of knowledge and depth of under-standing—but don't let him throw you and overwhelm you. Make him slow down a bit and force him to explain to you what he's talking about when, for example, he starts bom-barding you with references from other *masechtas.* It will be good for you and good for him.

Obviously, a delicate balance must be struck between people who study together. This does not mean, however, that the two persons must be equivalent in ability or knowledge. For some students equal ability makes for a productive relationship, but others may find it necessary to study with someone either more or less capable than themselves. One *bochur* may need to feel that he is "teaching" the other. Another may not be quite ready to handle the give-and-take of most *chavrusa* relationships.

A good *chavrusa* is crucial for success in the yeshiva. Without one, the student will most likely be ill prepared for the class. Allan Rudolf spent eight years studying in various yeshivas while also fulfilling the requirements for a Ph.D. in Economics at Col-umbia University. Asked to evaluate the importance of the *chavrusa* in the yeshiva, he replied:

> AR: It played a central role. You really needed it. To get the most out of a *shiur* you had to prepare and review, because often, even the *rebbe* himself was very vague. It was very complicated stuff. If you tried to prepare by yourself you'd be fooling yourself because you'd be limited by your own abilities. On the other hand, another's viewpoint is always a little different and this way it would be much richer, almost like a third viewpoint, a combined result. As far as choosing the *chavrusa* goes, it's like choosing a wife. There are so many things involved.
>
> WH: Did you find Talmud different from other disciplines?
>
> AR: Well, the way economics is taught in college, it's just facts.
>
> WH: Did you like the idea that *Gemora* was not "just facts"?

AR: Yes, I really enjoyed the idea that you could just keep analyzing and analyzing. In college you never had that sense.[10]

Sometimes friends will work well together, but more often than not friendships will create problems for there may be a temptation to relax and joke around with the *chavrusa*. Rabbi Yehuda Jacobs, director of admissions at Lakewood, provided further insight into this and related problems when he noted:

> Often if you're too friendly with a guy, it might just be a good reason not to learn with him. At the same time you have to be able to maintain a minimum degree of friendliness with the other guy. I would characterize it as a friendly business relationship. The question of equals is also very complex and you can't generalize. Sometimes a top guy feels he doesn't want to hassle with equals. He would much rather study with someone not as good as him but who will permit him to take a leading role in the *chavrusa*.[11]

At Lakewood Rabbi Jacobs is, in part, responsible for matching students with each other through a process involving instinct more than specific criteria:

> I don't sit down and figure out the criteria—that A has these characteristics and B has those. I see the person and I get a feel for him. I have a hunch the combination will go. You're sometimes right and sometimes not.[12]

The average student spends at least ten hours a day with one or another learning partner. Besides the *chavrusa* from his class, he is likely to have a different learning partner in the afternoon or evening. He may study with a less advanced student from another class who is having difficulty following the lectures, or he may learn together with someone whose level of understanding is higher than his own because he believes it will aid him in his own development. The right *chavrusa* will often make the difference between a good or bad year for a *bochur*. The *rebbe* may have to change *chavrusas* for his students eight or nine times a year within a class of 20 students before he finds the right combinations.

We have already detailed the second major form of study, that of the classroom teacher, or *rebbe*. At the basic levels the class is presented in a manner allowing for a great deal of give-and-take, with the *rebbe* encouraging the boys to think both on their own and on their feet. At the highest level, the *rosh yeshiva*'s class, the presentation is more in the form of a discourse. By this time the student has generally mastered many of the finer points of the talmudic method and is capable of working entirely on his own. In this situation, the *rosh yeshiva*'s functions include giving lectures that are models of erudition and originality and presenting insights that may have escaped even the advanced student's attention. Knowledge of the text and most commentaries is assumed at this level. Indeed, those who are unfamiliar with the text will be unable to follow the discussion after only a few moments, though, since no questions are asked of those attending, it is quite possible that no one will notice their ignorance.

A third form of study is the *chabura*. This is a cluster or group of students (usually six to twelve individuals) at the advanced level who form seminars and meet weekly. At these seminars students present an oral discussion based on a portion of the Talmud. Members of the *chabura* critically evaluate the thesis, challenging the presenter to defend his ideas. Sometimes the group is headed by a *rebbe* of the yeshiva and sometimes by one of the more senior students. Generally, this form of study takes place at the higher levels of the yeshiva.

Finally, there is the "tutor," usually a graduate student assigned by the yeshiva to help a student who is having serious problems keeping up with his classmates. Sometimes parents of a student who is faltering will privately engage a graduate student to help their son with the material, paying him a fee for the service. Although it varies from yeshiva to yeshiva, the tutor is generally not part of the official hierarchy and his role differs from one institution to another.

The Purpose of Talmud Study

In the larger sense, Talmud study is seen as an end in itself, the fulfillment of God's divine will. Still, the yeshiva regards such study as having a number of practical objectives and outcomes. In the first place, the yeshiva attempts to produce a graduate knowledgeable in the laws of the Torah to the point where he can be of help to others in the Orthodox community and assist in the religious development of his children. By studying the Talmud intensively, the individual acquires an understanding of the Torah that goes far beyond simply knowing what a specific law is. He assimilates into his lifestyle both the ideas and the ideals of the Bible. He knows how the law was developed, what ethical and moral considerations may have been responsible for its formulation, and how it is related to what is essentially an interconnected system of laws, customs, and moral imperatives. This is crucial for the well-being of the entire community in the eyes of the yeshiva, for without people who are thoroughly conversant with the tradition, both the spirit and the letter of the law are likely to be adulterated and, in the final analysis, abrogated.

A more general but equally important goal is the development of character. This is gained both through familiarity with those portions of the Talmud containing specific maxims and appeals and through general knowledge of the Talmud, since so many arguments that focus on strictly legal questions are intertwined with ethical issues as well. In addition, scattered throughout the Talmud are biographical anecdotes illustrating how the various sages conducted themselves in their personal affairs. The following statements taken from the tractate *Avot* typify the Talmud's concerns in these areas:

> Who is rich? He that is satisfied with what he has.
>
> *Avot* 4:1

> Who is wise? He that learns from all men, as it is written (Psalms 119:99): "From all my teachers have I gained knowledge."
>
> *Avot* 4:1

> There are four types of character: Easy to provoke and easy to appease—his loss is cancelled by his gain; hard to provoke and hard to appease—his gain is cancelled by his loss; hard to provoke and easy to appease—he is a saintly man; easy to provoke and hard to appease—he is a wicked man.
>
> *Avot* 5:15

> He who learns from his friends a single chapter, a single law, a single verse, a single expression, or even a single letter, must pay him honor.
>
> *Avot* 6:3

> Let the property of your fellow man be as dear to you as your own.
>
> *Avot* 2:17

He whose deeds exceed his wisdom, his wisdom endures;
but he whose wisdom exceeds his deeds, his wisdom does not
endure.

Avot 3:12

As a result of becoming familiar with these and hundreds of
similar aphorisms, the student of the Talmud becomes acutely
aware that talmudic wisdom without an exemplary life is a con-
tradiction in terms, if not fact.

A perhaps unintended but striking outcome of talmudic
study emerges in the patterns of interaction. Among those in the
yeshiva world there is a certain kind of banter, perhaps one could
call it verbal roughhousing, that often takes place and is usually
done in a kidding manner. I found myself both taking part in and
occasionally benefiting from my familiarity with it. For example,
I had wanted to obtain some information from the *mashgiach* of a
certain yeshiva and found myself getting nowhere with him. He
would either delay, neglect to return my calls, or simply be
evasive. Yet he was always cordial, and I eventually got the impression that he was enjoying himself at my expense. Finally,
after a phone conversation that had proven particularly frustrating, I said to him: "Okay, we seem to be reaching a dead end.
Can you think of any reason why I should call you?" "Yes," he
said. "I think you should bother me some more and we'll be able
to work something out." "I don't want to bother you," I
replied. "But I want you to, and if you're a gentleman you'll
respect my wishes," he responded. "All right," I said. "So
when will you call?" he asked. "I'm not saying," I answered,
"because if I did I wouldn't be bothering you." "Now *that's* a
good answer!" he exclaimed, laughing heartily. "So why don't
you come see me in two weeks." I did so, and found him most
cooperative. Such combativeness may well be a reflection of the
pilpul, or intellectual jousting, that marks talmudic study but,
whatever its origin, it is an important aspect of the culture. In
this instance I suspect that the *mashgiach* wanted to see if he could
compel me to abandon my role of professor and meet him on his
own terms before he would agree to help me.

A more narrowly defined but explicitly articulated goal of
Talmud study in the yeshiva is the development of a love for such
study to the point where the yeshiva graduate continues to learn
for the rest of his life. This attitude is inculcated in a variety of
ways through teachers, peers, and others in the community, but

it is also as a result of intensive study under proper guidance. Basic to achieving this objective is teaching the student how to work independently.

In addition to these reasons for Talmud study, there is the almost mystical notion that in studying Talmud one is somehow enhancing the survival of the Jewish community as a whole. The nineteenth-century leader Rabbi Israel Salanter said, in effect, that when a Jew in the town of Vilna, Lithuania, diverts his attention from study of the Talmud, a Jew in Paris converts. This conception of the benefit of talmudic learning is important because it demonstrates quite clearly that there is a religious component to both the actual study and its motivational forces that cannot be easily separated from the intellectual and practical goals. Such a belief gives a sense of immediacy and urgency to what might otherwise be regarded as a merely intellectual endeavor, and it is an important factor in explaining the hold the yeshiva world has on many of its adherents.

The Teaching of Ethics (Mussar)

Ethics is treated as a separate area of study by most Lithuanian yeshivas today.[13] The yeshiva student is exposed to *mussar* not only in his talmudic study but also through the perusal, usually for at least a half hour a day, of various ethical works, written mostly by medieval and postmedieval Jewish scholars. This is usually done together with one or more students who discuss the precepts and philosophical approaches advanced in these writings. As part of an effort to reach a more profound understanding of the faith, advanced students may also study major philosophical works of Maimonides, Saadia Gaon, and other important thinkers on their own. The writings of these and others attempt to deal with the basic issues of life after death, reward and punishment, free will, redemption, revelation, and many other similar matters.

These works are rarely an established part of the curriculum because of the general view by those heading the yeshivas that the study of philosophical works ought not to be undertaken until the student has thoroughly immersed himself, over a long period of time, in talmudic study. To do otherwise, it is argued, exposes the young man to ideas about Judaism that he cannot properly absorb and that may then lead him to question the faith. What is not often acknowledged by those in the yeshiva is that shying away from such study often leads to a *lifelong* avoidance of such works, even when the individual has reached what the yeshiva considers "intellectual and spiritual maturity." This is unfortunate since Jewish philosophy, as represented by the works of Maimonides, Saadia Gaon, and others, is an important part of the Jewish tradition. Those in authority in the yeshiva are well aware that their graduates will not be knowledgeable in this area. They have, however, made a calculated decision that neglect of this topic, while not an ideal solution, will help insure the preservation of their way of life and approach to the Jewish religion.

A central feature of the *mussar* program in the yeshiva is the *mussar shmuess* delivered weekly, usually by the *mashgiach*. Focusing, as a rule, upon specific observances and values—for example, the importance of observing the Sabbath, obeying one's parents, and so on— the *mashgiach* will draw upon biblical and talmudic sources to buttress his position in urging the student to be evermore sensitive to those around him. Frequently he will use contemporary examples to illustrate his points, as the following description of such a *shmuess* by a young yeshiva student demonstrates:

> Of short stature, he [the *mashgiach*] would sit in his chair in the classroom looking out at us, his favorites clustered in a semicircle around him, with the rest of us seated behind in chairs or on the window sills, and the late-comers standing in the back. As the twilight gave way to darkness in the small room, Reb Eliezer's tiny figure became a silhouette outlined against the wall, recognizable only by the gray beard that bobbed up and down as he gesticulated to emphasize his arguments. He knew just when to pause and when to speak, when to raise his voice and when to lower it. We all listened intently, for in his words lay not only wisdom, not only the key to understanding the philosophy of the Yeshiva, but also irony, wit and empathy with the hard road we had chosen. . . .
>
> Reb Eliezer managed to weave into his discourses such topics as sports, college and world politics. For us, encased in our cocoon, such discussions were fascinating, and we hung on every word, eagerly absorbing whatever was said. . . . How this man was able to find time to learn about baseball I will never know, yet he managed. He once talked for an hour about the game.[14]

Often, the student perceives the *mussar* talk almost as a respite from his talmudic studies which, by comparison, are far more strenuous mentally, requiring intense concentration. The *shmuess,* in which stories are interwoven with the presentation of guidelines for daily living, is a welcome change of pace that serves to relax the student. In the questionnaire, more than a third of the alumni who responded cited the talks given by the yeshiva's *mashgiach* when asked the open-ended question: "What aspects of your yeshiva experience did you find most satisfying and/or of the most lasting effect?" Considering the large range of possible responses, this is a strong indication of the importance of this experience in the life of the yeshiva student, an impression strengthened by the interviews with graduates from various yeshivas.

While the major ethics talks are given by either the *mashgiach* or the *rosh yeshiva,* the classroom teacher will frequently supplement them with discourses of his own. Since the class is intended primarily for Talmud study, these are generally of short duration. Sometimes the members of the class, particularly if they are learning about a difficult topic, will attempt to shift the discussion away from the textual analysis into spiritual and moral areas. The *rebbe* may become annoyed at such efforts or he may go along, depending on his own mood and predilections. The content of such discussions varies from admonitions against acquiring secular values to efforts at improving the level of learning in the class. Typical of the latter were the following comments made by my *rebbe* one day in the yeshiva where I carried out the participant observation phase of this project:

> The key thing in succeeding in the yeshiva is involvement. This means that you don't stop thinking about the *Gemora* when the class ends but let it always remain in the back of your mind ready to be called forth at any time. The key to success is not in being a genius. The *yeshiva velt* [world] is full of geniuses who never made it. A genius may be able to cheat in the sense that his intelligence will enable him to get by without fully concentrating but sooner or later it'll catch up with him. If not in this class, then in a higher class.
>
> The chief problem is laziness and you overcome it through involvement in learning, studying *mussar,* or through fear of punishment. I wouldn't like to use the last method but whatever works is the best way. And if you're

bored with learning, it means you're improperly motivated.
The only time the Chofetz Chaim got bored and fell asleep
was when he heard *loshon hora* [negative gossip].

In this manner, the yeshiva inculcates its members with its
philosophy and way of looking at things. Moreover, talking
about geniuses "who never made it" provides succor to those
who must work hard at comprehending the *Gemora* while warning
the better endowed that sharp wits are no substitute for hard
work. In this and virtually every other area of yeshiva life the
rebbe tries to be a model for the students, leading by example, not
simply by exhortation.

While the individual who is known for such qualities as
humility, sensitivity to others, generosity, and so on is respected,
real success is measured and status attained primarily through
virtuosity in the application of talmudic knowledge. Mental acu-
ity is highly prized; those who have it receive admiration and
even accolades from both peers and teachers. This may be con-
trasted with the values encouraged in the more monastic and less
intellectually oriented environment of the convent. In *The Nun's
Story,* by Katherine Hulme, the main protagonist, Sister Luke, is
given a number to replace her name as she enters the convent.[15]
This is part of the expressed goal of the convent to remove all
vestiges of pride, selfishness, competitiveness, and worldly
desires. The yeshiva, while viewing these qualities as important,
does not stress them as much. As a further case in point, Sister
Luke is encouraged to fail an examination on one occasion so as
not to make another nun feel badly. In the yeshiva, competitiveness is actually encouraged with the implicit hope that the good
students will serve as models for the others. Mention is often
made by those in the community of the talmudic maxim: "The
competitiveness of scribes breeds wisdom."

The overemphasis in this area is understandable in a community where so much time is devoted to thinking, arguing,
reasoning, and analyzing but it is nonetheless inconsistent with
the ideals of the faith, and those in the yeshiva are aware of the
problem. Evidence of this concern is apparent from the very fact
that *mussar* talks dwell so much on the need to develop one's
character. Translating such awareness into concrete action is,
however, difficult for several reasons.

First, the yeshiva, despite its efforts to remove itself from negative outside influences, cannot succeed entirely in doing so. Its students are frequently exposed to outsiders while on vacation, through whatever limited contact with the media they may have, and from a variety of other sources. Second, people are generally predisposed to respect that which is difficult to achieve, and in the yeshiva community talmudic erudition represents the greatest challenge. *Mussar* is not considered unimportant—it is simply not the sort of thing one focuses on all day in terms of study. The prevailing attitude is somewhat analogous to those in the physical sciences who look askance at the social sciences, characterizing them as ''soft'' in the negative sense of the word. Every yeshiva has students who spend what is considered a disproportionate amount of energy and time on *mussar*. Although they are not likely to be criticized openly, they are likely to be admired only if their knowledge in this area is matched by their ability to learn in general.

Yet another issue revolves around the difficulty of making clear to some students the need for the study of ethics. They often tend to regard it as something that does not require repeated study once its essentials have been grasped. In any case, some students have argued, many of the prayers recited daily in the yeshiva consist of statements regarding personal conduct and deportment. In interviews with a number of students, it became clear that many found the ascetic philosophies expressed in some of the readings difficult to relate to. Typical was the following response from a student in a New York City yeshiva:

> I think you need much more than just reading books. I was learning *Mesillas Yesharim* [*The Path of the Just,* by Moshe Chaim Luzzatto] with my *chavrusa* and after about a month or so we got sick of it. It was *lehavdil* [not to compare it with pornographic movies], too ''hardcore,'' you know, real fire-and-brimstone kind of stuff and it depressed me too much. It was written hundreds of years ago and it's hard to relate to.

The problem, upon further probing, ran deeper than simply the issue of relevance. There was skepticism about the utility of *mussar* in general, prompting this same student to observe:

> I believe *mussar* only helps people who want it to help. If a person learns *mussar* with the intention that he's going to change, then he will. But if he's learning it just for *limud* [the sake of study] then it won't affect him.

This statement does not so much challenge the efficacy of studying ethics as it points up the need for a proper approach to the subject.

Some yeshivas stress *mussar* more than others, and students may even change schools because of such an emphasis. One young man who transferred into the Telshe Yeshiva from another school remarked: "I don't like learning *mussar* and I don't feel it's something you can sit down and learn. It's extremely boring after a while. I'd much rather learn *Gemora*."

Another problem stems from the differing attitudes of those within a given institution. In a variety of ways, some subtle, some not, the faculty and administration can convey their sense of what a student's priorities ought to be. This may range from determining how much time is to be allotted in the schedule for a certain activity to words of praise directed at individuals who, it is felt, exemplify the school's ideals. Allowing only thirty minutes for the study of ethics speaks for itself, although some yeshivas such as Chofetz Chaim in Queens encourage their students to spend far more time on the subject. In one of the more prominent yeshivas, several students asserted that *mussar* was not taken seriously by the staff, which tended to look the other way at the lack of interest in the topic by most of the students:

> MORDECHAI: There's a *mussar seder* [program] but it's a big joke. I mean at 9:45 P.M. someone will bang on the table in the *beis medrash* and yell *"mussar seder!"* and everyone will laugh at the guy who said it. There's only a token few who learn it.
>
> MICHOEL: Yeah, most people just stop learning at 9:45 and bull around for fifteen minutes.
>
> WH: Why is this the case?
>
> SIMCHA: Learning or a talk doesn't seem to make an impression. I remember someone telling me a story about a guy in a New York yeshiva who said sarcastically: "We will now have fifteen minutes of silence in honor of Rabbi Yisroel Salanter [the founder of the *mussar* movement]." I think that people today just don't go for that anymore.

Do the students ultimately acquire a sense of morality and sensitivity that is substantially different from that of the population at large? This is an exceedingly difficult question to answer on the basis of available data. We can only make some preliminary observations based upon some firsthand observations of the community. While studying in the yeshiva, I noticed that the students exhibited a great deal of concern for one another's welfare. If, for example, a student had a cold, others would urge him to take care of himself, to rest more, and so on. On one occasion, a young man tore his pants as he brushed by the edge of a wooden table while walking through the *beis medrash*. Upon seeing this a *bochur* jumped up from his seat and, walking over to the student, said, "Don't worry, I have a needle and thread." In general, the students treated each other with respect and consideration. In making the arrangements for my stay at Beth Medrash Govoha in Lakewood I learned that, as a matter of course, whenever a person with an apartment leaves Lakewood for a weekend or longer he makes his apartment available to any guest of another member of the community. While staying at such an apartment, I found it necessary to use the phone. As I lifted the receiver off the hook I noticed a sticker pasted onto it that read in Hebrew, Yiddish, and English: "This telephone is for *mitzvas* [good deeds] only. Beware of *loshon hora* [negative gossip]!" Taken individually, such instances may not mean much, but observation confirmed that they were part of a pattern of behavior in a subculture governed by a strict code regulating human relations in many areas of life. It is difficult to pinpoint how such interaction is connected with ethical principles learned in the yeshiva. Nevertheless, there is no doubt that the laws of the Torah form the basis for such action and are frequently cited by members of the community to support their behavior. And if this is so, then the yeshiva may be doing an effective job in inculcating such values. Rabbi Elya Svei, head of the yeshiva in Philadelphia, pointed out that it is not easy for the student himself to notice the effect *mussar* has upon him:

> Everybody likes to see results right away. But *mussar* isn't like that. You don't get up and suddenly become a better person. But over a long period of time you definitely see results. Even a small change in a person's character and feelings takes a long time. And because it's such a slow process, the individual often doesn't see it happening to him.[16]

All this is, however, as one knowledgeable observer called it, merely the "etiquette of *mussar*." Given the emphasis on morality within the yeshiva, it is fair to ask whether it extends to areas beyond social interaction into matters such as business ethics and sexual morality. Here the record is far from clear. Over the years numerous articles have appeared in the media detailing various crimes by persons identified as Orthodox Jews. No one has established empirically what proportion of offenders come from the Orthodox community as opposed to other sectors of society. Furthermore, no breakdown is available of what percentage of those individuals labeled as Orthodox Jews are Modern Orthodox, Hasidic, or, as it has been defined in this study, Strictly Orthodox. Nevertheless, putting aside the matter of numbers, yeshiva graduates have been among those accused of criminal behavior, both in the nursing home scandals of the mid-seventies and in misuse of government funds. That such behavior occurs to *any* extent raises serious questions about how morality and ethics is taught in the yeshiva. Furthermore, while there are no studies on whether more Orthodox Jews cheat on their income tax returns than Reform or Conservative Jews or than any other segment of the population, no responsible member of the Orthodox community has ever claimed that no such cheating exists among Orthodox Jews (or those who studied in yeshivas). If such behavior is as much a fact of life among the Orthodox as it is among others, then one must wonder if the yeshiva system has failed in its efforts to inculcate ethical behavior among its members.

If the facts are difficult to ascertain with respect to fiscal probity, they are even harder to determine with regard to sexual morality, since such conduct is not necessarily a matter of breaking the law. True, one rarely reads of Orthodox Jews accused of rape, sodomy, and pornography violations, and the community can be very favorably compared to other communities in these areas. But what of adultery or promiscuity? Allowing for the relative nature of such judgments, most psychologists and therapists with whom I spoke asserted that marital infidelity, while by no means unheard of in the Orthodox community, was far less common than among their non-Orthodox or non-Jewish clients and that, in general, respect for traditional family values—that is, lack of adolescent promiscuity—was very high. Thus it would seem, based on impressionistic but nevertheless informed observations, that this is one area where moral precepts are generally adhered to. This entire subject, however, needs to be researched far more thoroughly.

Prayer and Meditation

No discussion of the faith would be complete without touching at least briefly upon the role of prayer and meditation in the yeshiva. In the Orthodox community at large, prayer three times a day is a basic tenet adhered to by all Jews who consider themselves observant. It would be safe to say that far more Orthodox Jews pray every day than study Torah every day. No matter how busy he may be, an Orthodox Jew will put on his phylacteries and recite the morning prayers. The press of business and other activities may, however, result in his spending little or no time engaged in study. In the yeshiva, students pray every day but the central activity in their lives is, as we have seen, studying the Law. Still, prayer itself is taken very seriously. Attending the services is considered very important. Although one can, according to Jewish law, fulfill the *mitzva* of prayer alone, certain prayers can only be recited with a quorum of at least ten males. At the high school level, the importance attached to this activity is brought home in some yeshivas by the imposition of monetary fines (which are then donated to charity) upon students who repeatedly miss group prayer or come late.

Prayer has a latent function in the yeshiva. It acts as a unifying force within the community for it is an activity in which all are judged equal.[17] Although the *rebbes* generally occupy seats in the front of the *beis medrash,* no one would take this as a sign that their prayers are more important than those of a beginning student. True, certain honors (i.e., taking the Torah out from the ark) relating to various aspects of the service are often given out with an eye toward the recipient's status,[18] but this too is secondary to the belief that everyone has the same ability to communicate with his Maker.

The emotional release of prayer is considered a very important part of the yeshiva experience. Open displays of feeling marked by hand motions, raised voices, and swaying are considered perfectly normal. As is the case among Jews everywhere, prayer assumes even greater significance during the High Holy Day period, the time during which Jews are urged to repent for their sins, as indicated by the following excerpt from an account of life in a yeshiva:

> The excitement in the Yeshiva was at fever pitch as everyone made his way to the synagogue to hear the Kol Nidre (All

Vows) prayer that marked the beginning of a twenty-four hour period of fasting and prayer.... All around me were males dressed in white, their heads covered with white skull-caps.... The gates of heaven had opened and we were now about to make one last, supreme effort to scale the heights and plead our cause.... I tried to absorb the meaning of every sentence.... My heart was beating very quickly.... For two and a half hours we prayed like this, singing, chanting, whispering and thinking. No one said a word to his neighbor. Each must find his own path. Yet there was a powerful, virtually unbreakable bond between us, for did we not worship the same Creator, follow the same laws, share a common dream, and strive for a common yet most uncommon understanding?[19]

Not surprisingly, quite a few respondents to the questionnaire sent to yeshiva alumni volunteered that the holidays and prayers in the yeshiva had been among the most meaningful experiences for them while they were there.[20]

The yeshiva student lives and functions in a community that makes tremendous intellectual and spiritual demands on both his time and energy. Given the opportunities for material well-being that exist in the larger society, the degree of commitment and self-sacrifice of those who make such a decision is remarkable. The types of people who enter the yeshiva and their motives for doing so is the topic to which we now turn.

CHAPTER 5

Yeshiva Students: Who Are They and Why Do They Go?

WHY IS A YOUNG MAN of eighteen willing to spend anywhere from two to ten years in a yeshiva studying the ancient tomes of the Talmud when he could be enrolled in a secular college, dating young women, traveling, playing sports, and doing everything else that goes with the lifestyle of today's youth? What attraction does a community which demands self-discipline and removal from most worldly pleasures hold for him? What type of young man is likely to enter this world?

As far as can be ascertained, most yeshiva students come from Orthodox backgrounds. Any of a number of persons with whom the young man has contact can be responsible for his decision but some, such as parents, play a greater role than others. To better understand this issue, we need to both listen to the students as they talk and examine the available data.

The Typical Student

On the basis of more than 70 in-depth interviews and questionnaire responses from 464 yeshiva alumni a general profile emerged of the typical student. He is most often of an Orthodox family background and has attended both elementary and high school yeshivas. American-born, he is likely to have parents who emigrated from Europe after World War II and who are lower middle class and, in terms of occupation and income, nonprofessional. More than half the students have fathers who attended a yeshiva.

David Greenbaum* is a tall, well-built young man of nineteen with a pale complexion which, like the thick glasses he must wear for reading, can probably be attributed to the long hours he spends hunched over the Talmud. He is my learning partner (*chavrusa*) in the yeshiva I have chosen to attend as part of this project. David's parents emigrated from Germany in 1938 and settled on Manhattan's Upper West Side. His father, a university professor, gave David what he describes as a "generally Orthodox" upbringing but did not insist that he attend a yeshiva beyond eighth grade. That decision came when David attended a yeshiva-sponsored summer camp at the suggestion of a friend from his local synagogue. Ordinarily, the yeshiva would not have permitted David, with his limited background, to spend the summer at the camp, but David's friend was one of the best students in the school and was therefore able to persuade the yeshiva to make an exception.

After an enjoyable two months at the camp, during which David "discovered the beautiful world of *Torah*," he joined the yeshiva as a full-time student, dropping out of the secular university where he was a third-year mathematics major. He now attends a branch of the City University two evenings a week in addition to yeshiva. Clearly, a number of factors played a role in David's decision—his traditional upbringing, some yeshiva background, a chance encounter with a friend, and an initially positive experience with a yeshiva community.

Like David, most students attending advanced *yeshivas* come from observant homes. In the Beth David Yeshiva study, more than three-quarters of the students grew up in homes where the laws concerning the Sabbath and *Kashrus* were strictly observed. A clear majority had fathers who had also attended yeshiva at one level or another. Moreover, 80 percent of the students had gone to both elementary and high school yeshivas prior to entering the *beis medrash*.

Articles have been appearing in recent years with increasing frequency about young men who have enrolled in special "yeshivas" (called "*baal teshuva*" yeshivas) who have little or no

* All pseudonymns are identified by an asterisk next to the name.

backgrounds, but these are actually special schools for beginners bearing little resemblance to the institutions we are talking about here.[1] Until about ten years ago quite a few students with little or no knowledge of Judaism were enrolled in special classes in the traditional yeshivas, where they were given the basis for eventually becoming part of the yeshiva proper. Some were able to make the difficult transition but many could not. In response to this need, and because of a general rise of interest in Orthodoxy, schools especially designed to meet the needs of such individuals were started. As a result, it is unusual to find someone without a strong grounding in the tradition in a regular yeshiva. As a rule, the advanced yeshivas discourage applicants who have not had a solid background in Talmud. They do, however, accept students from the special *yeshivas,* provided that they can function at the scholarly level of the *beis medrash.*

Chaim Rabin* is a bespectacled youth of nineteen whose face appears to be fixed in a perpetual scowl. This is deceptive, for he is quite friendly and easy to talk with. His father is a diamond dealer who always wanted his son to go to Lakewood. (Among those in the yeshiva community acceptance at the Lakewood Yeshiva is a source of enormous pride for the parents, equivalent to the "my son the doctor" of American secular-Jewish folklore.) Chaim talked freely about his family and their influence upon him:

> I was the youngest and my three older brothers had all gone to yeshiva so why should I be any different? My father came here after World War II and I grew up in Williamsburg. I went to Torah Vodaas Yeshiva and had a very sheltered life. My parents were very demanding and wanted me to get top grades in school, which I did. But my father's main goal was to have his sons go to Lakewood and he stayed up every night with us when we were small, going over the *Gemora* with us to make sure we understood it. He had gone to yeshiva in Europe and really knew how to learn. All four of us have gone or are going to Lakewood.

Moshe Ben-Yoseif,* also a student at Lakewood, represents a somewhat different case. He was born and reared in Morocco and graduated from a yeshiva high school in Casablanca. Before coming to Lakewood at age twenty-nine, he attended an advanced yeshiva in England for eleven years. He says he came to America because "I couldn't find a girl to marry. You see I'm

Sephardic and I was looking for someone with a similar background and in this country they have a big Sephardic community." Actually, quite a few young men from foreign countries attend American yeshivas. In 1973 there were 63 students from foreign countries (not counting Israel) at Lakewood, including nine from Germany, four from Morocco, and seven from South Africa. Today there are 130 foreign students.

Avrohom Gross * is part of the growing number of Hasidic youths who have decided to study in a Lithuanian yeshiva. Most attend Lakewood, where they constitute a community within the yeshiva. They retain their traditional way of dress and are therefore highly visible. I met Avrohom over a glass of tea in the Lakewood Yeshiva dining hall:

> I came here because I was very good in *Gemora* and my father felt I should have the best chance possible to become a *talmid chochom* [scholar]. He's a Satmarer and is a big shot in the community but our yeshivas [in the Satmarer community] are not as good as Beis Medrash Govoha.

Avrohom's father puts in long hours at the grocery store he owns in Williamsburg to pay for the education of his seven children but, as his son puts it, "It's the most important thing for him." Figures supplied by the yeshiva indicate that most of the students do not come from well-off families. More than two-thirds of the parents queried in 1973 reported incomes of less than $15,000 a year.

The yeshiva at Lakewood is somewhat atypical in that most of its entering students are twenty-one or older and previously have studied intensively at another yeshiva. According to Rabbi Jacob Bursztyn, the school's registrar, less than 10 percent of the students arrive at the yeshiva with a college background. The other yeshivas generally admit their students upon completion of high school and, in the majority of cases, the young men will attend college classes during or after their stay at the yeshiva.

Many of those attending yeshivas come from homes that would be considered Modern Orthodox. Often, as they make their way through the system, the students find themselves at odds with their parents, who are seen as lax in their observance of the various religious laws and customs. Mayer Kroner * is a case in point. A student at the Mirrer Yeshiva, he shifts uncomfortably in his seat as I ask about his family. Adjusting his black hat so that the upturned brim fully covers his hair and tugging at his dark blue jacket, he says, somewhat self-consciously:

> You know, you'd never believe it from looking at me but my family is a real "Young Israel" type family; you know, mixed dancing, knitted yarmulke, women not covering their hair. I'm sort of the black sheep of the family. They think I'm a real *chunyock* [religious fanatic], and will tease me by doing things like trying to get me to shake hands with a girl at a bar mitzva party or something when they know that as a *frum* [religious] person, I wouldn't do it. Obviously I don't get along with them. They sent me to a coed elementary school yeshiva. I then went to Yeshiva University High School and while I was there I became interested in *Gemora* much more than my English studies and that's why I'm at the Mirrer Yeshiva now.

Sometimes the reverse happens, with a student from a very religious family enrolling in a more liberal yeshiva. Gershon Schechter* went to Mesivta Chaim Berlin for high school but then decided to attend Yeshiva College, where he is a student in RIETS, the rabbinical division:

> I was not especially good in *Gemora* though I wasn't terrible either. I guess I just wasn't that interested. What really intrigued me was science, especially biology, and it was made clear to me [by my parents] that if I wanted to go to college I could only do so at night [while learning in a yeshiva during the day].

According to Rabbi Mordechai Willig, who teaches the first-year class at RIETS, most of the yeshiva students who come from the right-wing schools enroll at Yeshiva because of a strong interest in secular studies, especially medicine and law.[2]

Reasons for Attending

Looking at the relatively ascetic life led by the yeshiva *bochur,* it is easy to think of him as a person who came to the yeshiva because he "saw the light" and seeks spiritual fulfillment. No doubt, there are at least a few who enter the yeshiva for precisely this reason and many individuals who do find such satisfaction within its walls. This phenomenon is, however, far more common among yeshiva students with no prior involvement with Orthodoxy, such as those in the *baal teshuva* yeshivas, whose students are of college age or older and who are making an independent decision to attend and perceive the institution as meeting precisely such needs.[3] In the traditional yeshivas, the young man's entry is more commonly the culmination of a long process of socialization, beginning in his family or the lower schools he has attended.

A spiritual awakening of sorts, where it occurs, usually takes place in the high school years. Often, it is the *rebbe* who serves as the catalyst for such an experience. Shaul Elman* is thirty-two years old, married with two children, and a student in the Lakewood *kollel.* "I have to give complete credit to my *rebbes* there [in the high school]," he said, speaking at the rapid-fire pace common to many who study the *Talmud* all day and night:

> My parents were very Orthodox but when it came to me and my brother going out of town they felt "Why should they go? There's a yeshiva high school right here and they're learning very well." But the *rebbaim* there knew that the quality of learning there [in my home town] and the *seviva* [environment] was not as good as at some yeshivas back east so they pushed my father to let me go. They weren't selfish, you see, about building up their own place. Rather, they sent those with real potential elsewhere if possible. So they sat next to my father when I gave my bar-mitzva speech and whispered into his ear: "Look at your son. If you don't send him to yeshiva, you'll bury him." And it worked because he sent me to Torah Vodaas in New York. They did the same thing with my brother, only they practically kidnapped him. They came to my father's house at 11:00 P.M. and said: "Why don't you send your son to yeshiva in New York?" "It costs too much money," he said. "We have a train ticket for him at midnight." And he couldn't say anything and he let him go. The *rebbaim* knew he had gone to yeshivas in Lithuania and that he would feel guilty about not sending him.

Shaul informed me that hardly any of those who graduated from his class in high school, a less traditional institution that concentrated more on Jewish history, Hebrew language, and Bible as opposed to Talmud, went to a *yeshiva gedola.* In general, those high schools that stress Talmud provide the bulk of students for the advanced yeshivas.

Relatives are often cited by students as a factor in their decision to attend yeshiva. What generally happens is an older brother is sent to a particular yeshiva, has a positive experience there, and sets the pattern for whatever male siblings follow him. Frequently, several members of a family attend the same yeshiva.

Friends sometimes influence the decision to go to a yeshiva, but more often they play a role in choosing one particular school over others. As one informant put it: "I had a choice of Mirrer or Chaim Berlin and most of my friends were going to Mirrer, so that's where I went." There are cases of boys who pressure parents to send them to a *yeshiva gedola* because it is the "in" thing to do among their circle of friends. A second-year student at Ner Israel stated:

> I'm from Los Angeles and went to a yeshiva high school there. Now the majority of kids there go to college but in my year many leaned toward a yeshiva education. So I was joining a bandwagon by going. Everyone else was doing it. As a matter of fact my parents didn't like it, but they gave in once they saw it was what I really wanted.

In this instance, the parents would have preferred their son to attend college full time. This is often the case with parents who are Modern Orthodox and place high importance on a secular education that leads to a desirable profession. They tend to view studying full time in a yeshiva at the advanced level as not very practical.

In general, however, our findings suggest that parents ultimately play by far the most important role in determining whether or not a boy enrolls in an advanced yeshiva. Because early education is so important both in shaping the student's outlook and in determining his preparedness to handle the rigorous program at the advanced level, the direct influence of the particular elementary yeshiva cannot be discounted. Still, it is the parents who make this decision when their child is only five or six, consciously and deliberately setting in motion a process of socialization that will greatly enhance the likelihood that the young man will enter the yeshiva. If the home environment is one where the laws of the faith are adhered to, the parental influence is likely to be even stronger.

Respondents were asked about their decision to attend a

yeshiva high school. The data on the accompanying Beth David Yeshiva sample tend to confirm the importance of the parental role, in addition to indicating the relative significance of other factors.

While only 17 percent attributed their decision to themselves, a far higher percentage would probably have given this answer had they been asked about their decision to enroll in an advanced yeshiva which, coming as it does at age eighteen or so, means that the individual is more likely to make independent decisions.

The answers to this question were examined according to dates of attendance in the hope that this would shed further light on the figures. Respondents were divided into three time spans—the prewar student (1933–1945), the postwar generation (1946–1965), and the most Americanized group (1966–1977). Some striking differences emerged among the three groups. The prewar group had the highest number of students who said their parents had influenced them, and the Americanized group had the lowest number in this category. Conversely, the prewar respondents were least likely to answer ''myself'' to this question while the Americanized group was most likely to list the decision as their own. Similarly, the influence of friends increases as one moves closer to the present era. The apparent movement toward self-decision on the part of students entering the yeshivas is in accordance with recent trends toward greater freedom for children and a lessening of parental authority.[5] The level of commitment toward such yeshiva education on the part of parents has probably remained constant since such education involves a considerable investment, financial and otherwise, no matter how the decision is arrived at, and it therefore requires their active support.[6] Thus, parental opposition should not be assumed simply because a respondent does not mention his parents as the prime source of motivation.

Beth David Yeshiva Alumni Questionnaire Response

Which person or persons had the greatest influence on your decision to attend your yeshiva high school?*

Parents	56%	Teacher(s)	18%	Relatives	6%
Myself[1]	17%	Friends	9%	Principal	1%

* Respondents were allowed to give multiple responses.

Predictably, a higher proportion of those whose fathers went to a yeshiva claimed that their parents influenced them than among those whose fathers did not attend yeshiva. Nevertheless, a significant proportion of those whose fathers did not go, approximately 42 percent of the respondents, gave their parents credit for influencing them in the choice. This is easier to understand when one considers why the father may not have attended yeshiva. He may not have been able to afford the cost and may have wanted his children to have what he was unable to secure for himself, a not unusual desire on the part of parents in general. Also, among the generation of parents who emigrated here after World War II, many who might otherwise have gone to a yeshiva found it impossible to do so. In fact, the majority of students who said their father did not attend yeshiva but influenced them to do so came from the postwar group (1946–1965). Furthermore, the father may have become Orthodox in later life and encouraged his children to attend yeshiva so that they would receive the perceived benefits of a complete religious education. Finally, in earlier years, especially in America, yeshiva attendance was not a crucial determinant of Orthodoxy. Whereas today hardly any self-respecting Orthodox Jew will deny his children a yeshiva education, it was not nearly as common or even feasible to do so forty or fifty years ago.[7]

The role of the teacher in the decision-making process did not change very much over time, remaining the second most important factor in all three periods. The teacher is probably seen as a role model by the boy.[8] The principal has minimal impact because greater administrative responsibilities make it difficult for him to become close to the students. Though hardly a significant number statistically, it is interesting that all four of the respondents who cited the influence of the principal attended yeshiva prior to 1945, when such schools were much smaller than in the postwar era.

While it was possible to evaluate the relative impact of different individuals upon the student, these persons should be seen as part of an overall socialization process. It was clear from the interviews that by the time a young man enters the *beis medrash,* the idea of going to yeshiva is so thoroughly ingrained in him that he tends to respond to the question: "Why did you come to the yeshiva?" in terms of choice of a particular institution. Typical is the following response given by a third-year student at the Rabbi Samson Raphael Hirsch Yeshiva (known as "Breuer's"):[9]

> I went to Breuer's because the learning was very good. Also, I knew the gang there because I'd gone to their high school. Besides, it was only a short walk from my house, so why should I look further?

Others gave answers indicating that a good deal of thought had gone into their decision and provided insight into why yeshivas have flourished in the United States. The reasons given by the *bochorim* illustrate the different approaches of the various yeshivas, and how they cater to the needs of somewhat different types of individuals. Consider, for example, the case of Noam Steinhardt,* who attended several yeshivas:

> I first went to Cleveland [Telshe Yeshiva] but I didn't like it there because it was too strict. They were always confiscating things there like record players. I also wanted to be closer to home because I've always been close with my family. So I came back and enrolled in the Mirrer Yeshiva but I found it was too big. Then I heard about a new yeshiva in Queens. It's a small place. Everyone can find their own spot because there's no pressure. I liked it and I've been there ever since.

A number of students stated that their decision revolved around the possibility of attending college at night. As one put it: "I feel learning is important and I think you wind up a real *am haaretz* [ignoramus in areas of religious knowledge] if you stop learning after high school; but I want to go to college at night so I can also get a decent job later on."

There are also differences in cultural background within the Orthodox community that may determine selection of a yeshiva. The case of Willy Strauss * highlights these concerns. His parents arrived in 1938 from Germany and settled in the Washington Heights section of Manhattan. A handsome fellow, with deep-set blue eyes and neatly combed blond hair, he spoke with great intensity about his reaction to life in a Lithuanian–style yeshiva:

> WS: You have to realize that a person from a German background looks somewhat askance at an East-European way of life. Meaning that etiquette is very different. They are unkempt and, to a certain extent, ill-mannered. Now I can see both sides, though. For instance, let's say the most aggravating point is being

on time. You call the *chasene* [wedding] for 6:30 and it starts at
7:30. Every Eastern European person going there knows that 6:30
means 7:30. But when a German person receives the invitation
and he comes at a quarter after six because he wants to be on time
and he has to wait till 7:30, he gets very annoyed. Of course
nobody is doing anything wrong because in each culture it means
a different thing. You just have to get used to it, but I had a very
hard time doing that. It's like a different language.

WH: What else bothers you?

WS: German people are very straight. They say what's on their
mind. They are also very polite. I was taught to hold the door for
a person. I could be *chutzpadik* [fresh] to my mother and get away
with it but if I walked through the door and there was an older
person behind me and I didn't hold open the door, that was the
end. And when you live away from home and deal with people on
a twenty-four-hour basis, living and eating with them, you notice
things a lot more.

Among the fifteen or so students interviewed with a similar
heritage, none of the others mentioned this issue. Still, there are
yeshivas that tend to attract Hasidic youths, others whose student body is primarily of Hungarian, Galician, or Sephardic
background, and still others where boys from certain neighborhoods or cities predominate. With one or two exceptions,
however, the student body in the various yeshivas tends to be
heterogeneous, with boys coming from a variety of ethnic
backgrounds and from different communities.

An attempt has been made here to isolate and describe some
of the factors determining why a person attends a yeshiva. An
even more important question is why students remain in the
yeshiva. While some do not, the number who remain for at least
a few years is undoubtedly far greater. The reasons for this are
crucial in explaining the survival of the yeshiva in a secular society, and they will be more fully explored later on.

Admission to the Yeshiva

Admission requirements and the degree to which they are
adhered to vary from school to school, depending on both the
yeshiva's policy and the ratio of applicants to available places.
Like colleges, those with better reputations are able to be more

selective. While the yeshivas claim that they do no recruiting, some do in fact seek to attract students, even going so far as to enlist their own students in the search. Despite individual differences among the institutions, we can at least talk about the types of criteria and procedures that are likely to be employed.

The prospective applicant will probably be asked to fill out a written application. Besides the usual requests for a medical history, names of schools previously attended, biographical data, and the like there will be questions of a religious nature. Some examples are: Do you attend *minyan* (prayer services) regularly? Are you usually on time or late? What *chavrusa* difficulties have you had in the past? What difficulties do you anticipate in keeping long hours studying *Gemora*?

Of greater importance is the personal interview with the *rosh yeshiva, mashgiach,* or other yeshiva officials. The interview is designed to assess the candidate's suitability in a number of areas. The interviewer may engage the student ''in learning,'' meaning that he will discuss a portion of the Talmud that the student has already learned to try to determine the student's level of understanding and what class he belongs in. Throughout the interview an effort will also be made to judge the applicant's character and personality, as well as his commitment to learning. Recommendations by alumni, former teachers, synagogue rabbis, and even students currently in the *yeshiva* also carry some weight in the screening process. Rabbi Yehuda Jacobs, director of admissions at Beth Medrash Govoha, described the school's attempts to judge applicants as follows:

> They take a *bechina* [test] of what this fellow is about in learning. And more than that we speak to him a little and ask him for some type of reference out of which we get a pretty good idea of what this boy is all about—his personal habits, the impression that someone makes. We look at his gait, his dress, his manner of speech. Say, for example, if he shows up in a flashy shirt. Wherever he's gone, we want to know what people said about him before.[10]

The requirements for admission to Lakewood, considered by many in the Orthodox community to be the ''Harvard'' of yeshivas, are probably more stringent than elsewhere. In general, however, admission to an advanced yeshiva does not pose a serious problem for the average graduate of a yeshiva high school. There is enough room in most yeshivas to accommodate all qualified applicants. Students are sometimes disappointed by the program and the general yeshiva experience. If this is their first experience away from home, they may find the adjustment too difficult. Others may have been pressured by parents or friends into enrolling only to discover that the program lacks sustaining appeal for them. Still others may be unable to make the grade scholastically, especially if they have come from high schools with lower standards.

CHAPTER 6

A Self-Enclosed World: Life in the Yeshiva

A yeshiva ought not to have magazines, newspapers, or radios. Guys should not go into New York City unless absolutely necessary. The Torah is not a course. It requires *kedusha, tahara,* and *amkus* [holiness, purity, and depth]. Anything that deviates from this doesn't belong in a yeshiva. A yeshiva is not a college. I'm not saying it's bad to know what's going on in the world. You have to be up to date. You have to know. But not while you're learning. Anybody who thinks differently, I think his *hashkofoh* [belief system] is wrong. He doesn't realize what Torah is. A yeshiva has to be a shelter from the world and anyone who doesn't see that should leave.

A 24-year-old student at
Beth Medrash Govoha in
Lakewood, New Jersey

THROUGHOUT THIS BOOK we have been referring to the yeshiva as a world unto itself, which is how its members tend to perceive their community. Although some yeshivas would not enforce the isolationist approach suggested by the quote above, all would agree with it as an ideal state. Many subgroupings in society, ranging from religious cults to street gangs, see themselves as separate and apart from the larger culture. It is now time to take a more careful look at the yeshiva to see if it qualifies for con-

139

sideration as a separate world.[1] This is crucial for understanding its members' views and behavior and the institution as a whole.

Life Away from Home: A Positive or Negative Experience?

No yeshiva locks its doors or has walls to prevent members from leaving. Some yeshivas are, however, located away from the urban centers in places relatively inaccessible except by auto. At Ner Israel Rabbinical College, for example, the location of the cluster of buildings in which the students carry on their daily activities, a forested area away from the main road, effectively separates the students from the outside world. This is especially true because most students and faculty live on the grounds of the yeshiva.[2]

Yeshivas such as Beth haTalmud Rabbinical College, Mirrer Yeshiva, Chaim Berlin, Kamenitzer Yeshiva, all in Brooklyn, or Chofetz Chaim in Queens, are situated in densely populated areas and have large numbers of young men who commute; yet even in these yeshivas many students spend almost all their time within the institution, venturing forth only when necessary.

With regard to the former type of yeshiva, it should be understood that the decision to be away from populated areas was a conscious one inspired by the view that isolation removed temptation and enhanced one's ability to concentrate. As Rabbi Mordechai Gifter, *rosh yeshiva* of Telshe, put it: "We moved here to get away from all the hubbub. In the city the problem is everywhere. You find it in the candy stores and the kosher pizza shops too. When Reb Elchonon Wasserman visited here from Europe in 1938, his driver took him through New York City's Times Square, and the smell made him nauseous."[3] It is well known that Rabbi Aharon Kotler established his yeshiva in Lakewood for the same reasons.[4]

Dormitory life has both positive and negative features. Students interviewed often observed that it gave them an opportunity to develop concern for others. A young man enrolled in the Telshe Yeshiva said:

> Like if I saw a guy was leaving the yeshiva because he was unhappy there—if I'm his roommate I see the problems and

> I care more. After all, I'm living with him. But if he's not in
> the dorm then I might say, "The heck with him. I don't
> learn with him. He learns downstairs and I learn upstairs."

Another perceived benefit is a feeling of independence not much
different from that often experienced by college students living
away from home. Said one student: "Your parents aren't bug-
ging you, standing over your head." And, of course, the
students themselves find that they can concentrate on their
studies better in an environment whose primary goal is to
facilitate such involvement.

But each of these benefits can become a disadvantage. In-
compatibility of roommates will result in the evaporation of a
spirit of cooperation. Immature students can find living on their
own unnerving and disappointing. The yeshivas have dormitory
counselors who try to help such persons, but sometimes even
they cannot deal with a student whose unpreparedness for group
living makes him a disruptive force. The following excerpt from
a case history provided by a private psychiatrist to whom a major
yeshiva refers students graphically demonstrates such a situation:

> I had a case the other day with a local kid who stayed in the
> dorm and was having trouble with his roommates; they
> "shortsheeted" [folded the sheet in such a way that he
> would have trouble getting into the bed] his bed and did a
> few other things. He went to his *rebbe* and the *rebbe* didn't do
> anything. He [the boy] felt he hadn't done anything wrong
> but he probably had since I see him because he's a dis-
> ciplinary problem who also goes home too often, even in the
> middle of the week. Anyway, he refused to yield to the pres-
> sure of the guys and asked the head of the dorm for a *din
> Torah* [Jewish court of law] from the school, which he got.
> The guys were at fault too since they were doing it not only
> because the fellow was making trouble but also because they
> had a good friend whom they wanted to have move in.

Homosexuality has often been cited as a problem in all-male
or all-female institutions.[5] Not surprisingly, no figures are available from yeshivas or any other sources on this problem. However, interviews with a wide range of persons, including teachers, students, administrators, psychiatrists, and social workers
suggest its incidence is very low in yeshivas. It should be noted

that, in addition to societal norms discouraging such activity and the fact that Orthodox Jews tend to be quite conservative in their attitudes and behavior patterns, the specific prohibition against homosexuality in the Bible is likely to further inhibit individuals from engaging in overt, clearly homosexual behavior. However, close friendships, occasionally involving displays of affection such as putting one's arm around a friend, do occur, and perhaps more often than would be the case in a mixed-sex environment.[6] The feelings that students have toward each other sometimes lead to anxiety when the individuals believe they are becoming too emotionally involved. One therapist who works with yeshiva *bochorim* reported:

> Sometimes I have students who come to me and express fear that their feelings of close friendship toward another student may mean that they're homosexual, but most often these fears prove groundless. Then there are the overt cases. I have found in my experience that almost all cases of this sort are with people who had troubled lives, i.e., broken homes, seductive mothers, and other pathologies, before they entered the yeshiva or if they developed while the student was in the school, had nothing to do with life in the yeshiva itself.

Most professionals reported a higher incidence of masturbation (which is considered a sin), sexual dreams, and sexual obsessions than of homosexuality. Students are expected to avoid even thinking about sexual desires; talking about them, whether to friends or members of the yeshiva faculty and administration, is not encouraged and occurs rarely. Yeshivas permit social contact with members of the opposite sex only when the stated purpose is to find a marriage partner. Physical contact of any sort, including the holding of hands, is strictly forbidden until after the marriage ceremony. In a community with such rigid taboos, the offending party may often be guilt-ridden and will be extremely reluctant to discuss any problems in these areas.

While the yeshiva is naturally concerned for the welfare of its students, several factors may prevent it from responding positively to the idea of professional help. One Orthodox social worker in New York City, who had attended yeshivas for many years, was especially critical.

> I feel that the world has changed so much in the last twenty-five years that the *rosh yeshivas* don't know how to deal with

this problem. I've had guys come in here where the *rosh yeshiva* said to them when they had a masturbation problem: "Have you tried stopping?" or "How about learning *mishnayos baal peh* [rote learning of Mishna, to take the individual's mind off his problem]?"[7] This happens to be one of the biggest problems that yeshiva guys go through, never spoken about.

Others in the field disagreed, arguing that most *rosh yeshivas* and *rebbes* were apt to respond more knowledgeably by reassuring the student that masturbation was no cause for undue concern—that is, that man is not perfect and that repentance will "cleanse" the individual. Still, even they conceded that certain yeshiva teachers and administrators were incapable of helping the student in such matters.

Generally speaking, the yeshiva administration will send a student for professional guidance only as a last resort. First, the yeshivas have a fear of relinquishing control over the student. This fear is not entirely unfounded for the advice given by a professional (who may be hostile toward religion) might conflict with yeshiva policy, thereby placing the school in a difficult position. For instance, the therapist may recommend that to resolve certain conflicts it would be good for the student to date girls, despite yeshiva rules prohibiting such activity. By allowing an outsider to become involved the institution appears to be making a commitment, although the yeshiva usually ends up strongly reasserting itself to the student when its authority is challenged in this manner, sometimes defeating its intended goal of helping the young man.

The idea of looking outside the community for personal help goes against the oft-stated view in the yeshiva that Torah study can cure all ills. Moreover, yeshivas, which view man's choice as limited only by God, have long been suspicious of the behavioral sciences, largely because they (the sciences) take the view that an individual's free choice is limited by his environment. Because of this view, yeshivas that permit students to take college courses urge them to stay away from courses in anthropology, sociology, and psychology. Another issue is that parents and other students often regard both psychological problems and treatment by professionals as a stigma. This not only increases the reluctance of both student and institution to consult with professionals but may create problems of self-image and social rejection.[8]

A number of yeshivas refer students with problems to professionals who are Orthodox in the hope that they not only will be sensitive to the unique setting in which the students function but will also take into account the yeshiva's position on various matters. This does not always work out because the helping professional, even if he adheres to the faith, usually has less regard for the yeshiva's particular interests than for the student's if they should conflict. That is, he may be observant and committed in terms of his personal life, but "professional" in terms of diagnosis and recommendation. Some schools prefer to send their students to a professional with a strong yeshiva background, perhaps even a graduate. However, as the yeshivas become more exposed to the outside world, such attitudes are changing. A Modern Orthodox psychiatrist who has worked with yeshivas over the past seven years described these attitudinal shifts as follows:

> PSYCHIATRIST: I think that in the past few years they've come to see me as an ally rather than as an adversary. For instance, I was recently called in connection with a *bochur,* or rather ex-*bochur* who remained close to the yeshiva. He was not a psychotic but he needed help of a mediating sort that went beyond rabbinic guidance.

> WH: What was the problem?

> PSYCHIATRIST: A very troubled family relationship. The father is extremely possessive, domineering, and controlling in a very severe way. The son tried not to have anything to do with the father and the yeshiva took the stance that "you must respect your father." I felt that the son should stay away from the father and that meant I was taking a stand opposed to the yeshiva.

> WH: How did Rabbi_____react to your position?

> PSYCHIATRIST: Well, he's a very powerful and confident man, but I told him I was making a clinical as opposed to a religious decision. Now the rabbi did not back off from his position, but he was able to respect that there was a choice here. And I think this represents quite a shift over the past few years. In the past they would have called in one of their own psychologists [a graduate] and he would have told Rabbi_____what he wanted to hear.

A number of professional and yeshiva administrators pointed out that, while problems of a sexual nature occurred in yeshivas, their incidence, however infrequent, was more common at the high school (*mesivta*) level than at that of the *beis medrash*. This was attributed to the fact that adolescence was a period in the individual's life when his emerging feelings in this area often presented difficulties. As one high school principal put it:

> When a boy is fourteen it's hard sometimes for him to restrain himself. He doesn't yet have the self-control. A boy is interested in girls or in other boys and it's a society where sexual contact is strictly forbidden. The problem is in handling it properly. The boy thinks he's gone, that he's condemned. And you have to explain to him: "You're not the first one and you won't be the last one. Work at it. But don't give up. You're still a good boy."[9]

What happens if professional treatment fails to help the student significantly? The response varies from school to school and from administrator to administrator, but generally the institution is compassionate and adopts a protective attitude toward the individual. There seems to be a feeling of communal responsibility that extends beyond the walls of the yeshiva itself. Thus, a person who is asked to leave an institution may be recommended to another yeshiva, which will not be told of the student's problems. The yeshiva justifies this practice with the arguments that it does not wish to besmirch the student's name and that it also hopes he will improve in a different setting. Unfortunately, more than a few such students become "flying Dutchmen," with some attending as many as four or five yeshivas before dropping out altogether. To the yeshiva's credit, expulsion is generally considered only in cases where the young man poses a danger to others, though the interpretation of when this point is reached naturally varies considerably.[10]

The Parents and the Yeshiva: A Question of Control

Many yeshiva students commute daily to the school or return to their homes on weekends. Even those who are away from home for long periods of time are as a rule in contact with their families by phone or mail and return home for vacations at various times during the year. Moreover, as we have seen, the family is usually a major factor in the student's decision to enter the yeshiva in the first place, having nurtured and supported the development of a religious belief system that harmonizes quite well with the goals of the yeshiva.

On the other hand, the very structure of the yeshiva, especially its capacity for physically isolating the student, enables it to create a degree of separation between a student and his family, should it so desire. This does, in fact, happen under certain circumstances and is not limited to children who come from non-observant homes. For example, Mrs. Jacobs* became deeply committed to the tenets of Orthodoxy as an adult. She provided her children with a good background in the ways of the faith, sending them to Orthodox day schools and following the laws at home as well. She is now very well versed in the various religious practices followed by the Orthodox community and is, in fact, something of a right-winger. In line with her beliefs, she sent her son to an out-of-town yeshiva which was strictly Orthodox.

When I interviewed her, she asserted that she was happy with the progress her son was making but she also indicated unhappiness with the *rosh yeshiva,* whom she described as "insensitive and domineering."

> He may be great for the kids but he isn't so nice to the parents. For example, he refused to let him come home for the entire Succoth holiday. Now we're religious people and I couldn't understand what was wrong with him being home for the holiday. But he [the *rosh yeshiva*] made a whole big thing about how important it was for Yitzchak to be in the yeshiva with the boys and I thought it was very inconsiderate of him.

Since the students live away from home, it is perhaps inevitable that various staff members of the yeshiva will sometimes become surrogate parents. Of the twenty or so parents with whom I spoke, several expressed resentment at what they perceived to be a certain loss of control over their children. In addition, they were disturbed that the students, now that they were engaged in intensive study, seemed to look down on their frequently less knowledgeable parents. None of the parents placed this in the context of attitudes toward parents often evinced by college-age students in the larger society.

There are instances, however, where sending a student

away to a yeshiva is seen as benefiting the student's relationship with his family, as in the following case, told to me by Meir Wikler, a social worker who works closely with yeshiva students and other Orthodox Jews:

> In one case the parents had a long-term marital conflict and the children were, in some ways, incorporated into that conflict. After numerous sessions, I recognized that the boy was having a problem making a healthy break from home. The parents came to me and said: "He wants to go away to yeshiva, out of town." I felt if he would go out of town and leave his parents at home, it would create enough distance so that he could probably work things out successfully.[11]

A Unique World unto Itself

Does the yeshiva resocialize individuals? To some extent, the answer depends on what the *bochur* was like prior to his arrival. Yeshivas that cater to newly observant young men (*baalei teshuva*) are likely to effect far more dramatic and drastic changes in the lives of those who attend them than yeshivas made up primarily of students from observant homes. Nevertheless, those who attend traditional yeshivas do develop attitudes, perspectives, and lifestyles which differ sharply from those of other Orthodox Jews and which are directly related to the yeshiva experience. Certainly attempts are made to insure conformity to the norms and values of the community. In fact, it is in the seemingly minor aspects of yeshiva life that we can gain a better picture of the degree to which the lives of its members are regulated. Let us briefly look at some of these aspects.

There is no official dress code in the yeshiva but that is because none is needed; students are very well aware of what constitutes proper dress. Starting at the top, yeshiva *bochorim* do not, as a rule, wear knitted or colored yarmulkes. That is for Modern Orthodox Jews. Their skullcaps are large, black, and usually made of velvet or satin. A dark hat is always worn for services and when the student ventures forth into the outside world. In the yeshiva style, its wearer allows it to perch on his head at an angle, or to be set back in such a manner as to indicate nonchalance about how he may look in it. The dark hat has become such a symbol of these students that the schools they attend are

often called the "black hat yeshivas" by others, especially
Modern Orthodox Jews whose children attend schools such as
Yeshiva University or secular colleges. The rest of the uniform
consists of a dark jacket and pants (not necessarily matching),
dark leather shoes, and a white shirt either open at the neck or
with a dark tie. Without going into greater detail, there are certain jackets, shirts, pants, and hat styles that are widely accepted
in the community. As a result, students from other yeshivas can
recognize each other as members of the same larger community
without verbal exchange should they see each other in the subway, in a park, or at a museum. This high degree of visibility
enables the institution to extend its influence beyond its
geographical boundaries, for the conforming student knows that
others recognize him as belonging to a distinct group.[12]

Yeshiva students use a certain argot, not only in the context
of talmudic study but in all social interactions.[13] Basically, it is an
amalgam of English, Yiddish, Hebrew, and an occasional
Aramaic phrase. The following remark by an American-born
yeshiva student is an extreme example of this linguistic pattern:

> When it comes to going to movies I *takeh* [really] *hold* [feel]
> that there's a real *sacanah* [danger] that something there
> could be *mashpiah* [influence] on you in a way that could
> undermine your whole *hashkofoh* [belief system]. Therefore,
> it's not *kedai* [worthwhile] to go and put yourself in such a
> *matzav* [position]. Do you *chap* [grasp] what I'm saying?

While most students would probably not lace their conversation
to this extent, no yeshiva student would have the least bit of difficulty understanding these statements. Terminology of this sort,
when used, enhances group solidarity. Its origins probably lie in
the community's relative isolation from society's mainstream,
plus the fact that the students speak in this fashion every day for
about ten hours while engaged in talmudic study. Certain terms
and concepts in the Talmud cannot easily be translated into the
contemporary idiom of a different culture, hence the combining
of several languages.

Within the yeshiva there is a deference pattern which, while
not compulsory, would surely result in ostracism from the community were it not followed. That is, students must demonstrate
respect for their teachers and for the *rosh yeshiva*. The pattern is to
address them in the third person ("I wanted to ask the *rebbe* if I

could speak with him") and to rise whenever they enter a room (unless they specifically decline the honor).[14]

Yeshivas are often characterized by a certain degree of internal tension. Those who run the yeshiva (generally called "the *hanholoh*" [Hebrew for administration]) are in a variety of ways perceived as having different interests than the students although such divisions are not nearly as sharp as those existing in prisons, mental institutions, or the military. One of the harsher descriptions came in the following discussion with a group of yeshiva students:

WH: How about the physical facilities here—dorms, food, etc.?

STUDENT ONE: It's [the facilities] the kind of thing you regret complaining about ten years later.

WH: Do you feel the yeshiva has your interests at heart?

STUDENT TWO: Many times not. Sometimes I feel they write off everybody except the guys who they think are going to make it really big.

STUDENT THREE: Yeah. There are guys in the dorm who are crying out for somebody to take them by the hand.

STUDENT FOUR: Do you really cry? (general laughter].

STUDENT THREE: I often wish somebody would come over to me after a rough week.

STUDENT FIVE: They [administrators] will; but they'll only talk to you about early curfew and then if you miss it, you'll have to sleep out in a car.

WH: How about the dorm counselor?

STUDENT TWO: He cares. He's one of the few, but he'll also come into your room and take away your radio.

WH: Why don't you go over to someone?

STUDENT FOUR: Because we don't think they'd care.

The fact that the student's social position in the school is often sharply different from what it is on the outside further underlines the separateness of the yeshiva world. In the yeshiva he tends to be judged primarily on his ability in talmudic study. Outside that community, his erudition is often not taken into account at all or, when it is, it is considered along with many other factors. At the superficial level he is judged by his physical appearance. In college, for example, other students see him as an

Orthodox Jew. His professors are highly unlikely to be aware of his proficiency in Talmud or, for that matter, his lack of it. His parents are likely to evaluate him on the basis of how he acts toward them, not in terms of his knowledge, unless they are especially learned. Later on, when he applies for a job in the secular world, his high or low status in the yeshiva community is similarly disregarded. On the other hand, when efforts are made by him or others acting on his behalf to find a suitable marriage partner for him, his reputation as a scholar will weigh heavily, although once he is married, other factors in the relationship are likely to supersede this qualification in importance. As a consequence of his differing social positions, he will have different roles to play both inside and outside the community.[15] Moreover, once he leaves the yeshiva, his social position in that world will never be quite the same again.[16]

In a prison, the punishments and privileges given out by the staff are often labeled in a way that lends support to the institution's goals. Thus, as sociologist Erving Goffman notes, solitary confinement may be described as "constructive meditation."[17] The yeshiva is, of course, a voluntary institution and is therefore quite different from the prison. Still, a parallel appears in the student's manner of handling aspects of the yeshiva which he does not like. One young man stated:

> So what if there are five guys to a room? That's not important and it's got nothing to do with why I'm here. In fact, the crowded conditions, the lousy food, and even the fact that I can't play ball as much as I'd like to, all give me an opportunity to develop my sense of values and priorities to a much higher level. It's really all a *nissoyen* [divine test].

In effect, this is a process of sublimation by which the *bochur* turns inconvenient features of yeshiva life into an opportunity to reach some of the overall goals of the yeshiva: to produce a spiritually oriented individual to whom material benefits are of minor importance.

Those in the yeshiva are fond of emphasizing how different their lifestyle is from that prevailing in the larger society. They will often make invidious comparisons between life on the outside and in the institution. The following comment by a well-known *rosh yeshiva* is typical:

> You want to know why we're so successful in attracting people? It's because there's so much emptiness in the world. It

used to be a nice idea thirty years ago that you went to college, that you became a man of culture. But today . . . college is terrible. There's no education going on there. It's not a place for study. Or take sex. There's no more the view that it's romantic. Forty years ago they thought of sex as something beautiful. It used to be poetry, at night, under the stars. But today the world is so *grub* [low, etc.] . . . so naturally, the *bochorim* come to us.

By taking the negative features of society at large such as heavy drug usage, crime, and violence, all of which are almost nonexistent in the yeshiva world, members of all segments in the Orthodox community find additional support and justification for a way of life that they know is radically different from that of the surrounding culture.

Teacher and Student: A Crucial Relationship

Although his involvement with the students takes place primarily in the classroom as the students argue and debate the *Gemora,* the teacher can be, and often is, far more than a classroom instructor. The closeness that often develops between students and *rebbes* is, in part, a result of the fact that they are in contact for an average of six to eight hours daily. Besides giving a one-and-a-half- to two-hour class, the *rebbe* is in and out of the *beis medrash* the entire day. In addition, as indicated in Chapter 4, Talmud study is a cooperative effort that demands involvement on the part of all and the dedication with which many *rebbes* approach their subject can be likened far more to passion than to detached intellectual curiosity.

Rabbi Velvel Perl, a former teacher at Ner Israel Rabbinical College, described the intensity that typified his interaction with the students in those days:

There was a guy who was the laziest guy in the world. He didn't do anything. So I tried to *be mekarev* him [motivate him through personal contact]. I learned with him eight or ten hours a day for a while and then I gave him over to other students to learn with him [at this point the rabbi's eyes lit up]. And you know? He was turned on! Then there was a really tall guy in the class. He towered over me and when I threw out a question, you could see him catch the *kashe* [question] in midair and [laughing with pleasure at the recollection] he would throw it back at me! I got them living and involved.[18]

Categorizing the various roles played by the *rebbe* is a difficult matter because they are intertwined. In no area is this more evident than in the intellectual domain. Because of the centrality of learning in the yeshiva, rapport in this aspect of the student–*rebbe* relationship is a highly personal matter, not simply a question of hearing a stimulating discourse. As an example, let us look at how a former student of one of the greatest Talmud teachers in the world, Rabbi Joseph B. Soloveitchik, views his *rebbe*. Rabbi Aaron Kahn teaches Talmud at Yeshiva University. He has been associated with ''The *Rav*,'' as Rabbi Soloveitchik is known, for more than fifteen years, first as a student and in later years as the person responsible for reviewing The *Rav*'s lectures with the class.

> The *Rav*'s bond with his *talmidim* [students] is very strong, very intense, but it has little to do with his personal relationship with them. In fact, very few students have developed such a relationship with him. The relationship has to do with other factors. We realize that the *Rav* has given us the key to a treasure. We thank him for what he taught us and also for what he did not teach us. By the second thing I mean that he did not convey to us anything that was wrong or trivial. He also taught us not to approach learning only through the writings of others but to become creative on our own, to develop a method that will allow us to analyze on our own.
>
> The students realize that they're next to a giant in Torah who also is a great orator and philosopher and who has had a major impact on *halacha*. Yet he relates to us on our own level. He'll say: ''This question [concerning the Talmud] will keep me up all night. Will it keep any of you up all night?'' Or he'll present something in class and, if the fellas don't react to it, he'll say: ''I've been working on this solution for days and you just accept it! It's not a problem for you!''
>
> There are quite a few people who see the *Rav* as their father, in a sense. They regard their whole exposure to Torah as coming through and because of him.[19]

The meshing of intellectual with personal is represented here in an almost ideal form. Those who are in Rabbi Soloveitchik's class are very advanced students. Because of this, their attitude concerning the importance of talmudic study is already highly developed and they regard it as one of the most important things in their lives, if not the most important. It follows, that they would look upon anyone who can contribute so much to their growth in this area as fulfilling a basic and, at the same time, highly personal need. In this way what seems to be purely a cerebral activity becomes one that deeply touches the emotions as well.

In the final analysis intellect alone is insufficient from the perspective of both the yeshiva and Orthodoxy. Since one is learning about a tradition requiring action, as well as under-standing, there must be a sense of commitment beyond knowledge. Those who have gained admittance to a class operating at the level of Rabbi Soloveitchik's, have, as a rule, ac-quired a sense of values and basic feeling for the faith much earlier in their student careers and do not need the personal at-tention that *rebbes* often give their students. It must be stressed that, were they to have only an intellectual comprehension of the Talmud, their development would be incomplete from the yeshiva's standpoint. The following case history makes it clear that for some, at least, emphasis on the intellectual is not enough to keep them within the yeshiva community.

Barry Deutsch* grew up in an Orthodox home. His parents sent him to yeshiva when he was six. Early in his education he gained recognition as a boy who excelled in talmudic studies. Because of his ability and his love for the subject, he gravitated toward a clique of friends who were similarly inclined. He re-mained friends with this group through his high school years, as well as when he began attending college at night while continu-ing in yeshiva by day. At the *beis medrash* level, he was admired and respected by students and teachers as a *talmid chochom* (scholar) of considerable standing.

On the surface he appeared as observant as his friends, but in fact he was simply going through the motions. As he put it:

> Praying was a big drag. It was an interruption in my day. I would do it simply because it was expected. I never got joy out of it. It was simply my duty.[20]

Yet he carried out the commandments to the letter of the law throughout those years. What kept him in the yeshiva was his love for talmudic study:

WH: How much of your learning was pure intellectual pleasure and how much for the idea that it was God's work?

BD: It was 100 percent intellectual pleasure, and the fact that you were going to earn your place in heaven was an added bonus. But if God would have told me to do it and it wasn't pleasurable, I would have probably broken away from the religion at that point, when I was still in high school. Mind you, there were periods in my life when I questioned religion, but each time I would say, *No, no, no,* deep in my head. I thought, *How do I know it's true?,* but when you're doing something you enjoy, you question it less. The analytical framework was fascinating to me and I just loved it.

After graduating from college with honors, Barry went on to study for his Ph.D., at the same time continuing intensive talmudic study. He dressed conservatively in the style of the "black hat yeshivas," ate only kosher food, prayed three times daily, and behaved like any other Orthodox Jew. After receiving his Ph.D., he moved to Israel. Within two years, at age twenty-seven he had ceased to be an observant Jew. He no longer kept the laws and, in fact, ridiculed them.

Barry's case is unusual in the sense that most yeshiva students who leave Orthodoxy do so at an earlier age, usually in the high school and sometimes the college years. Still, his case is instructive because of his reasons for liking and leaving this way of life. When asked how he became irreligious, Barry responded:

BD: I never really believed in it. But inertia kept me within the fold. I had grown up this way. My friends were religious, my parents were, and that was the environment I felt comfortable in. I just drifted along. Sure I had questions but I didn't have anyone I felt I could ask and because I enjoyed the learning part so much, I didn't feel pushed into doing it. But I never had the belief, just the intellect. Then when I got to Israel I was able to break away from my past, start again, where no one knew me. In short, I was learning and God was just a part of the world I had been social-ized into.

WH: What happened in Israel, specifically, to make you change?

BD: I was hating the *davening* [praying] more and more. And other interests began to crowd out the *Gemora*. I no longer enjoyed Talmud study. I was interested in my own field of research. I met many people who were irreligious; I had known almost none in New York. I went through a crisis with a religious girl who said she wouldn't marry me. At the same time, I was lucky enough to have a roommate who was going through the same thing vis-à-vis religion and we sort of supported each other. For example, he would put on the light on Shabbos and I would clap.

This case raises many questions that cannot be answered here. Why did Barry feel unable to confide in his friends or *rebbes*? Was it because of the sort of people they were, or was it because of his own psychological makeup? What about the influence of the yeshiva itself? What role did his parents play in the socialization process? Why didn't Barry rebel earlier?[21] His story is presented in brief here as a way of demonstrating what can happen to an individual whose attraction to the yeshiva stems primarily from a love of talmudic study that differs little from the appeal philosophy, English literature, or physics might have for an undergraduate at, say, Amherst College. In the all-encompassing yeshiva world, however, it is not enough.

Problems of a personal nature are the other area in which the *rebbe* plays a major role. Both he and the administration view it as one of his primary responsibilities to be available for consultations with his students. The degree to which the students interact with their teachers varies greatly from yeshiva to yeshiva and from teacher to teacher. There are individuals who feel a sense of mission in this area and who are also capable of relating well to students. One *rebbe* of this type portrayed his level of involvement in the following manner:

> I am available to them. There's no such thing as office hours. I'll never say—"You can see me between three and four in the afternoon on Tuesdays and Thursdays. When I'm not giving *shiur* I'm often still in the yeshiva. Sometimes I'll tell them I'm busy, but, by and large, if someone wants to see me, they can. At night they can call me at any time and many do—as late as one or two o'clock in the morning.

This is by no means universal. Many students complained that their *rebbes* were not sufficiently interested in them. While no teacher would openly admit to a lack of interest, in many cases their comments made it clear that they too felt a communications gap. Although there were quite a few exceptions to this rule, generally speaking, the older, European-trained *rebbes* had greater difficulty in this area. Those with whom I spoke tended to blame the students for the problem.

Rabbi Moshe Turin* is a teacher in a somewhat liberal New York City yeshiva. Born and raised in Europe, he came here shortly before World War II and has been a *rebbe* for over twenty-five years. In his late fifties, he speaks pessimistically about most of his students:

WH: Do you see your students outside the classroom?

MT: I personally don't much. I try to but it's not easy. Not only because it's hard for us but because the students don't seem to want it somehow. It is very difficult to gain the confidence of the students.

When I asked Rabbi Turin why this was so, his choice of words was in itself an indication of the distance between him and those whom he taught:

He's [the student] always on the alert, worried there may be something more to it than the eye meets. The students do not confide in us. I find it on a personal level and I see it among my colleagues. The boys are suspicious because they identify us with the establishment. I pray to God we can overcome this.

Interviews with a number of *rebbes* in this yeshiva revealed that certain colleagues did indeed feel this way, but others, all of them younger, disagreed sharply. Rabbi Asher Smolinsky* is in his thirties, American-born and -trained. He has a close relationship with his students. He will invite them to his house on various occasions and spends many hours advising and counseling them:

Last year I had a Chanuka party at my house for the students. It was almost an existential experience. We talked about Torah and we sang songs too. There was a real glow that evening besides the Chanuka candles. I felt extraordinarily close to them and they to me. In fact, they presented me with a set of *seforim* [religious books] that cost well over $100 and inscribed it with a moving dedication. It's hard to describe the almost mystical relationship I had with them. The closer you get to an emotional and religious experience the more words fail you.

From numerous conversations with *rebbes* in different yeshivas, it became clear that there was a general feeling of "burnout." In all likelihood, those younger individuals who are excited about teaching now will not feel this way in twenty years. Rabbi

Chaim Krupnick* has been teaching Talmud for more than thirty-five years. I approached him because I had heard he was an excellent instructor, noted for both his pedagogical abilities and his interest in his students. I was somewhat surprised to discover that, while he still enjoyed teaching a great deal, this was not the case with regard to his involvement with the students:

> WH: How involved are you with the *bochorim*?
>
> CK: Are you asking me about today? Ten years ago?
>
> WH: However you choose to answer the question.
>
> CK: Well, ten, twenty years ago, I was very involved. I'm not as interested in that as I used to be. My focus is more on intellectual matters now, though it's hard to say why. They still come to me for advice on occasion. But do I take them for a walk around the corner? No, but I used to years ago.

It seems reasonable to assume that as the age gap widens it takes more of an effort by the faculty member to bridge it. When only a few years separate the two groups, their interests are far more likely to coincide, whether it be in terms of leisure time activities or even career aspirations. Concerning the latter, one young faculty member at Yeshiva University's RIETS division said: "When they see a young person like me standing up and giving a class, it gives them hope, especially those considering a career in Jewish education or even the rabbinate, that a young person can make it and end up giving a high-level class."

The older *rebbe* has other advantages, however. He is more likely to be respected because of his age and because he has had more time to develop a reputation. This would be true in a college as well, but there is another factor at work here that has to do with his own background and community values. In the yeshiva world, tradition is prized and the older *rebbe* is seen as a link with the great European yeshivas where he was usually a student. Even if he is not an especially renowned scholar, mere contact with the greats of a bygone era is sufficient to give him a certain status, one that makes the students overlook his failure to understand their world and speak in a more contemporary idiom. One alumnus asserted:

> What I liked best about the yeshiva was coming into contact with the greats. I had been brought up on stories about the

European yeshivas like Slabodka, Volozhin, and the like and simply to be in the class of someone who was actually there and understand what they represented—it was a great feeling.

Some *rebbes,* acutely aware of this feeling, cultivate it by telling stories about the yeshiva and by insisting on a certain degree of respect. One man said:

> I feel that the students have to learn respect for the *rebbe,* to know that he represents a certain tradition. I don't even let a guy lean back in his chair. Even though I'm an older person, though, they trust me because they know I pour out my heart to them.

The fact that they have attended famous yeshivas with long traditions and are established scholars may have nothing to do with encouraging a nineteen-year-old student to speak with the *rebbe* about his personal problems. But it must be stressed that there are older *rebbes* who can gain the trust of their students in this area and there are younger ones who cannot. Moreover, a *bochur* who feels unable to approach his teacher can usually find others such as the dormitory counselor, an older student, the *mashgiach,* or even a former *rebbe* in the same school to talk with about his problems.

Although age emerged as probably the most crucial factor there were other considerations too. *Rebbes* who lived close to the school seemed able to develop better rapport with the students. Most yeshivas require their teachers to live near the yeshiva but some do not, and where this is the case it can be a significant disadvantage. Obviously, a *rebbe* who chooses to live far away from the institution may do so because achieving a close relationship with his students is not an overriding concern for him. Responses to the questionnaire revealed that school size and class size can also be factors for many students, with a significant number (about 15 percent) indicating they would have preferred a more intimate setting that would have allowed for closer student–faculty relationships. Another consideration was college attendance. Those teaching at yeshivas where students attended colleges, as well as *rebbes* at Yeshiva University, where college studies are a required part of the program of study, frequently noted that this meant the students were less involved and concerned with talmudic study in general. As one *rebbe* at RIETS said:

They're very *farnumen* [preoccupied]. They're concerned about getting into medical or law school, passing the Graduate Record Examination. This makes it harder to get closer to them in general. In high school they have less on their minds and obviously, if they don't go to college there's more room for Torah and this also affects how they see the person who teaches them Torah.

The types of problems which a student asks his *rebbe* about generally fall into one of three categories: dating and marriage, intellectual matters, and questions regarding religious faith. In a community where contact between boys and girls is quite limited, the *rebbe* is frequently seen as a knowledgeable person. After all, he has a family and by virtue of age is more experienced in such matters. Sometimes his function in this area is far more specific, for many teachers serve as matchmakers. Since they are in close and constant contact with young, eligible men, members of the community will ask them to recommend someone for their daughter, or a friend's daughter. This is almost always done without a fee, with personal satisfaction the major incentive. One *rebbe* told me with pride: "I've already *rett* [recommended] ten *shidduchim* [matches]."

The *rebbe's* involvement in matchmaking provides him with a broader perspective than that of the student. Since he has seen failure and success, he is perceived by the student as one who can give counsel. The specific questions posed by students range from when to get married to what qualities to look for. The following observations were made by a *rebbe* who has successfully advised a number of young men:

> They'll ask me what kinds of girls they should date. Or the fact that they don't have any dates. They'll tell me a girl is from a certain background and do I think she fits for someone who's going to be a rabbi out in the sticks. Someone who came to religion on his own where his family wasn't that religious will want to know if I think he should marry someone who was brought up very Orthodox.

In the final analysis students will be more likely to confide in their peers, among whom this is often a major topic of conversation. Still, the *rebbe* is often very important in the lives of the students, if only because he frequently has the ability to actually introduce them to eligible young women.

The second problem area concerns the student's studies, the

focal point of yeshiva life. A young man may ask his *rebbe*
whether it is time for him to leave the yeshiva. Such a question is
a loaded one for the student may know from the response
whether or not the *rebbe* thinks he has the talent to "make it" in
the yeshiva world by becoming an outstanding scholar. Of
course, the *rebbe* may advise him to leave for other reasons—that
is, he is not suited for intensive study as much as for bringing
people closer to the faith. A *bochur* may ask his *rebbe* whether it
would be better for him to try to cover ground in his studies or to
concentrate on obtaining a deeper understanding of a particular
tractate in the Talmud. He will consult with the *rebbe* about difficulties with his learning partner, problems in understanding the
lecture and so on.

The third area revolves around belief in God and the tenets
of the faith. This is the least discussed area at the *beis medrash* level
because most students have already resolved or at least thought
through this issue by the time they have completed high school.[22]
Those who have decided they do not believe in the Orthodox way
of life will usually drop out after high school.[23] Nevertheless,
doubts do crop up and, on occasion, if the *bochur* cannot get
satisfaction from informal rap sessions with his peers, he may
seek out his *rebbe* for guidance. This, however, requires excellent
rapport between student and teacher because questioning basic
beliefs at this advanced stage is seen as rather odd. A former student who did have questions of this nature recalled:

> Questions of faith bothered me a lot. Yet there wasn't
> anybody I felt I could go to. I could never have raised such a
> question and the *rebbe* would have said: "That's fine as long
> as you keep it [the physical act of obeying the Torah, i.e.,
> eating kosher food only, etc.]." I remember that once or
> twice, I thought about even running to the Village [Green-
> wich Village] and seeing what life was like there but it was
> just a thought. I never seriously considered becoming ir-
> religious. It would come up once or twice a year and that
> was it.

As one of the dominant figures in the institution, the *rebbe* is
the focus of much conversation among the yeshiva *bochorim*.[24]
Stories are told about his class and what goes on there, his
younger years, where and with whom he studied, his family, and
his interaction with other students. All his actions are noted. At
prayer time the students will notice how long it takes him to say a

certain prayer and how much emotion (*kavana*) he seems to put into his entreaties to God. They observe how he speaks to and about others, how he dresses, how he walks.

In all these areas, the students are searching for clues to how he will react to them on a personal level. The teachers, for their part, are acutely aware of the close scrutiny to which they are subjected. They frequently respond with attempts to demonstrate how in tune they are with the students and their extracurricular interests, particularly sports. Contrary to popular opinion, sports are an important part of life in the yeshiva, not in terms of participation, since the student's day is occupied mostly with his studies, but in terms of interest in the subject. Many students are intimately familiar with the names and vital statistics of the local professional hockey, basketball, and baseball teams in their city.[25] They also place considerable importance on excelling in sports in the limited time they have to engage in such activity, though, of course, it cannot replace the status accorded to those expert in Talmud. Therefore, a *rebbe* who wants to show how "hip" he is may bring sports into a class discussion:

> I'll talk at times about sports to show them I know as much about it as they do, though I really don't. In this way they feel that I can relate to their needs.
>
> A *beis medrash rebbe* in New York City

Another *rebbe* explained that he used sports analogies to hold the students' attention: "I tell them 'You're rounding third base' if they're near the right answer to a question."

Corny? Perhaps, but if nothing else, a message is conveyed to the young man that the *rebbe* cares and can be approached. Interviews with students supported this assumption. One, a college professor who had attended Ner Israel Yeshiva, recalled:

> Isaacson* [a *rebbe* at the yeshiva] was pretty normal, not a *chunyock* [religious fanatic]. He played basketball, had a broken nose from playing ball. Stuff like that. He was definitely cool. He was Zionistic, ended up going to Israel. Other *rebbes* were really out of it. You couldn't talk to them at all because they took things to an extreme. Everything was *bitul zman* [a waste of time in that it diverts one from studying Torah]. Now to the outside world Isaacson was a right-wing, fanatical, Orthodox Jew, but to us he was a pretty liberal spirit.[26]

Many *rebbes,* however, especially those in the right-wing yeshivas, view such efforts as beneath their dignity. In general, such instances are more apt to take place at the high school (*mesivta*) level, where sports and other extracurricular interests are more likely to be a strong focus of student attention. In their efforts to appear "relevant," some teachers may also bring topics other than sports into their class discussions, most notably current events. Besides heightening student interest, this has the effect of demonstrating to the *bochorim* that, despite the *rebbe*'s obviously intense involvement in Talmud study, he manages to know about other things too. In the yeshiva that I observed intensively, the students often took great pains to demonstrate to me both their own awareness (which was quite limited) and that of their *rebbes* concerning world affairs. Typical was the following statement: "You'd be amazed at how much the *rebbe* knows. Once I was talking to him and you could see he knew everything the *Times* was saying." (I did not ask him how he was able to ascertain this in light of the fact that he had asserted at an earlier point that he [the student] almost never read a newspaper.)

Student Life and Culture

Despite their rigorous program of study, students find time to relate to one another on a casual basis. Very few can study Talmud all day without some diversion, whether it be talking to their learning partner about matters other than talmudic study or simply walking out of the *beis medrash* for a few minutes. While such activity is not encouraged by those in authority, it is certainly tolerated, within limits. On one occasion, I was engaged in a conversation with my learning partner unrelated to talmudic study when I noticed the *rebbe* walking toward us. When I informed my partner he replied: "So what? He knows whether or not you're learning. You can't fool him. As long as we learn *most* of the time, he won't say anything."

Certain activities fall into a gray area. For instance, in New York City, there are sellers of religious books who travel from yeshiva to yeshiva in vans. Upon their arrival at a school many students leave the *beis medrash* to examine their offerings. Browsing through the available stock can take up a half hour or even more while at the same time providing an opportunity to talk with friends or the bookseller.

If we are to understand the uniqueness of the yeshiva *bochur*'s social world it is necessary to examine what he talks about. Yeshiva humor, for example, not only reveals a certain degree of insularity but serves the important function of increasing group solidarity, the feeling that one belongs to a real community. Consider the following joke related to me by a student:

> A *baal teshuva* [one who has recently returned to the faith] was sitting in class for the first time and he asked the *rebbe* for the literal meaning of a word in the *Gemora*. "I don't know the exact meaning of the word," the *rebbe* said. "Oh, I'm sorry, *rebbe*. I didn't mean to stump you" [replied the student].

The joke is that certain words in the Talmud cannot be literally translated by anyone, no matter how knowledgeable. Yet the novitiate thinks he has embarrassed the teacher by demonstrating that he cannot explain a word in the text. Relating this story to others while knowing that an outsider would fail to see the humor in it solidifies the group. The choice of topic, namely Talmud and the newly observant, is an indication of topics important to the community.

Even more revealing are the stories told about yeshiva life in general. The following story told to me by a student demonstrates how the yeshiva *bochur* thinks the larger society perceives him:

> The policeman in town came over to one guy and he can't understand the *yeshivaleit* [members of the yeshiva community]. "A guy got a ticket a few months ago," he said, "and I asked him how long have you been in the school?" and the guy said, "Fifteen years." "Wow! You must be the dumbest guy in Lakewood. You've been in school fifteen years and you haven't graduated yet!"
>
> Then he told the guy another story: "Everything the rabbis do until now I understand. But I saw one thing last night, I'm never gonna start up with these guys again. They're like a different breed. Last night I was on patrol. I was driving down Madison Avenue. It was raining and two o'clock in the morning. There was this real downpour and

you could barely see out your window. The streets are deserted. Suddenly I see a guy walking down the yellow stripe in the middle of the road. I rolled down my window; he's wearing a black hat and black coat, and I tell him to get out of the street, and you know what? He just waves to me and keeps right on walking."

Besides underscoring the distance between members of the yeshiva community and those among whom they live, such stories reinforce community values. As we saw in Chapter 4, the goal of Talmud study is study itself. One does not complete a program of study that automatically leads to a formal degree except in the most modern yeshivas, certainly not in Lakewood, where this idea was particularly stressed under the leadership of Rabbi Aharon Kotler and continues to be emphasized today. Therefore, one who has studied in Lakewood for fifteen years is not only not "the dumbest guy in Lakewood"; he is, by virtue of his long tenure at the institution, probably one of the most accomplished.

The second story deals with yet another point, one that recalls the stereotype of the "absent-minded professor." Amplifying upon this story, my respondent explained to me: "You see, this guy was one of the big *illuyim* [geniuses] in the yeshiva and he was probably *farteefed* [deeply engrossed] in some *inyan* [a portion of the Talmud]." Within the yeshiva world such stories are legion. The protagonist usually does something that appears bizarre but that is totally understandable once it is explained that he was thinking about "Torah." This again reinforces yeshiva values. In a culture that repeatedly urges its members to consider Torah study of paramount importance, it is highly useful to indicate that certain otherwise eccentric forms of behavior are totally excusable because the person was thinking about such matters.

Another student related a similar story to me:

> Reb Aharon [Kotler] once locked himself out of his room in the dormitory. Reb_____was with him. There was a transom on top of the door. He asked Reb_____to climb in and open the door for him. So Reb_____ climbs in the transom and opens the door and climbs right back out [the transom] again. He's totally absent-minded because he's always thinking about the *Gemora*.

In a society where the types of permissible extracurricular activites are rather limited, telling stories of this sort is an important activity. Exchanging such stories after the evening *seder* (session) has ended at 10:00 P.M. is a staple of life in the yeshiva.

The fabric of life in the yeshiva becomes clearer when we look at the issues discussed by students among themselves. Such discussions usually revolve around aspects of the learning process, tenets of the faith, or personalities in the yeshiva. To the insider it is an exciting and highly stimulating world. A student will say to his friend: "I just saw this new *sefer* [religious work]; it has fantastic interpretations on *Kesuboth* [a tractate in the Talmud], things we never thought of. You gotta get it!" One student may say to another, "My *rosh yeshiva* says listening to this record is *assur* [forbidden] because of some of the thoughts expressed by the singer," and this will generate discussion about what is and is not permitted in this area. Sometimes students will discuss conflicting views of different *rosh yeshivas,* or news about where they stay for the summer, or what they do in general. Sometimes there will be gossip about why a *rebbe* resigned from his position at a certain school and what the political issues were. On other occasions people will talk about "success stories" in the yeshiva; "Naftoli Birnbaum*—remember what a lazy guy he was in our class at Chaim Berlin? Well, he went to Telz and now he's the smartest guy there." Students will on occasion discuss politics and general developments in American society, but even there the topics are likely to be limited. Students are more apt to talk about the government in Israel than about the current American administration.

Students are sometimes even more critical of the yeshiva than those in authority assume. Once, during lunch at a yeshiva, a boy expressed his views about a teacher in the institution:

> STUDENT: I've heard some really terrible things about Rabbi Levy's* *shiur.* Sometimes he'll let you say the wrong *pshat* [simple translation of the talmudic text] as long as your logical thinking is good even if he knows there is a *Maharsha* [the name of a well-known talmudic commentator] whose explanation clearly proves the incorrectness of what you're saying.
>
> WH: Why is that so terrible?
>
> STUDENT: Because then you might repeat it to someone else! For example I know of someone in that class who told a wrong *pshat* to

Rabbi Savransky* and he took him down about ten steps [severely criticized him] for it, saying: "How can you say such a thing?" Imagine that!

At this point, others at the table murmured their agreement. Such matters are of great concern and interest in the yeshiva. Yet conversations with administrators revealed little awareness of the extent of the students' concern over such issues.

Issues dealing with religious laws and how they are to be applied are often an important concern. Expressing such concern to the *rebbe* or *rosh yeshiva* is regarded as an indication of a young man's *"frumkeit"* (concern for proper adherence to the laws). To the outside world these problems may appear of minor importance but in light of the Orthodox viewpoint that every *mitzva* (commandment) is of equal value, proper application can assume great significance. Typical of such concerns are: What do you do if a strange woman sits down next to you in the subway, or if your female cousin insists on shaking your hand? What is the correct reponse if your aunt, who you know keeps a basically kosher home, offers you a cookie? Do you ask to see the ingredients of the cookie box? What do you do if your father, with whom you are spending the evening while on vacation, turns on the TV and for some reason you can't leave the room? Do you dare be disrespectful and tell him to turn if off? Many students look the other way when faced with such dilemmas, but many others take them very seriously indeed.

The intensity of such a lifestyle can exact a heavy toll on people, especially when they are undergoing at the same time the adjustment process that occurs between adolescence and adulthood. For some, who may have been unstable to begin with, the effects can be traumatic, and the yeshiva has often been criticized for not being sufficiently aware of such problems in students until it is too late. Some students do "crack up" under the strain. One student who has been studying in various advanced yeshivas for over sixteen years remarked:

I know from Torah Vodaas, Philly, Lakewood, at least nine or ten people who cracked up. You got guys who think they're *moshiach* [the Messiah]. You know what I think? Everybody knows that in yeshiva you're waiting for *moshiach*. You know if you could be *moshiach*, you've got it made. But what's really going on? These people are dying for some *hakoroh* [recognition]. Either because they're good and nobody recognizes them for that or because there are so many that are good that they just don't care about this guy. I mean the guy is walking around like this all day and sleeps with it and he eats his heart out inside. All of a sudden one day he has a nervous breakdown because he gets no recognition from anyone.

This comment touches on an issue that we will discuss later in greater detail (Chapter 10), the intense desire to be a great scholar, fostered by the yeshiva, and the reality that very few actually achieve such a state. This discrepancy between goals and realistic expectations is a serious problem for yeshivas, and some of its consequences are quite evident to the students. Many in the community feel that severe mental disorders, when they do develop, are only extreme manifestations of the general stress felt by many *bochorim* in this area.

Yeshiva students, while they may have particular affinities for their own institutions, see their schools as belonging to a larger constellation of similar institutions. This manifests itself not only in their conversations, but in the assumptions they make about members of other yeshivas. Each yeshiva has its own features, but the features that they have in common far outweigh the distinctions. Students from different schools, when meeting for the first time, immediately establish a strong bond once they learn that they have gone to one of the traditional yeshivas. They have an implicit understanding that they live in a world with similar values and standards of conduct. This is, to some extent, true of Orthodox Jews in general but among yeshiva students there is a further recognition of similar experiences in terms of study, social life, and specific goals. When the respondent quoted above talks about students at other yeshivas he does not identify these schools by their proper names. He says, "I know from Torah Vodaas, Philly, Lakewood," mentioning the first school by its name only because Brooklyn has more than one such yeshiva. To him what matters most about these cities is that yeshivas are located there.

A Time to Relax: From Pizza to Purim to Woodbourne, New York

Considering the constraints imposed by his tight schedule and the prohibitions imposed by the yeshiva, the average *bochur* has a rather surprising range of leisure-time activities.[27] Reading is a major source of pleasure for students. Quite a few yeshivas do not allow their students to read popular news magazines, or even the daily newspaper, arguing that they contain too much material of an "inappropriate" nature—that is, articles about, say, "the new morality," prostitution, drug use, and crime, and photographs of women in various suggestive poses. Over and above this is the feeling that even general news items are a waste of time. Typical of such attitudes was the following response by a student in Lakewood:

> STUDENT: I'm not of the opinion that newspapers are worthwhile reading. There's really nothing to read in them. Anything important I'll hear about.
>
> WH: When will you hear about it?
>
> STUDENT: Whenever. If there's a war in *Eretz Yisroel* [Israel], that's the important news that counts.

There is, however, a good deal of variation from yeshiva to yeshiva in this matter. Obviously, a student who does not live in the dormitory has far more opportunity to read secular books, magazines, and newspapers. Not only is he in greater contact with the outside world but the yeshiva has less control over his life. Interviews with commuting students at Rabbi Samson Raphael Hirsch Yeshiva in New York City's Washington Heights section revealed a pattern of leisure-time activity substantially different in almost every aspect from that prevalent in the out-of-town yeshivas. The following responses were representative of such views:

> WH: What sorts of things do you read?
>
> STUDENT: I personally don't subscribe to anything, but my parents, with whom I live, do. I read the *New York Times* a day late or sometimes *Time* or *Newsweek*. On *Shabbos* [the Sabbath] I'll read the *Jewish Press* or the *Jewish Observer*.
>
> WH: What about nonschool books?
>
> STUDENT: I don't get a chance to read much during the year. I read mostly during the summer. Basically when I read it's those with a Jewish theme. Like I read Chaim Potok's *My Name Is Asher Lev* and I read *The Boys from Brazil,* dealing with a Nazi.

Some boys will read books on non-Jewish themes (i.e., *The Godfather*) and some subscribe to magazines that address themselves to a special interest, such as *Popular Mechanics, Sports Il-*

lustrated, or magazines about chess. One student at Lakewood confessed to having, as he put it, a *taaveh* (weakness or desire) for books on psychology. The most popular magazine in the yeshiva community is the *Jewish Observer.* Published by the Agudath Israel of America, it contains articles on topics of interest to the Strictly Orthodox community, many of them dealing with yeshiva life: for example, the goals of yeshivas, their history, problems involved in reaching out to the nonobservant community. They are written almost exclusively by people affiliated in one way or another with the community, including prominent *rosh yeshivas.* On more than one occasion students compared it favorably with the *Jewish Press,* which is considered, on the whole, to be a publication of lesser quality.

There is a certain category of books referred to as *apikorsus* (heresy) that almost no student in the right-wing yeshivas will read. In its most obvious form, this refers to works of philosophy and religion that challenge fundamental beliefs of Orthodox Judaism. One former yeshiva student, who is currently a Ph.D. candidate in economics, reflected on what this meant in the yeshiva environment:

> I had so little contact with other ideas. Yet even if I had been exposed I would have dismissed it out of hand. Like I knew that Bertrand Russell made fun of religion and that he was a brilliant man. But even there it wasn't really a threat. I simply said that he didn't know what *Yiddishkeit* [Jewishness, in the religious sense] was all about.

"*Apikorsus*" is not limited to non-Jewish works. It includes anything written about Judaism that does not conform to Orthodox beliefs as defined by the yeshiva community. Rabbi Joseph Elias, a board member of the *Jewish Observer* and book reviewer for the magazine, will frequently reject a book on such grounds:

> B. Stadtler, *The Holocaust* . . . is meant as a history book for children but fails totally to convey the values of *Kiddush Hashem* [sanctifying God's name] with which we are concerned; there are many clichés—and a blunt statement that "rabbis and community leaders were no more or less human than other people."[28]

Well-known scholarly works such as Salo Baron's *A Social and Religious History of the Jews* and Heinrich Graetz's *History of the Jews* are similarly accused of "lacking in proper Torah *hashkofos* [perspectives].'' Once a book is so classified, almost no one in the community will even glance at it.

As a rule, students can leave the yeshiva for any length of time only after 10:00 P.M. or on Friday afternoon until the Sabbath begins at sundown. On evenings, especially Saturday night, students may go to a local kosher restaurant or kosher pizza shop for a welcome change from the monotony of institutional cooking. Such excursions also offer opportunities for socializing with students from other nearby yeshivas. Students generally avoid places where they are likely to encounter girls, at least in part because the school disapproves of such socializing. Thus, *bochorim* at the Chofetz Chaim Yeshiva in Queens currently patronize a pizza shop on nearby Queens Boulevard rather than similar shops in the neighboring Orthodox community of Kew Gardens Hills, partly because there is less mixing of the sexes at the former establishment.

At Rabbi Samson Raphael Hirsch Yeshiva, policies are somewhat more liberal.[29]

> WH: What do you do in your spare time?
>
> STUDENT: Sometimes during the week I go to Yeshiva University [Y.U.] for lunch.
>
> WH: Why there?
>
> STUDENT: It's a good meal. You can go to the pizza shop. Go to the game room at Y.U. and shoot some pool.

Such behavior as shooting pool is not approved of by the yeshiva, but because most students are commuters it has less power to regulate student activities. At the same time, yeshivas such as Chaim Berlin and Torah Vodaath, which also have large numbers of commuting students, tend to attract more right-wing students who are less likely to engage in such activities even were they to have the opportunity to do so.

Few yeshivas specifically prohibit their students from moviegoing, largely because they find it unnecessary to do so. It is assumed that a young man would not be likely to enter *beis medrash* at a right-wing yeshiva such as Lakewood or Telshe if he regarded moviegoing as an acceptable pastime. At some of the more liberal yeshivas, many students will go to the movies though they are likely to use discretion in what they see (i.e., they are likely to avoid films with explicit sexual scenes). Many yeshiva high schools specifically prohibit this activity, with the result that the *beis medrash bochur* has already been socialized not to go. Still, there are quite a few young men in right-wing institutions who violate this norm, especially during periods when they are away from the school, such as summertime. The extent to which this occurs is difficult to ascertain because students are often reluctant to confide in any but close friends, for fear of being looked down upon. Still, it does exist, and it is an indication of how difficult it is for the yeshivas to control the lives of their students in an open society. One student at Mesivta Tifereth Jerusalem stated:

> STUDENT: I go to movies because I don't see anything so terrible about it. It depends on what you see.
>
> WH: What wouldn't you see?
>
> STUDENT: I wouldn't go to an X-rated movie because it lacks plot and it's *schmutz* [dirt].

At one yeshiva in New York City where movies are frowned upon and where the *rosh yeshiva* speaks out against them, students queried estimated that almost half of their classmates saw an occasional movie.

Attitudes toward television are similar, although news and sports programs tend to make this a less criticized activity. Those who live on the grounds of the yeshiva can generally watch television only when they are home on vacation. Given their more cloistered existence, it is not surprising that they seemed on the whole to take a more negative view of watching television than the commuters who often came from homes where others in the family watch television.[30] Yet even this latter group felt guilty in doing so. David Goldschmidt* is a third-year college student who attends Rabbi Samson Raphael Hirsch Yeshiva. His father is a businessman with rather conservative views about modern society. Although he owns a set, the father has not watched television since it broke about two years before—a very positive development in his eyes. David shares his opinion:

> Television in my mind is really an addiction. You watch one show this week and then you want to see the continuation the next week. Or you see the previews—and before you know it, you're watching regularly. I feel guilty when I'm watching it, almost as though I'm doing something against

the law. Frankly, it's better not to have it in the first place.
Then you're not tempted.

His views were echoed by a commuting student at the Chaim
Berlin Yeshiva who does not attend college:

> I used to watch too much but then my *rebbe* pointed out to me
> how you could become like a zombie sitting in front of it.
> *Boruch hashem* [blessed be the Lord] now I've begun to see
> [realize] it and I don't watch nearly as much as I used to.

It is of interest that the number of adults with yeshiva backgrounds who neither own nor watch television is extremely high
relative to the general population. Only 66 percent of the Beth
David Yeshiva sample own a television set, compared to at least
97 percent in the larger society.[31] The figures with respect to
movie attendance among yeshiva alumni are also very low. Fifty-
three percent of the respondents reported that they attended
movies only "rarely or never," 33 percent did so several times a
year, and only 14 percent went once a month or more often.
These figures indicate that avoidance of such leisure-time activities continues long after the student has left the yeshiva.

A leisure-time activity that *is* permitted is listening to Jewish
records or tapes of Jewish music. It is not uncommon to hear
such music wafting through the halls of a yeshiva dormitory late
in the evening when the students have completed their daily
studies. On the other hand, listening to rock'n' roll, soul, country and western, and popular music in general is forbidden, because of the secular as well as sexual themes present in many of
the lyrics. This also falls into the category of unnecessary secular
activities.

Participant or spectator sports are also a permissible activity, and one that many *bochorim* pursue enthusiastically. It is not
at all unusual to see boys playing basketball or baseball in a
yeshiva schoolyard during the lunchtime break, though it is more
common at the high school than at the *beis medrash* level. In
Joseph Heller's recent novel *Good as Gold,* the protagonist, a
rather assimilated Jew, marvels at the sight of such high school
athletes:

> Returning . . . by way of Coney Island Avenue, he came
> upon a softball game in a schoolyard played by boys wearing
> *yarmulkes,* and he left the car to watch. Athletes in skullcaps?
> The school was a religious one, a yeshiva.[32]

In a community where so many activities are proscribed on religious grounds, sports is a quite noticeable exception. The participant runs no risk of meeting girls before marriage, seeing lewd pictures, or becoming involved in the drug culture. Even the argument that it takes time away from learning is at least partially offset by the belief that what keeps the body healthy will be good for the soul as well. Yeshivas do note in their catalogues and other literature the availability of various sports programs. Some even have modest gyms of their own or nearby facilities that they can use. But the amount of time the student can spend in active sports is limited to one half hour or less a day, plus, at some yeshivas, Friday afternoons. Since there is so little leisure time many students, especially those not athletically inclined, do not avail themselves of even these opportunities, using their time instead to pursue other interests. Thus the image of the yeshiva *bochur* as an unathletic, pale, and not very healthy young man is not entirely inaccurate.

Vacations afford opportunities for a variety of activities. The major breaks during the year coincide with the Succoth and Passover holidays, usually in October and April, respectively, and generally last from two to three weeks. Most dormitory students go home to spend the holiday with their families. Although they generally make an effort to continue Talmud study, even if only for an hour or two a day, they also pursue other activities that they cannot ordinarily squeeze into their busy schedules at the yeshiva—for example, excursions to parks, boating, bowling, and the like, and simply spending time with the family.

Such periods away from the school can sometimes have a latent function as well. They allow the young man and his family to view each other in a different light. The student, especially if he has been away from home for any length of time, tends to judge his parents and siblings by the standards of the yeshiva. This can lead to friction since even Orthodox parents often fail to measure up. It can also result in mistaken perceptions in another direction. For the student, vacation periods offer a chance to sleep late, turn off, and in general escape from the regimen of yeshiva life. Parents, however, judge their son on the basis of what they see. And they wonder, *Is this what I have been sacrificing for?* The parents will attempt to see how their son has changed while at the school. Has he become more of a *mensch* (person who has made something of himself)? Is he tolerant of others? Does he show concern and respect for his parents? And so on.

A number of students go to camp during the summer vacation period (see pp. 91–93). If the camp emphasizes study as well as rest and recreation, then it is essentially a limited sort of yeshiva with some sports activities mixed in. As already noted, most such camps are in New York's Catskill Mountains. In recent years a variety of stores have sprung up in the local communities to meet the needs of a clientele that has shifted from the Modern Orthodox Jews of the 1950s and 1960s to a more religious element, of which yeshiva *bochorim* are a part. The main center is the village of Woodbourne. On a Saturday night its four-block-long main street is packed with vacationers from the camps and bungalow colonies (to which many students also go with their families) in the surrounding area. There is a kosher pizza shop, four restaurants (all *glatt* kosher, of course), and a Judaica bookstore, which reflects the literary bent of its customers by staying open until past midnight. The town attracts both young men and women who are Strictly Orthodox, and this provides yeshiva students with a rare chance to converse with members of the opposite sex. Because of this social aspect quite a few camps have declared the village off-limits, though many students pay no heed to such edicts, hoping that their presence will go unnoticed or unremarked.

In the center of town is an amusement arcade, the "Lucky Dip," which also sells a variety of hot and cold kosher dairy products. This is the central gathering place for yeshiva *bochorim* who, along with adult members of the Orthodox community, avidly play the pinball machines, shoot pool, and try other games. The arcade is open until 3:00 A.M. on Saturday nights, an indication of its success in attracting large numbers of people. On the occasions when I met persons from the yeshiva community there, either alumni or students, they were uncomfortable at being seen. One older man, a prominent rabbi, claimed he was only watching the "*meshugaas*" (craziness) that went on there, though I later saw him playing a pinball machine. Those who frequent this establishment represent a small proportion of the total yeshiva population, but they indicate that even in the yeshiva world certain people must find outlets.

Not all students spend their summers away from home. Many stay in the city, perhaps helping in their father's business while maintaining a *seder* (program of study) with a friend from their yeshiva or a similar institution. Others may volunteer a good deal of time to collect money for the school. In such cases the yeshiva supplies them with a list of potential donors in their area, and they go from home to home making personal appeals to well-to-do members of the community. Occasionally, they may go away for a few days to vacation areas such as the Pennsylvania Dutch country or the Adirondacks, taking along the necessary kosher foods. Such trips are one of the few times where *bochorim* have opportunities, however superficial they may be, to interact with those living outside their own culture.

Besides breaks during the year, there are various special events which provide a change from the routine of yeshiva life. Weddings, the birth of a baby to one's *rebbe* or a married student, or a bar-mitzvah celebration for a relative are legitimate reasons for leaving one's studies. Weddings, in particular, are very lively affairs with much singing and dancing, giving the yeshiva *bochur* a legitimate opportunity to rejoice and let go. As in the larger society, such religious ceremonies reinforce group solidarity and the sense of belonging.[33]

One of the most important events of the year is the annual convention of the Agudath Israel of America. The three-day convention features speeches by well-known leaders and scholars in the community, including most of the leading *rosh yeshivas*. The atmosphere is serious and purposeful, as reflected by the topics discussed at the various panels that are held. The 1979 convention included a symposium on "The New Immigrants: What Are Our Obligations?", referring to Russian and Iranian Jews, along with their coreligionists from other Near Eastern countries. Another topic was "Applying Torah Standards to Everyday Life: Home and Community; Business and Professions."

Over 4,000 people, including hundreds of yeshiva students, attend the convention, a very large figure considering both the size of the community and the ability of other groups within the Orthodox community to attract participants. For example, the annual convention of the Union of Orthodox Jewish Congregations, a group that appeals more to the Orthodox Jewish community in general, draws hundreds but certainly not thousands. This disparity may be due, in part, to the fact that the Strictly Orthodox have fewer social outlets, for the Agudah convention is as much a social as a religious event. While hundreds sit listening to educators, administrators, and community leaders expound on various subjects, hundreds more mill about outside, sometimes because they cannot obtain seats but also because the convention gives them an opportunity to renew old friendships and make new ones. Held in Rye, New York, only a forty-five-minute drive from New York City, the meetings attract large numbers of people who do not stay at the hotel, and many Strictly Orthodox Jews who are not in the yeshiva community but simply form part of the larger support system for the yeshivas. The convention itself serves as a forum for the entire community, one in which issues of importance to it are brought up, debated, and sometimes resolved.

Visits to the yeshiva by prominent figures constitute yet another break in the daily program. These are not extracurricular activities since the talks these visitors give usually deal with intellectual topics studied by the students as part of the curriculum. It may be useful to recount one such visit by the head of the Telshe Yeshiva, Rabbi Mordechai Gifter, at the school in which I had enrolled.

There was a strong sense of anticipation in the air on the appointed day. Several changes were immediately visible. The yeshiva library, a rather modest, one-room affair, was immaculate, with all the books on the shelves in perfect order and the chairs neatly pushed in at the tables. The dormitory was spotless as well. Everyone had been told that Rabbi Gifter might come into the room to observe the class, and there was a feeling of tension as the *rebbe* began speaking. We were discussing a point in the Talmud when the door opened rather suddenly and Rabbi Gifter walked in, accompanied by the dean of students and the executive director. Everyone sprang to his feet to show respect as the renowned *rosh yeshiva* strode briskly to the front of the room.

"*Sholom aleichem!* [Peace be unto you!] Please sit down," he said. We all sank into our chairs as I thought to myself: *Who will be asked to read?* I did not have long to wait. "Yerachmiel, read the *Tosfos* [a commentary on the Talmud]," said the *rebbe*. Yerachmiel, who was probably the best student in the class, began reading in a slightly quavering voice. After about two minutes he suddenly began to falter, and I found my own heart beating a little faster, out of sympathy or shared nervousness. Miraculously, it seemed to me, he got out of trouble and continued reading, sounding more like the self-confident young man I had come to know.

A discussion developed with some of the students participating. Yerachmiel asked a question which the *rebbe* began to answer in a matter-of-fact manner. Suddenly Rabbi Gifter's voice rang out: "He's asking a terrific question. This case here is an example of how we establish the truth of what the individual is saying." We all turned to stare at the *rosh yeshiva,* surprised by his active participation in the discussion. The *rebbe* began to demur, saying that he did not believe this was the gist of Yerachmiel's question. "Well," responded Rabbi Gifter jestingly, "that's what he *seems* to be saying. Whether he knows what he's talking about is another matter." Eventually, the *rebbe* inquired if that was what Yerachmiel meant to ask. "No," he said reluctantly in a soft tone, but his answer was partially lost in the confusion, and I was not certain that Rabbi Gifter had heard him. When, after several moments of back-and-forth debate, the discussion moved on to a new aspect, Rabbi Gifter got up and, as he was leaving, remarked: "When my grandfather, *olov hasholom* [may his memory be blessed] heard such a question in class, he said it was a great question. Be well and continue learning!" Everyone rose again as he left and, as the door closed behind him, the class breathed a collective sigh of relief.

"Why didn't you make it clear right away that this wasn't your *kashe* [question]?" asked one of the *bochorim.* "Because," responded Yerachmiel, "if Rav Gifter sees a great question hidden inside my question, then why should I deny it?" We all burst out laughing (including the *rebbe*).

Following class I went into the dining room, where everyone seemed to be talking about Rabbi Gifter's visit—"Do you know what happened when he came into our class? Well, Shimon [a student in the class] asked a real hard *kashe,* and when the rebbe answered him . . ." One student observed somewhat cynically: "Look . . . to him this is all a game. I mean, he knows the *Gemora* inside out. He can see flaws in almost everything you guys would ask. Let's not blow the whole thing out of proportion. We're just novices." The others accused him of being a spoilsport and went on talking in animated tones, relishing the experience as they told each other of what had happened in their respective classes.

In their catalogues and other literature describing the institutions, most yeshivas define the holidays that occur while school is in session as extracurricular activities that are nonetheless integral features of life in the institution. This is true because, although the celebration of such holidays is not part of the daily schedule, they are a crucial part of the yeshiva experience for most youths. Each holiday has its rhythm and cadence, its own special attraction for the students. There is, for example, the spirit of learning that characterizes *Shavuoth,* which, among other things, marks the giving of the Torah. As is customary among Orthodox Jews in general, students stay up until the wee hours of the morning to study Torah, with many poring over the Talmud until dawn, when services are held. Only then—about 7:30 A.M.—do they go to sleep.

Of all the holidays, Purim, commemorating the deliverance of the Jews from the Persian vizier Haman, is the most memorable. Within the walls of the yeshiva it occupies a special place that far transcends the religious significance of the holiday, a rather minor one compared to Succoth or Passover. The focus on the central activity of the yeshiva, namely study, tends to obscure the youthfulness of this population and their need to let go occasionally. Purim serves as a mechanism for the fulfillment of this objective.

In the evening, after the Purim story has been read before the entire school in the *beis medrash,* bottles of whiskey and wine appear almost magically, and the festivities begin. Tables and chairs are pushed aside and an area is cleared for dancing. The students and their *rebbes* form circles, whirling around to the accompaniment of music, usually played on an accordion or guitar. Inside the circle students do *kazatskas* (a Russian dance) while balancing bottles on their heads. One young man may hold a handkerchief in front of another student's face, while the latter pretends to be a charging bull trying to attack a bullfighter. The room becomes crowded as more and more join in the festivities, and presently a line of revelers leaves the *beis medrash* and snakes through the halls of the yeshiva singing and dancing. At some point during the evening each class will go to the home of its teacher, where they will hear "Purim Torah" presented by the *rebbe* and fellow students. This is a satirical presentation that parodies (within limits) that which is taken seriously throughout the year. For example, the students may offer novel interpretations that "prove" the relationship between the *rebbe*'s age and the expected arrival of the Messiah. Others will add up the numerical value of words in the Talmud and use it to explain why the food in the yeshiva is so terrible. While they are generally abstainers, the *bochorim* do their best on this occasion literally to fulfill the rabbinic injunction of drinking so much that they are unable to distinguish between the Hebrew phrases "cursed be Haman" (the villain of the story) and "blessed be Mordechai," the hero of the historical event on which the holiday is based.

The high point is reached late that evening or the following day when the students put on a play lampooning the institution, its faculty, and the facilities. No one is spared. Student spies who inform the administration about wrongdoers are roasted. The quirks and failings of the various *rebbes* and even of the *rosh yeshiva*, generally the most revered figure in the institution, come in for some kidding in original lyrics set to familiar Hebrew tunes, through satire, imitations, the recitation of poems and telling of stories, plus the costumes worn by the students themselves. The faculty eagerly attend, curious to known how they are truly perceived by their disciples. Even if they are hurt by an unflattering portrayal, they must feign amusement or at least unconcern, for almost anything goes on this day.

We have, in this chapter, tried to provide a glimpse into the social world of the yeshiva student. It is a complex and multifaceted world with a unique set of values, norms, and expectations. The ways in which people in this community relate to one another are not entirely clear but it is obvious that they share a world view that sees the rest of society as quite different.

The reader may have noticed that no mention has been made of how the yeshiva student relates to outsiders. This is no accident, for there is very little interaction between members of the yeshiva culture and those who are not a part of it, except on the most superficial level. Why this is so and its consequences will be discussed in a later chapter. Here we simply indicate that the insularity of the yeshiva community is part of its general philosophy, and that its effects are especially noticeable in the attitudes and lifestyles adopted by its members when they leave the protective environment of the institution to make their way in the world.

CHAPTER 7

Making It
in the Yeshiva

Every community has its pecking order, and the yeshiva is no exception. Why some people are looked up to in the yeshiva and others are not is a complex issue that could easily be the subject of a separate study. To begin with, there are considerable variations from institution to institution; some emphasize character development and others intellectual attainment. Within each yeshiva there are those on the faculty and in the administration who are impressed more by a student's intuitive grasp of abstract concepts, while others give greater credit to the *bochur* who makes up in effort what he lacks in ability. Similarly, among the students there is no unanimity about who is looked up to, although there is general agreement concerning what criteria are of importance. Certain criteria seen as important by teachers are given little attention by the students, and vice versa.

Bearing in mind the wide variation possible from school to school and among those persons constituting the community, I want to present some of the *general* criteria by which people in the yeshiva are judged, and to discuss in preliminary fashion some of the consequences of such status within the institution. Although my investigations do not permit definitive conclusions, what follows should at least suggest some further lines of inquiry. The fact that the yeshiva is an institution with a rather fixed authority structure, one that emphasizes conformity over individuality and whose members are in basic agreement with its general goals, makes it easier to generalize from what we know about it. When sociologists use the word "status" they refer either to a socially defined position in a community (i.e., *rebbe*, executive director, advanced student), or to a person's prestige.[1] In this case the focus will be on the latter as we try to understand what and who counts in the yeshiva.

"He's a Genius"

All those enrolled in the yeshiva have at least one status, that of student, upon their entry. Before long, however, they acquire reputations as good, average, or poor students in the academic sense; as fine or not so fine persons; as "nice guys," "bums," and so on. Generally speaking, the highest status among the students in the yeshiva is accorded to those who "learn well," the term of praise used to describe a student who studies hard and has a thorough understanding of the material. The teachers, with a few exceptions, also seem to place this attribute ahead of all others, including ethical behavior (*middos*), although most *rebbes,* when asked, would probably respond that being a "good person" is of greater importance than talmudic erudition.

The significance of learning is readily apparent from the almost exclusive focus on study throughout the entire day. Those students who do not attend college at all are generally accorded higher status than those who do. Not attending is viewed as a sign of one's *hasmodoh* (dedication to Talmud study). This dichotomy is most apparent where practice with regard to college attendance varies widely among those in a particular institution, with some going two, three or four evenings a week and others not at all. Nevertheless, while diligence in one's studies is highly valued, the brilliant student receives even greater recognition. It is common for both students and teachers to describe others in terms such as "He's a genius"; "He really knows how to learn"; or "This *rebbe*'s class is very deep." This is so important a criterion that students will sometimes go to great lengths to persuade others of their mental prowess.

An example of this sort of "impression management," as Goffman calls it,[2] occurred with one of my learning partners. The fellow had been in the yeshiva for only a short time and gave the impression that he had a limited talmudic background. Yet he seemed very knowledgeable and often complained that the pace in the class was too slow for him. Over a period of time it became clear that he had not only studied extensively at other yeshivas prior to his arrival but was quite familiar with the tractate being studied, having been exposed to it previously at another school. He had apparently played down his previous experience because of a desire to gain a reputation as a really bright fellow among both his peers and teachers. The following observations made by a twenty-two-year-old student at Ner Israel Yeshiva indicate both awareness and concern about status:

> When I came here I found out there were two ways to be recognized, to make it. One, *of course* [emphasis added], was to get in on your smartness—and when I mean recognized, I mean dealt with on a personal level by either your *rebbe* or the *kollel* guys [older, married students whose place in the hierarchy is just below that of the faculty]. Then your name goes around on a grapevine. The other way is to do something very *shticky* [cool or idiosyncratic]. If you catch on, then you're liked, there's something about you that's very special, that stands you out, which is basically the *pshat* [literally, explanation, but as used here it means "the way it is"] in a competitive society.

These comments were made in the presence of five other students, none of whom disagreed with the assessment.

The value placed on doing something "*shticky*" may be due, in part, to the lack of emphasis on individuality in the yeshiva. Being "*shticky*" may range from wearing a special sort of hat (within the bounds of propriety, of course) to using certain pet expressions which for one reason or another catch on and become a way of showing that one is "in" or "hip."[3] Certain phrases and forms of expression become associated with different yeshivas to the point where former and current students can relate to each other through a common frame of reference. For example, at one school, the meat served in the institution has been called "slabs" for over twenty-five years!

A student who helps others in their efforts to understand the material derives a certain degree of status from them independent of his intellectual virtuosity. On occasion, however, students will be motivated to help others as a way of demonstrating and verifying their own abilities, both to the recipients of such aid and to their own peers and teachers.

Character and Religiosity

A second major determinant of status is character (*middos*). There are several hundred laws in the Bible governing how one ought to act toward one's fellow man. Thus, a person who is considerate of others fulfills a religious precept as well as one judged important by general standards of human interaction. People in the yeshiva will often characterize someone by saying, "He's a great *baal middos* [literally, master of ethical behavior]." The degree of respect accorded such individuals varies. At schools such as the Chofetz Chaim Yeshiva and the Rabbi Samson Raphael Hirsch Yeshiva, which have a tradition of emphasizing this area, it matters a great deal. Conversations with members of both institutions confirmed that such attitudes are ingrained in the minds of the students:

> The main thing in this yeshiva among most of the *bochorim* is the person who's sincere and friendly and honest and gets along nicely with people. The ones looked up to are also those who manage to learn without using the "*frumer shtick*" [religious oneupsmanship], like: "Don't ask me to clean up the *seforim* [books] in the *beis medrash* because it's going to take away time from my learning." Or, they'll say: "Don't ask me anything except about learning because I'm too busy to bother with nonsense."
>
> A twenty-one-year-old student at the
> Rabbi Samson Raphael Hirsch
> Yeshiva (Breuer's Yeshiva)

An individual who is intellectually well endowed but who is a braggart may find his abilities disparaged in retaliation for such behavior:

> There's one guy who went to Cleveland [the Telshe Yeshiva] for a year. He knows how to learn well but he's really obnoxious. He's a *baal gaavanik* [conceited] and he always talks *chutzpadic* [in a disrespectful manner]. He hardly gets along with anyone. In the morning he learns with the older guys. He tries to make out like he's one of those big learners. But he's not that brilliant.
>
> A twenty-year-old student at
> Breuer's Yeshiva

Modesty and the avoidance of gossip (*loshon hora*) are key virtues, partly because they are difficult to adhere to. This is especially true in the yeshiva, where one's abilities are on almost constant display in the classroom and in the *beis medrash* and where the limited options for free time activity plus institutional insularity make talking about others a favorite pastime.

A certain degree of status can sometimes accrue to one who is extremely religious. Nevertheless, since being quite religious is a prerequisite for membership in the yeshiva community, only extreme displays are likely to draw attention. Thus, a bochur who takes twenty minutes to say a prayer that others recite in ten or fifteen minutes will attract attention. He may also make the others uncomfortable, for it is an implicit statement about the devotional level of the individual as compared to that of his peers. Still, when seen as sincere, it will rarely evoke criticism. Such behavior is perfectly acceptable when it comes from someone who is generally perceived to be on a higher plane, such as a *rebbe*. In fact, it is almost expected that the teachers in the school will spend more time saying their prayers than the students, an expectation that is usually fulfilled.[4]

There are other ways of demonstrating religiosity. A young man may wear ritual fringes (*tzitzit*) that are very large or sleep all night in a *succah* (branch-covered hut) on the festival of Succoth rather than simply have his meals there. More often than not, his religiosity will be evaluated as part of his overall personality. Others will take note of his sincerity in areas other than rituals—that is, is he as careful not to speak ill of others as he is in ritual aspects of the faith?

The "All-Around Guy" and the *Meshoress*

Another source of status is a reputation of the student as an "all-around guy." This is usually synonymous with ability in sports. Interestingly, the *bochorim* may look up to a teacher who has a reputation for such skills. One can speculate that a *rebbe*'s reputation for proficiency in this area is a double-edged sword. While it reduces social distance between teacher and student, the *rebbe* must insure that this does not result in a loss of respect on the part of the students. Whether or not this will be an important basis for status in either direction depends on both the individual and the school. In general, the more liberal the institution the more significant such criteria. Thus, a student at a New York

City yeshiva, where most of the students attend college and where the enforcement of regulations relating to dating and seeing movies is lax, said:

> I play basketball, so I'm always arranging the games and everything. But it isn't just me. Guys who are good ballplayers are admired by the other guys because it's something they'd like to be good at. Yet it isn't only that. If a guy has a good sense of humor, if he's an okay guy, not a squealer, these things count too.

Students at the more right-wing yeshivas asserted that such characteristics, especially ability as a ballplayer, were, by and large, rather irrelevant.

There are also students who fall into the category of *meshoress* (literally, he who serves). This refers to individuals who act as aides to either the *rebbe* or the *rosh yeshiva,* driving them to weddings, important meetings, and so on. If the man they serve is ill, it can involve giving him his pills or preparing his meals when he is away from home. Their role also includes shielding the person from unnecessary or unimportant matters. This is especially true in the case of the head of the institution who is often besieged by persons wanting to see him, each of whom insists his matter deserves the highest priority.

Students who function in this capacity are not necessarily the best students. In fact, it is sometimes because they are not such good students that they gravitate to this area. Often, they also have a gift for administrative detail. Some *rosh yeshivas* are literally surrounded by a phalanx of such individuals, some of whom are students and others who work in this capacity on a formal basis and are paid for their services. Tension may develop among the various persons who carry out such tasks as they jockey for a position that will make them more powerful. Power, in this case, usually means having the *rosh yeshiva*'s ear on certain matters and controlling who gets to see him and who does not.

Wealth and the "Right" Family: Does It Matter?

Most yeshivas are hard pressed for funds. They are therefore open to pressure from wealthy parents who want their son to be admitted. Schools in poor financial shape will have more students who might not pass muster were it not for substantial contributions made by their families. This situation has, however, improved tremendously in the past twenty years or so. Formerly, yeshivas could ill afford to turn *anyone* away. Today, a young man might be admitted to certain institutions under such circumstances, but he would probably be asked to leave if he became a disruptive force affecting morale in the school. On the other hand, family wealth counts for little among the students in what is, after all is said and done, very much a meritocracy. Such students often become the subject of unfavorable remarks:

> Now you take Asher. He's a real "bum." He doesn't learn; he doesn't come to *minyan,* goes to movies and look at the way he dresses—flashy shirt, tight pants. I mean, he doesn't belong here. But this is a poor yeshiva, and you have to let him stay here for a little while. His father's on the board. It's just a shame he had to have a son like that. You know, this is his third yeshiva in three years.[5]

Needless to say, "bums" without money or family lineage fare rather poorly in the yeshiva community.

In Chapter 3 it was pointed out that *rosh yeshivas* are frequently from distinguished rabbinical and scholarly families. Such criteria are often applied to students as well, who may, in fact, one day occupy positions of importance in the yeshiva world partly, though not solely, because of their family backgrounds. In the yeshiva community, membership in such families gives the bearer a certain degree of prestige. First, it implies that a student from such a family has had the benefit of highly desirable role models. If his father is a *rosh yeshiva,* for example, he has presumably been socialized into the values and norms of yeshiva life at an early age and has presumably profited from such exposure. On a more subtle level, it is assumed that there is a better than even chance that some of the family's talents in scholarship have been genetically passed on to its descendants. Success on the part of such individuals may be noticed more rapidly, with credit being given to the family lineage. ("What do you expect? He's a Soloveitchik.")

Sometimes, as in the case of a not-so-talented student, membership in a distinguished family can be a liability. A young man of average capability may feel tremendous pressure to be outstanding. In some cases, the matter is resolved by sending the *bochur* to a yeshiva other than the one with which his family is connected. This is often considered a good idea, even in cases where the student is quite talented since it gives him the opportunity to grow independent of other factors.

As indicated previously, learning is more highly prized than money and family prestige.[6] Yet, as the following remarks by a former student at a New York City yeshiva suggest, the last two can and sometimes do tip the scale:

> STUDENT: One of the things that bothered me for a very long time is that it was a very prestige-conscious world. There was very little learning *lishmo* [for the name of God and for no "practical" reason]. It didn't bother me in the areas I was good in, like learning, but in the areas I was weak in. For example, I didn't have *yichus* [family prestige]. I always felt bad because my father was a nobody. He was just a salesman. And you would see how the *rosh yeshiva* would talk to other guys, guys whose fathers were *rosh yeshivas*, more than to me. *They would get better dates* [with girls]. I was considered good but not top material. Rich guys were also respected.
>
> WH: Who was respected most?
>
> STUDENT: Learning came first. Then money and family. I remember one fellow though. He learned exceptionally well. He got the best. Certainly it wasn't a pure world. There was a lot of jealousy. It's not heaven after all. I expected it to be better but there are rivalries and jealousies in the academic world too.

The above respondent mentions that those with higher status were rewarded by getting better dates. This brings us to the question of the consequences of status in the yeshiva. Having considered the basis for status in the community, it is appropriate that we turn our attention to the rewards resulting from high position in the community as well as some of the negative outcomes that are part of the system.

Some Results of Status

By way of introduction, it may be useful to begin with an examination of clique formation among yeshiva students. The group a person belongs to may be an outcome as well as a predictor of his status. Thus, good *bochorim* may become friends with others who are already good students or they may be motivated to become good students because they belong to such a group and are influenced by its values. For example, student A comes from Memphis, Tennessee, to an eastern yeshiva where there are six other students from Memphis of about the same age, all of them good students. Student A is slightly above average, although he has a propensity for fooling around occasionally. Upon arriving, he encounters students B and C who were close friends of his from childhood days. They introduce him to the others from Memphis, who knew him only slightly at home but now consider their common origins of great significance in an environment of young men from every part of the country. Accepted by a group in an unfamiliar setting, student A tries his best to fit in, adopting the norms and values of those closest to him. In addition, he is perceived as a "good guy" at the outset by others merely by association and may be referred to as one of "the Memphis contingent." In this way, membership in a group may encourage a person to act in a status-raising manner while at the same time conferring status upon him.

Student D comes from a small town in Minnesota where his father is the local rabbi. He has been sent to the same eastern yeshiva because his father knows the *rosh yeshiva* from the old days in Europe. He arrives with no reputation and no friends. A studious young man, student D throws himself into his work. Fortunately, his teacher notices his diligence and not inconsiderable mental abilities early in the term. He matches him with one of the best students in the class, one who has numerous friends in the institution, partly as a result of having been there since high school days. The two *bochorim* hit it off almost immediately and, as a result, student D is introduced to his learning partner's circle of friends, who are also excellent students. These young men become his friends too. In this instance group membership confers status. It differs from the first instance in that achievement in a key area preceded acceptance. Both examples illustrate the interplay between the sources and consequences of status.

These factors operate in similar fashion among poor students. Someone who does not adjust well to the yeshiva regimen is likely to find himself limited to friends of similar bent. On the other hand, the poor student may prefer their company because he has more in common with them. Nevertheless, membership in such a group both affirms his status in the institution and at the same time denies him many of the benefits accruing from high position.

Cliques often form on the basis of who one's roommates are. Thus friendship may have nothing to do with considerations mentioned earlier. Room assignments are sometimes made because the dormitory supervisor feels particular individuals will have something in common. In other instances, such decisions may be motivated by the supervisor's hope that an excellent student in a room with those who are not studious may positively influence them. Whatever the case, it is generally recognized that one has a responsibility toward one's roommates that transcends personal preferences. As Thomas Blass notes in his study of the social structure of a yeshiva: "Demands were made on roommates that would not be made on others. A student expected his roommate to lend him money when the need arose. When a student became sick, his roommates felt obligated to bring him his meals."[7] Over a period of time, a student comes to identify closely with his roommates who often become his confidants and who play a significant role in his development at the yeshiva.

Because one can belong to different groups within the institution, situations can arise where the student experiences a certain degree of role conflict.[8] A student may have a friend from his local community who is performing poorly in the yeshiva, while he is friends with certain students who, like himself, are very studious. The desire to retain his old friendship may result in diminished esteem from his newer friends. Similarly, an individual's roommates may violate certain rules of the institution such as listening to the radio. His membership in a small circle of friends who study privately on an extracurricular basis with the dean of men may cause him great discomfort, especially when the dean tells him that there is a problem involving radios in the dormitory.[8]

Being a good student can bring about a number of rewards. Some yeshivas have journals in which scholarly articles by students (*chiddushim*) are published. Publication is considered a great honor. Good work also results in promotion, in itself a tangible mark of achievement. In the classroom setting, a good student may have his status acknowledged by being called on to read a particularly difficult portion in the text. Sometimes

criticism is an indication of high status. As a member of the class
to which I belonged as a participant observer explained to me:

> The fact that the *rebbe* puts him down doesn't mean that he's
> asking the wrong questions. It just means that he can take
> being put down more. If you're handled gingerly it may well
> mean that the *rebbe* doesn't feel you're ready yet for rougher
> treatment.

Within the system students carefully observe how the
teacher relates to each of their peers. Relationships between good
students and the *rebbe* are usually more relaxed. In addition, the
rebbe may invite the better students to his home more frequently.
Among the students high status can result in being asked for help
by others, and receiving certain honors in the synagogue. Finally, minor infractions, such as coming late to services, are
more likely to be overlooked if the student learns well. Even a
major violation will not result in as severe a punishment for a student whose behavior is otherwise exemplary as it would for one
who is seen as a so-so student.

Special treatment for various students may bring about resentment in others, particularly when it is accorded on the basis
of inherited rather than achieved status. Thus, one young man in
an out-of-town yeshiva voiced the following bitter complaint:

> There's a lot of politics. Like we were leaving for vacation
> and I was supposed to leave early. The *mashgiach* found out
> about it. So what did he do? He screamed at me and said it's
> not fair that I should be allowed to leave one day before the
> New York guys do. On the other hand, there's one kid
> who's loaded; he's got a stereo and a gorgeous car—I think
> it's a Cadillac—and he gets away with it.

As indicated earlier, differential treatment on such a basis varies
greatly from one school to another. It is a potential source of
trouble in maintaining morale and high motivation.

Competitiveness in the Yeshiva:
Pros and Cons

Dispensing privileges to those who study well is a different
matter, for the yeshiva can justify its actions as based on a desire
to provide incentive for others to do better work. Yet, when such

privileges are given out because of a student's accomplishments rather than his efforts, it can have negative effects, for not everyone is similarly equipped to compete successfully in the yeshiva world. Meir Wikler, a social worker who counsels yeshiva students, often at the request of the institutions themselves, had this to say when asked about the problems confronting the "average student":

> Because of the emphasis on producing an elite there is a tremendous pressure on performance and achievement. Yet the blessing we make on the study of Torah is *laasok bedivrei Torah* [to be involved in the study of Torah], regardless of the outcome. Thus the message is not supposed to be how much Torah you know, but how hard you try to learn. Sometimes others around him will say, "You really try. That's great." But the one who is really praised is the one that *chaps* [stumps] the *rosh yeshiva.*[9]

Defenders of the system have argued that competitiveness makes the student try harder. One former *rebbe* said: "If you try to be Mickey Mantle you'll at least be Hector Lopez." He claims that the teachers often pay attention to "so-called average students" by helping them realize potential they may not believe they have. This *rebbe* does not touch on the question of what happens to those who simply do not have such potential, answering such a query with "It's a difficult problem." Wikler agrees that the yeshiva makes strong efforts to reach everyone but argues that they do not proceed in a professional manner:

> It's not that they ignore the average *bochur.* They don't. What they do is they make him feel he's missed the mark, that he's failed. They do this by making it clear that the overall goal is to be *boki beTorah* [very knowledgeable in the Torah]. When a student gets a C he really feels that he failed. It would be better to say: "Try your best, and if you do, you'll get an A." I'm not saying that's easy to do. In elementary schools, where there is more emphasis on pedagogical expertise and training . . . they have ways of rewarding children for their efforts, for making a child feel good about his work.[10]

It may seem reasonable to ask why the student who cannot compete successfully does not simply leave. This is, however, not an easy matter, as Wikler points out:

> They stay because the insular nature of a yeshiva places a
> stigma on anyone who leaves. You may have no status in the
> yeshiva because you're an ignoramus . . . but you're made
> to feel that you're one of the in-crowd because you're there,
> and once you leave, you've lost even that.[11]

The value of being in the "in-crowd" should not be
underestimated. As we saw earlier, the average yeshiva student
has been socialized into this world from an early age, a process
which virtually excludes consideration of other ways of life. His
parents, teachers, friends, and relatives have shaped his perceptions of the yeshiva community as *the* place to be and of superior
learning skills as the highest attainment possible. It is not easy for
him to turn his back on such a world for he has little preparation
or even inclination for another way of life. Moreover, as noted by
Wikler, this is a world that offers certain psychic benefits ir-
respective of one's location within its status hierarchy. Leonard
Topp, a psychologist and ordained rabbi who attended the Rabbi
Jacob Joseph Yeshiva for many years, attempted to express what
was essentially an emotional feeling about membership in the
community:

> You couldn't get this anywhere. The *kovod* [honor] that you
> got from learning in a yeshiva. There was just a total aura in
> some sense.[12]

This "aura" comes both from the yeshiva itself, which inculcates pride in its students by instilling in them the conviction
that they belong to an elite group, and from the community
which gives respect to yeshiva students. A student need only
mention to other Orthodox Jews that he attends an advanced
yeshiva to be respected. This is especially true for top-ranked
schools such as Lakewood and Telshe. Not only do the students
benefit, but their parents and friends receive reflected prestige.

The long-range effects of yeshiva life on the individual will
be assessed later on. It is, nonetheless, relevant to point out that
those who do succeed in the yeshiva sometimes find adjustment
to the outside world difficult because the very criteria by which
such success was judged do not apply beyond the yeshiva. Thus,
a person who has enjoyed high status because he is a talmudic
scholar may find that his colleagues in the clothing industry are
not in the slightest bit impressed by what they regard as a non-
marketable skill. His status in an accounting firm will depend

upon the clients he brings in and how he handles them, not in whether he was one of the best students in his *rosh yeshiva*'s class. Such status loss often comes as a rude shock to the recent alumnus and the adjustment can be painful. The situation is probably exacerbated by the fact that the competitive nature of his yeshiva experience may cause the young man to place great importance on success in general.

What can be done to alleviate such problems? If, as some maintain, competitiveness is a necessary element in developing outstanding scholars and community leaders, it would seem that there should at least be a stronger recognition that, notwithstanding differences in ability, all are working toward a common goal of understanding the material and that this must be a cooperative process. It is, nevertheless, utopian to believe that all students are capable of demonstrating such selflessness of purpose in these endeavors. Moreover there will be those, as we have indicated, who simply lack a certain degree of ability, no matter how hard they try. To satisfy *their* needs, the yeshiva must confer status in both tangible and intangible ways on those who exhibit a high level of ethical conduct and who try their best to comprehend the talmudic texts.

Whether or not a student "succeeds" in the yeshiva may have as much to do with his attitudes toward success as with the view of the particular yeshiva. Social worker Yaakov Salomon emphasized the role of the individual in discussing his own yeshiva experience:

> The people who cope best are those that sort out other areas for competing. It wasn't "If you can't beat em, join em," but, "If you can't join em, go someplace else." [within the yeshiva]. Guys used to stand out in different ways. One guy became the expert in *mussar* (ethics). He couldn't learn so well, so that's what he did. Another person who couldn't learn that well would try to hang around with the high school guys to influence them. One became a *gabbai* [the one who takes care of administrative duties in the synagogue] in the *beis medrash*.[13]

There are many possible roles for students in the yeshiva, and the degree to which students can adjust to their strengths and weaknesses plus the willingness of the school to aid them in doing so will ultimately determine the success of both.

CHAPTER 8

"Out on the Next Bus": Deviance in the Yeshiva

Imagine a society of saints, a perfect cloister of exemplary individuals. Crimes, properly so called, will there be unknown; but faults which appear venial to the layman will create there the same scandal that the ordinary offense does in ordinary consciousness. If then the society has the power to judge and to punish, it will define these acts as criminal and treat them as such.[1]

Emile Durkheim, 1895

THE IMAGE OF THE YESHIVA as a place where all fit into a mold ordained by the school administration is incorrect. In almost all societies there is some deviance, and the yeshiva is no exception. Measuring this is difficult because those who break the rules are not, for obvious reasons, always willing to talk about their activities.

When sociologists use the term "deviance," they mean behavior that does not conform to the expectations of society. This can mean many different things depending on what segment of society is making the judgment.[2] To those in the yeshiva community, refusing to shake hands with a woman to whom one is not married is not only perfectly acceptable but is expected; outsiders, however, may think such behavior strange. Conversely, bringing a television set into a dormitory is likely to be viewed as a deviant act in all but the most liberal yeshivas.

194

Considering the fact that the yeshiva is a voluntary institution made up primarily of "true believers," there is a surprising amount of activity that runs counter to its philosophy. Such activity can be broken down into three broad, sometimes overlapping categories, each of which deserves to be examined separately. These are restrictions based on religious laws, explicit biblical prohibitions, and school regulations.

If I Don't Date, I'll Be Socially Inept

The first category is rules and regulations that are based on interpretations of religious laws. The interpretation advanced by the yeshiva may sometimes be stricter than that of the Orthodox community at large. An act that may not appear to some to be a religious violation may be thought of as such in the yeshiva because it is seen as one that *might* lead to a violation of the religious law.

Almost all yeshivas forbid dating unless it is undertaken for the specific purpose of finding a marriage partner. Social dating as an end in itself is taboo. Although talking with a girl is not considered a violation of the faith, it is discouraged for another reason related to the religion. According to Jewish law, masturbation is not permitted since the Bible forbids wasting semen. Therefore, young men are not allowed to put themselves in a position where they might become sexually aroused and, out of frustration, violate this precept. Of course, dating for the purpose of marriage can result in the violation of the law too, but here common sense and current mores take precedence. Since marriages are not prearranged in yeshiva society (although dates for the purpose may be arranged by matchmakers), dating for the purposes of marriage is considered a necessary "evil." It is also argued that purely social dating takes the student's mind away from Torah study. This line of reasoning, which can obviously be used to ban sports, leisure reading, and the like, is not often employed since the first argument is thought of as sufficient justification.

At more liberal institutions such as Yeshiva University, most students date regardless of the proscriptions. Interviews with members of the community, including students, suggest that prohibitions against touching girls, for instance, are routinely violated. One *rebbe* at the school described some of the arguments advanced by his students along with his responses:

REBBE: A boy shouldn't go out with a girl until a year before he's getting married.

WH: How does he know when it's a year before marriage? He has to first meet the girl.

REBBE: Well, you know if you're eighteen and just starting college, you're probably not going to get married for another four years. Now the point I make is that the biggest problem here is what if you do meet the right girl at eighteen? To go with a girl you love for four years and not do anything except talk to her is a very difficult thing. So it's better to avoid putting yourself in this position until you're serious. But what they [the students] always say is: "I want to date early because if not I won't be able to handle myself with the opposite sex. If I don't date I'll be socially inept." My answer to that is either you have it or you don't and it doesn't matter when you start. I don't have any statistics but it's my impression that those who start late have as good marriages as those who start early.

Yeshiva University is unique among talmudical seminaries because it has a women's school, known as Stern College, within its system. Stern is located at least seven miles from the men's center and functions as a separate institution with its own dormitory, deans, faculty, curriculum, and so on. A four-year liberal arts college with a religious studies program as well, it has no coed classes and has nothing to do with RIETS. Nevertheless, both the men's school, Yeshiva College, and Stern jointly plan, sponsor, and hold social events, including activities such as blind-date parties. As a result, dating among those in the school cannot be considered as an example of deviance.

Unlike Yeshiva, most yeshivas have explicit regulations against dating and other social contact with members of the opposite sex. Such rules are not written but are orally transmitted to the student body by faculty, administrators, or other students. As one dean put it: "We don't have to write down rules about dating and movies. A student who gets this far knows what's *assur* [forbidden] and what's not." Although there are no figures, observation and interviews indicate that while actual dating among those not actively seeking a marriage partner is unusual, there is social contact. One young man, a resident of Baltimore, who attended the Ner Israel Yeshiva in that city, described it as follows:

> I didn't have any real dates. There was a girl on Park Heights Avenue and usually we'd go over to her house, my friend and I, or to her friend's house, and just talk. I guess we could have occasionally drifted into a movie too. But it wasn't a formal date . . . you know: I call her up and say, "I'll take you out next weekend."

Those who live at home cannot be supervised as closely, but even those who dorm have opportunities to socialize in the summer months or while on vacation. It would be incorrect to assume that the average yeshiva *bochur* has almost no contact with girls as he grows up. In addition to casual meetings, he has relatives such as sisters and cousins with whom he can speak. Still, most students have far less contact with young women than is true of young men in general.

The prohibitions in this area are a reinforcement of a socialization process that begins in the Orthodox Jewish home environment and is emphasized in elementary school and high school. Among the Strictly Orthodox, these are all-male or all-female institutions. One psychologist told me that an elementary school girl was instructed by her teacher not to attend New York City's annual Israeli Independence Day parade because "there are boys and girls holding hands there." A sixteen-year-old high school student at an out-of-town yeshiva made the following observations:

> WH: What do you do when you go off the grounds?
>
> STUDENT: You can go to the shopping center and buy things. There's also a kosher pizza shop. The Bais Yaakov [local girls high school for the Strictly Orthodox] girls also hang out in the plaza.
>
> WH: What happens if the yeshiva catches you talking to the girls?
>
> STUDENT: If you're caught, you're dead.
>
> WH: Do you try to?
>
> STUDENT: Of course.[3]

The popular perception of the yeshiva *bochur* as shy when it comes to approaching members of the opposite sex may have more than a kernel of truth, but it is certainly not true of all students. Sexual promiscuity does exist in the yeshiva community. As far as can be ascertained, however, its incidence is quite low. Because detection by yeshiva authorities would result in immediate expulsion as well as social ostracism by the larger Orthodox community, the subject is rarely discussed.

Those who engage in such behavior are likely to seek out similarly inclined young women who also belong to the Strictly or Modern Orthodox community. They are also apt to, if only for the sake of outward appearances, observe the various laws and rituals adhered to by Orthodox Jews. They will not, as a rule, eat nonkosher food or violate the Sabbath. Their dress will not necessarily differ from that of the average yeshiva student, and they will probably pray with seeming fervor and sincerity. Those willing to discuss this topic with me (many feared it would be improperly presented to the outside world) seemed to feel guilty and hypocritical about their *"taavehs."* In a society as demanding as that of the yeshiva it is understandable that a small minority will find themselves unable to function without succumbing to temptation in varying degrees. Such occurrences may be due both to human nature and to the impact of the sexual revolution that has been taking place in American society as a whole over the past two decades.

At some yeshivas, such as Lakewood or Telshe, such forms of entertainment as movies, plays, or rock concerts are regarded as taboo while at schools like Chaim Berlin and Torah Vodaath, students will sometimes make a distinction between an "R" rated film and one receiving a "G" rating. Still, even among those who go, there is general acceptance of the idea that such behavior is not appropriate for a yeshiva student. One young man who admitted seeing an occasional movie or two, described his reaction to a group of fellow students who went to a concert in the following terms:

> Last year there was a bunch of guys who went to a singing concert—Olivia Newton John. They didn't see anything wrong. When I heard they were going, I was very upset. There's a certain line you draw. You go to the movies, that's one thing. But you're dealing here with listening to *kol isha* [the voice of a woman singing, which is prohibited according to the strict interpretation of Jewish law, because it might result in sexual arousal on the part of those listening]. That's number one. Number two, you're going into a place that's

not for Orthodox Jews. Even movies isn't something a yeshiva *bochur* should do. He has to have a little higher standards than everybody else.

This passage indicates, first, that some students do violate the
norms, although the respondent noted at a later point in the interview that they were a small minority. Second, we see that
members of the community internalize such values. Third, this is
another instance of the interrelationship between religious laws
and normative expectations. While the concert is cited as ex-
pressly forbidden, moviegoing is seen merely as incongruent
with the general lifestyle of the yeshiva student.

We have noted that many yeshivas do not allow students to
read *Time, Newsweek,* or the daily newspaper. This policy is ignored by large numbers of *bochorim.* Unlike the previous categories, the yeshiva recognizes an implicit value in being at least
minimally knowledgeable about world and national affairs. It ob-
jects to articles dealing with topics that do not promote what is
sees as a "Torah view" of life. The students justify such reading
on the ground that they are selective in what they read. To what
extent this is true is hard to judge. There is, incidentally, a
separate category in the yeshiva of good "bathroom literature"
such as *Reader's Digest Condensed Books.* In explaining this, one
young man at the Beth haTalmud Yeshiva observed: "It's not
vulgar like the *New York Post* but it's too secular to be placed in a
bookcase in the dining room."

Dress code is another area of a seemingly secular nature that
is actually based on religion (see p. 147). Conservative attire is
considered the "right way for a *ben Torah* [son of the Torah] to
dress" and flashy clothing is seen as at best an unnecessary accommodation to materialism and secular values and at worst as
indicative of a lack of religiosity. Styles of dress are inculcated at
an early age. Since the *beis medrash* student is regarded as an adult
and this is not, in any event, a serious violation of school policy,
a flashy dresser may be frowned upon and some may draw conclusions about the sort of person he is, but he will not generally
be rebuked. At the high school level, on the other hand, a boy in-
appropriately attired may be called into the principal's office and
told to alter his dress habits.

College attendance is another area where religious interpretation is employed to support restrictions. The general argument
is that the atmosphere at a secular college is not conducive to re-

ligious observance (i.e., scantily clad women, showing of films), that heretical ideas are sometimes discussed in the classroom, and that college attendance takes away time from Torah study. Policies with respect to college attendance vary among the yeshivas. At some, such as Yeshiva Beis Shrage in Monsey, New York, and the Telshe Yeshiva, even limited attendance is prohibited. At the Chofetz Chaim Yeshiva, Chaim Berlin Yeshiva, and other schools students can attend on a limited basis, usually two nights a week, and at Breuer's Yeshiva students can go to college four nights. Regardless of the restrictions, there seem to be a significant number of students who disobey the rules by going to classes more often than the school permits. A student with whom I occasionally studied while enrolled in the yeshiva wanted to take a certain course that met daily. Since this was forbidden, he arranged to take a class that met from 8:00 A.M. to 9:00 A.M. before regular classes began at the yeshiva.

And Thou Shalt Love Thy Neighbor as Thyself

A second category is certain laws that the yeshiva feels need to be stressed despite their explicit presence in the Bible itself. These laws deal with how one ought to conduct oneself in one's personal relationships with others. Thus, the yeshiva will urge its members (some feel not often enough) to constantly be aware of the biblical prohibition against speaking ill of others or of the importance of not embarrassing someone in public. These views are communicated both through private conversation as well as in talmudic discussions and *mussar* classes given by the *mashgiach*.

Does the incorporation of such exhortations into the very fabric of the learning process and its emphasis by members of the yeshiva hierarchy mean that very few stray from the "straight and narrow path"? Not at all. In fact, *mussar* was established as a separate area of study because it was seen as an area where everyone needed improvement. We deal here not with an area where limits are clearly defined but with qualities that are often as elusive as they are difficult to measure. For instance, while it is apparent to the average yeshiva *bochur* that conceit is not a virtue, it is difficult to determine the line between vanity and pride in accomplishment. Similarly, in the yeshiva's view, while all ought to strive to reach as high a moral and spiritual level as possible, the point at which such efforts reach a level of acceptable or desirable behavior is hard to assess.

It is, however, possible to obtain a picture of the extremes and thus to define deviance in this area. A student who is occasionally abrupt with his friends may be thought of as a bit unfriendly. If, on the other hand, he is downright surly, his actions can be defined as deviant. One who lends his roommate money is seen as doing a good deed. If he does so for anyone in the school who may ask, he may be characterized as unusually generous. Generally, efforts to improve one's character are seen by the yeshiva as part of a never-ending struggle against what it defines in religious terms as the evil inclination (*yeitzer hora*) present in all human beings.

Laws such as eating only kosher food, not violating the Sabbath, or not eating bread on Passover are not emphasized, because it is taken for granted that anyone attending yeshiva at the advanced level adheres to them. Violation of such rituals, when it occurs, is more likely to have serious consequences in the yeshiva than, say, lack of concern for others. Someone who breaks a dietary law such as eating meat together with milk or who fails to pray every day will be expelled far more quickly from the yeshiva than someone who is known to speak ill of others or who has a tendency to embarrass others in public. Only a gross violation of human decency such as stealing from another can result in a student being asked to leave.[4]

The dichotomy drawn by the yeshiva and the Orthodox community in general between explicitly stated laws of ritual and laws of human relations raises the question of why the latter set of injunctions seems to be violated more frequently and taken less seriously. Some have argued that the laws relating to general conduct toward others are much more difficult to follow than the rituals. But the difficulty of adhering to the laws is not in itself sufficient explanation for failure to do so. Perhaps in a community where observing the laws is so important, the rituals are taken more seriously because they are the laws that make Judaism different from other faiths. It is no doubt true that if one considers only the moral and ethical laws, Judaism is not much different from the other faiths, all of which embody such ideas. There is, however, no empirical evidence that persons in the yeshiva, or in the larger Orthodox community, for that matter, take such distinctions into account on either a conscious or sub-conscious level. What is known is that among those in the ye-shiva the laws between "one man and his friends" (*bein odom lachavero*) appear to be transgressed more often than those be-tween "man and God" (*bein odom laMokom*) and that the yeshiva, recognizing this, makes an effort to raise the level of con-sciousness in this area.

Movies, Radios, Burger-Makers, and *Newsweek*

The third grouping of regulations concerns rules established by the yeshiva that are, at best, only tangentially related to re-ligious imperatives. These are regulations such as cleaning one's room every day, going home for a weekend only with the ye-shiva's approval, and going to bed at a reasonable hour. Some-times a general religious stricture such as respecting one's elders or guarding one's health may be invoked to justify a particular regulation, but by and large these rules are meant to insure the smooth running of the institution and to establish its authority over the students.

For those at the *beis medrash* level such rules are generally conveyed as guidelines. An eighteen-year-old *bochur* is regarded as mature enough to know when to go to bed. Still, a *bochur* who repeatedly comes late to morning services because of too little sleep will be noticed and reprimanded. Generally speaking, how-ever, such rules are emphasized much more at the high school level. There the regulations are clearly stated and violation is often seen as a direct challenge to institutional authority. Most students tend to abide by such restrictions, but there are quite a few who find them intolerable. Typical of such individuals is Binyomin Davis,* who attended an out-of-town yeshiva in 1978 and was finally forced to leave because of this problem:

WH: What was it like in the yeshiva?

BD: Well, they were pretty strict. They said no radios but I figured I'd sneak one in. Do you know I wound up having seven radios taken away from me in one year?

WH: You're kidding.

BD: No, I'm serious. Five to ten times a year the *mashgiach* [in this case, the dean of the high school division] went through the dorm on raids.

WH: Why?

BD: Oh, looking for radios, magazines like *Time, Newsweek.* One time they even took away a book I had by Elie Weisel because they didn't like the cover.

The yeshiva was rather tolerant of this young man's behavior in giving him so many chances, perhaps because he was a fairly good student. Often, such a situation turns into a game where the student tries to outwit the administration.

BD: I have a burger-maker that I had to build a special slot for in the wall behind the closet in my room. When I asked why we couldn't have a burger-maker, the dorm counselor said: "Because if you had one, then you'd be wasting time thinking, *What am I going to make to eat this evening?* and so on, and this would affect your concentration in learning." Now, do you think every housewife in America spends the whole day thinking, *What am I going to make this evening?* That's ridiculous. Now eventually I was told it's a fire hazard. At least that's a reason.

Binyomin eventually left the yeshiva and enrolled in a more liberal institution on the West Coast. Comparing the two places, he said, "At _____ you're a robot. Here you can have radios, go to movies. The *rosh yeshiva* understands you have a *taaveh* [temptation] to do certain things." The existence of a variety of yeshivas with different approaches and standards is a major factor that accounts for their success. Were the standards uniform throughout, students such as Binyomin would be compelled to leave the community.

Although deviance among faculty and administrators is not the focus of our discussion, it can be noted in concluding this section that it does exist, though to what extent cannot be determined. The following comment by a yeshiva *rebbe* at the high school level is unusually open:

I haven't seen a movie in three years. Not that I would want to but what if my *talmidim* [students] would see me going into one? Or to give you another example: I love reading science fiction, especially after twelve hours in the *beis medrash.* I do it to relax. But if the bell to my apartment rings, I must drop

> what I'm doing and grab a *Shulchan Aruch* [Code of Jewish
> Law] or a *sefer* as I come to the door for otherwise what kind
> of example would I be setting?

While it is not being suggested here that such disingenuousness is
rife among the faculty of yeshivas, there is no doubt that they too
have temptations to which they sometimes succumb.

Why Deviance?

In the high school setting, the lives of the students are
closely regulated and supervised. As in any boarding school, the
administration takes its role of *in loco parentis* rather seriously.
The majority of *bochorim* chafe at the restrictions but abide by
them. Some, however, see entry into the *beis medrash* not only as a
confirmation of intellectual and emotional maturity but as an opportunity for the release of the tensions associated with close
supervision. They may express their relief by reading certain secular magazines, going to an occasional movie, or violating other
minor regulations here and there. For such persons admission to
the *beis medrash* may be seen as a reward for playing by the rules.
When deviance is motivated by such considerations it is usually
temporary or very sporadic. Typical of such students was one
who made the following observation:

> When I first came into the *beis medrash,* I used to sneak out
> and go bowling, which I happen to have a big *taaveh* for.
> After a while though, I stopped and in thinking about it I
> realized that part of the reason I wanted to go so much when
> I was in high school was because I had been told I couldn't
> go, that I would be suspended if I did because it wasn't a
> *yeshivishe* [appropriate activity for a yeshiva student] thing to
> do. Now I realize this on my own.

The last statement is important for it indicates a self-sustaining
mechanism of social control. This is what the yeshiva strives
for—to have the student conduct himself in accordance with the
yeshiva's wishes because *he* feels it is the right way. By and large,
it seems that those who manage to make it through the high
school have internalized, at least in principle, the values and
ideology upon which the various proscriptions of the yeshiva are
based.

At the same time, there are those who stifle their desire to engage in unacceptable behavior only because certain aspects of the yeshiva experience appeal to them so much that they are willing to forego some pleasures in order to remain within the community. For example, a student may enjoy the learning process but also have a "weakness" for movies. At the high school level, he refrains from attendance because he knows detection can have rather unpleasant consequences. Yet at the *beis medrash* level, where the rules are not so strictly enforced and the institution does not monitor the behavior of the *bochorim* so closely, he will feel free to take greater liberties. Although such individuals may be able to keep up with their work, their activities can have unintended and sometimes negative consequences for their success in the institution. For one thing, it may bring them into contact with others in the yeshiva who have made a generally poor adjustment to yeshiva life. If, as a result of his one deviant act, the *bochur* is drawn into closer contact with this marginal group, it can affect the perception of him held by others who look down upon such people. Such a student is often labeled as deviant despite the fact that, except for this "weakness," he is like all the other "good students." Responding to a label such as "bum," he may accept it and fulfill the expectations of those who have defined him as deviant in a general sense.[5] Whether or not the process described here takes place depends on the individual and the institution. Certain people seem to have a knack for getting away with mildly deviant behavior while others do not. This may or may not be due to their own personality and other factors relating to their background, friendship networks, and so on.

The bulk of serious deviant behavior by yeshiva standards comes from those students who cannot attain the goals of the institution but crave the status accorded those skilled in this area. In response, they may form a subculture within the yeshiva community.[6] As one young man who had attended Beis Moshe Yeshiva in Scranton, Pennsylvania, asserted:

> I couldn't learn as well as the other guys but I wanted to be somebody too. So I became friendly with the bums in the yeshiva. I didn't really want to be part of their group at first because I knew everyone else looked down on them but at least I felt like I belonged somewhere. And after a while I got to like the guys and the things they did. I guess that's why I didn't make it in the yeshiva *velt* [world].

The nature of yeshiva life itself probably contributes to some of the behavior of which it disapproves. It is a way of life demanding a great deal of commitment, discipline, and conformity. Virtually every aspect of the student's life is governed by either law or custom. For some, the pressure can be intolerable. One young man who left the institution said: "It was driving me crazy. Everything had to be done a certain way and I was always worrying about whether or not I had done it right. Like should the brim on my hat be two or three inches wide? What is the yeshiva *rade* [way] on this?" Others who have a need to assert their individuality, to break out and have a little fun, engage in behavior that will get them attention. This is especially true if they are not among the select few whose scholarly achievements set them apart from the rest. The following caper, recounted by a thirty-three-year-old man who still studies full time in a yeshiva as a member of its postgraduate division (*kollel*), is an example of the bizarre behavior that occasionally occurs in yeshivas:

> I was such a wild guy. There wasn't much you could do and I wanted to be noticed. _____ was a yeshiva where you had to be a soldier, really toe the line, but I used to step out of line once in a while. Once I wanted to have a little fun at four o'clock in the morning. I was walking outside and there was a Christmas tree lying on the ground. I brought it into the dormitory. The guys were sleeping. This was unheard of in _____. You want everybody to get up and have a laugh. The guys woke up and they cracked up. There were snitchers who told the *rosh yeshiva* . . . but he couldn't believe it and the next night it was still there.

Bringing an overtly religious symbol such as a crucifix or a religious statue into a yeshiva would have been sacrilegious. Bringing in a Christmas tree was simply regarded as a "wild" thing to do. Such antics, besides testing the limits of tolerance of the institution's authorities, are largely an escape valve.

Sometimes letting go is directly related to the rigors of yeshiva life, almost as if the individual is trying to balance the scales. The following story told by a former student at another yeshiva (and verified by several others who were students at the time) is an example of this phenomenon:

> Thursday night we were supposed to stay up late learning. I don't think it was official, but if you missed *davening* [prayer

services] Friday morning without saying it, well, wow, you must have been learning all night. So we didn't miss just *davening*—we missed everything. I mean we slept right through. The way it was done, once you got into May and it was hot enough, a couple of guys who wanted to look sun-tanned and all that would go up to the roof of the dorm and fall asleep there. By the time they got up in the morning, late I mean, they were really tanned. And then they'd go and play a good game of baseball or basketball. You always knew who they were because the tan would give it away.

Stories of this sort provide us with a multidimensional view of those who attend such institutions. Though they spend most of their time hunched over a tome of the Talmud, they are subject to many of the same temptations that characterize other youths their age.

Finally, deviance for some may simply be a response to insecurity about how the larger society perceives them. The typical yeshiva *bochur* travels, reads, attends college, and listens to the radio often enough to be at least somewhat aware of what is going on in the larger society. And he is also sensitive to criticism that he is unaware of the outside world. He may therefore choose certain recreational activities partly because he enjoys them but also because they give him a feeling that he is "with it" or "cool." The following example of this pattern took place not long ago in an out-of-town yeshiva known for its "other-worldliness":

You can always tell the *rosh yeshiva* you need the tape recorder for *shiurim* [classes]. My roommate was playing Simon and Garfunkel music. I happen to think it's beautiful . . . like "Bridge over Troubled Water." As an instrumental it could pass for a Yiddish *niggun* [melody or song]. In fact, when I learned before in another yeshiva my *chavrusa* used to hum it while he was learning and the *rebbe* picked it up and he thought it was beautiful.

Anyway, *bekitzur* [in short] one of the guys next door told the *mashgiach* that this guy plays rock, *goyishe* [non-Jewish] music. So the *mashgiach* comes over to me and asks me. Now I couldn't care less what my roommate does. They're not going to change him anyway. So I said he probably plays the *Yiddishe niggunim* but he *zicher* [surely] wouldn't play rock music. When the *mashgiach* came over to me the second time, I had to tell him *something*. I told him he plays these former *yeshivaleit* [yeshiva students], Shimon and Garfinkel. They made a couple of *Yiddishe zachen* [loosely: songs or numbers]. "Oh, good," he said, "as long as he doesn't play the rock music."

What is significant here is not that an authority figure within the school was made to look foolish. A *rebbe* or a *mashgiach* is not supposed to know about such matters. In fact, it is to his credit that he does not know the difference between Simon and Garfinkel and Shimon and Garfinkel. What does matter is that the yeshiva *bochur* cloistered away in the *beis medrash* knows who they are and what they do. Nevertheless, such awareness is somewhat tempered by the slightly defensive tone, as the student says, "It could pass for a . . . *niggun*," and "I happen to think it's beautiful."

The Yeshiva Response: From Exhortation to Expulsion

> After people are here for a while, they just get different ideas of what could be reached. We can't force a person to learn. No one looks down your back here. But if you're in a place like this you just do. There's a different idea. You see a bigger, better, nicer-looking example.
>
> Rabbi Yehuda Jacobs, Director of Admissions,
> Beis Medrash Govoha[7]

Group pressure is perhaps one of the strongest forces against deviance in the yeshiva. The majority of students conform to the demands of yeshiva life, thereby exerting considerable influence over those who do not. In the yeshiva anonymity is not possible. The lifestyle adopted by the yeshiva *bochur* ultimately becomes known to his peers and, in all likelihood, to those who run the yeshiva.[8] As one student at the Talmudical Yeshiva of Philadelphia observed:

> A guy who doesn't learn well usually packs up. He can't last long here. He won't get *chavrusas,* and no one will want much to do with him.

Said a student in a Chicago yeshiva:

> There's a lot of pressure from your peers about *shiurim.* People work on *shiurim.* If you're not sitting in the back of the

beis medrash in the evening listening to a tape of *shiur* and working on it, then you're really out of it.

Students who do not fit in rarely have a prolonged stay in the school. They are either forced out or leave of their own volition.

Community norms often extend beyond the walls of the yeshiva to affect the behavior of those belonging to it. A well-placed word here or there can have a highly beneficial or disastrous effect on the intellectual career of a yeshiva student. One *rebbe* spoke of such efforts in critical terms and the example he cites, while perhaps not that common, demonstrates the mixed motives that can result in such actions:

> I once learned privately with a *baal teshuva*. He became very good and decided to go to Lakewood. And the head of the yeshiva said to me: "He wants to go to Lakewood, but, you know, he's nervous, he's this and that, he has problems, he's a little strange. I don't think we should do it. So we're going to warn people at Lakewood about him." So I said: "Here's a *bochur* who gave up everything to learn. Yes, he has a myriad of problems. His parents are both doctors and don't like the way of life he chose and he doesn't make friends easily. For these reasons you'll destroy his reputation?"

As the *rebbe* went on to explain, the yeshiva was concerned that its own reputation might suffer if it recommended an individual who, although he learned well, somehow did not "fit" their view of the ideal yeshiva product. It was ready, as the teacher put it, "to sacrifice the *bochur* on the altar of the prestige of the yeshiva."

Other types of group pressure are more informal. At one of the more modern yeshivas, an eighteen-year-old Manhattan resident described his reluctance to go to the movies as follows:

> I don't feel movies are wrong. The only thing that keeps me from doing it is that I'm afraid what other people will think about yeshiva guys when they see me. I have an untrimmed beard and I wear a big *yarmulke*. So Orthodox people will see me go to the movies and what will they say about yeshiva guys in general? That it's okay with them.

Group pressure sometimes militates *against* strict observance in those yeshivas where the Strictly Orthodox are not so numerous. In the following statements, made by a *rebbe* at

Yeshiva University's RIETS division, we see how the *rebbe* is cast in the role of defender of the faith against the students:

> I try my best to influence them. I discourage them from going to concerts at Stern College. I know I had an effect because one kid asked for a refund. Of course, he was a short kid and wasn't too good-looking, and I guess he felt he wouldn't get too much out of it anyway. This shows there was pressure from the other kids and he was just going along with the times. But I've seen that kids who get involved with girls . . . it almost precludes serious learning. There's four hours for a date, long phone conversations, and all that.

Mussar talks, while they focus more on general issues, can also dwell on specific forms of behavior. A student at Breuer's Yeshiva described the content of the *rosh yeshiva*'s *mussar* talks as follows:

> WH: What kind of topics does he touch on?
>
> STUDENT: Reading newspapers, reading magazines . . . you shouldn't. Watching television. He says, nobody watches television here, of course. Watch your eyes in the summer when there are pretty girls in the street. These are the more interesting things. About coming to *seder* on time, about cutting classes. Every week it's something different. Sometimes he'll say have more *kavana* [devotion] when you *daven*.

At Yeshiva University, where attitudes and practices tend to be somewhat more liberal, one *rebbe* said:

> I talk about the general moral climate. That they shouldn't date *so often* [emphasis added]. I'll talk about *Saturday Night Live,* which I never saw, but I know all about it from my students.

Sometimes offenders are singled out in a *mussar shmuess.* Although their names are rarely mentioned, a recounting of the incident usually makes it easy to identify them since what transpired is generally known to all in the school. Those guilty are, in effect, lectured about their misdeeds, often suffering group censure because of such disapproval by authority figures.[9]

Talking, however, is not always enough, and the yeshiva may sometimes be required to take concrete action. Even Lakewood occasionally has problems in this area. One of the administrators gave this assessment:

AMINISTRATOR: The *mashgiach* walks around the room and he finds things that shouldn't be in the yeshiva. He'll pick them up and deposit them in the garbage can. If he knows to whom it belongs, he'll have him know he's very dissatisfied.

WH: Like what things?

ADMINISTRATOR: Novels, soft-backed junk out of the drugstore. It seldom happens but we're not immune to it. And even when we crack down, that doesn't mean it disappears totally. It just goes into hiding.

WH: Do you sometimes keep an eye on people to make sure they come to *minyan*?

ADMINISTRATOR: Sometimes. We do have to know what a fellow is doing, but this yeshiva is run on too adult a level that you dress a guy down for not coming to *minyan*.

Many of the regulations of the yeshiva are, as we have seen, related to the religious laws and serve merely to reinforce them. In the final analysis, however, it is the faith itself that often serves as the brake on deviance. Even were there no specific rules and regulations set down by the yeshiva, most students would feel obligated by what they interpret as the tenets of Judaism. Socialized as he is from early childhood into believing that the Torah is his supreme authority, the yeshiva *bochur* often experiences tremendous guilt even for feeling a desire to violate a law.

WH: If you were in a subway and there was only a seat next to a pretty woman, would you decline to sit down next to her because you didn't want to feel a desire for her?

STUDENT: I never was at the stage where I wouldn't sit next to a girl, although others in my *shiur* were. Yet I would castigate myself for having sexual desires and not trying to get rid of them through becoming very religious. After all, my world was the yeshiva world.

Naturally, to prevent any wavering, the religious laws are backed up by those charged with defining and clarifying them. And, as one writer and teacher, himself a graduate of Breuer's Yeshiva, noted: "Questioning and challenging the right of authorities to lead and direct is alien to a tradition that equates the authority of parents, teachers and rabbis with the authority of G-d."[10]

Nobody likes a fink. Yet he too is part of the mosaic that

makes up the yeshiva community. It would be unfair to say that the yeshiva has a system of informers. There are those, however, who feel it their duty to let the administration know who is breaking the rules. When they do so it is most often their own idea, not that of the yeshiva authorities. Every yeshiva student has his own story about how such a spy was outwitted or made to look foolish:

> My *chavrusa* bought bell bottoms. He was a fancy dresser, *shtaatz* [cool]. So they went into the *rosh yeshiva,* a representation of guys who feel it's their job to spy on others. So the *rosh yeshiva* said: "What's the *avla* [terrible thing]? I also wear wide pants." So the guys said: "No, but these are wide on the bottom and the *rosh yeshiva*'s are wide on top." So the *rosh yeshiva* asked: "Is it because they're wide on the bottom or because they're narrow at the top?" The final outcome was nothing. There are many stories like that where people came in and made a tumult.

Despite the fact that such persons are widely disliked among the students, their presence is effective in that it makes people more careful in what they do and in what they tell others about what they do.

Formal sanctions are unusual at the *beis medrash* level. In high school students may be fined for repeatedly coming late to prayer services, they may be "grounded" (not allowed to leave the yeshiva) for breaking curfew, or have other privileges taken away from them. College-age students are considered too old for such treatment. In the words of Rabbi Yaakov Ruderman, *rosh yeshiva* of the Ner Israel Yeshiva:

> We have a *shita* [philosophy] that you don't send a student away from the yeshiva unless he actually does harm to others because we have a responsibility to the rest of the students as well.[11]

As implied here, some yeshivas are stricter than others, often reflecting approaches that date back many years. The Telshe Yeshiva is known as a no-nonsense institution that stresses strict adherence to its rules and regulations and asks those who fail to do so to leave. What is interesting is that it had the same reputation in nineteenth-century Eastern Europe. One of its earliest *rosh yeshivas* was described in the following terms by Rabbi Mordechai Gifter, present head of the institution:

> Rav Joseph Leib Bloch, head of the Telshe Yeshiva in Europe, was so punctual in all his ways that one woman in

the village reportedly set her clock according to his daily walks. He would pass her house every day at exactly the same second. He once told a student: "If I call a *shiur* for 4:00 P.M. I don't mean it to begin at 3:59 P.M. or a minute after 4:00 P.M."[12]

Formal sanctions are more likely to be applied in schools where conformity to the system is a highly prized virtue. Yet even in such institutions, when a student's behavior calls for some action to be taken it is usually done so reluctantly, for it is not only a source of mutual embarrassment but an indication that the yeshiva has failed to reach the individual. Rabbi Jacobs explained the circumstances under which disciplinary action would be taken at Lakewood:

WH: Did it ever happen that you had to tell someone to go home?

RJ: Certainly. And it can be a major turning point in a person's life. Being kicked out of Lakewood is *modne* [strange], *nicht geshmak* [unappetizing]. This is an adult place. It's not like they threw him out of grade school.

WH: What would result in a person being asked to leave?

RJ: A person who does something scandalous, I don't know what . . . but it gets into the papers. Or a person who just isn't doing anything here. He isn't learning at all. Sometimes we'll let him stay as long as he doesn't hurt anyone else. If, however, we see it's fruitless, that we can't help him, then we'll ask him to leave. Ask him to change yeshivas for his own good.

WH: That's being diplomatic.

RJ: He knows what we mean. We tell him in case he doesn't understand. And at the end of the *zman* [semester] he just happened to leave. People always come and go and he's one of those who went. In general, though, we try to avoid this.[13]

Expulsion is a last resort, and the threat of such action is in itself often sufficient. This is so not only because the individual will be forced to leave but also because others outside the yeshiva may discover what has occurred, thus bringing disgrace upon him and his family. Aware of this, the yeshiva student is likely to take great pains to see that it does not happen to him.

Our understanding of formal sanctions would be incomplete without mentioning that quite a few students are forced out of yeshivas in informal ways. If a student is labeled undesirable his *rebbe* may ignore him, except perhaps for a perfunctory greeting; students may make him feel unwelcome by refusing to become his learning partner or to share a room with him. Isolated and rejected in this manner, the student leaves "voluntarily," but in reality his departure is due to group pressure.

Controlling Deviance: The Costs and Benefits

The yeshiva goes to quite a bit of trouble to prevent deviant behavior. Are such efforts necessary or even desirable? Such a question cannot be easily answered, for deviance in the yeshiva, as in the larger society, has both positive and negative outcomes. Let us first look at the negative results of allowing deviance to go unchecked.

Perhaps the greatest problem is that if the yeshiva fails to punish those who deviate from its norms it risks breeding disrespect for the system as a whole, greatly reducing the likelihood that its members will conform to institutional expectations. In addition, when large numbers of people disregard the rules, the trust on which a closely knit culture depends begins to disintegrate. Moreover, since the yeshiva is a place where individuals are supposed to devote themselves to intellectual and spiritual pursuits, the diversion of administrative resources toward controlling deviance can disrupt the effective functioning of the yeshiva as it strives toward its overall goals. For these reasons, the yeshiva must exercise control over those who attend it.

But deviance can have positive results too. When tolerated to a limited degree, deviance acts as a safety valve for dissatisfaction. Very few students find the yeshiva a utopian institution, and allowing them sometimes to violate certain minor rules—reading a secular book, listening to a record by a folk-singing group, and so on—may prevent more serious violations from occurring.

Deviance can also be the catalyst for changes in an institution. One major yeshiva, for example, was opposed to having its students attend college in the 1950s. Despite this, several students began attending clandestinely. The school eventually became aware of these infractions but chose to ignore them rather than make an issue of them. Over the years more and more students began attending college, arguing that they needed to do so in order to acquire training for entry into the job market. In response, the yeshiva gave students permission to attend on a limited basis. Today, this yeshiva informally advises the students on what courses to take so that they can best profit from the college experience.[14]

Ultimately, the most significant outcome of defining certain behavior as deviant is that it indicates the limits that will be tolerated by the yeshiva. As is true of all societies, students in the yeshiva require a sense of how far they can go without running afoul of authority. By setting down rules and regulations, the yeshiva gives its members concrete guidelines to acceptable behavior. As a corollary of this, identifying deviants strengthens the values and norms of the community and enhances its solidarity. Students are able to point to others who break the rules with scorn and to their own conformity with pride.[15]

Interviews and observation indicate that the majority of students do conform to the demands of yeshiva life. In addition, there is other empirical evidence suggesting widespread acceptance of the yeshiva's authority. In a fascinating study, Uri Sondhelm, a *rebbe* in a Modern Orthodox yeshiva in New York City, distributed a questionnaire to tenth- and eleventh-grade high school students in six different types of yeshivas to assess their general attitudes toward authority.[16] Among his findings were that students exhibit less respect for the authority of religious leaders in the yeshiva as the modernity of the school increases. One of the items on which students were asked to agree or disagree was: "The principal and religious faculty should have a say in the choice of secular literature read in high schools." Three-quarters of the boys attending schools that had an all-day *beis medrash* agreed, as compared to only half of those enrolled in the more modern schools. Those in the more traditional yeshivas were also more likely to believe that parents should have the final say in all family matters, and that laws against capital punishment and policies that "hindered" police effectiveness should be changed. Their opinions on enforcement of drug laws were equally conservative. Taken together, Rabbi Sondhelm's findings demonstrate high acceptance of the general legitimacy of authority in a wide range of areas.

In the questionnaire sent to yeshiva alumni as part of this study, respondents were asked whether or not they found anything lacking in their yeshiva experience and, if so, what. Of the eight types of responses given, the restrictions of yeshiva life was the answer given *least* often (6%). This suggests that, when the student reflects upon his yeshiva experience, he does not see its restrictiveness as a very negative aspect of it.

The system that works well for most does not work at all for some. There are students who do not respond well to an authoritarian approach. They may agree with the school's objectives but resent the coercive manner in which it enforces them. Many yeshiva administrators and teachers seem to believe that allowing such individuals to flout yeshiva rules so jeopardizes the legitimacy of the system that it does not pay to be flexible toward them. One former *rebbe,* Rabbi Velvel Perl, who disagreed with this attitude, told of a young man with whom the disciplinarian approach had failed:

> There was a guy in the yeshiva named Kronenberg.* He was a genius and wanted to learn in Lakewood, but the parents insisted he go to college so he came to this yeshiva because here he could go to college. This was in the early sixties. And when he came to the yeshiva, they decided to knock out his *gaaveh* [conceit]. They made a project of it. They were going to cut him down to size. So they cut him down to size. He became an *apikorus* [heretic]; he married a *shikse* [gentile]. And he would have become a *gadol* [great Talmudic scholar]. They said things like: "He doesn't come to *minyan*; so what's his learning worth?"[17]

According to Rabbi Perl, once a yeshiva admits a student it has an obligation to meet his needs, including a responsibility to adopt an approach that will be most helpful to him, even if such an approach runs somewhat counter to yeshiva policy. This should not be seen as the polar opposite of the "shape up or ship out" approach. Neither Rabbi Perl nor any other member of the yeshiva community would argue that a student who, say, violates the Sabbath ought to be permitted to remain in the yeshiva. The question of what to do arises in cases of minor infractions such as missing an occasional group prayer service, sneaking out to see a movie, and so on. It is here that pedagogic stands are taken and differences in overall philosophy emerge.

A small but significant minority in the yeshiva community expressed the view that nonconformists should be viewed with considerable tolerance. One prominent *rosh yeshiva* explained his position on this issue as follows:

The majority of students are conformists. Those you get along with nicely. You enjoy them and they enjoy you. One should never neglect them and take them for granted. Yet on the other hand, they're the least neglected precisely because the *rebbe* enjoys them. As a result they frequently get more attention than they need. This is unfortunate because it is the nonconformists who usually have greater potential. They have more drive, vision, curiosity, initiative. They're the ones with breadth who will investigate and who will care more deeply about things. The conformers create the dictator because they're willing to let someone else make the decisions. You'll find in the biographies of the *gedolim* that most of them were nonconformists. In the long run they develop into greater people. The challenge lies in dealing with them. I think there is only one way and that's on a warm, personal basis. These people need someone whom they feel genuinely cares about them.

As indicated before, the fact that an individual can switch schools and still remain within the yeshiva orbit stems the widespread revolt and/or defection from Orthodoxy that might occur were such alternatives not available. The following remarks from a piqued member of the faculty at the RIETS division of Yeshiva University demonstrate the range of options available. Although his perceptions of the other institutions may not be entirely accurate they do represent their overall policies:

FACULTY MEMBER: There are guys here who are involved in mixed dancing. That I know for a fact—RIETS guys. Telshe also has its problems, but there *a guy is thrown out on his head* [emphasis added]. Here he's thrown out, he's not thrown out. In Baltimore, *he'd be out on the next bus* [emphasis added]. In the other yeshivas stuff goes on too, but not inside the walls of the yeshiva. A guy might go to a sweet sixteen party but it's not inside the yeshiva. No one would put up a sign, like they do here, announcing a coed ski party. Why I've had the chairman of the blind-date party in my class! Now I know in Philly they smuggle in radios even though the school doesn't allow them.

WH: What would you do if you were in charge of setting policy?

FACULTY MEMBER: I would allow radios, tape recorders, and newspapers, but not TV and movies. There have to be some kind of restrictions. Not like here where on a bulletin board you find announcements for a Satmar rally and a disco party side by side.

Aware as they are of the different policies, students opt for the yeshiva that best suits their talents and proclivities. Yet problems sometimes occur as a result of poor choices by the students or bad judgments by parents, who sometimes pressure their children to go to a yeshiva because it has a good reputation even though it might be too restrictive for them. This is not easy to determine, involving as it does a prediction by either the student or parent that is not based on any hard evidence. Possibly the young man may *think* he can handle a program, only to discover later on that he has erred. The yeshiva, which all too often fails to take an individual approach toward the student, is not likely to be understanding of such mistakes, thus compelling the *bochur* to go through the embarrassment and pain of transferring out.

It can also happen that an individual finds the *freedom* existing at a certain school intolerable. One such young man at Ner Israel Yeshiva had the prescience to recognize this in advance:

> To tell you the truth, I couldn't last for two months in a place like Yeshiva Kerem in California where they allow you to have a radio or hang up posters because I can't see a person who can be cool and still be a *ben* Torah [literally, "son of the Torah"].

This student feels that rules such as no radios are necessary to "create a proper atmosphere." His friend, happily enrolled in Yeshiva Kerem, believes that such rules are counterproductive, arguing:

> Do they really think that after you leave yeshiva you're not going to listen to the radio because they prevented you from doing so while you were here? Such rules just breed resentment that is translated into resentment against everything, including the learning for which you go to yeshiva in the first place.

No yeshiva has as yet devised an infallible method for selecting students who will conform to its own particular *Weltanschauung*. Moreover, it cannot control for all the factors that affect an individual's decision to attend a certain school. Partly because of the intrusion of the larger society into the yeshiva world, largely through the mass media, and partly because no society can be totally free of deviant behavior, this area will continue to be something of a problem for most yeshivas.[18] The extent to which such behavior can be controlled will have an important bearing on the success of these institutions.

CHAPTER 9

Preparing for Life Outside the Yeshiva

F OR ALL BUT THE SELECT FEW who spend their entire lives there, the yeshiva is only a temporary home. Sometime between the ages of twenty-one and twenty-eight the majority of students leave its protective environs to make their way into the world, a world that presents them with a host of problems and challenges that must be overcome if they are to lead happy and fulfilling lives. Among them, perhaps no two are more important than those of preparing for a career and finding a suitable marriage partner.

As we have seen, the yeshiva *bochur* is taught early that Torah study is the most important activity in his life and that there are no limits on how much time should be spent in it. It is therefore expected that most yeshiva students will, especially at first, view deciding on an occupation to be at best an annoyance and at worst irrelevant. Yet they must, sooner or later, take steps in this direction. Along with the usual career considerations, the students face problems unique to those who follow Orthodox practices. Jobs that entail working past sundown on Friday or coming in on Saturday cannot even be considered.[1] The geographic mobility of observant Jews is limited by their need to live in a community that has kosher food, a *mikva* (ritualarium), yeshivas for their children, an Orthodox synagogue, and other religious amenities. A large number of yeshiva graduates go into business; most study for careers calling for a college education such as law, accounting, teaching, and so on. The need for college attendance has long been one of the major problems for the yeshiva community, and will now be examined in detail.

College Attendance:
Primacy of Religious Study

Despite the general decline in the prestige of a college education in recent years, thousands of yeshiva students eventually go to college. Among the alumni responding to the questionnaire, 48 percent had completed some form of graduate training, 23 percent graduated college only, 15 percent attended but did not graduate, while only 14 percent failed to go beyond high school. Although no statistics are available, it is likely that even those yeshivas, such as Lakewood and Telshe, which forbid college attendance for those in residence at the school, have substantial numbers of alumni, perhaps even a majority, who attended college either before they enrolled or after they left the yeshiva.[2] While the yeshivas prefer that their students not do so, there is a realization among those in authority that college is for many a necessity. This awareness has affected their position considerably. Rather than announce their clear-cut opposition to secular education, a number of schools have adopted a policy of permitting it on a limited basis without "officially" approving it.[3] A few yeshivas have formally given their approval while others have remained unalterably opposed to college study.

The yeshiva does not denigrate secular knowledge in general, taking the position that all knowledge stems from the Torah. It does, however, distinguish between the Oral and Written Law, which it considers holy and of far greater immediate importance to Jews, and that body of knowledge which is indirectly based on the Torah. In support of their position, the yeshivas draw upon numerous sources in the Bible and Talmud which view secular and preprofessional study as permissible only when necessary for one's livelihood.[4] There is, nonetheless, considerable variation in emphasis and approach to the issue among the different *rosh yeshivas*. Thus, Rabbi Shmuel Berenbaum of the Mirrer Yeshiva stated unequivocally, "The whole idea of college is terrible,"[5] while Rabbi Yaakov Ruderman took a more moderate position, saying, "College gives a person *parnoseh* [a livelihood]."[6]

Determining the age at which a young man is ready to pursue college studies is not easy. Some mature earlier, some later. While the yeshivas have specific rules regarding college attendance, a number of them exercise a certain degree of flexibility in allowing some individuals to attend more often or at an earlier age.

Besides opposition on strictly religious grounds, yeshivas are against college because it detracts from involvement in talmudic study. The yeshiva believes that true Torah study requires total immersion, and that anything extraneous will dilute the quality of such study. In an interview with the writer, Rabbi Shneur Kotler differentiated between religious and secular studies as follows:

> It's important to understand that Torah is not like an exact science. It's not a discipline that you examine and learn about. Torah is a complete way of life and the learning is one part of it. You have to be in it completely. It's even, *lehavdil* [one should pardon the comparison], like saying to a doctor: "You should study a little engineering." Even in such a case he would laugh because engineering is a big subject. Then it's certainly true of Torah which is a total way of life.
>
> Today the main center of Torah knowledge and Jewish tradition is the yeshiva. It is very hard to put an "atmosphere" into words, but that's what the yeshiva has to be. There has to be a twenty-four hour a day commitment to become a great scholar and to become part of the tradition of scholarship that goes back from generation to generation for thousands of years. *Rosh yeshivas,* older and younger students, interact with one another and they create an electric, enthusiastic, ambitious atmosphere where nothing matters but advancement in learning, development of piety and character, and scrupulous performance of *mitzvas.*[7]

Thus, we see a distinction between what is purely intellectual study and what is both studied and lived.

In addition, there is the view that *because* secular studies require, in many cases, mental concentration, the energy expended on such activities will affect the individual's ability to focus on the talmud. A student at the Telshe Yeshiva explained it this way:

You can't compare someone who learns *Gemora* fourteen hours a day and studies English literature one hour a day with someone who learns fourteen hours a day and sleeps the extra hour; because once you put *interest* [emphasis added] into something, then it has to decrease from the other thing. That's why even a little bit is dangerous.

Cultural Influences and Heretical Ideas

Another problem is the atmosphere prevailing on many college campuses. Even though he attends on only a part-time basis, the student is likely to be exposed to a variety of influences foreign and perhaps even threatening to his way of thinking. Though he may decline to participate in rallies for all sorts of causes, he may stop and listen to a speaker during club hour, and has the opportunity to see a film on campus, wander through the cafeteria and lounges, watch a TV program, and meet people whose views on religion, sex, parental authority, and so on differ radically from his own. Most students consciously avoid social interaction and participation of this sort. Defending college attendance on the part of his students, Rabbi Henoch Leibowitz, *rosh yeshiva* of the Chofetz Chaim Yeshiva, said: "We've found that, *boruch Hashem* (thank God) students are sufficiently protected against secular influences by seeing in a comparative way the beauty of Torah which dwarfs everything else that the secular world has to offer."[8] Rabbi Mordechai Gifter, head of the Telshe Yeshiva, takes a less tolerant view. Although the example he gave was that of a full-time college, his observations could apply to many evening schools as well:

> Now you take college. This is a part of modern-day culture too. . . . It's not an intellectual question today. It's a question of the atmosphere. I once went to Columbia University to address the Yavneh group [an organization made up primarily of Modern Orthodox college youths] and I saw, as I walked, people lying on the gound in the grass, kissing and hugging and worse. And the *rosh yeshivas* who allow college—they don't know. I told them . . . Come, let's visit a college campus. They don't know what it's like. *Takeh* [indeed], they're alien to these things. A fellow told me that he went to a college class and there's this man, a math instruc-

tor, he's naked to the waist and barefoot, the room is dark
and he's burning incense. Is this an environment for a *ben
Torah* [son of the Torah]?[9]

Another aspect of the problem concerns that which is taught in
certain college courses. The matter of intellectually foreign ideas
and the social environment cannot be separated. In the yeshiva's
view, they combine to create a person who questions accepted
positions and regards that which he does not understand with
skepticism. With the support of new-found friends from different
cultural backgrounds it is possible that he may begin to doubt the
validity of the yeshiva's world view, one predicated upon unquestioning acceptance of certain principles that permits questioning only within a limited framework. Those in the yeshiva
community most adamantly opposed to college feel that such
problems are best avoided by erecting high and impenetrable
barriers to contact with such ideas.

On the other hand, those yeshivas that allow students to
study secular subjects often believe that heretical ideas can be
avoided if the student is selective in what he takes. Thus there is a
tendency to avoid courses in the behavioral sciences, especially
psychology, anthropology, and sociology, where ideas concerning evolution, sexual repression, and so on are discussed which
are often at odds with those of the yeshiva. Since a sizeable
number of Orthodox Jews with yeshiva backgrounds have become social workers, psychiatrists, and psychologists, it is clear
that at least some use can be made of these disciplines. Nevertheless, as noted earlier, Orthodox practitioners in these areas
are often regarded with some suspicion by right-wing Jews.
Needless to say, philosophy courses are strictly taboo, inasmuch
as they present the views of heretical thinkers such as Kant,
Hegel, Spinoza, Socrates, Plato, and so on. The fact that great
Jewish philosophers such as Maimonides were familiar with
Greek philosophy is not considered a valid argument in support
of such pursuits, since yeshiva students are thought to be on a
much lower level, in terms of both belief and understanding,
than such great scholars. Partly because of the nature of what is
taught in these areas and partly because of their own inclina-
tions, yeshiva students who attend college gravitate toward the
hard sciences, mathematics, and economics, taking only an occasional course or two in political science or history.[10]

Some Consequences of the Anticollege Attitude

The negative view of college can have undesirable consequences even from the yeshiva's standpoint. Some students will
denigrate college to outsiders to the point where their position
reveals a total lack of understanding of what is taught there. The
following remarks, made by a young man at the yeshiva where I
had enrolled, are illustrative of this phenomenon:

> Psychology is total nonsense. I know a fellow studying to be
> an industrial psychologist, and do you know what they want
> him to do when he gets out? This guy will have to figure out
> where they should put the toilet paper in the bathroom so
> that the person isn't embarrassed and doesn't have trouble
> reaching it.

Although this is perhaps an extreme case, it is representative of a
view among more than a few yeshiva students that college, and
the social sciences in particular, is worth very little indeed.

It is a testament to the strong hold that the yeshiva has over
those who stay in it for any length of time that views concerning
the superiority of talmudic knowledge over other areas persist in
later life, even among those who have been heavily exposed to a
secular environment. Acceptance of this view is often emotional
as opposed to rational:

> I always believed that if you could do *Gemora,* you could do
> anything. I know it may not be true, but I still believe it at a
> gut level. After all, *Gemora* is good training for the mind. I
> was just at a conference of advanced mathematics and the
> majority of the people there had yeshiva backgrounds. I've
> always felt that the power of our tradition to survive against
> all odds, and that includes the validity and logic of the
> *Gemora* as well, is a sort of proof of its power. It's almost a
> mystical thing when I think of how old it is.
>
> A thirty-eight-year-old mathematics professor

Another problem is that of cheating. Because of the tendency to put down secular study as only a necessary evil from
which very little of intrinsic value can be gained, cutting corners

becomes legitimate in the eyes of some. The yeshivas do not attempt to justify such behavior but, by emphasizing the goal of getting a college degree for the purpose of earning a livelihood while at the same time criticizing the means by which this goal is achieved, they invite deviation from those means. Those who engage in such behavior are, in all likelihood, a minority and do not have the support of the yeshiva hierarchy. The problem was described in the following manner by an Orthodox psychologist:

> I have a friend who teaches at Brooklyn College. And he told me some incidents in his class where yeshiva guys and very religious women with *sheitlach* [wig worn for religious reasons] were cheating. He's a religious guy, a psychologist. He asked them to please stop. Then finally, on the final, he saw them and he said: "You're going to have to sit separately." So they said, "No, don't worry." So while he was standing there a friend of his came in and said: "You know, there's cheating going on in the back." So he gave them all Ds and Cs. So the guy got a call from the husband of one of the girls who said, "How could you do this to one of your own? It's just a college course, *limudei chol* [secular studies]. It's nothing." That's the attitude.[11]

Some members of the community adopt a defensive posture in explaining behavior of this sort, such as one who said: "Everyone does it. Christians, Hindus, and Moslems all put themselves on higher pedestals and they're all just as crooked." From the yeshiva's perspective, and probably from that of leaders of the above-mentioned faiths, such an answer is not acceptable. All available evidence indicates that Orthodox Jews make strenuous efforts to incorporate moral precepts into actual practice. In fact, there is a separate term referring to behavior that brings shame upon the community because it is noticed by outsiders (*chillul Hashem,* or desecration of God's name). Many community leaders are concerned about this problem. In addition to what has already been said, they feel that tolerating such behavior may lead to general dishonesty and cynicism. As one Orthodox therapist put it: "When you say it's okay to pull *shtick* [a quasi-legal or illegal activity] in one area, it can lead to other things—food stamps, job training, or whatever."[12]

The Need for College:
"Something That Had to Be Done."

Despite their misgivings, most yeshivas agree that college can be justified on the grounds that it will help the student to become financially self-supporting, especially if he goes on to study in graduate school. In one *rosh yeshiva*'s words: "This way, the boys don't have to kill themselves for a job. In other yeshivas they say: 'He'll go into business.' But if he doesn't make it there then all is lost. Anyway, in business, you often have less time to learn than if you're a professional."[13]

Once the decision has been made to attend college for employment purposes, the question of status enters into the picture. While the students themselves may make deprecating comments about college, they recognize that it carries with it a certain degree of status. Whether this is seen as status solely on economic grounds or is also related to how an individual with a college education is perceived in the larger society is not certain. In an article in the *Jewish Observer,* Dr. Bernard Fryshman, who himself has a Ph.D in physics, argues that there are alternate occupations to those requiring a college education. In his discussion, he acknowledges the status factor when he says:

> Is there any reason that a young person should be pressed into devoting the best years of his life . . . in the hopes that he will eventually gain admittance to a medical school, and then at the age of 30 or thereabouts begin to earn a fine living with "stature" in the community? Why should the same young person not be encouraged to spend many more years in the yeshiva and then become a tradesman? . . . since when do recognition and stature in a Torah community depend on anything *but* Torah scholarship and contribution to the community welfare?[14]

In another article asserting that the answer lies in vocational training, which will eliminate the problem of exposure to an unwholesome environment and involve less time spent away from the yeshiva, another writer presents figures citing the demand for persons in various occupations. Among those listed are automobile mechanic, plumber, machinist, and carpenter, hardly traditional Jewish occupations.[15]

In fact, such options do exist for the strictly observant.

Agudath Israel has a program called Project COPE (Career Opportunities and Preparation for Employment). Federally funded, it both counsels and trains Orthodox men and women. The program attracts yeshiva students (as well as others) who have not gone to or completed college and are not interested in or capable of making it in the business world. Among the types of job training offered are bookkeeper–manager, foreman in a jewelry factory, salesman, computer programmer, electrician, and paraprofessionals in a wide number of areas. Those running the program report that they have placed hundreds of persons successfully. It is supported by the yeshivas themselves because the reduced time required for career training when compared to college studies means the student will have more time to devote to talmudic study.

Despite its availability, relatively few yeshiva *bochorim* opt for vocational careers. Were the argument that college is attended by yeshiva students *only* out of economic necessity really true, then yeshiva *bochorim* would probably gravitate toward vocational training. In fact, social status also plays a significant role. Vocational employment will become a realistic alternative only if the market in other areas undergoes complete collapse.

To some extent, the unwillingness of yeshiva students to forego college indicates the inability of the institution to shut out the demands of the dominant society. It may, however, also be due to general values of success fostered in the yeshiva environment which are then transferred into other areas of concern. The way in which this is sometimes resolved is revealed in the following comments by a former student of Yeshiva Torah Vodaath who is today an attorney:

> College was treated as something that had to be done. I looked at somebody who went to Columbia or Harvard like they weren't *frum* [religious] even if they wore a yarmulke on the campus there. A *frum* guy—all right, you go to City College. That was good enough. But to go to Columbia?— that's *really* college.

Once the yeshiva makes a decision that college is permitted it will sometimes take steps to smooth the way for the students, perhaps working out an arrangement allowing them to receive college credits for Talmud study. In an age when youths receive credits for ''life experience,'' such agreements are more favorably received by colleges than in the past. In some cases the connection is a formal one, while in others the students merely go from department to department and see if the courses given match up with any of the "courses" they have "taken" at the yeshiva. Typical of the former is the relationship between Ner Israel Yeshiva and Loyola College of Baltimore where students receive credits in philosophy for studying Maimonides and Luzzatto, credits in history for becoming familiar with responsa literature, and general credits for theology. The latter pattern exists at Queens College (City University of New York), where students can petition individual departments. They are likely to be most successful in the Hebrew and Jewish Studies departments, although they can perhaps also obtain credits for, say, medieval history, in the History Department. Of course, there is only one "course" at the yeshiva and that is Talmud, but, as we saw in Chapter 4, the Talmud encompasses a wide range of subjects.

The effect on those yeshivas allowing college study is usually quite noticeable. Generally, one can say that the quality of a yeshiva as measured by the community itself is inversely correlated with the amount of time its students are permitted for college study. Students who might not otherwise attend may be more likely to do so in a school where many of their peers go. This dilutes the quality of the Talmud program and changes the atmosphere in the institution from one of total dedication to a life goal to one of accommodation with "reality." In some yeshivas, the *beis medrash* is virtually empty during finals week at the local college.

Ultimately, the yeshivas stand to gain a great deal from the fact that many students attend college. To the extent that such an education will provide prestige, financial advantage, and general stature in the Orthodox community at large, it means that the yeshivas will have people sympathetic to their interests in key positions throughout the community, lay leaders who will support the synagogues and Jewish day schools. In many cases they will sit on policy-making boards of Jewish organizations that determine the direction to be followed by their members. In this way, such individuals are a cadre of core supporters whose influence will affect the support given yeshivas at various levels. In addition, their college training and contact with outsiders will give them the knowhow to help the yeshivas in crucial areas—for example, in writing proposals for government aid, supplying legal advice and representation, and providing financial support.

Yeshiva University and the Right-Wing Yeshivas: A Crucial Issue

Besides the choices of a college environment not in keeping with the yeshiva's philosophy or no college attendance at all, there is a third alternative—Yeshiva University (Y.U.). Every student at Y.U. must be enrolled in one of three morning divisions: Erna Michael College, which concentrates on such topics as Jewish history, Bible, Hebrew literature, and Hebrew language; the James Striar School, which offers a variety of Jewish courses for students with little religious background; and Rabbi Isaac Elchanan Theological Seminary (RIETS), the advanced division for talmudic studies (also known as the Mazer Yeshiva Program). RIETS is the equivalent at Yeshiva to the other yeshivas discussed here, but its students can and do, as part of Y.U.'s overall program, take a full complement of college courses leading to a B.A. or B.S. College classes are held under the same roof and generally begin at 3:00 P.M. Our concern here is with RIETS, the "yeshiva" part of the school.

Despite its rigorous program of study, RIETS has engendered fierce opposition from the other advanced yeshivas. Much of it is intertwined with the traditional yeshivas' more general disapproval of the compromises they feel Modern Orthodoxy, which forms the backbone of Yeshiva University's support, has made with the dominant society. This issue has important ramifications for the Orthodox community as a whole. The question is not whether Yeshiva University's talmud division is a yeshiva; for most of its opponents in the larger yeshiva community would agree that it is. What is at issue is the *type* of yeshiva it has become since its inception more than seventy-five years ago.[16]

In its most general sense, the conflict here is between those who favor only limited contact with foreign ideas and those willing to risk exposure to them. With its full program of college study (students take an average of 16 credits a semester),

Yeshiva's stance regarding the value of such pursuits is self-evident. This view was perhaps best summed up by Rabbi Norman Lamm, its current president:

> We are committed to secular studies, including our willingness to embrace all the risks that this implies, not alone because of vocational or social reasons, but because we consider that it is the will of G-d that there be a world in which Torah be effective; that all wisdom issues ultimately from the Creator, and therefore it is the Almighty who legitimates *all* knowledge.[17]

Yeshiva University's general position has been that notions challenging Orthodoxy should not be avoided, but studied and dealt with from a critical standpoint. In practical terms, the differences often boil down to the emphasis placed on the secular. Students from the right-wing yeshivas do read newspapers, attend college, and often enter the same professions as Yeshiva University graduates. Yet emphasis is regarded by many as a crucial determinant of one's commitment to the faith as a whole.

Over the years Yeshiva University's approach has come to be called the "synthesis philosophy," a concept espoused by Bernard Revel and Samuel Belkin, its first two presidents. "Synthesis" in this context refers to the development of an individual well versed in both secular and religious knowledge, not to an integration of the two in the classroom.[18] Unfortunately, many in the Strictly Orthodox community are under the impression that religious and secular ideas are brought together in a sort of melting pot from which a new and totally alien philosophical approach to the tradition results.

Another point of emphasis with substantive implications concerns the program itself. During the undergraduate years, the student at RIETS studies Talmud for "its own sake" (*lishmo*) just as his counterpart in, say, Yeshiva Chaim Berlin does. At the end of this period, however, he will be eligible for admission into the ordination (*semicha*) program, a formal course of study leading to a series of examinations and the conferring of a rabbinical degree. The other yeshivas deal with this much more informally. While at some yeshivas ordination is granted following an examination, the course of study is not generally as clearly defined as at Yeshiva. In other yeshivas, a young man may be granted the title of rabbi without a formal examination simply because, throughout his stay, the faculty has become well acquainted with his abilities. As a rule, a student will ask for such a degree only if he needs it for a job he seeks—that is, becoming a pulpit rabbi or a teacher in a Hebrew day school. The key difference here is that by not formalizing the requirements as much as RIETS does, the right-wing yeshivas underline their belief that learning should be for a higher spiritual goal, not only for obtaining career skills. In practice, however, many graduates from the traditional institutions enter Jewish education and, to a lesser degree, the rabbinate and many at RIETS study *lishmo.*[19]

A crucial area of dissension has to do with the atmosphere at Yeshiva University, which the Strictly Orthodox regard with great disapproval. While many RIETS students are quite Orthodox, there are many in the other divisions of yeshiva whose views and practices differ sharply. It is not unusual to see young men and women socializing together on the campus. Many students wear shorts and tiny *yarmulkes,* watch television and sometimes play cards in the dormitory, and are much more caught up in the cultural milieu of the larger society. The right-wing yeshivas feel that constant exposure to such values will take its toll even among those students who are Strictly Orthodox.

Proponents of Yeshiva University argue that the student who can survive in the open society will emerge stronger in his faith. They maintain that, whatever its shortcomings, the environment at Yeshiva *is* Orthodox and that this is far preferable to a completely secular college. Paradoxically, the Strictly Orthodox favor the secular colleges precisely because they believe that the distinctions between the Orthodox lifestyle and that pervading the college are so clear that the student will not be tempted or confused by them, whereas at Yeshiva he might believe that whatever is done there is sanctioned by Orthodox law. "If this is true," counters one Yeshiva administrator, "how come we have both very religious and some not so religious students? They should all be the same. We let our boys think for themselves, at least up to the point where they don't blatantly violate religious principles."

Besides ideological differences and the question of the proper environment, there are several other factors rarely discussed openly. One is the animosity toward the dominant intellectual figure at Yeshiva University, Rabbi Joseph B. Soloveitchik. No one in the right-wing yeshiva community questions Rabbi Soloveitchik's scholarly credentials. In fact, many believe he is one of the greatest scholars in the world. It is his approval of secular studies and his generally liberal approach that irk them, especially since, in the words of one rabbi, "He should know better." Stories about Rabbi Soloveitchik's delivering a lecture on talmudic matters to a group of women at Stern College (he did), and his views concerning secular subjects are frequent topics of discussion in the yeshiva community. His adherents claim that the vehemence of the right-wing opposition may be motivated by jealousy. Said one: "For us mere mortals, jealousy may exist over material things. But at the higher levels, even among the *rosh yeshivas,* it'll more likely show in matters of *kovod* [honor] and who knows more. That's their *yeitzer hora.*" It should be noted that, despite some of his ideological positions and his close involvement with the Modern Orthodox Rabbinical Council of America (RCA), Rabbi Soloveitchik is very much a part of the yeshiva world. He is related to Rabbi Moshe Feinstein, and in a community where family ties are very important such a connection is significant. Moreover, he is far more interested in talmudic studies than in politics, as anyone who has ever been a student of his knows. It is ironic that he has come to symbolize the intellectual leadership of the Modern Orthodox, a role he has acquiesced to most reluctantly, if at all.[20]

Jealousy may play a role in other areas. Interviews with administrators at Yeshiva University indicated that many of them believed this to be the case. One stated: "We pay our *rebbes* on time and we pay more." Another added, "We also have better facilities for the students." Envy for these reasons, though it may exist, is probably not a primary cause of opposition, since, there are plenty of genuine differences in philosophy and approach between Y.U. and the other yeshivas.

One important area in which there are significant differences is in attitudes toward the State of Israel. Without going into great detail on this complex issue, Yeshiva's position is representative of the general Modern Orthodox view—Israel is the fulfillment of a dream held by the Jews for thousands of years and deserves their full support. The school encourages students to study there, work on kibbutzim, and emigrate if they so desire. The right-wing yeshivas' attitude is somewhat more ambivalent. It has granted Israel some form of recognition by supporting a political party that has joined the ruling Herut Party —namely, Agudath Israel. It also sends many students to study in Israeli yeshivas and does not discourage settlement there. In our study of yeshiva alumni, 18 percent reported that they planned to emigrate to Israel but 39 percent said they were not sure. Of the 43 percent who said they would not emigrate to Israel, quite a few were opposed to the idea because the government does not give primacy to religious law. Some expressed the view that the Jewish dream for a homeland will be realized with the arrival of the Messiah, and not before.[21]

Although our focus is on yeshivas in this country it is important to note, even briefly, that the recent increase in the number of American youths attending Israeli yeshivas is bound to have implications for both Y.U. and the right-wing schools in the United States. This development may be due simply to the appeal of Israel; it may be that study there is seen as an opportunity to be independent, or that Israeli yeshivas are perceived as superior; but, whatever the case, such a pattern could result in a significant brain drain from the American yeshivas. The loss of students is also bound to bring economic hardship on the schools in this country. Furthermore, as such study grows in popularity, there is likely to be a spillover here of the religious norms and values that prevail in Israel. These range from an emphasis on intensive study of Talmud at the high school level to attitudes toward the State of Israel.

Until recent years, Yeshiva University was unquestionably the preeminent educational force in the American Orthodox community. While it still remains very powerful, the winds of change are in the air and developments within the school itself reflect an awareness of and responsiveness to them. Rabbi Lamm's sensitivity to this was apparent in the following remarks:

> But I fear that with Orthodoxy's well publicized move to the right—which I hail, admire, and applaud insofar as it presages more thorough study, greater punctilious observance of both ritual and ethical laws—there have emerged concomitant phenomena that are negative and disturbing and even destructive.[22]
>
> From a speech given at the 1979
> Convention of the Rabbinical
> Council of America

There is little doubt that RIETS has also been moving to the right. What is interesting is the pride which some of those run-

ning the school take in this development. Rabbi Zevulun
Charlop, director of the RIETS program, stated emphatically to
me:

> Things are altogether different than fifteen years ago. Boys
> learn until one or two in the morning. For the evening ses-
> sion we often have three to four hundred students learning.
> Their whole outlook, sexual, religious, anti-college except in
> the narrowest, most utilitarian sense, is completely different
> from what it used to be. True, the majority still want to at-
> tend professional schools, but we have definitely moved to
> the right.[23]

Others at Yeshiva are not so enthusiastic about the rightward
trend. At the moment, the right-wingers are a growing and vocal
but still small minority among the students, drawing both fire
and support from various administrators and faculty members.
Indicative of some of the struggles going on were the following
comments made by a *rebbe* in RIETS:

> Do you know there's constant pressure in Yeshiva at the
> undergraduate level to have mixed classes? Charlop and
> Hecht [a former dean of the college] have held it back so far.
> The administrators, some of them, say: "If you have two
> girls at Stern wanting a course in biochemistry and three
> boys here wanting the same thing, you can save a lot of
> money by combining them. And at Stern College, a teacher
> in the Hebrew division gave an interview to the student
> paper about who he thought were the four greatest
> luminaries of the twentieth century, and none of them were
> religious—Buber, who married a *shikse* and Yechezkel Kauf-
> man. I'm telling you—my blood boiled over.

Right-wingers in the yeshiva world tend to take credit for
Y.U.'s move to the right. When I mentioned to Rabbi Yitzchok
Hutner that the institution which he roundly condemned (he
said, "When they put the word 'University' in, they spoiled
everything") had become more traditional in recent years, he exclaimed: "And where do you think they got the idea from? Wall
Street? We made them do it!"[24] Some at Yeshiva University feel
that the rightward shift is part of a worldwide phenomenon while
others say that the increasing popularity of study in Israel, where
there are numerous truly outstanding yeshivas, has also contributed to the change.

At the moment, Yeshiva finds itself struggling to attract students. This must be viewed in the larger context of dropping college enrollments all over the country. Moreover, it is possible that those sending their children to Yeshiva today have smaller families than was the case twenty years ago. Also, some students decline to attend Y.U. not on ideological grounds but because they want to take courses (at an evening college) in areas not offered by the school. Another deterrent for some is the tuition charges, which are considerably higher than those at public institutions. Finally, an unknown number of students have been attracted to Touro College, a recently established institution with an Orthodox orientation. Conversely, Yeshiva, because of its program, attracts some students from the right-wing yeshiva high schools because they wish to pursue careers in medicine or law and to attend full time while continuing their Talmud studies.[25]

The conflict between Yeshiva University and the other yeshivas is important because it is a mirror of the struggle in the Orthodox community between the Modern and Strictly Orthodox. At stake is the direction Orthodoxy will take in the future. Is rapprochement between Yeshiva and the other institutions possible? At the moment no effort is being made, although it is Yeshiva which increasingly seems to be on the defensive in the Orthodox community. Thus, Rabbi Lamm stated recently:

> This constant constriction of the community is clearly catastrophic. . . . After you exclude those who are pro-secular education and pro–Israel . . . and pro–Agudah and even pro–Satmar, what is left?''[26]

The general tone of his remarks reflected pessimism that such unity could be achieved and an unwillingness to compromise on firmly held beliefs:

> I refuse to accept the proposition that . . . Judaism to be authentic must be intolerant. I do not believe any of us is ready to make such concessions. More devoutness . . . certainly; more bigotry—certainly not.[27]

For their part, the Strictly Orthodox appear equally unyielding.

Many of those responding to the questionnaire mailed to alumni cited the lack of unity as one of the most important problems facing Orthodoxy today. If these two segments of the Orthodox community can resolve their differences both would probably benefit. It seems at this point, however, that neither side is willing to make the necessary adjustments to bring this about.

To those unfamiliar with the Orthodox community, it may appear as though these differences are minor and as if they could be settled were both sides willing to give in a little. This assumption would be incorrect on two grounds. First, both sides believe they are doing what God wants them to do, so that compromise of any sort would involve renunciation of a divine commandment. While the Modern Orthodox might appear to have compromised in their practices already, it must be remembered that they too base their liberalism upon scriptural interpretation and do not say, at least on the ideological level, that they are "easing up."[28] Like the Strictly Orthodox, they will invoke passages in the Bible and Talmud to account for their leniency in certain matters. Thus, both sides adhere to a literalist philosophy that makes flexibility very difficult.[29]

An even greater barrier to a meeting of the minds is rooted in the culture of the community. The student of the Talmud is trained to notice and question every "jot and tittle" in the Torah from the time of his first exposure to its concepts in elementary school. "What does the *pasuk* [verse] in the Torah *really* mean?" he is asked by his teacher, or "What are Rashi and Tosfos trying to tell us in this *Gemora*?" Every point is analyzed and debated and every small detail counts. This too contributes to the difficulties involved in bringing together those with opposing viewpoints.

Touro College

Another institution in the Orthodox community that has had an impact on the yeshivas is Touro College. Founded in 1970 by Dr. Bernard Lander, a former dean at Yeshiva University, it has a regular college curriculum with a Jewish studies program requiring a minimum of six hours' attendance a week. Dr. Lander characterizes it philosophically as "somewhere between Yeshiva University and Brandeis University," explaining that it "is not a yeshiva but rather a college with a Jewish emphasis for religious men and women." Touro has numerous divisions and programs, ranging from the liberal arts and sciences to courses of study geared to the needs of senior citizens and Russian immigrants. It is, however, the Flatbush Evening Career Program for Men that has created a major dilemma for the right-wing yeshivas. It offers programs leading to degrees in accounting, management, finance, mathematical sciences, and economics, precisely those areas studied by most yeshiva students at evening sessions in the secular colleges. The difference is that they are given in an Orthodox institution staffed by Orthodox professors and run by Orthodox administrators, and that the program is for males only and is attended only by Orthodox Jews. Unlike Yeshiva University, Touro does not maintain that secular knowledge is valuable for the sake of knowledge but stresses it as a necessity to earn a livelihood. In Dr. Lander's words:

> Not every individual can become a *rosh yeshiva* and this way they have *parnoseh* [a livelihood]. The tragedy is that a lot of yeshiva families have been broken up by lack of *parnoseh*.[30]

For these reasons the yeshivas are unable to oppose Touro on the same grounds they use to challenge Yeshiva University or the secular colleges.

What, then, is the problem? Put simply, Touro makes college so appealing that the yeshivas are afraid that more and more students, including many of their best students, will opt to go there. At the root of the yeshivas' opposition is their desire to create a community where young men study day *and* night. According to Dr. Lander, however, "A man who can become a *gadol beTorah* [giant in Torah scholarship] is not likely to become an accountant because Touro exists. If he has such talent we can't attract him and if he doesn't [have such talent] he'll go to college anyway." One prominent *rosh yeshiva* echoed this view, though he refused to be quoted by name:

> I personally feel it's a good idea to have such an institution. This way they can prepare for a job without the awful atmosphere of Brooklyn College. The idea that by giving Touro a *hechsher* [seal of approval] more will go, is naive and foolish. A guy who wants a secular education is going to go anyway.

Dr. Lander asserted: "I went to every *rosh yeshiva* before I opened Touro and only one objected." Yet no *rosh yeshiva* would acknowledge this. Their predicament was perhaps best summed up by Dr. Lander himself, who observed:

> Officially no *rosh yeshiva* can agree to college. He has to take the position that you study Talmud day and night. But in fact very few opposed us.[31]

Touro's program in Brooklyn has been growing, and there are currently between 80 and 100 students from various yeshivas enrolled in it. Their attendance, impossible without the yeshiva's knowledge, means that the yeshivas have chosen to look the other way. Those opposed to Touro have described Dr. Lander as a man who has "no qualms about ruining yeshivas."[32] In response, Dr. Lander has called his opponents "extremists," stating:

> We have a proper environment for yeshiva students, and I am not going to desist because of a small minority's opposition.[33]

Becoming a Jewish Educator: A Matter of Choice—or Lack of Choice?

One of the two professions most directly related to a yeshiva education (the other is the rabbinate) is teaching in the yeshivas themselves at various levels. Slightly less than one-third of the alumni respondents entered Jewish education. Since Beth David* is a school with a higher proportion of persons in the field than most yeshivas, it may be assumed that the number of persons not selecting Jewish education would be significantly higher if all the yeshivas were polled.[34] There are a sufficient number of jobs available in the field, and this is not a viable explanation for the relative lack of interest. When asked why they declined to enter Jewish education (*chinuch*), the most popular replies were "not suited for it" (39%) and "financial reasons" (30%).

The responses were open-ended rather than imposed by the research instrument and hence are probably representative of the range of feelings on the subject. Most persons who felt unsuited for the job did not specify why. Among those who did elaborate, the most common answers were lack of patience to teach children

---

*As noted in the Preface, this is a fictional name.

and inability to transmit knowledge to them on an elementary level. Those who gave other reasons alluded to general problems in the field for which there may or may not be solutions. Chief among them was the poor pay. In the New York City area, where competition is stiffest, a *rebbe* in a day school is likely to make $9,000 to $14,000 a year for his four or five hours a day, hardly enough to support a family. This is ironic, observed Rabbi Elya Svei, because "each one of our teachers has an education greater than that of a Ph.D. Yet they don't get the salary of a Ph.D."[35] As a result he must take a second job and this, as we see from the comments of a yeshiva student whose father is a *rebbe,* presents other problems:

> My father teaches from 8:30 to 1:30. That's his day. People say he could have another job—drive a bread truck, deliver newspapers, or teach Talmud Torah. I have met a number of people who do that. And these people, after ten years, they're *shmattes* [rags]. If you do two things at one time you get satisfaction from neither.

Rabbi Yoel Kramer, principal of the Prospect Park Yeshiva, and former President of the National Conference of Yeshiva Principals, offered the view that for people concerned about income, the solution may lie in teaching outside the New York metropolitan area, where the pay is usually much higher:

> For a young couple, it's the smartest thing. If the young man has had a year's experience, he could earn anywhere from $18,000 up. Generally, the smaller the town, the further away, the better.[36]

But teaching in "out-of-town" schools entails other problems. For the strictly religious Jew it means accommodating to a lifestyle where religious observance is difficult. Kosher food may have to be imported from outside the community (for the yeshiva graduate it must, as a rule, be *"glatt,"* as opposed to "strictly" kosher), the synagogue may not be Orthodox enough for him, and there will be few people with a background like his to serve as friends for him, his wife, and his children. As a result, the average yeshiva graduate looks to such schools as a temporary solution at best. Moreover, although the salaries at out-of-town schools may be better than the pay in New York, they are not necessarily attractive. As Rabbi Gifter of Telshe Yeshiva put it:

>Even if a teacher is paid $20,000 a year it doesn't really do much good because he often lives in a community where 20,000 isn't enough to live on and support a family.[37]

The American Jewish community is a generally affuent one.[38] The teacher, for both social and religious reasons, must live in the community (i.e., he must be within walking distance of a synagogue) where the homes are usually more expensive and the lifestyles of his neighbors may make him feel relatively deprived.

Another factor is a significant change in the number of jobs available to Sabbath observers. Years ago yeshiva graduates felt that positions in Jewish education had the advantage of enabling them to lead a strictly religious life. Many opportunities in law, accounting, and government hinged upon the willingness of the person to be "flexible" in his observance patterns. With the advent of strictly enforced civil service regulations barring discrimination against Sabbath observers and the like, the argument that one cannot lead a truly religious life in certain professions no longer holds true. As a result, many yeshiva graduates feel less hesitant about looking for openings in areas previously considered closed to them, and this has brought about a brain drain from the field of Jewish education. It is ironic that the successful efforts of the Orthodox community in pressuring employers and agencies that had discriminated against Orthodox Jews in the past has in part been responsible for a seeming dearth of qualified applicants in another area also crucial to the community's well-being.

The question of money is inevitably tied in with prestige considerations. No elaboration is needed on this point beyond indicating that numerous yeshiva students with whom I spoke and many respondents to the questionnaire felt strongly that day school teachers were looked down upon because they tended to be poorly paid.

What about other sources of prestige? Does it not stand to reason that in a society where education is so highly valued, an individual charged with transmitting that culture will be respected? What about idealistic motivations? A sense of dedication and responsibility? Perhaps looking at some of the other reasons given by respondents for not choosing Jewish education can provide some answers.

One of the major problems has to do with the course of study prevailing in the advanced yeshivas themselves. They do not offer a specific program geared to produce teachers. Rather, they emphasize intensive Talmud study with the aim of producing knowledgeable scholars. If an individual studied exclusively for a position as, say, a fifth-grade Talmud instructor, he could complete his training in Talmud itself in less than half the time that is devoted to the subject now. The rest of his training could encompass intensive courses in pedagogy and child development, and in how to teach Bible, Prophets, and Jewish laws and customs. Instead, he studies as if he were training to be a *rebbe* at the *beis medrash* level. Unfortunately, there are very few positions that open up in advanced yeshivas or even high schools (*mesivtas*), both of which are far fewer in number than the elementary school yeshivas. The result is a person vastly overqualified for the positions available to him while untrained in the specific pedagogical skills necessary for the teaching of small children.[39]

Exacerbating the problem is the fact that it is often those who have been in the yeshiva longest and who are therefore most likely to notice the disparity between their training and their occupation who end up teaching in the day schools. One *bochur* at Lakewood described what happens:

> A person can admit he'll never be Einstein but he'll be somebody. He'll get a good job at Bell Labs. But in the yeshiva you're forced to admit you didn't make it big and then you're twenty-five and you've got to get a job. You're asking a person to admit that he'll never have acclaim . . . that if he goes into *chinuch* he'll never have any money to make up for that lack. And it's too late in life to try anything else. He's twenty-seven and he's got two or three kids. It's too late for him to go to law or medical school.

These are often people who gambled that they would get one of the few jobs available at the high school or *beis medrash* institutions and who lost that gamble. It is for them a bitter and humiliating experience.

Moreover, school officials sometimes fail to appreciate the emotional adjustments facing a graduate of a top-notch yeshiva who regards teaching in elementary school as a sign that he is a failure. The situation cannot, incidentally, be compared to one where a young man studies in a secular college for his M.A. in education and becomes a second-grade public school teacher. In such a case, he has usually decided in advance and on his own that this is what he wants to do. He has also received training in how to approach small children and get them to learn.

Some will place the blame on the advanced yeshivas themselves for failing to set realistic objectives. This will be discussed in greater depth when we deal with the overall goals of the yeshiva in the next chapter. For now, it can be noted that the yeshivas do neglect to prepare their students adequately for teaching at the lower levels. And although no one would speak for attribution, almost everyone—students, administrators, faculty, and community leaders—acknowledged that most yeshivas discourage their best students from going into Jewish education because they feel it is a dead-end job financially. In addition, they believe the poor pay will make it necessary for the young man to work so hard that he will have little time left for private study, which is a major goal of the yeshivas. Even the idealistically inclined are reluctant to enter a profession where they feel obliged to prove to others in their community that they did not select it because they were regarded as less than "top material" while in the yeshiva.

Largely owing to the efforts of Dr. Joseph Kaminetsky, former head of Torah Umesorah (National Society for Hebrew Day Schools), there has been some improvement in the situation over the years. Programs known as *machons* have been established by Torah Umesorah at several yeshivas, with varying degrees of success. Students enter the *machon* for a period of up to two years, where they are taught pedagogy and other relevant subjects while continuing their talmudic studies in the *beis medrash*. Still, a great deal depends on the individual yeshiva's interest and its willingness to place its best students in the program. At yeshivas such as Chofetz Chaim and Ner Israel Yeshiva, positive attitudes on the part of the administration have encouraged many graduates to go into Jewish education.[40] At other schools the programs have been less successful.

Summing up, numerous problems stand in the way of the young man who wishes to become a teacher in a yeshiva. Salaries are low, and there is the tremendous letdown experienced by the student when, after years of studying Talmud at a very high level, he must teach beginners how to read Hebrew. Furthermore, there is the low status accorded those who enter the field by their own peers in the yeshiva and by those who run it, a feeling that they didn't really "make it." Finally, there is the relative lack of financial support for Jewish education by the Orthodox community itself, a curious anomaly, given the importance that Orthodox Jews place on such education.

The Rabbinate: Its Limits and Potential

If it is true that young men reject the prospect of becoming educators because of the low pay and prestige and their lack of interest in teaching at an elementary level, what about the rabbinate? Here is an area where the pay is better, the job more prestigious, and the challenges seemingly broader. Yet today most yeshiva graduates, with the exception of those from Yeshiva University, which produces many of the rabbis currently hired by Orthodox synagogues, have eschewed this field.[41] While Yeshiva University has a highly organized and efficient placement office, at other yeshivas placement is much more haphazard, in itself an indication of the lack of priority given to the rabbinate.[42]

One reason for the lack of interest is the nature of the job itself. The right-wing yeshiva graduate requires a synagogue where there is a separation between the men's section and that of the women (*mechitza*). More than that, he wants a congregation where his obligations will not be primarily social, where he will not be a psychiatrist for his congregants, and where he will not be expected to make speeches on political and other contemporary issues.[43] Rather, he wants to preside over a congregation of *talmidei chachomim* (scholars) where he is first among equals and can give lectures presupposing intimate familiarity with the Talmud. Unfortunately, such congregations are relatively few in number, and where they do exist, their members are unlikely to feel the need for a rabbi to guide them, relying instead upon their former *rosh yeshivas* for guidance. The lack of an appropriate environment becomes even more manifest when the student thinks of an out-of-town position. As Rabbi Gifter observed:

> In one East Coast community, I sent a young man where he
> built up a community from nothing. Unfortunately he felt he
> had to leave because of the *chinuch* needs for his children.
> The problem was no one replaced him and the whole community went down the drain.[44]

For these reasons, many yeshiva students tend to look down upon those who accept pulpits in synagogues. They wonder what compromises the rabbi was compelled to make, how much time he has to teach and learn Torah, what with all his other responsibilities, and how much influence he actually has over his congregants. Rabbi Emanuel Feldman, a well-known pulpit rabbi who graduated from Ner Israel Yeshiva, attempted to portray such characterizations in a positive light:

> The unfortunate tendency among some of the students must be understood for what it is: an extension of their total commitment to *shlemut* (perfection) and study and service of God which views apparent professionalism and careerism with a jaundiced eye. The researcher in medicine frequently looks down upon the practicing physician as one who has left the tower of ivory in favor of the fleshpots. Although I know the great achievements for Torah which can be accomplished in the active rabbinate, I am willing to forgive any yeshiva student his looking down on me, for I know his soul and it is a Torah soul, and as he matures he will come to the understanding that the so-called career rabbi is no less concerned with God and Torah than he.[45]

Another factor reducing the appeal of the rabbinate has to do with the shape of the power structure within the Orthodox community in America. In Europe the rabbi was generally the leader of his community in both the religious and political spheres. Here he must compete with the *rosh yeshiva* as the yeshiva movement continues to gain in power and influence. With the involvement of the *rosh yeshivas* in activist groups such as the Agudah-supported Moetzes Gedolei Torah and the Torah Umesorah–supported Rabbinical Administrative Board, has come a perception by many in the community that these individuals are not only great scholars but also knowledgeable activists. Awareness of this situation makes the rabbinate even less attractive for yeshiva graduates.

Nevertheless, the rabbi's position can be an influential one. The average rabbi does command the respect of a substantial number of his congregants. Moreover, unlike the yeshiva *rebbe,* he has a power base from which to operate and he is better paid. Though he may be denigrated by his former classmates, they are not, at least in the large Modern Orthodox synagogues, the people with whom he deals on a daily basis. He also has the opportunity to bring people closer to Judaism.

The leaders of the Strictly Orthodox recognize the potential of the rabbinate, and several *rosh yeshivas* expressed the view to me that more of their students ought to consider it as a serious option. Rabbi Moshe Sherer, President of the Agudath Israel, expressed his concern over what he felt were lost opportunities to influence the larger community:

> Many don't want to go into public Jewish life because they want to spend more time studying Torah. But if we are really engaged in a struggle to survive, something has to give. The alternative is that millions of *neshomos* [souls] that heard the *Aseres haDibros* [Ten Commandments] on *Har Sinai* [Mount Sinai] will enter churches. People have to go into the rabbinate to save them.[46]

Although the number of positions available in establishment-type Orthodox synagogues has probably decreased, it seems that in the Strictly Orthodox community congregations are springing up, some with seventy-five or even more families, made up of persons with extensive yeshiva backgrounds. Known as ''*yeshiva minyanim* (congregations),'' they have been appointing outstanding scholars as rabbis. At present there are several congregations of this sort in the Flatbush section of Brooklyn and the Kew Gardens Hills section of Queens. The need for such rabbis, despite the influence of the *rosh yeshivas,* was prophetically outlined in 1964 by Rabbi Nosson Scherman in the *Jewish Observer:*

> The ties of the alumnus to the yeshivah grow weaker as time goes on until the concept of a vibrant Torah life . . . fades into a Shangri La of hazy nostalgia. The unbending ideals of old grow flabby and flexible and much too accommodating to the stresses of job, home, and neighborhood. . . . His [the *rosh yeshiva's*] influence on daily life is ended with his disappearance from the day-to-day existence of his students. Here is where the *Rov* [Rabbi] is needed.[47]

Conditions are now ripe in the Strictly Orthodox community for congregational rabbis. If the present growth trend continues, we can anticipate, first more and more congregations in the Orthodox community whose direction, including the type of

rabbi they employ, will bear the imprint of the Strictly Orthodox. Second, in the same manner as the Moetzes Gedolei
Torah, these rabbis will sooner or later band together in an
association that will rival established groups such as the Rabbinical Council of America, or they will take control of these
groups. Finally, the appeal of the rabbinate as a career will increase sharply among yeshiva students whose institutions will
respond by offering courses in rabbinics and homiletics.[48]

Dating and Marriage: How to Meet, Where to Go, and What to Do

Young men in the Yeshiva community usually begin dating
between the ages of twenty and twenty-three. For young women,
seventeen or eighteen is considered the proper age in accordance
with both religious and social custom, and few wait beyond nineteen. In all cases, dating is permissible only for the purpose of
finding a suitable marriage partner.

The *shadchan* (matchmaker) still plays a role in yeshiva society. He or she not only makes introductions but investigates the
backgrounds of the families with respect to lineage, wealth,
religiosity, and general reputation in the community. While
matchmakers often charge a hefty fee for their services, most
parents consider it an eminently worthwhile investment. *Shadchanim* operate ''marriage bureaus'' as opposed to ''dating
bureaus.'' They see their services as eliminating the problem of
''the rat race.''[49] In addition to screening the families, the matchmaker must weigh the probable compatibility of the prospective
bride and groom. Among the important questions are: Does the
young man wish to study Talmud or enter business immediately
after the wedding? Does it matter to him that his wife has (or has
not) gone to college? Does he prefer someone of German or
Hungarian or Polish background? How about a girl from a
Hasidic background or one from a Modern Orthodox family?
How large must the dowry be? How important are looks, personality, and so on, and so on?

Far more common are introductions made by members of
the family or their friends, the *rosh yeshiva,* the *rebbe,* or even the
young man's contemporaries. There are people in the commu-

nity who recommend (*rett*) matches gratis, taking pleasure in the accomplishment. Because community norms severely limit the yeshiva *bochur*'s opportunities to meet young women, having others make the arrangements does not carry the stigma it may evoke in the Modern Orthodox community. When nonprofessionals are involved, the prospective date is not always thoroughly investigated. Mr. X, who is a member of the Diamond Dealers Club, on 47th Street in Manhattan, may casually suggest to Mr. Y with whom he has done business for fifteen years, that he and his family, including his eligible son, come visit on Sunday afternoon, so that they can meet Mr. X's daughter, who is "ready"; or the *rosh yeshiva* may suggest to one of his students that Mr. D has a daughter who might be an ideal match for the young man. Given the *rosh yeshiva*'s position, such a suggestion is rarely ignored.

Marriages are not arranged in the American yeshiva community, only introductions. No matter how suitable a prospective match appears to be, custom dictates that the boy and girl date for a period of time and arrive at their own conclusions concerning compatibility. The days when parents decided are gone, as are the days when decisions were based on a submitted photograph. Interestingly, there is some leeway in how introductions are made that allows for a certain amount of initiative to be exercised by the young man and woman. If the parties meet in a college class, at a wedding, resort hotel or at an informal occasion and are smitten by each other they may begin to date; or they may approach their own parents, a *shadchan,* or some other third party and ask them to arrange a formal meeting so that the match will be acceptable to the respective families. In this manner, the chance meetings that are common in the larger society acquire greater legitimacy and respectability. Despite these avenues, therapists familiar with the community have reported quite a few patients who claim not to know how and where they can meet someone of the opposite sex. As a rule, such individuals tend to be somewhat shy and withdrawn. They probably turn to *shadchanim* for help because the community does not approve of mixers, parties, computer matches, and similar approaches used in other cultures.

By the fourth or fifth date pressure from parents and others begins to make itself felt. According to informed members of the community six to ten dates are about average before an engagement is announced, although there are instances where the young man and woman see each other as few as two times or as many as twenty. Double dating, incidentally, is frowned upon since it carries the implication that the couple is simply going out "for fun" rather than *tachlis* (for a specific purpose).

It is a measure of the distinctiveness of the yeshiva community that a number of customs have sprung up in the area of dating, some of which also exist in the contemporary Hasidic community. For example, one or two weeks after the engagement, the girl's parents give a party called "a congratulations" on a Sabbath afternoon. Many young men (or their parents) also purchase a leather-bound set of festival prayer books (*machzorim*) with the future bride's married name engraved in gold on the cover. Often, gold watches are exchanged. The girl's parents generally give the young man a prayer shawl (*talis*) with a gold or silver embroidered collar plus a complete set of the Talmud, which is later prominently displayed in the newlyweds' apartment. These practices are not uniform and frequently depend upon the financial ability to carry them out. Nor are the various customs necessarily permanent; new wrinkles constantly appear in the yeshiva version of "keeping up with the Joneses."

Since movies, concerts, trips to the beach, and so on are considered religiously inappropriate, couples are somewhat limited in their recreational choices. Still, it is possible to go to a museum, or the planetarium, to eat in a kosher restaurant or just take a ride. A number of places have become popular among yeshiva students that would hardly constitute a date in other communities. There is an "airport date" where the couple drive to the airport and simply walk around, perhaps dropping into the cocktail lounge for a drink. In fact, cocktail lounges have become popular in their own right. If the girl is properly bred (or coached), she will order a coke while her date indulges in something a bit stronger perhaps. The more religious students will wear their black hats even inside a bar while the "freer spirits" are likely to favor a yarmulke of an inconspicuous color. "In-dates," where the couple stays in the girl's house for the evening, are not the norm in the yeshiva world, but they are common in the Hasidic community. Wherever they go, the couple must, according to Jewish law, avoid being alone. If they should find themselves in such a situation, they will keep the door open.

Finding the Right Person:
The Things That Count

The Jewish Single—Twenty-two and over the Hill

Dear *Rebbetzin* Yungreis:*

I am somewhat embarrassed to write to you because my problem is of a personal nature, but I'm so terribly hurt I feel that I must pour out my heart to someone who might be able to give me some advice. I only ask that you please keep my name confidential.

My daughter is a graduate of a well-known yeshiva, 22 years old and single, a tragedy in our Jewish community. Most of her classmates are already married and have babies, and my daughter has been left behind. She is a very pretty girl and holds a fine position . . . , but somehow, I don't know why, she has no *mazel* [luck] and lately she has become very nervous and depressed. . . . So my problem is, where can she meet a nice *balabatish* boy [loosely, one from a background with which the girl will feel comfortable]? And believe me, Rebbetzin, the competition is stiff. We are not rich people. . . . It seems that in our religious community, if you don't have big money, you can't make a *shidduch* for your daughter. I have discovered that some of these boys are not interested in marriage, but in a financial merger, and I find that the mothers of the boys are the major culprits. They have such demands and pretensions for their sons. . . . The girl has to be not pretty, but gorgeous, outfitted in designer clothing and name brands. Lately [my daughter] has been talking about . . . taking her own apartment in the city. . . . On Simchas Torah she just stayed in the house and refused to walk out on the Avenue [Brooklyn's 14th Avenue, where Orthodox Jews go to see and be seen].

Rebbetzin, what do I do? Should I let her take her own apartment . . . or should I try to pressure her to remain at home?

A Heartbroken Mother†

This lightly edited letter, reminiscent of the Bintel Brief column that appeared in the *Jewish Daily Forward* starting in 1906, is

* *Rebbetzin* is a term identifying a rabbi's wife.
† From "Rebbetzin's Viewpoint," *Jewish Press*, December 1, 1978, p. 26.[50]

typical of a certain genre of letters addressed to *Rebbetzin* Esther Yungreis or to psychologist Dr. Morris Mandel, each of whom has his or her own column.[51] The *rebbetzin*, predictably perhaps, advises the mother not to allow her daughter to move out, observing that it will damage the young lady's reputation. In an implicit criticism, she urges the various *rosh yeshivas* and *rebbes* to "speak out on the problem."

By the time the student reaches marriageable age, he has assimilated into his own outlook many yeshiva values, one of the most important of which is that study is a lifetime endeavor. He will therefore judge a lifestyle and occupation with an eye toward whether or not it will allow him enough time to "learn Torah." The same considerations enter into his choice of a wife, and he is likely to care a great deal about whether or not the family is wealthy enough to support him while he learns full time for a few years after marriage in a *kollel*. Anyone familiar with the yeshiva community knows that he who learns well is frequently rewarded with the opportunity to marry a girl whose dowry will provide for the couple while he sits in the yeshiva. This practice is defended on the grounds that those who are most capable should be allowed to pursue their studies. True, there are many young men who marry girls of more modest means and still manage to devote several years to full-time study in a *kollel*, but, as we shall see, they face a difficult struggle in doing so.

In light of this situation, it is perhaps not surprising to find some students who speak of marriage in disparaging tones. As one commented to me: "I don't want to get married yet. I'd rather have a few years to give just for learning. Unless you're lucky and marry rich, all you get is a *shas* [set of the Talmud] and then you have to go to work." For Orthodox girls who are not lucky enough to have wealthy parents this state of affairs has bred a great deal of resentment. Typical is the following description by a graduate of a post–high school girls' seminary:

> I went out with a guy who didn't want to marry me because I wasn't rich enough. Actually he was willing, but his mother wasn't. I think it's really disgusting because eventually you have to go to a *shadchan* who charges $3,000–$4,000 to find someone decent and my parents can't afford that.

This situation often causes the family to overextend itself financially in its desperation to find a good match for their daughter.

There are other criteria, too. For the very religious, the fact that the young man or woman has gone to college may be seen as a negative factor, implying that he or she is "too interested in secular matters." One young graduate of a women's seminary informed me: "I had to explain to a *shadchan* why I wouldn't go out again with a fellow. He just wanted to go to the movies. He was a good student but I just didn't like his outlook on things." Conversely, the more modern members of the yeshiva community will view a college background and/or secular interests as a plus. Some young women prefer a student who will study for a few years after marriage, regardless of the financial hardship, while others want a "more practical" fellow.

To a greater degree than in the larger society, family background and general reputation are considered to be important. Rabbinic leaders in the family, wealthy relatives known for their generosity to Jewish institutions, and respected community leaders are taken into account. The fact that a person has siblings who are not observant may sometimes be held against him or her. A young man who proclaims his interest in marrying only a young woman from a wealthy family may acquire a reputation as someone who "only cares about money." Like universities, yeshivas confer a status of their own upon those who attend. Thus, "a Lakewood boy" can automatically command a higher dowry even if his proficiency in Talmud is somewhat lacking, just as a Harvard graduate steps into the economic marketplace with certain advantages.

Preparation for Marriage: Are They Ready?

Despite the established and widely accepted patterns of courtship in the community there are strong indications that all is not well in this area. Interviews with a wide range of persons in the community, including psychiatrists and social workers, revealed rising concern about the problems facing numerous yeshiva families after marriage. Although family life is remarkably stable, compared to the dominant society, with a low divorce rate and little incidence of pathology, the absolute rate of problems appears to have increased significantly in the past decade. To what extent this is due to general societal developments such as the women's movement and the general rise in the divorce rate is not known, but these factors are undoubtedly important. The *Jewish Observer*, almost always a reliable barometer of yeshiva norms and priorities, has printed a number of articles on this subject in the past few years. Moreover, numerous conferences and meetings have been held at which community leaders have debated the increase in marital discord. In this context, I want to touch briefly on the question of readiness for marriage, which ultimately bears upon the success of the relationship. These issues are, as we shall see, unique to the community itself.

One of the major problems revolves around the disparity between the attitudes toward members of the opposite sex inculcated during the grade school years and throughout adolescence and later expectations. Boys and girls are cautioned repeatedly against having contact with each other, even on a superficial level. Then suddenly, without formal counseling or any other sort of preparation, they are told that they have reached the age at which they should actively seek a mate. By way of illustration, I want to quote from a lecture given to a class of students in an advanced yeshiva who ranged in age from seventeen to twenty:

The *rebbe*'s face appeared very stern. He began speaking in a low and deliberate tone, choosing his words rather carefully:

> I've been asked to talk about a very serious matter by the *rosh yeshiva*. Perhaps the best way to begin would be to refer you to the laws concerning women in *Ibn Haezer* where it states that a man has to be very, very careful to stay away from women. "It is forbidden to engage in light-hearted talk with them and to look upon their beauty." This sin is harder to stay away from because it involves lust, emotions, and when you deal with lusts, discussion doesn't help much. By their very nature, emotions aren't open to reason. This has "an atomic power" and can bring about a person's total downfall.

Then, raising his voice, the *rebbe* continued:

> We know that some of the boys are talking to the girls at the college and we've heard that a few are even giving them rides home. The yeshiva cannot and will not tolerate such behavior in its midst and we will ask people who do this to leave the yeshiva if it doesn't stop immediately. We are living in an age of moral degeneration and decay. The last thirty years have been worse than any period in the

preceding 5,000 years. You may think innocent socializing is okay but you should know that one step leads to another.

The *rebbe,* who is in his late thirties, married, with several children, continued in this vein for almost an hour. Throughout the lecture, the students sat silently, their faces impassive. When the *rebbe* had finished he called for questions. Only one student, a young man with a reputation for rebelliousness, spoke up. "But *rebbe,*" he asked with a faint smile, "why do you have to stay *so* far away from this?" "Such a question requires no answer," the *rebbe* replied curtly. "You can see me after class if you want to continue the discussion. Now let's go on with the *Gemora.*"

The fact that these students were close to or of marriageable age is significant for it highlights the very short transition period mentioned earlier. If these same students were introduced to an eligible girl by a *shadchan* the following week, the yeshiva would encourage them to pursue the matter. Yet how is the student to recognize the subtle distinctions between what is totally forbidden in one context and desirable in another, especially when the Orthodox girl he encounters in college is the same one he might meet on a formal basis a month hence?

Obviously, there are many students for whom such an adjustment is no problem. They will take such moral exhortations with a grain of salt and go their own way. For others, there may be a greater need to elaborate. After class, I spoke with some of the students and discovered widely differing reactions. One student said to me, somewhat sarcastically, "I guess that's why I'm Dovid Elbaum* and he's Rabbi Margolis,*" indicating at the same time that he thought the whole thing had been blown out of proportion. Another student, a serious and intense young man of twenty, took a different view:

> You know, maybe someone outside the yeshiva world who hears about this would say: "What are you trying to do? You can't close yourself off from the outside world." But this obviously has no place here. It's as though a yeshiva student would eat *trefe* [nonkosher food]. It would just be shocking. If the yeshiva's purpose is Torah anything else is a distraction.

Such attitudes raise important questions: To what extent do they affect general attitudes toward women *after* marriage? Is marriage itself unduly hastened as a result of the repression of physical desires? A number of respondents indicated great difficulty in this area, describing how apprehensive they felt when the time came to date for *tachlis*. Said one who attended Mesivta Tifereth Jerusalem:

> What I remember most about these dates is my heart pounding before I called them up. There was the fear of rejection. And then the date itself. I couldn't touch her and was afraid to anyway. But I couldn't imagine having sex with someone after marriage when I wasn't allowed to *think* about it before.

In an excellent article that appeared in the *Jewish Observer* Meir Wikler, a social worker with a practice in Brooklyn, quotes a girl whose views are almost identical:

> Somehow, I find it all so confusing. For 18 years it gets drummed into my head that I'm not suposed to talk, to look at, or even *think* about boys. Then all of a sudden, literally overnight, I'm supposed to be able not only to go out with boys but also to feel relaxed on a date.[52]

Drawing upon his own experiences, Wikler presents numerous case studies that reveal a range of problems. He argues that they are widespread and concludes that all sectors of the community—parents, teachers, and leaders—should redouble their efforts to resolve them.

Another aspect of the same problem is that the average student is away from home for long periods of time. If he dorms, it means that he will not have the opportunity to observe how his parents interact, nor will he have the chance to interact with the opposite sex siblings as he passes through the crucial adolescent years. Even those boys who commute are away most of the day and evening. Some have argued that because girls are home more they learn through observing role models how to interact on this level, and are therefore better prepared for the give-and-take of marriage than their male counterparts.

Mention must also be made of the strong bonds of male friendship that develop as a natural result of extended contact on a twenty-four hour basis. This may make the yeshiva student apprehensive about adjusting to the different interests and ways of socializing common among young women. Perhaps alluding to this, one young man informed me that he was waiting until he was twenty-four to look for a girl because "I still want to get

more established in learning, and also *I think I wouldn't be able to
have as much fun with the guys if I got married*" (italics added).

Parents, while sometimes serving as a source of support, are
in many cases not helpful. Frequently they pressure the children
to get married, fearful that failure to do so by a certain age will
reflect negatively upon their success as parents. In fact, living as
they do in a highly status-conscious community, they may even
push their children into an ill-advised match because of the inor-
dinate value placed by the community upon such things as the
"right" family. As the principal of one of the largest girls' high
schools said:

> The parents have to get into the act. They're all involved
> socially: "Is this the proper match? What kind of in-laws are
> they? Will they make a nice house? Will it look good?
> What's the *yichus?*"

Another trouble spot related to community mores is the
reluctance of the parents to allow their children much independence. Because the nuclear family in the Orthodox community is so closely knit, reflecting as it does the European values
of the postwar immigrant generation, there is a tendency to interfere with the couple's lives even after they get married.
Sometimes the attachment is welcomed by the children, and this
can lead to other problems. Yaakov Salomon, a social worker
with a large clientele of Orthodox Jews, explained it in the
following terms:

> The families want to hold on to their children so badly that
> they mix in as a way of staying in touch. Frequently there
> will be the feeling expressed by the parent—"Remember, if
> the going gets too rough you can always come back home."[53]

According to Salomon and others, this is especially true of
parents who survived the Holocaust and who are, as a result,
often eager to hold on to their offspring even as they send them
out into the world. The lack of research on the community in
general, and on the post–World War II immigrant experience in
particular, means that assumptions such as these must remain,
for the moment, a matter for speculation.

If not the parents, then perhaps the yeshiva can play a more
assertive role in this area. As noted in earlier chapters, the
yeshiva faculty and administration often serve as surrogate

parents. As such, they are in a position to advise and counsel the young man. Yet many therapists, rabbis, and former students lamented the lack of institutional involvement. Hardly any yeshiva today has classes that prepare the student for his marital responsibilities. This is not simply because there is a dearth of capable instructors (though it is admittedly no easy task to find men who can win the respect of the American yeshiva *bochur* in this sensitive area). It is also due to the yeshiva's perception that its role is not to prepare a young man for marriage but to teach him Torah. There is also the feeling that focusing attention on this matter might inflate the problem. The girls' yeshivas are not in the same situation since Torah study is only one part of their objective, with the overall goal being more one of preparation for life in general. As a result, they spend more time on these issues. Yet even there, with one or two notable exceptions such as the Prospect Park Yeshiva for Girls in Brooklyn, the emphasis has been on laws relating to family purity—important, but not sufficient.

There is, however, some movement in the direction of genuine counseling within the community, with the tacit support of the yeshiva community. Rabbi Label Katz of Boro Park gives what is called "a *choson* [groom] class" that deals with the underlying dilemmas facing the yeshiva student. This is only a beginning and there is hope among community leaders that those who head the yeshivas will recognize their responsibility to provide guidance for those who will, for better or worse, be known as alumni of their respective institutions. In a society where separation of the sexes is rigidly enforced until shortly before marriage such counsel is imperative.

We can perhaps conclude this section with the observation that attitudes and practices with regard to marriage point to the intrusion of secular values into the lifestyle of the community. The very idea of dating is an American phenomenon, as is the feeling that one must "go somewhere." It is doubtful that any *rosh yeshiva* living in Lithuania in the nineteenth century would have dreamed that a twenty-four-year-old yeshiva *bochur* could take a prospective mate to a cocktail lounge for drinks. Despite the efforts of those who run the yeshivas, such contact is unavoidable in an open society. The student who opens the newspaper may not look at the movie section, but is one to assume that he has not heard of Farrah Fawcett or seen a photograph of her as he glanced at an advertisement? And does this not affect his idea of what constitutes a pretty wife? What about the emphasis on self-gratification? The fancy car, the pretty dress, and the beautiful home furnishings all bear the marks of the materialism that prevails in the larger society. Try as it might to eradicate such temptations, the yeshiva can only hope to minimize them. The question is, Do these accommodations represent adjustment or compromise? It is a question to which we shall turn later on.

The *Kollel* (Graduate Division): "Learning in His Blood"

An increasingly important component of yeshiva life in America is the *kollel*. Although there were *kollels* in Europe (the most famous in Kovno, Lithuania) and in Palestine in the early part of the twentieth century, the institution has reached its zenith in this country.[54]

Basically, a *kollel* is a place where married yeshiva students pursue full-time talmudic study as they did during their years in the yeshiva but with a greater degree of autonomy.[55] Most *kollels* are attached to yeshivas that have undergraduate divisions and were, in fact, founded to provide continuity for those students who wished to continue studying after marriage. The central goal of the *kollel*, as envisioned by its leaders, is to promote the intellectual and spiritual growth of its members. *Kollels* vary in their requirements for admission. Some, such as those at Yeshiva University and the Rabbinical Seminary of America (Chofetz Chaim Yeshiva), require their students to have completed a formal course of undergraduate study prior to entry while others ask only for a general commitment to learning. There is no such thing as "graduating" from a *kollel*; the length of stay can be anywhere from one year to twenty. Most, however, study between two and five years. Students admitted to the *kollel* often receive some support from the institution itself but must invariably supplement it from other sources.

In 1950 there were no more than 50 to 100 persons studying in *kollels*. Today there are at least 1,000 such individuals, evidence of profound quantitative and qualitative changes in the character of higher Jewish learning in America. There are *kollels* in all parts of the continent. Besides the major yeshiva centers of New York City, Baltimore, and Lakewood, New Jersey, *kollels* have been founded in Mexico City, Toronto, Los Angeles, South Fallsburg, New York, Scranton, Stamford, Connecticut, and Deal, New Jersey, which has the only *kollel* in the United States established specifically for Sephardic Jews. Some *kollels,* possibly because of their small size and isolation from large Orthodox communities, are more closely knit than others, such as those located in New York City itself.

In recent years quite a few *kollels* have been deliberately established in the midst of major Jewish communities. Known as "community *kollels,*" they represent a departure from the earlier, inwardly oriented *kollels.* In addition to full-time study, members of these *kollels* are committed to reaching out to the larger community. Among their activities are studying with interested Jews who have little background, raising funds for elementary school yeshivas, helping families observe various Jewish laws, opening Judaica libraries, and so on.[56]

The daily schedule of study is arduous. The young man rises about 6:30 A.M. for services at the yeshiva and returns home for dinner around 6:00 or 7:00. By this time his wife, who often has a job, even if she has children, has already prepared supper for him. After spending an hour or so relaxing with his family, it is back to the *kollel* for the evening session. Those in the *kollel* are treated as adults with little or no supervision. It is assumed that they are there because of idealistic motives.

Besides Talmud study, the *kollel* members serve another, very important purpose if their *kollel* is attached to a yeshiva with a *beis medrash.* By acting as role models they stimulate and motivate the younger students. The nineteen- and twenty-year-old undergraduates carefully observe the behavior of the *kollel* members since they know that in a few years they may be in a *kollel* themselves. *Kollel* members, particularly the younger ones, frequently become study partners on a limited basis with undergraduates. Studying with a *kollel* member, unless it is for a remedial purpose, is often seen as a status symbol among undergraduates. On an informal level, they act as shoulders to cry on and people to confide in. Sometimes they will admonish the younger students, asking them: "Do you think it was right to walk around talking during *mincha* [afternoon prayer service] or during the *rosh yeshiva*'s *mussar shmuess* [ethics talk]?" Some of the boys accept such remonstrations with equanimity while others are resentful.

Perhaps 70 percent of those attending *kollels* receive financial support from the school. The amounts vary from $40 to $75 a week in the more established *kollels,* while the newer ones, seeking to attract qualified applicants, offer up to $150 per week. For the most part, support is given equally though need and, to a lesser extent, merit are also taken into account. In some instances, the *kollel* will provide other means of support such as subsidized housing and free trips back home for those who live in far-away cities.[57] Finally, *kollel* members may receive government aid such as food stamps, Medicaid, Section 8 housing, and other benefits.

Life in a *kollel* presents a variety of challenges and dilemmas. To learn how people cope with some of them, 14 *kollel* members from several yeshivas and 12 wives of *kollel* students (only two were married to the *kollel* members with whom we spoke) were interviewed at length. The general description of life in this community is drawn in large measure from these discussions.[58]

Since the stipend given by the *kollel* is rarely enough to support a family, the wife generally works in jobs ranging from secretarial work and keypunch operating to teaching in a Talmud Torah. When the first child is born some of the wives stop working but many, unable to afford this luxury, take off for perhaps a month or two and then return to work, putting the child into a day care center run by either the yeshiva or a private group, or leaving him with relatives. Cases of women with three or four children working part-time are not uncommon. Kollel students will also enroll in work–study programs at the yeshiva such as working in the kitchen, library, handling the mail, and so on. The financial burden is somewhat eased during the first year of marriage as the couple draws upon wedding gifts. Of course, there are many things to be bought at first, but here the parents generally help.

There are those fortunate enough to have wealthy parents to tide them over during these years. Some parents will support their children only up to a point whereas others spare nothing, buying expensive furnishings, clothes, and food. In a community where people live in close proximity and share many common experiences, everyone knows who is supported by parents and who is not, and those who engage in conspicuous consumption often arouse envy in others. One young woman, who, like many others, considered a washing machine and dishwasher as luxury items, expressed her scorn in the following manner:

> I feel that someone who is sitting and learning and depend-
> ing on their parents' money, they shouldn't buy the most
> beautiful dining-room set. If you're dependent on someone
> else why squeeze them for all they have? I'm not saying you
> shouldn't buy, but is it necessary to run around and try to
> match everything up just so?

Another wife of a *kollel* member stated:

> We buy the cheapest meats. We don't buy steak—we get
> chicken by the case or we eat fish. My parents wanted to give
> us money but Dov doesn't want to. He says it's not right.
> Our furniture is second hand.[59]

On the other hand, a woman whose home was beautifully decorated said:

> Why shouldn't we live well? My husband doesn't take
> money from the *kollel* because he doesn't need to. But he's
> been learning for six years and will continue learning for a
> while. Should we live like paupers? Besides, my parents are
> happy when we take the money. They feel that a man who
> learns should live as well as a businessman since his "work"
> is for *Hashem* [God].

The yeshiva tries to make matters easier for those not as blessed as this couple. There is a fund called "*gemach*" from which needy students can draw. These are short-term loans repayable at no interest, usually within a year. In some places there is a store where groceries may be purchased at slightly more than cost. The profits are used only to pay the employees. All in all, it should be recognized that their financial situation is such that most *kollel* families cannot afford vacations, trips, eating out in restaurants, or anything else beyond the basic necessities of life. The few that can are often singled out by other Orthodox Jews as "living off the fat of the land."

Why, then, is *kollel* not only popular but becoming increasingly fashionable? In the interviews, both men and women expressed the view that inasmuch as marriage was a lifetime commitment it was crucial that it be established on a strong foundation. Given their value system, learning fulltime was an excellent way to begin:

> I really think the first year or two sets the pattern for the rest of your life. Even if my husband goes to work later he'll never change. He'll be a person who has learning in his blood, not just for an education.
>
> A nineteen-year-old woman living in
Lakewood, New Jersey

Rabbi Aharon Schechter, the present *rosh yeshiva* of Chaim Berlin, emphasized the education of Strictly Orthodox girls in the development of such attitudes:

> You have to give a great deal of credit to the Bais Yaakov [Beth Jacob] schools which ingrained in their students the idea that it's right for the women to work so that their husbands can continue to learn Torah after they're married.[60]

Again, it must be emphasized that the majority of *kollel* families come from Orthodox backgrounds, with parents and older siblings who placed great value upon study. Moreover, they continue to receive moral as well as financial support in many instances from their families.

Another significant factor is the general appeal of the lifestyle, one whose positive aspects are often seen as more than compensating for material deprivation. In most cases, there is a genuine sense of community that draws people closer together. This is especially true in out-of-town *kollels* where the families generally live near each other, usually in yeshiva-subsidized garden apartments. For the men, it is, in effect, a continuation of the isolation from the larger society that was their experience during the yeshiva days. For the wives, who have been brought up to value learning but given only a limited role in the learning process, it is a way of sharing in that life. Moreover, there are the tangible benefits of living and raising one's children among people who share a common outlook and similar values. One woman described it in the following terms:

> I come from New York City and I have found that here people really care about others. Let's say a woman comes home with a newborn baby, everything is taken care of. They cook the meals, they take the children for the day. Anything to

save the next person money. When someone goes shopping
they ask: "Can I get you something?" It's like having an extended family and I feel privileged to live here.

Others cite living away from parents as an advantage. As one
man put it: "I'm not saying you shouldn't visit them, but if you
live near your parents, somehow you can't become fully involved
in Torah."

The adjustment is not easy for everyone. Some noted the
lack of privacy—"Everyone's always looking in your *chulent* [a
Jewish dish eaten on the Sabbath] pot," while others complained
that those who had been in the *kollel* longer were "snobby" to
newcomers. A common observation was the lack of contact with
spouses, although most learned eventually to accept it. One
young woman explained:

> At first I used to get upset that Chaim was hardly ever
> around. Let's say my parents wanted to make a Chanuka
> party, he'd say, "You go; I have to learn this afternoon."
> And I didn't want to take the train by myself. But in think-
> ing about it I came to see that this was part of the sacrifice I
> had agreed to make when I married him.

Others did not seem to mind the lack of time together as
much. "I'm so busy with the children and everything," remarked one woman. "I love him, but I have my friends and lots
of things to do." To better understand this perspective, one
needs to know a bit more about the average wife's life as a single
girl, a life sharply divergent from the usual experience of most
young, unattached American women. Virtually her entire youth
has been centered around relationships with other girls. She has
little or no contact with boys until shortly before marriage. Thus,
in spending most of her time with other married women, she is
continuing a long-established pattern. Unlike the typical American housewife, she sees little of her husband in the evening when
he is in the *beis medrash* and not much more of him on the
weekends (except for the Sabbath meals and Friday evening)
when he is either praying or studying. Similarly, her husband
has had little social contact with women throughout his life. As
noted by social workers in the community, his difficulty in
relating to women is sometimes complicated by a chauvinistic attitude that sees women as "silly things" to be appeased with

clothing and furniture or, at best, as people who exist to work and raise children so that he may learn.[61]

Obviously, many, perhaps even most, *kollel* couples do not fit into this category, but for those who do one wonders if their relationship would be improved by a lifestyle which allowed them long blocks of time together. In a sense, a latent and unintended function of the *kollel* may be to give the couple a chance to make the emotional transition to married life slowly. By the time the husband is ready to leave the *kollel*, they feel more comfortable being with each other. While hypothetically possible, this assumption needs to be tested.

The *kollel* also represents an opportunity for sacrifice and idealism, perhaps even more for the women than for the men. Almost every woman interviewed identified this as a key source of satisfaction. A typical comment was: "It gives me great happiness when I go out to work that I'm supporting someone who is learning." For the men it is a further opportunity to prove to the yeshiva, the community, and themselves their dedication and devotion to a life of study. It is perhaps precisely because they realize that with marriage the time to leave the cloistered world of the Talmud comes one giant step closer that *kollel* becomes for them a way of making the transition to the outside world while at the same time postponing it for just a little while longer.

This brings us to what becomes for many *kollel* members a troubling issue: when to leave. As the years go by and his family grows, economic need may precipitate his departure. In other cases he may feel that he can accomplish more on the outside. The dilemma was summed up by one yeshiva administrator:

> YA: Whenever someone comes up to us and says this is his last year in the *kollel* we try to help him find a job. However, if *we* approach a young man and tell him it's time to start looking it is a most devastating experience for him. It breaks him down spiritually and morally.
>
> WH: Why?
>
> YA: These young men go under the assumption that they must learn as long as possible, and therefore the initiative to stop must come from them. When we tell him, it means we are voiding his standing as a *kollel* member, that we are voiding his existence as a potential *gadol hador* [great scholar of his generation] which he may

never achieve. We are saying we don't believe in his future. He feels often that he has made great sacrifices, foregone economic opportunities, and that his learning is just not appreciated.

These words underscore what is for so many an exceedingly difficult problem. Just as people in every walk of life must at some point face their limitations, the yeshiva *bochur* must often learn to accept the fact that he will probably not be a "*gadol hador*," that in leaving the *kollel* and entering the job market he is almost certainly closing the door to such hopes. For those who harbored such dreams leaving is a most painful and depressing experience.

There are others for whom such disappointments do not exist, because they never hoped to achieve such high levels. Just as the quality of students in the yeshivas varies so does the caliber of *kollel* members. Those in the middle level accept the fact that they are studying for a reasonable period of time to increase their level of understanding, or to prepare for entry into a related field such as the rabbinate or Jewish education. There is, nonetheless, a development in the community that has disturbed most of its leaders. With the growing success of the yeshivas in general and the idea of learning in particular, studying in a *kollel* has come to be seen by many as a status symbol, almost a *rite de passage*. A student at Ner Israel Yeshiva accurately expressed the prevailing community sentiment, when he noted:

> Any guy in the yeshiva who's truly *choshuv* [important] will have to learn in *kollel* and any decent girl will want to marry a guy in *kollel*. Today *kollel* is not for the elite . . . it's part of your membership in the "Torah Club."

This development is a radical departure from twenty years ago when *kollel* attendance was for outstanding scholars only. It can perhaps be called the proletarianization of the *kollel*. Others believe that those incapable of sustained participation in the *kollel* are at least gaining *something* from their additional exposure to study, but even these individuals have voiced concern about the overall effects of this on the institution. This shift may have significant ramifications for the community as a whole in two important areas. First, the idea that everyone is entitled to attend *kollel*, regardless of ability, may result in a serious decline in the level of scholarship both because the students will not, on the average, be as well endowed intellectually, and also because many who attend will be reluctant to leave and lose face even though they may discover that *kollel* life is not for them. Unfortunately, their way of coping with their inabilities may be to sit and not study or simply not to show up, both of which are likely to have detrimental effects on other *kollel* members.

The second area is more hypothetical but of potentially greater concern. If the idea of *kollel* study maintains its increase in popularity, then an entire generation of young men will be supported in varying degrees by their families. Their years in *kollel* will deplete their family's wealth and limit their earning possibilities in terms of job training, except for those who enter the family business. Even there they may find, after the many years spent hunched over a *Gemora,* that they are temperamentally unsuited for business. The question is, What will happen when their own children grow up? Who will supply the funds for their education if they want to follow in their parents' footsteps? Will they have to leave yeshiva earlier and enter business or other fields so that *their* children will have what they themselves did not? Many in the current generation are having large families, and this is bound to increase even further the economic pressures. Whether or not these and other pressures will cause a basic shift in the pattern of study in the yeshiva remains to be seen.

CHAPTER 10

Is the Yeshiva Successful in Reaching Its Goals?

> The perpetuation of Jewish peoplehood depends on the development and growth of authentic Torah scholars. . . . In the absence of Torah scholars, Jewry lacks the great teachers who are the links in the great chain of Tradition, spanning the ages. It lacks the educators to instruct the coming generations in the purity, wholeness and perfection of Judaism. And it lacks those who can intuitively articulate the unique wisdom and insights of Torah and make them relevant and available to Jewish youth.
>
> Rabbi Aharon Kotler, founder
> of Beth Medrash Govoha in
> Lakewood, New Jersey[1]

THESE WORDS, WRITTEN BY the dominant figure on the yeshiva scene in the post–World War II era, encompass the general objectives of the advanced yeshiva in America. Yet, as shall become evident, clarifying and isolating the yeshiva's goals is a difficult and complex task, for different yeshivas stress different areas and, within a stated objective, there are often minimum and maximum levels of achievement.

Transmitting the tradition, developing persons capable of being professional educators and religious leaders, and bringing Jews closer to the faith are the three major goals of the yeshiva. However, they are articulated in different ways by different yeshivas, and there is often sharp disagreement on how they can best be realized and which should have priority. Since the *rosh*

266

yeshiva controls the institution in most cases, his views on these matters are crucial and we will therefore focus especially on them.

Learning for Its Own Sake: How Long Does It Last?

The yeshiva is primarily a centralized, organized, and institutionalized form of studying the Torah. It is not set up to be a school for the training of Hebrew teachers and rabbis. That is only an outcome of its teachings. Those who run the yeshivas and most of those who attend them view Torah and Talmud study itself as the fulfillment of a commandment that needs no other justification.

The ideal result of such study is the exceptional Torah scholar, known as the *gadol*. Complete immersion, day and night, in "the sea of the Talmud" is regarded as the only way in which great scholars can emerge.[2] The development of such individuals is crucial for the survival of the institution of the yeshiva as a whole. For this reason alone, it is therefore understandable that the yeshiva promotes the total involvement approach to study.

The yeshiva recognizes that very few can attain such status. Still, the study of Torah itself is a divine command and, even if those who study do not achieve greatness, they will at least have acquired the tools with which to continue studying on their own after they have left the yeshiva. Rabbi Yaakov Perlow, former head of Breuer's Yeshiva, summed it up as follows:

> The occupation of a yeshiva's graduates is secondary, regardless of whether the yeshiva calls itself a rabbinical seminary. It's not there as a *semicha* factory. It's not there to produce rabbis or Hillel Foundation directors or teachers. A yeshiva exists to educate Jews who will be committed to the best of their abilities. It should foster the study of Torah with the underpinnings of *yiras shomayim* [fear of God]. Torah study without *yiras shomayim* is like a sack that's full of holes. You can pour whatever you want into it and it all spills out.[3]

The emphasis placed on *Torah lishmo* (study for its own sake) varies from school to school. Rabbi Yaakov Kamenecki of Torah

Vodaath indicated this in his response to the question of what the *major* goal of a yeshiva ought to be:

> There are those who believe that the goals of yeshivas should be that all sit and learn and nothing else but I don't agree with them. I feel that if certain people have a talent in engineering they should do that and those with other abilities should at least go into occupations where they'll have the opportunity to learn three hours a day or whatever. I give a *shiur* Sunday morning to a group of professionals who were once my *talmidim* [students].[4]

Rabbi Kamenecki is not in disagreement with the idea of *Torah lishmo,* but he recognizes that not every student is capable of long-term intensive study. In so doing, he reflects the philosophy of Yeshiva Torah Vodaath. Although the school has produced its share of very prominent Torah scholars, it has always been known for its commitment to the training of knowledgeable laymen (*baalei batim*).

Interviews with students indicated almost universal agreement with this goal. The following quotes are typical:

> I want to feel that when I leave the yeshiva I'll be able to learn just about anything on my own. I feel that I'm getting the desire to make learning a basic part of my life after I've left even though I plan to enter the insurance business.
>
> > A twenty-year-old student at the
> > Telshe Yeshiva in Cleveland

> For me it's important that I'll be able to study on my own. That I won't open up a *Gemora* and not know what's going on.
>
> > A nineteen-year-old student at the
> > Rabbi Samson Raphael Hirsch Yeshiva

> It would be good if people went into *chinuch* but training for it shouldn't go on inside the *koselei* [walls] of the yeshiva.
>
> > A twenty-five-year-old student at Beth
> > Medrash Govoha

Implicit in all this is the goal of cultural transmission. The yeshiva emerges as the place where the Oral Law has life and vitality. In continuing the unbroken chain of tradition from teacher to student, the yeshiva perceives itself as carrying on the work begun on Mount Sinai. Learning for its own sake is, in the eyes of the institution, the process by which this is best accomplished.[5]

Has the yeshiva been able to impart such values to its students? Whether or not it has done so depends on the lifestyle adopted by its graduates, for the yeshiva wants to make a permanent impact, not one that merely lasts as long as the young man is enrolled in the school. To determine the yeshiva's influence in this area, alumni of one major yeshiva (the one identified in the Introduction as Beth David Yeshiva) were asked various questions concerning how much time they spent on talmudic study.[6]

Slightly less than two-thirds of the 464 alumni who responded (62%) said they study Talmud almost every day, and an additional 19 percent study Talmud once or twice a week—providing ample evidence that the yeshiva has succeeded in instilling one of its core values into its graduates. The accompanying illustration tells us with whom and how often such study takes place.

Further support for the conclusion that Talmud study is part of the alumni's lifestyle comes from the fact that only a small minority of those who study almost every day or once or twice a week do so with their children. Such study, important as it may be for the children, possibly indicates nothing more than that the parent is helping his son with his homework, hardly definitive

Beth David Yeshiva Alumni Questionnaire Response

With whom and *how often* have you studied *gemora* in the past year or so?

	Almost Every Day	Once or Twice a Week	Several Times a Month	About Once a Month	Several Times a Year	Rarely or Never
Alone	38%	18%	6%	4%	5%	29%
Friend(s) (chavrusah)	32%	22%	4%	1%	5%	36%
Children	8%	14%	4%	1%	6%	67%
With a class	19%	19%	5%	2%	7%	48%
Other, please specify	—	—	—	—	—	—
N = 426						

proof of commitment to an ideal. Another sign of high commitment to learning was that approximately 40 percent answered in the affirmative when asked if they were studying with a Talmud class apart from in a professional position, as a teacher in a school.[7] A somewhat higher percentage of positive responses to this question was given by teachers and rabbis. Nevertheless, the respondents came from many other professions as well. Interestingly, those who had been away from the yeshiva for a long period of time were somewhat more likely to study often than those who had completed their stay in recent years. This lends further support to the positive long-term influence of the yeshiva experience.[8]

Only 9 percent of those who returned the questionnaire acknowledged that they studied "rarely or never." Preliminary analysis of their responses revealed no pattern with regard to income, occupation, age, secular education, or background in Orthodoxy, that would distinguish them from the rest of the alumni. They were, however, less strict in their religious observances.

Adhering to the Tenets of the Faith

The yeshiva has always felt that simply producing an observant Jew is not an acceptable goal at the *beis medrash* level. Adherence to the laws is taken for granted. Still, there has never been any effort made to determine whether even this minimum level is achieved by such institutions. The results of the survey prove the yeshiva to be more or less justified in its assumptions. Let us look first at laws of the religion that leave no room for interpretation within Orthodoxy.

According to rabbinic law, it is forbidden to carry any object from one domain to another on the Sabbath. Ninety-five percent of those responding claimed that they complied fully with this prohibition. Similarly, 97 percent stated that they did not eat nonkosher meat. With respect to the various laws concerning family purity (i.e., abstaining from sexual relations at certain times of the month), 90 percent described themselves as "strictly observant" and 7 percent as "generally observant."

Although it is not a biblical commandment per se, attending synagogue on the Sabbath is certainly the norm in the Orthodox community. An individual who failed to attend regularly would, unless there were extenuating circumstances, certainly not be considered Orthodox by most members of the community. Considering the other results, it is not surprising that almost all the respondents attended Sabbath services. A more significant measure of commitment was that 79 percent did so several times a week besides the Sabbath. For the working man this means that he must rise at about 6:00 A.M. or even 5:30, since most services are held about 6:30 or 7:00 A.M. Although there is no available evidence, I suspect that the proportion would be considerably lower among Orthodox Jews who did not study at the *beis medrash* level. In addition to religious commitments, such attendance may be seen as part of the socialization process. All yeshivas expect their students to attend daily prayer services on the premises even if they do not dorm, and certainly if they do. If they do not do so at the yeshiva because they live far away, it is taken for granted that they have gone to a *minyan* someplace near their home. It can safely be assumed that the young man who has gone to yeshiva at the *beis medrash* level attended such services on a daily basis for several years beyond the age of eighteen. In continuing such activity in later life he is following a pattern established in early adulthood, not simply something he did as a child.[9]

Several other indices, such as the giving of charity in accordance with biblical injunctions, produced similar results. The only exception was the law against speaking evil about others (*loshon hora*). When asked how closely they adhered to this precept, 34 percent indicated "sometimes," 31 percent said "often," and 31 percent "almost always." Four percent claimed they never engaged in *loshon hora*.

In the chapter on deviance in the yeshiva, it was pointed out that laws dealing with human relationships seem to be violated more frequently than those involving rituals and that, recognizing this, the yeshiva must make an effort to raise awareness among the students that such behavior goes against the spirit and law of the Torah. The relatively high number of persons who indicated that they "sometimes" spoke ill of others may reflect not the frequency of this occurrence so much as a heightened consciousness that it is a transgression. After spending years reading and listening to lectures on this subject in an environment where he may be chastised for making the slightest negative comment about someone, the alumnus is likely to develop a much stricter interpretation of the term and what it encompasses than the average individual, whose only restriction is that "it's not nice." Naturally, that 62 percent claim adherence to this law "often" or "almost always" may be an indication that the school has succeeded to a considerable extent in this area.

The Lifestyles of Yeshiva Graduates: A Socioeconomic and Cultural Profile

The largest proportion of yeshiva alumni, approximately one-third, entered fields related to their yeshiva background. These included the rabbinate, teaching in a yeshiva, yeshiva administration, and fund-raising for yeshivas, with most selecting teaching. This was followed by business and sales, which together totaled about one-quarter of those responding. While no single type of business predominated, those most often mentioned were the garment industry, the diamond and jewelry lines, and the travel business. The high concentration in business may be a reflection of the culture insofar as Jews, particularly recent arrivals to this country, have traditionally been well represented in business, especially the garment and diamond trades. The choice of a business career was not related to college attendance. More than nine out of ten respondents who entered business had attended college and more than half had graduated college, with quite a few having received advanced degrees in business.

The next four most popular professions selected by alumni were accounting, computer programming, systems analysis, and law. Besides offering the student the opportunity to learn a profession in four years, the logical systems employed in both mathematics and talmudic study might be a factor in the appeal of the first three areas. Law, while not mathematical, is even more closely related. Not only does it require logical thinking, but the style of debate and the use of specific cases to develop general principles bear a striking resemblance to the manner in which the Talmud is studied and its content. As one alumnus put it: "Law school was just a continuation of the yeshiva but in a secular context. I was used to the *pilpul* [talmudic study characterized by extensive debate, casuistry, and great attention to minute details] of the yeshiva and was actually ahead of my classmates in law school.'' These features may account for its relative popularity among yeshiva alumni, even though law requires three years of full-time study beyond an undergraduate degree.

Other areas of some interest to yeshiva alumni were teaching in a secular school or college (5%) and to a lesser extent (2½%) psychology, counseling, and social work. The decision to pursue careers of this sort may be due, in part, to the long period of time spent in educational institutions and the emphasis within them on human relations.

Hardly any alumni entered medicine or dentistry. Aside from the long training period, the problem of Sabbath observance is probably a major factor. While a doctor or dentist is permitted, in fact even obligated, to work on the Sabbath should there be a question of saving a human life, many Strictly Orthodox Jews are reluctant to enter a profession where they know in advance that breaking the Sabbath will be required of them. Dr. Arthur Feinerman, a Forest Hills, New York, gastroenterologist, is a graduate of Yeshiva College and Downstate Medical Center who defines himself as a ''Modern Orthodox'' Jew. He described the difficulties of being an Orthodox Jewish doctor as follows:

> When you're an intern or resident you're likely to be on call every second or third night which means you have to come in on the Sabbath fairly often. While I know I can answer the phone on Shabbos or write a prescription in an emergency it just goes against the grain and that's what's so hard. You're brought up for twenty-five years that you don't answer the phone on Shabbos or take an elevator or turn on a light and then you end up doing it—it requires an adjustment and many people would prefer not to do it. And when you're a doctor with a private practice people call you all the time.[10]

Hardly any of the respondents entered blue-collar occupations, and of those who did none were typical of the average yeshiva alumnus. Harry Brecher* is a thirty-four-year-old meat packer. He lives in a small city in Ohio. He did not attend college because, as he put it, ''I wasn't the intellectual type; they should have given me vocational training at the yeshiva instead of all that *Gemora.*'' Harry has no observant friends and is a confirmed

bachelor who watches TV about three hours a day, mostly
"popular and variety shows." Other occupations selected by
only a few persons included engineering, pharmacy, probation
officer, photographer, and editor.

Beth David Yeshiva permits but does not encourage college
attendance. Among those responding to the questionnaire, the
breakdown of college attendance was as follows: 48 percent completed some form of graduate training, 23 percent graduated college only, 15 percent attended but did not graduate, while only
14 percent failed to go beyond high school. The years covered
were from 1933 to 1978. Interviews indicated that the overwhelming reason for college attendance was the feeling that one
could obtain a better-paying job with a degree or specialty.

Respondents were asked to indicate their total income from
all sources. Thirty-six percent reported incomes of above
$25,000 a year, and more then half said they earned over
$20,000 annually. Such figures are not especially high, but it
seems reasonable to speculate that quite a few of those answering
may have underreported their income.

The residential distribution of the sample was as expected.
Almost all respondents lived in cities with Orthodox Jewish communities. About half of those on the list lived in the New York
metropolitan area despite the fact that the school was located
elsewhere. Of those that did not, about 90 percent resided in major North American cities or in Israel.

In the larger sense, it is impossible to separate the yeshiva's
goal of study for its own sake from that of molding an individual
who will conduct himself with dignity and integrity in his personal life. True, one studies because the Torah is God's word
and not because one has an express desire to be a noble person;
yet the thousands of moral and ethical precepts found in the
Written and Oral Law are presumed to have an exemplary effect
on those who study them. Thus, when the yeshiva says it wants
to produce people who study and follow the Torah, character
development is a basic part of this objective. Rabbi Shmuel
Berenbaum, head of the Mirrer Yeshiva, explained this goal in
colorful terms:

> SB: Here you have a person who's a liberal-minded individual.
> He's a free-thinker. He's Jewish but he doesn't know or keep any
> laws. But he's a nice man. He doesn't rob; he doesn't kill any-

body. But he lives in a culture alien to Torah. Should one condemn him?

WH: I imagine that would depend on one's own perspective.

SB: Look, there are coed dormitories in colleges across the country. So? Big deal! Some people, I heard, say that because *odom horishon* [Adam] walked naked that we should also. You're a college professor. You should know.

WH: How would the *rosh yeshiva* respond to such a person?

SB: The point is that after *odom horishon* [Adam] sinned, he didn't go naked. He had developed *taavehs* that he had to control. He wasn't just an animal. Our response is that man was created in God's image and he must remember that at all times. A horse eats out of a leather bag. Does a person stick his head into a leather bag to eat? Of course not! Human beings are on a higher level. Our yeshivas try to teach boys how they should act in this world by teaching them Torah.[11]

The mode of life alluded to here involves being scrupulous in one's private and public life, showing kindness to others, and making every effort to transmit these values to one's children. In his attempts to conform to such expectations, the yeshiva graduate must make many decisions, small and large. He must determine what he will read in his spare time, how he and his wife will dress, how much money he will give for charity, who his friends will be, what type of education he will seek for his children, whether or not he will go to the movies or watch television, and how much time he will spend helping others in the community. In short, the Torah must serve as a guide, whenever possible, in all his actions.

A number of questions asked of the alumni addressed themselves, either directly or indirectly, to how they spent their free time. The results indicated that, by and large, the respondents reflected the viewpoint of the yeshiva in their daily conduct and in their attitudes. As we saw earlier, the yeshiva student is discouraged from reading secular literature, watching television, and going to the movies. The accompanying illustration (next page) reveals the long-term effects of such policies.

These figures strongly suggest that leisure-time pursuits are judged in terms of their usefulness, and that those which are purely pleasurable tend to be avoided. Interviews lent credence to this assumption; many respondents noted that they read the

Beth David Yeshiva Alumni Questionnaire Response

In your free time, how often do you engage in the activities listed below?

	Almost Every Day	Once or Twice a Week	Several Times a Month	About Once a Month	Several Times a Year	Rarely or Never
Read a daily newspaper	63%	19%	6%	2%	2%	8%
Read weekly or monthly magazines	16%	39%	19%	8%	8%	10%
Watch TV	29%	18%	10%	3%	6%	34%
Attend movies	—	—	6%	8%	33%	53%
Read popular novels	1%	1%	5%	7%	20%	66%
N = 428						

paper or watched television largely because they felt it important to be informed about developments in society as a whole. Even those who watched television favored news programs by a very wide margin.

An interesting question is what type of yeshiva graduate is more or less likely to watch television or go to the movies. Our efforts here were limited to correlating such activity with level of education. The stereotyped notion that the less educated watch TV more or go to the movies more simply did not hold true for the sample. In fact, the pattern was the reverse. Among those who watched TV almost every day 6 percent were high school graduates, 30 percent had attended college, and 32 percent had gone to graduate school. Among those who rarely or never went to the movies the breakdown according to education was similar: of those with only a high school secular education, 92 percent stated that they rarely or never attended, far more than the average rate of 53 percent for all respondents. Similarly, more than a third of those responding did not own television sets, an extremely high figure compared to the general population, where almost every household has at least one. Among those who went no further than high school only 27 percent owned sets. Among those who completed graduate school the figure reached 78 percent.

The negative relationship between education and mass media entertainment can perhaps be explained as follows. Many of those who did not finish college were engaged in religious occupations, such as teaching in a yeshiva or the rabbinate. Conversely, those who completed formal secular training at the college level or beyond are more receptive to the offerings of the dominant culture. If this interpretation is true, it would support the yeshivas' general opposition to college as a strong secularizing influence. Which came first, however, the desire to attend college or a secular outlook, is an open question. Regardless of how one interprets the figures, we have here a population of which an inordinately high number of persons are not exposed in any systematic fashion to certain basic forms of the mass media. Further, they are rearing a generation of children who will not be influenced by this crucial agent of socialization in our society.

Limiting the time spent on television and movies is not the only way by which the yeshiva alumnus seeks to prevent outside influences from encroaching upon his values and lifestyles. He also keeps his contacts with nonmembers of the Orthodox community to a bare minimum. This is clear from the responses to the questionnaire inquiry shown below.

Most striking perhaps is the relative lack of contact with nonobservant Jews. It is in itself an indication of how important the religious way of life is to this population, and how determined they are to maintain it. At the same time, one wonders how the lack of social contact with both nonobservant Jews and gentiles affects the outlook and perceptions of those belonging to this community. It is likely that certain gaps in their knowledge about other cultures that existed when they were in the yeshiva remain because of their unwillingness to engage in social interaction with outsiders.

Beth David Yeshiva Alumni Questionnaire Response

Think of your four closest friends. Of these how many are:

Observant	84%	Not Observant	15%	Not Jewish	6%
N = 446					

Whether or not the way of life pursued by the yeshiva alumnus is perpetuated depends, in large measure, on how successfully it is transmitted to the children. Judging from the type of schooling selected by parents, it is apparent that they are making every effort to pass on their traditions. Ninety-seven percent reported that their children would attend a yeshiva day school or were already enrolled in one. The vast majority expressed satisfaction with their overall experience at Beth David, noting that they intended to send their children to the same type of advanced school. Some, however, said that this depended on whether their children were suited for a program as rigorous as that offered by Beth David. From the questionnaire it was obvious that most parents would prefer their son to be a fine product of a top-notch yeshiva than an outstanding graduate of an Ivy League university. Ninety-two percent disagreed with the statement: ''For a son, a good secular education is more important than a religious one.'' They also expressed considerable optimism regarding the future of Orthodoxy. When asked to complete the statement ''In all likelihood, the next generation will be————,'' 49 percent said ''more observant than my own,'' 32 percent replied ''as observant,'' and only 19 percent answered ''less observant.''

Training Jewish Educators and Rabbis

As noted before, the yeshiva does not regard itself as a center for training professionals because it feels that once pedagogy or homiletics become important concerns, the quality of talmudic study is bound to become diluted.[12] Yet the training of teachers and rabbis must still be viewed as a goal for three reasons. First, it is a fact that most of those who hire teachers and Orthodox rabbis consider study in the yeshiva as the primary qualification for such employment. Second, the majority of persons currently in these fields received their training in yeshivas. Finally, the yeshiva recognizes that, in teaching Torah, it is giving the students the basic tools required for proficiency in these areas.

There is, with one exception, no serious full-time program leading to a degree that qualifies one to teach in a yeshiva. Only Yeshiva University's teacher training division, known as Erna

Michael College, fulfills this role, offering courses in pedagogy, Jewish history, Bible, Talmud, Hebrew literature, Prophets, and the Hebrew language. But although it awards degrees in Hebrew education to its graduates, very few of them enter Jewish education, for the various reasons indicated in Chapter 9. Despite the problems—low salaries and prestige, lack of encouragement from the yeshiva for various reasons, and the feeling that one is overqualified for this profession—enough persons enter the field to fill most of the available positions. Those officials involved with placement of teachers and principals agreed that there were enough teachers but complained that there were not enough good pedagogues.[13] A preliminary analysis of those entering Jewish education who responded to the questionnaire lends support to this claim.

Those who did not go further than a high school education were more than three times as likely to enter Jewish education than other professions. This may mean that those who enter Jewish education sometimes do so as a last resort. It certainly means that as the secular level of one's education increases one is less likely to go into the field, and that those who do enter are, by and large, less educated than their fellow yeshiva alumni.

No empirical evidence is available to support the contention that the yeshiva tries to dissuade its best students from entering teaching, but there was a consensus among all segments of the yeshiva community that this was indeed the case. When asked what they liked most about the yeshiva experience, those who became educators were twice as likely to cite the ritual aspects of the experience, such as prayers, holidays, customs, and so on. We may note that these are probably more important areas at the elementary school level than Talmud. They were considerably less likely to mention the pleasures derived from the study of Talmud itself, although a good number did so. It cannot, of course, be proved that those who most enjoyed the learning part of the yeshiva experience were the best students, but there seems to be at least a good possibility. In any event, the question of why those who most enjoyed their own Jewish education are relatively uninterested in transmitting it to others is a fascinating one. At the same time it must be remembered that even if the best students in the yeshiva do not enter Jewish education, the talmudic erudition that defines the outstanding student is not necessarily the most important qualification for teaching at the day school level. One can argue that relating to and being interested in others are far more important considerations. On this score, there is indirect evidence from the questionnaire. *Rebbe*-student relationships were more important than the learning process in his yeshiva years to the present-day educator.

The problems with respect to the rabbinate are somewhat different. Several yeshivas, including Yeshiva University and Chofetz Chaim, offer programs leading to formal ordination. In reality, however, all yeshivas offer training for the rabbinate, and there are rabbis in every part of the country from yeshivas such as Ner Israel, Chaim Berlin, Mirrer, Telshe, and so on. Most graduates do not, as a rule, use the title "rabbi" unless they accept a position in a synagogue or school where it is professionally appropriate for them to do so. At this point, they may seek to formalize their achievement through a document from the yeshiva attesting to their competence. Despite the fact that yeshiva alumni have formal training in this area most do not enter the field. The reasons for this, mainly the difficulties in finding a pulpit in a truly Orthodox synagogue, the lack of time for private talmudic study, and the myriad of social obligations, have already been evaluated (see pp. 243–246).

Until the early 1960s the right-wing yeshivas produced a significant number of graduates who became pulpit rabbis. This has declined in the last fifteen years or so. Some have attributed it to the rightward movement of the yeshivas and the resultant reluctance among their graduates to assume positions where their standards might be compromised.[14] The study of alumni, however, offered no clearly discernible evidence that those going into the profession were more liberal in outlook.

There is, in any event, some indication that the yeshivas are becoming interested in having their graduates enter the rabbinate although, to be sure, this interest is confined only to strictly observant synagogues. Rabbi Shneur Kotler's observations on this topic shed light on the reasoning behind such a shift:

> The problem with regard to the rabbinate was different when I came here in the 1940s. Then the trend was toward modern rabbis who "fit right in" and spoke English well, dressed in the right clothes. So where did it get them? Many [congregants] left the religion because the rabbis didn't have high enough standards. Many were willing to overlook that the synagogue didn't have a high enough *mechitza* or none

at all. We lost a whole generation to the Conservatives. But
through the years it was demonstrated that compromise is no
solution. If you want to succeed you can't give in.

Today things are different. There's a community that
wants the rabbis to tell them to be more religious. And
because there are such people, yeshiva graduates should
enter the rabbinate again. It is because the yeshivas have
become the strongest centers of Jewish life that the *rosh
yeshivas* have come to assume the leadership of Torah Orthodoxy. We do not denigrate the rabbinate; far from it. But it
is a simple observable fact that the yeshivas are now our
most vibrant institutions.[15]

There is, however, a major problem: there are hardly any
jobs available. There is very little movement among today's Orthodox rabbis, and graduates of the right-wing yeshivas would
not consider a Conservative congregation. Perhaps recognition of
this reality prompted the *rosh yeshivas* at a recent convention to
issue a statement urging every synagogue to appoint a rabbi.[16]
This was obviously directed at those synagogues which have a
right-wing, yeshiva-style constituency that feels no need for a
rabbi. Besides giving congregants someone to turn to, the appointment of more rabbis would increase the opportunities for
those in the yeshiva inclined in this direction.

Reaching Uncommitted Jews

"Have you prayed today? No? Why don't you step into this
van and we'll help you." "Excuse me, ma'am, but do you know
that tonight every Jew is supposed to light candles for the Sabbath? Take these candles as a gift from us and use them in good
health." Thousands of Jews living in urban centers throughout
the United States would recognize the source of these statements
as representatives of the Lubavitcher Hasidic movement. Pro-
selytizing among nonobservant Jews is a primary goal of the
Lubavitcher, and their vans, called "mitzvamobiles," have
become a common sight in New York City. Earnest young men
approach passersby on busy streets and invite them to come inside, say a prayer or a blessing, and accept some literature
describing the faith.

The yeshiva's approach to the uncommitted is not quite so

dramatic but it has become an increasingly important activity in recent years. Since the role of the *rosh yeshivas* in the community is so important, it is worthwhile to present their views below and indicate the near unanimity of opinion concerning the importance of this issue:

> There is a world of work. One can't be satisfied with what is, both in quality and quantity. There is a world full of children, a world full of people who, unfortunately, know nothing.
>
> Rabbi Moshe Feinstein
(Mesivta Tifereth Jerusalem)[17]

> The yeshivas have made quite an impact in recent years. Yet most of the Jews in this country have no contact with them. They are assimilated and we have to reach them.
>
> Rabbi Joseph B. Soloveitchik
(Yeshiva University)[18]

> We lull ourselves into a false sense of security by the fact that we have thousands studying in yeshivas. But there are so many more who are not.
>
> Rabbi Mordechai Gifter
(Telshe Yeshiva)[19]

> A certain portion of every yeshiva person's time and energy should be spent trying to satisfy the instinct for *klal* [community] work.
>
> Rabbi Gedalia Schorr*
(Yeshiva Torah Vodaath)[20]

There is plainly no disagreement that reaching out is important, desirable, and necessary. The problems, from the yeshiva's perspective, are under what conditions it should be done and how much time and effort should be devoted to it.

One of the most often mentioned caveats is that one should not engage in such activity without a very solid grounding in the tenets of the faith. According to Rabbi Henoch Leibowitz, whose Chofetz Chaim Yeshiva is heavily involved with such work, this takes many years:

> I'm trying to follow on the imprint established by my father . . . that Torah can reach everywhere if it is carried by people who are great scholars. It isn't enough to be infused with a kind of emotionalism and to feel "we want to disseminate

* Deceased.

Torah.'' We try to send men out to the field who have spent between twelve and fourteen years at the yeshiva . . . devoting themselves to the profundity of Torah.[21]

While Rabbi Leibowitz did not elaborate on his criticism of emotionalism as the primary impetus for such activity, there is a widely held perception in the yeshiva community that many Lubavitcher Hasidim who try to bring others closer to Judaism do so without a deep understanding of the basis and meaning of the religion. One study of the Lubavitcher community concluded that those whose beliefs require the most strengthening are often precisely the ones sent out to urge others on. The act of persuading others becomes a way of reaffirming the validity of the belief system.[22]

The yeshiva's approach is the reverse. It believes that one cannot be relied upon to transmit the faith accurately without many years of preparation. Thus, Rabbi Kotler stated:

> One must be careful who one sends out. You have to be ready to teach. It's like a first-year medical student. Do you say to him: ''Why don't you go out and do some open-heart surgery''? He's not prepared to. He has to study more. One of the prophets speaks of clouds becoming full and pouring rain on the earth. That is the story of yeshiva students. Only after they have become filled with Torah and authentic Jewish attitudes can they pour their knowledge into others.
>
> People criticize us for not training teachers and administrators. They miss the point. Jewish education can only flourish if genuine scholars are in the field. Our alumni are not only knowledgeable; they are motivated and enthusiastic because they are totally committed to the cause of Torah. Come to a Torah Umesorah convention or look at the teaching staffs of the best day schools. *Our* graduates are the ones who are making the revolution in Torah education. Only someone who truly cares can influence others.[23]

These disparate views must be understood within their historical context as reflecting the differing approaches toward religion of the Hasidim and those in the Lithuanian yeshivas as they developed in Eastern Europe (see pp. 3–6).[24]

Despite the yeshiva community's active participation in reach-out activites, the perception of study for ''a higher purpose'' again dominates its thinking on such matters. The prevailing belief is that the more Torah one studies, the better job one will do if one selects community work as either a vocation or spare-time activity. *Kiruv rechokim* (literally, bringing nearer those who have strayed) is seen as a secondary objective for the yeshiva, one that often emerges as a *result* of Torah study. Some in the community expressed the view that such study alone contributed to *kiruv rechokim,* even if one did nothing specific in this area. As one student at Lakewood explained it:

> STUDENT: We do not know what God's motives are and how He works. It is entirely possible that my keeping my *Gemora* open five minutes longer will result in God influencing someone to become a little more interested in being religious.
>
> WH: Do you feel that you therefore do not have to go out and engage in such activities since your learning accomplishes it?
>
> STUDENT: I certainly think it's possible. Look, if God could create the whole world, could create something as complicated as a human being, making someone a little more religious is easy compared to those things.

Others expressed reservations about whether such work was worth the effort. One student at Beth haTalmud Yeshiva in Brooklyn said:

> It should be considered that we've probably already lost most of these people. They're beyond redemption. They were lost forty or fifty years ago when their grandparents became irreligious. We could have saved the grandparents because they still knew what *Shabbos* was. Today, when they get turned on to Reverend Moon, this is the logical conclusion. We may only be able to save 2 percent. Is it worth the effort when instead I could be doing the holiest work in the world, that which God created man for? What about those who went out into the boondocks and eventually became Conservative rabbis? There are all sorts of risks. Who knows how strong his faith is until the day it is tested? And then it's too late.

The comments of other students indicated that they felt unprepared and insecure in their ability to answer the questions that their unknowledgeable coreligionists might pose to them. Said one:

> The yeshiva didn't really prepare me to answer the questions that the average nonobservant Jew asks. Like I know a guy from work and he asked me: "Why do the *shuls* have to

charge so much money to get in on the High Holy Days? Don't they realize it turns people off?'' Or he wants to know how God could allow six million people to be killed. I can't tell him: ''You have to believe.'' He's not ready for that. On the other hand, I don't know what to tell him.

Such students are often even less prepared in areas where they might well be challenged by skeptical secularists. They know nothing of evolution, are unfamiliar with the works of Aristotle or Plato, and rarely, if ever, read anything critical of religion. Students will often adopt a defensive posture that automatically rejects such topics as *apikorsus* or will decide, without being specific, that *kiruv rechokim* is not for them. Unless the yeshivas are content to focus their efforts only on those whose knowledge of these areas is as deficient as that of their students, they will have to make an effort to educate students in these subjects before sending them out.[25] This is, however, unlikely, not only because the yeshiva's general approach has always been to avoid such topics but also because they lack qualified personnel who, while Orthodox, can refute arguments concerning evolution, the origin of the world, and so on, in the idiom used by the scientific community.

It must also be noted that the elitist character of the yeshiva, while promoting group solidarity and instilling a higher sense of purpose among its members, sometimes brings about a disdain, even contempt, for those who do not belong to that world. This is not likely to be acknowledged publicly, but it can be observed that in the yeshiva, as in most insular and highly committed societies, there is a feeling of smugness about the superiority of the lifestyle that often results in intolerance toward outsiders. This attitude makes many in the yeshiva community unwilling to extend themselves to such persons. A student at the Chofetz Chaim Yeshiva offered an opposing view:

> STUDENT: I feel that making people more religious is the fulfillment of my existence. I am not the type who can sit all day and learn and even if I were, I would feel an obligation to save souls. There are so many people out there waiting to be instructed in the beauty of Torah.
>
> WH: Are you afraid of losing your own faith in the process?
>
> STUDENT: I believe that God won't let that happen to me. I don't think He would punish me for trying to show other people what's right.

It should be apparent that there is both ambivalence and a variety of viewpoints concerning this issue and, although many in the yeshiva do not work with those outside the community, an equal, if not greater, number do. One project is the Jewish Education Program (JEP) run by Agudath Israel. Volunteers from the yeshivas take participating Jewish students from the public schools to nearby synagogues and yeshivas where they are offered religious instruction.[26] They also place children in Orthodox summer camps and aid them in transferring to yeshivas if they so desire. Students from nonobservant homes are also invited to stay in Orthodox homes for the Sabbath. JEP also produces a magazine designed for seventh- and eighth- graders with a circulation of several thousand. Another undertaking is the Summer Educational Environmental Development Program (SEED) sponsored by Torah Umesorah. This is an effort to promote the study of Torah by sending young men into local communities for three to seven weeks during the summer—where they study full time together with those living there.

One of the most successful Orthodox reach-out programs at the high school and college levels is that of the National Council of Synagogue Youth (NCSY), sponsored by the Union of Orthodox Jewish Congregations. With close to 500 chapters throughout the United States and Canada, NCSY sponsors a wide range of activities designed to bring young boys and girls closer to Orthodox Judaism as well as to provide a religious social and cultural setting for those already Orthodox. The organization conducts seminars, runs social activities, and arranges for participants to spend weekends, known as *Shabbatons,* in communities other than those in which they live. Some 20,000 to 25,000 people, mostly teenagers, participate in its programs each year. Although the majority of its members and leaders are affiliated with the Modern Orthodox and attend schools such as Yeshiva University and Touro College, many attend the more right-wing institutions too. Because NCSY has many coed activities, it has drawn some fire from more conservative elements in the yeshiva community but such criticism has been limited, for the most part, to private comments since it is recognized that the organization is attempting to reach unaffiliated youngsters who might reject a more rigid approach to the faith. *Rosh yeshivas* such as Rabbi Leibowitz of the Chofetz Chaim Yeshiva and Rabbi Yaakov Weinberg of Yeshiva Ner Yisroel have addressed meetings of NCSY and other *rosh yeshivas* have urged students who they feel are qualified for this type of work to become involved with the organization.[27]

Basically, these are voluntary programs. There are, however, certain professions which can be seen as fulfilling the objective of reaching out, such as when a young man decides to become a teacher in a community removed from the centers of Jewish life. It is here perhaps that the yeshiva alumnus faces the greatest test of his commitment in this area. A significant proportion do quite well but many fail, and the following remarks by one such individual provide a glimpse into some of the reasons:

> Look at me. I was a Hebrew teacher. Everybody pushes you around and you're bitter because you feel you could have been a doctor or a dentist, make money, and still be *frum* [religious]. But no. I wanted to be *mekarev* people [bring them closer to religion]. My father-in-law warned me: "Don't you dare go," he said. And where does it get you being stuck in this little town in Pennsylvania? Your kids go to a crummy yeshiva where they get no *chinuch*, not a word of *Gemora* which is the main thing. The institution doesn't give a damn about Torah. Judaism means gefilte fish. The kids ride to *shul* on *Shabbos* and it's usually Conservative or Reform. There's a *mechalel Shabbos* [violator of the Sabbath] butcher. The principal is a big phony. He has to give the parents what they want or out he goes—coed activities and what-not. There's no way he can last and remain sincere to the principles of the yeshiva in which he studied. After a while he rationalizes and he's not the same man who went in. Your wife has no friends. They think she's weird or exotic because she covers her hair. I couldn't take it and I wouldn't advise anyone else to do it.

Such a life is difficult for any Orthodox Jew, but it is especially hard for one who has spent most of his life in the intense environment of the yeshiva. He is often ill prepared for such challenges and unwilling to compromise. He is ready to tell people about his faith but he cannot meet them halfway, for to do so would contradict the total involvement demanded by that faith.

Despite this, many do go out to the "boondocks." Some simply view such work as an apprenticeship and look forward to the day when something will open up in a city with a large Orthodox community. In response to this dilemma some yeshivas send out groups of students so that they form a community of their own, giving each other the strength to meet the challenges posed by such a life.[28]

A more fruitful profession perhaps is working with *baalei teshuva,* literally those who repent. Beginning in the 1960s hundreds of young Jewish men became interested in Orthodoxy as a way of life.[29] To meet the need, special yeshivas, located mostly in Israel, were set up to teach them. They could not be conducted along traditional lines since the students had no background in Talmud. As a result, new and more varied curriculums were designed. Those who headed and staffed such yeshivas were primarily drawn from the right-wing yeshivas. Although it is not clear what the long-range prospects are, teaching in these yeshivas, both here and in Israel, is a source of employment for numerous yeshiva graduates. In addition, graduates of yeshivas and their wives often teach in day schools where the children come from nonobservant homes. This too can be classified as *kiruv rechokim.*

Yet another area is working with Russian–Jewish immigrants. One of the chief problems has been absorbing Russian children into the yeshiva day and high schools. The schools have been reluctant to accept such children out of fear that with their lack of background they will not adjust rapidly enough to the program. To meet their needs, an independent group of concerned Orthodox Jews established a special yeshiva for Russian–Jewish children. Known as Yeshiva Be'er Hagolah, the school, which has about 400 students, rents space in various yeshivas throughout New York City and conducts separate classes for its students. Its board includes several prominent *rosh yeshivas,* and the school is seen as a transitional institution whose aim is to prepare students for entry into the traditional yeshivas.

Notwithstanding the steps taken by the yeshivas and their graduates in this sphere, most of the "reaching out" by Orthodox Jews in the United States is done by the Lubavitcher Hasidim. This is a major goal of their movement, and they are far more heavily involved with Russian immigrants than any other group. They have also attracted countless individuals to Orthodoxy through their work in every part of the country. The collective efforts of the Lithuanian yeshivas pale by comparison although, considering their priorities, that is to be expected.

Where Has the Yeshiva Failed?
Former Students Speak Out

When one looks at both the high percentage of alumni who continue talmudic study after they have left the yeshiva and their leisure patterns, it is evident that the yeshiva has succeeded in instilling many of its values to a remarkable extent. These effects appear to be long-lasting, affecting those who left twenty-five years ago as much as the recent graduates. Yet the yeshiva cannot be rated an unqualified success. Open-ended questions elicited many complaints about various aspects of yeshiva life and the educational approach of the school. The greatest area of dissatisfaction concerned teacher–student relations, with a smaller but significant number of persons expressing criticism of the way in which Talmud was taught and the lack of emphasis placed upon Prophets, Jewish history, and the Hebrew language. Students were also critical, though to a lesser degree, of life away from home, the yeshiva community in general, lack of preparation for the "real world," and institutional restrictions on their activities. Let us look a bit more carefully at the nature of the two most often cited complaints.

The major source of unhappiness with the *rebbes* was the lack of a personal relationship with the teacher. The following remarks were typical:

> I felt the *rebbe* and, for that matter, the administration, was not really interested in me enough as a person.

> I could not develop personal relationships with most of my teachers. They seemed distant.

> There was a lack of personal attention. I did not make any waves.

Many students expressed resentment at what they felt was a tendency to favor the good students. This is, of course, a general problem in education at all levels and in all types of schools, but we have seen that it may be more pronounced in the yeshiva. Others faulted the *rebbes* for not discussing and counseling them in terms of preparation for life in general, and some felt the school was too concerned with producing *gedolim* instead of focusing on those with more limited objectives.

Further study of the questionnaires revealed, however, that most who noted this problem were satisfied, on the whole, with the yeshiva experience. Significantly, *rebbe*–student relationships and the learning experience itself were the two most often cited factors when persons were asked to identify the *most* satisfying aspects of the yeshiva experience. The following comments were representative of the feelings of many regarding their teachers:

> My *rebbe*, when he said a *shiur*, his face lit up. He was excited; this was his life. His talks in *hashkofoh* [religious-spiritual outlook] instilled in me a love of learning and of our fellow man that has lasted until this very day.

> I loved the close relationship between *rebbe* and student. They were always available to discuss educational and personal matters. Without my *rebbes* I would be nothing today.

The large number of alumni who claimed that *rebbe*–student relations were either the most or least satisfactory aspect of their yeshiva years indicates, it would seem, that this area is of crucial importance to the average student.

The emphasis in the yeshiva curriculum is overwhelmingly on talmudic study. Classes in Bible and Prophets are rarely given except at Yeshiva University. The major reason is the yeshivas' belief that the subject matter can be studied on one's own if a student is sufficiently advanced to be in a *beis medrash*. Yet more than a fifth of the alumni claimed to feel insecure in their knowledge of Bible and Prophets. Since the question asked people to volunteer information concerning the yeshiva's shortcomings instead of asking them to select from a fixed number of choices, it is possible that an even greater number than those specifying this deficiency felt likewise but gave priority to other areas. Some responses were:

> There was too much emphasis on Talmud. I would have benefited from some formalized *Tanach* [Prophets] program.

> There was very little learning of *Chumash* [Bible] and *Tanach*. I'm not talking about simple explanation. It's true perhaps that we could have learned this on our own, but we could have and should have studied it in-depth with all the *meforshim* [rabbinical commentaries]. Now I know the advanced things without some of the basics and have to grope my way through it with my own children. Frankly, each year I'm

away from the yeshiva I feel these deficiencies more and more.

There was a total lack of emphasis on *Chumash* and *Tanach* with the false assumption that we were expert in them.[30]

The interviews revealed further that students were often embarrassed to admit to their own teachers that they were not proficient in these subjects. Although the Talmud is based on the Bible and Prophets, it is possible to conceal lack of knowledge in this area because the Talmud deals only with selected passages at a time. Naturally, if a person knew the entire Talmud he would, of necessity, be well versed in the Bible, but this is not the case with students who spend four or five years in a yeshiva *beis medrash*. They are familiar with only a few tractates of the 63 that comprise the Talmud. If the yeshiva bases its decision not to focus on these topics because students are familiar with them, the results of the questionnaire should give pause to those making this assumption. It can perhaps be argued that the yeshiva elementary schools are doing a poor job in teaching this subject, at least those that send their students on to the right-wing yeshivas. There may be some truth to this, but it needs to be understood in its proper perspective. Several principals complained to me that they were being pressured by right-wing parents to start instructing boys in Talmud at an age where the children could not comprehend it. As one educator put it:

There may be one or two kids in the fourth or fifth grade who can handle it but most can't. They should be studying *chumash*. But what can I do if the parents insist? I only work here. The terrible thing is if you expose someone to *Gemora* at too early an age, they'll be turned off to it forever.

Quite a few respondents bemoaned the lack of instruction in Jewish history and in the Hebrew language, stating that outsiders within the Jewish community took it for granted that they were expert in these subjects because of the many years they had spent in the yeshiva. One talked about the discomfort he felt when at a meeting of his local yeshiva's board of directors he was asked to prepare a short talk on how European Jewish history should be taught. Others felt that the yeshiva did not focus enough on the portions of the Talmud that dealt with practical law. One of the most often mentioned criticisms was the yeshiva's failure to approach the study of Talmud in a systematic fashion, or at least to explain its relationship to the period in which it developed. Said one former student, an accountant who was in the *beis medrash* for seven years, and who studies Talmud several times a week:

> I loved the *rebbes* and the chance to absorb their wisdom. However, I never understood where everything fit in. For two years I walked around not knowing when the *Amoraim* [later sages] and when the *Tanaaim* [earlier sages] lived, until I found out many others didn't know either. Finally I took out a book on Jewish history, by Solomon Grayzel. The same thing was true about the time of Rashi and the Rambam. Oh sure we heard about their lives from the *rebbes* and the *mashgiach* but it was all bits and pieces, never presented in an organized way. Now I'm an adult and I have to *phumpher* [fumble] my way around.

There are books on these subjects available, mostly in Hebrew, but careful study of them is not considered important in the yeshiva. It is something one does when one has time, which is almost never the case in an institution where Talmud is studied day and night. Moreover, largely because the yeshiva views the Talmud as based on divine revelation and independent of time and place, it does not regard its historical location as very important.

One area conspicuously absent in the criticism of the curriculum was comments about the subject of ethics. Very few respondents mentioned it as a subject needing greater attention. In our discussion of ethics (*mussar*) (pp. 116–123), it was noted that *mussar* is not regarded as a topic one can or ought to spend all day studying. It appears that, in the student's view, whatever was taught in this yeshiva was sufficient. Evidence supporting this assumption comes from the fact that 19 percent said that the emphasis on moral–ethical development was among the things they liked most about the yeshiva.[31]

It should be remembered that the various criticisms were more than likely offered by respondents as ways in which the yeshiva might improve, not as evidence of its failure. Perhaps the most telling proof is that when all was said and done the overwhelming number of respondents indicated that they were pleased with the yeshiva experience (see figure opposite).

To encourage respondents to be critical, choices likely to

Beth David Yeshiva Alumni Questionnaire Response

How satisfied are you today with your yeshiva experience?

Very much	39%	Pretty much	43%	Not too much	18%
N=408					

create reluctance to commit oneself, such as "It failed" or "I was dissatisfied," were avoided and the more innocuous "Not too much" substituted. That only 18 percent checked off that response is therefore quite revealing.

Rebels and Malcontents

What about those whom the yeshiva failed to reach? It is almost a sociological dictum that the case of the deviant teaches us about the norm. Fifteen such individuals were interviewed. While no clear pattern resulted, some of the cases raise interesting questions about both the yeshiva and its influence upon the different types of individuals who attend it. In giving their reasons for leaving the fold the informants do not mention things such as curriculum, but it must be remembered that such matters may seem minor to those who last were in a yeshiva many years ago and are today completely irreligious, even if these were considerations at the time they attended.[32]

Jeffrey Portnoy* was born in 1946 into a family of Holocaust survivors. He lived in Manhattan and attended all-boys' yeshivas at the day school and high school levels. He was ritually observant but began doubting his commitments shortly after entering college. He studied in the *beis medrash* of the Rabbi Jacob Joseph Yeshiva by day, choosing as friends others who were also marginally committed. When I asked him why he went to the yeshiva he said:

> You have to understand that to my parents, especially my father, religion was the most important thing in the world. He had kept kosher in the concentration camps and I couldn't bear to tell him that I didn't believe in all this stuff, particularly since he acted as though he would have a heart attack every time you questioned something. So I pretended to be Orthodox so as to make him happy.

Jeffrey managed to persuade his father to allow him to drop out of yeshiva after two years of college, arguing that "I'll never get into graduate school if I don't go full time." Today he is not at all observant and has no qualms about working on Saturday at his job as a research biologist. Looking back on his experiences, he observed:

> I finally broke the news to my father that I wasn't religious and I was amazed to discover that he didn't care as much as I thought he would. He said to me, "Well, at least you're a *mensch*," though he keeps on telling his friends that I'm Orthodox. Perhaps I could have broken it earlier but I just didn't realize it.

Jeffrey expressed no regret about having gone to yeshiva, saying that it gave him a good background in Jewish culture. He will not, however, send his children to yeshiva because his wife, who comes from a Reform background, thinks religion is an anachronism. Jeffrey noted, with a trace of sadness in his voice, that his wife discouraged friendships with any former comrades from the yeshiva days:

> I think she feels threatened because invariably we talk about old times and it makes her conscious that I come from a world she was never in and could probably never enter. As a result she gets defensive and puts me down. You have to remember that her parents are very antireligious.

Jeffrey does not belong to any synagogue and attends only on the High Holy Days. When I asked him why he did not join a Conservative or Reform temple, he responded: "The way I was brought up I know that's a lot of baloney. If you don't want to be religious that's one thing, but don't legitimize it by saying that the Torah really didn't mean what it says." Why, then, did he not affiliate with an Orthodox synagogue? "Because," he replied, "I would feel too guilty about belonging and not observing. Sooner or later I would meet people from my childhood and it would be embarrassing. They would ask me why I never come."

Stanley Kahan* is a bitter man. He grew up in Brooklyn and attended Yeshiva Chaim Berlin for two years in the early 1950s. His parents sent him to yeshiva because "that's what they always did. Follow the crowd. Their friends from the old country did it, so they did it too." Like Jeffrey's parents they had come here after World War II, surviving because they were deported to Siberia from Poland by the Russians. They moved to Boro Park because Stanley's cousin owned an apartment building there. Stanley disliked yeshiva throughout, asserting, "These guys didn't know how to teach. I remember the elementary school principal was like a Hitler. He would walk around and slap you in the face if he didn't like what you were doing." Upon graduating from high school, Stanley was admitted to City College but his father refused to allow him to go:

> He said: "Nothing doing. You will go to Yeshiva Chaim Berlin where Uncle Abe sends his kids. I won't have you going to City and becoming a goy. If you want to go to college you can go to Brooklyn at night."

Stanley did so for two years but then, in what he described as "a terrible fight in which I said that I didn't believe that God had created the world," his father threw him out of the house. Stanley went to work on Wall Street as a senior order clerk. He never finished college and while he is today a successful shoe salesman, he feels that his father, now dead, and the yeshiva, are responsible for his never having realized his lifelong dream—to be an engineer. Stanley belongs to a Conservative temple because in the suburb in which he lives "that's what everyone else does and I want my kids to have friends." He displays great hostility toward observant Jews, describing them as "brainless fanatics" who want to impose their way of life on other Jews. He opposes federal aid to yeshivas, thinks that Jews should discard their "outmoded" religious practices, and does not keep kosher at home.

Harold Goldman* is a professor in a major university. He was born and raised in New York City where he attended yeshivas all his life, including an advanced yeshiva for four years. For the first two of those years he studied all day and night, entering evening college only because of pressure from his parents. His family had come here in 1908 and was Modern Orthodox. They wanted their son to become a doctor but he felt otherwise:

> I loved studying *Gemora*. It was a real challenge to understand all the arguments and conclusions. The yeshiva was very happy with me. They were sure I would become a *gadol*, and so was I for that matter. I didn't want to become a doc-

tor because to me that didn't require *real* intelligence. You just had to be a technician who worked on humans instead of machines, and if you were a grind and had a good memory you could make it. I wanted to use my creative powers.

Harold's decision to leave the yeshiva was precipitated when he took a course in philosophy as a sophomore in college. The instructor was "the first person outside the yeshiva world whose mind I could respect and, don't forget, it was the yeshiva that taught me to respect the mind." The instructor exposed him to the works of Kant, Hegel, and others and he found their ideas so fascinating that he began to question the validity of Orthodoxy.

Further probing revealed that this was not the entire story. Harold had also observed that other students for whom greatness had been predicted did not quite live up to expectations. He recalled how one young man, four years older than he, had been unable to find a job as a high school *rebbe* and had become instead a third-grade teacher in a day school. This made him pessimistic about his own future:

Sure, they said I'd be great, but that's what they said about the other guy too and look where he wound up. I didn't want to have that happen to me. Even then I realized that, smart as I was, there were others in the yeshiva and elsewhere just as smart.

Harold laughingly describes what he teaches as *apikorsus*. He does not feel comfortable talking about the yeshivas because he feels he let them down, though he also asserts they would have let him down had he stayed. He recounts how ashamed he felt when, eating a hamburger in a nonkosher luncheonette in midtown Manhattan, a former classmate, now a prominent leader in the Orthodox community, walked into the establishment to make a telephone call. "I cringed. I felt trapped. Our eyes met and he looked away." This happened fifteen years after Harold had left the institution. Summing up his decision to leave the yeshiva world, he observed: "Since everything ultimately rests on faith, I can't help but wonder if somehow they might not be right."

A strong sense of guilt characterized some of the respondents. This is not surprising in light of the fact that all had spent more than twelve years in such schools. Some felt anger at the intolerance of their teachers. This was especially true of those who attended in the 1950s and early 1960s, when yeshivas were not as good as they later became. The *rebbes* were often men whose lives had been broken by the ravages of life in Europe under Hitler. They were frequently impatient and sometimes incompetent. The prevailing perception of Orthodoxy was also very different in those days. The immigrants who would be remembered with fondness twenty-five years after their arrival were then seen as "greenhorns" even by their own children. Several informants admitted that they felt ashamed of being religious, and were embarrassed by their parents' accents and foreign ways. Finally, the community then was much smaller and Orthodoxy was strongly identified with low socioeconomic status by other Jews. Although there are no statistics, one suspects that these years produced the highest number of defections.

Most of those answering had good jobs, high education, and seemed quite intelligent. The majority were not poor students; their reasons for rejecting the faith seemed rational rather than emotional. Some were very hostile but most were not. Quite a few expressed disappointment and frustration at having come so close to what the yeshiva defined as greatness without quite making it. One observed in a somewhat deprecating fashion, "You see, in the Lithuanian yeshivas the deviants are intellectuals, philosophers, and doctors. Among the Hasidim if they deviate it's not heresy and irreligiosity but dishonesty in business." Exploring the different forms in which deviance emerges among both communities would indeed be an intriguing topic, though there is no evidence to support this individual's generalizations on this score. Some interesting questions are: What happens to such individuals as they pass through various stages of the life cycle? What factors in the larger society influence them? What is their psychological makeup? How does the yeshiva experience affect their behavior in nonreligious areas?[33]

Conflicting Goals?

Implicit in our discussion until now is the fact that the priority given to study for "a higher purpose" often conflicts with and impedes the realization of the other two major objectives. That this creates problems has been alluded to throughout the chapter. For all sorts of theological and historical reasons, the yeshiva must give primacy to the goal of *Torah lishmo*. Because of this emphasis, the curriculum is, in most instances, geared toward the student capable of intensive Talmud study but, in fact, many of its students are not. This was noted in an article by Rabbi Yisroel Belsky, a prominent member of the faculty at Yeshiva Torah Vodaath:

> It has been observed that many individuals with a passive interest and weak enthusiasm in the *Bais Hamedrash* possess major talent and organizational capability. Channeling these energies into . . . [dissemination of Torah] can do wonders for the community.[34]

This is easier said than done for several reasons. First, there is no simple way to determine who is most fit for this sort of activity. The problem does not arise with the brilliant student. He clearly belongs in the *beis medrash*. Nor does it come up with the student described above. It appears among the great mass of students who make up the middle; those reasonably capable of serious study. Keeping in mind that the yeshiva's major objective implies that persons go into the community only if they are less gifted in talmudic study, on what basis is such a decision reached? How can a *rosh yeshiva* know for certain at what point a young man has achieved his potential in scholarship? Furthermore, there is the problem of how to tell an individual that he is most suited for communal work or for teaching elementary school. He has, after all, spent half his life hoping and dreaming that he may be one of the few who achieve intellectual greatness.

Some might see a solution to such a dilemma in the creation of yeshivas committed to the goal of sending out proselytizers into the community or specializing in the training of teachers. But since such work is often viewed as second rate compared to becoming a *rosh yeshiva* and because, for reasons already mentioned, opportunities are limited in these fields, a yeshiva that proclaimed these goals would be shunned by most students. In fact, certain yeshivas do produce more persons who enter these fields than others, but all pursue all three goals simultaneously, and it often creates serious pressures on the students. If the yeshiva is unable to initiate significant changes in its curriculum lest it endanger its overall objective of Torah study at the highest level possible, it can at least move in two other directions. First, it should develop ways to deal with the lack of fulfillment expressed by large numbers of students in a variety of areas. Second, it ought to, wherever possible, exert pressure on the community to raise the status and material rewards of the teaching profession. Giving greater attention to these issues would be an important first step in reducing the strains discussed above.

CHAPTER 11

Why Has the Yeshiva Survived?

IN THEIR LANDMARK STUDY of Jewish acculturation in America, the sociologists Marshall Sklare and Joseph Greenblum wrote that the Jewish community was drifting away from traditional observances and redefining religiosity as moralism rather than sacramentalism.[1] In taking the opposite approach, the yeshiva has adopted a position at odds with that espoused by most American Jews today. That the yeshiva community and the larger Orthodox community of which it is a part would be highly committed to Old World traditions at the time of immigration is to be expected. That it has retained these values thirty-five years after most of its leaders landed on these shores is inconsistent with the pattern followed by most immigrants. What is the drawing power of this community for thousands of college-age youths in a society where anti-Semitism is not a powerful force, where the State of Israel constitutes a highly visible and potent rallying point, and where opportunities abound for Jews in virtually every area of life? That is the central sociological question of this study.

The yeshiva cannot be considered apart from the Orthodox community which supports and maintains it through contributions of both financial aid and students. Thus, at least some of the factors that might account for the yeshiva's survival can be applied to the larger Orthodox community, especially the Strictly Orthodox.

The historical chain of events and the larger societal factors that might explain the transplantation and reinvigoration of a centuries-old culture onto alien soil are a basic part of the picture but they are not the whole story. The other crucial component is that the yeshiva satisfies both basic human needs and, in many cases, the lofty aspirations that motivate its supporters regardless of the shifting currents of history. Let us now look at some of these complex factors that have affected the yeshiva in its efforts to maintain itself.

Leadership

As Chapter 3 details, the *rosh yeshiva* is most often a charismatic leader who combines highly unusual qualities of character, personality, and scholarly erudition in such a manner as to inspire awe and reverence among his followers. In addition, his authority is institutionalized by the yeshiva itself.

During the post–World War II period, the major period of growth of advanced yeshivas in this country, several *rosh yeshivas* who had arrived during or immediately after the war began the task of rebuilding and reestablishing in the United States the European yeshivas that had been destroyed in the Holocaust. This monumental task demanded men of exceptional talents and energies. That such individuals came to the fore at this time is one of the most important factors in the growth of yeshivas in America. In Rabbi Moshe Feinstein's words:

> When [after World War II] the great people started arriving—the *rosh yeshivas* and *menahalim* [administrators] the people began to see that there was a different type of learning, not the sort they had thought of earlier. It wasn't simply that one knows a little *chumash* [Bible], a little *Gemora*. They began to see that one can become great from such study.[2]

The most prominent of these extraordinary men was Rabbi Aharon Kotler. Rabbi Kotler's personality and character had been shaped and tempered by his experiences in the yeshivas of Lithuania, and he was determined to re-create as close an approximation of that culture as possible. Besides establishing his own yeshiva in Lakewood, he took it upon himself to spread the idea of full-time learning in a yeshiva for its own sake. Rabbi

Kotler was joined in these efforts by other prominent *rosh yeshivas,* among them Rabbi Elya Meir Bloch of Telshe and Rabbi Avrohom Kalmanowitz of Mir, who also set up yeshivas in this country. In addition to their unique abilities, these men derived a great deal of prestige from the fact that they had come from what were universally acknowledged as the greatest yeshivas in the world.

The Character of the Immigrant Generation

The presence of such men on the American scene raises an interesting question. The prewar American yeshiva community was by no means leaderless. Besides Rabbi Shraga Feivel Mendlowitz of Yeshiva Torah Vodaath and Dr. Bernard Revel, the first President of the Rabbi Isaac Elchanan Theological Seminary, perhaps the two most important figures in this period, there were other prominent leaders such as Rabbi Yitzchok Hutner of Yeshiva Chaim Berlin, Rabbi Dovid Leibowitz of Yeshiva Chofetz Chaim, Rabbi Yaakov Ruderman of Ner Israel Yeshiva, and Rabbi Shlomo Heiman of Yeshiva Torah Vodaath. Yet these men were unable to generate the same degree of enthusiasm that marked the postwar period. It was not, however, a question of their capacity to lead. Their problem was the nature of the community itself and the times in which they lived. They had taken the first step in establishing yeshivas in the United States, but conditions were not yet ripe for the full transformation of Jewish education at the higher levels into a mass movement.

In his description of the Jewish immigrants who came to America in the 1880s, Irving Howe called them "the *luftmenschen* without trades or roots, driven to take a chance across the sea."[3] Although the impetus for leaving the old country was often persecution, the emigrant was frequently eager to leave his home simply because America was seen as the land of opportunity. Thus, his reluctance to abandon the familiar was often accompanied by a nascent willingness to accommodate to the demands of the new society and discard what was often only a nominal adherence to tradition. Devout Jews, on the other hand, resisted the lure of the New Land because they saw it as a place where they would be required to give up deeply held religious values and practices. And so they stayed until the Holocaust uprooted them and turned them into reluctant immigrants. Though largely poor, they had built up strong educational and cultural institutions in Europe, for years operating them relatively free from state interference. Those who survived the Nazi horrors and retained their faith must have been even more determined not to allow their standards of religious life to disappear or even be eroded in America. As Rabbi Yaakov Kamenecki put it: "Post-Holocaust parents were not satisfied with the quality of Jewish education they found when they came here. They came from the land of the *gedolim.*"[4]

While the leaders gave direction to their followers, they were aided by the fact that communities of scholars who had continued to study during the war years, mostly in Shanghai, came here and provided a model for others to emulate. The most notable case was the Mirrer Yeshiva, which had remained, more or less, intact through the war years, and which reestablished itself as a unit in Brooklyn, New York. The sight of men in their thirties and forties studying full time was an inspiration for younger students, who viewed them as culture heroes from a world known to them only from stories told by their teachers or parents. Rabbi Shraga Moshe Kalmanowitz, a Mirrer *rosh yeshiva,* gave a vivid portrayal of how the yeshiva was set up in America:

> Today people have contact with the outside world. In China we were isolated and this was good because it strengthened our commitment. As a result we were able to preserve our *ruach* [spirit]. Since we were many, American boys had to adapt to *us* and little by little they did. You know, of course, that it was unheard of in America that boys learned after marriage. But we did it, as did others. Those that came had real dedication. There was a fellow who suffered terribly from migraine headaches and the doctor told him he needed more ventilation than there was in the *beis medrash;* but he said: "I can't learn in a room by myself. I have to learn with everyone else." So he bought two little fans that he put on both sides of him in the *beis medrash* and they blew on him and everyone saw what he went through to learn.
>
> There was also the case of a Hungarian Jew who wanted to give a *bochur* $10,000 and bring him into the business if only he would marry his daughter and stop learning. But he refused and the man went to every *bochur* in the

beis medrash and not one took him up on his offer because
they wanted to continue learning after marriage too. Since
he was Hungarian he was used to the idea that prevailed in
that country—that you learned until you got married.[5]

The influence of the Hasidic communities such as Satmar, Ger,
Belz, and Bobov, many of which came with their *rebbes,* also cannot be discounted, inasmuch as they demonstrated that right-
wing Orthodoxy could be successfully transplanted to the *treifene
medinah* (literally, nonkosher country).

It must also be remembered that the masses of Orthodox
Jews who immigrated in this period had no need to develop a
sense of group solidarity, a meaningful and viable set of values
and norms. The history of Orthodoxy and its institutions on the
European continent was over a thousand years old, and the
yeshiva had been an institution of cultural transmission in one
form or another for an equal length of time. Along with that, the
Orthodox immigrants had developed a prestige hierarchy that
looked upon the *rosh yeshivas* as authority figures who embodied
their beliefs, hopes, and aspirations, and they therefore strongly
supported the call to expand higher Jewish education in
America.

Had the new immigrants trickled into this country over a
long period of time, maintaining their culture would have been
inestimably more difficult. That they came en masse, with their
leaders, greatly increased their resistance to the blandishments of
the larger society. Moreover, the very factors that set the new immigrants apart from the larger society—that they and their
children wore skullcaps or conservative hats in public, that their
children attended special schools from the age of six, and that
they were not allowed to play in the street on the Sabbath—increased the suspicion traditionally reserved for newcomers,
bringing them even closer together.

Changing Attitudes Toward
Cultural Identification

Attitudes toward immigrants in postwar America were also
crucial. Prior to World War II the prevailing view among
American government officials, intellectuals, and others was that

all incoming groups were expected to give up their cultural traits and become totally absorbed into the dominant society. This was not an unimportant perspective, since it colored the activities of settlement houses, public schools, industry and business, and various government agencies.[6] By the end of World War II, there was a gradual realization that forcing the immigrant to give up his ways often resulted in a social and personal disorganization that disrupted the family structure and impeded the acculturation process.[7] Moreover, many immigrants met the efforts to devalue their culture with increased resistance rather than assimilation. A new view emerged, known as "cultural pluralism." Simply defined, this held that those aspects of one's culture that did not conflict with the national interest ought to be retained. Ethnic identity came to be seen in a more positive light as a way of smoothing the transition from the old to the new. In its broader sense, cultural pluralism favored the coexistence of different minority groups within the larger society.

The evolution of these attitudes created a situation favorable to the newly arriving Orthodox Jews. They found a society that was at least somewhat receptive to their needs. True, they encountered much individual prejudice in the areas of first settlement, but the various government agencies, as well as many influential figures in politics, business, and community life were, on the whole, sympathetic to their needs.

Hospitality to new and "different" groups of immigrants, which had hardly been characteristic of Americans or American institutions before the war, was also fostered by the impact of the Holocaust on the public mind. In the larger sense, the newcomers benefited from identification of their suffering at the hands of the Nazis with that undergone by Americans in general. After all, Germany had been America's wartime enemy too.

The Role of the American Jewish Community

The larger American Jewish community played an important role in facilitating the adaptation of the post-Holocaust Orthodox Jew. As part of its larger interest in all Jews who entered the United States at that time, it helped meet their needs through organizations such as the Joint Distribution Committee (JDC) and the Hebrew Immigrant Aid Society (HIAS). It worked hard both to bring them here and to help them adjust to a new way of life.

The pace of the yeshiva's growth was greatly accelerated by the fact that a viable Orthodox community already existed at the time of the postwar migration. This meant, among other things, that there were already yeshivas at various levels for children, Orthodox synagogues to attend, and neighborhoods to live in where they might associate with other Orthodox Jews. Many of the new arrivals had relatives among the Orthodox members of the Jewish community as well as among those who were not observant and their support often speeded up the resettlement process.

The new immigrants began to make their presence felt as they enrolled their children in the yeshivas and began to participate in school activities. They also became involved with the synagogues and other organizations in the Jewish community. Above all, they persuaded many native-born American Jews that the level of religious life in this country needed to be raised, although others were made to feel uncomfortable and defensive by the complaints of the refugees and responded with antagonism.

The immigrant Orthodox were not a monolithic group. They came from many countries and the cultural baggage that they carried with them often reflected this diversity. Jews who had lived in Belgium, Holland, or Germany between the two world wars had different perspectives from those of the more isolated Hasidim from, say, Poland. The Orthodox from Budapest did not see eye to eye with the Hasidic groups who had lived elsewhere in Hungary. Each grouping managed, however, to find its own niche with some sending its children to the already established right-wing yeshivas while others chose the more modern institutions. Many immigrants underwent dramatic changes in their own religiosity after their arrival, with some turning left and others right.

Ethnically, the post war Orthodox immigration can be divided into two distinct phases. The first, immediately after the war, saw Jews coming from Galicia, Poland proper, the Ukraine, Hungary, and Czechoslovakia. Substantial numbers of Jews came from Western European countries too, especially Belgium, Holland, Germany, and France. But most of them were culturally Eastern European and had either migrated to

Western Europe between the two world wars or had fled there during the second war itself. The second wave, which arrived in the wake of the 1956 Hungarian Revolution, came from Hungary and Czechoslovakia.

It is interesting that although the *yeshiva gedola,* with its emphasis on learning for its own sake, is a Lithuanian transplant, most of its students come from the above-mentioned backgrounds. Attitudes toward talmudic study were far more utilitarian in Hungary, Czechoslovakia, and Galicia. One studied until marriage and then it was time to leave the yeshiva. Although immigrants from these countries influenced yeshiva life in a myriad of ways, the basic mode of study has been that which was customary in the Lithuanian yeshivas.

All this remains an unexplored field. Without a great deal of empirical research, it is impossible to assess fully either how the Europeans changed the face of American Orthodoxy or how they were themselves affected by the prevailing assimilationist tendencies. There is no doubt, however, that this wave of Jewish immigration breathed new life into a culture and community which, while not threatened with extinction, was not undergoing tremendous growth.

The Day School Movement

The traditional value placed on education by Jews is a crucial factor in comprehending the survival and growth of the yeshiva. While this is an important value among all Jews, the Orthodox place greater priority on religious education than on education in general. Immigration therefore accounts for much of the current strength and impressive growth of the day schools and, to a lesser extent, the high schools.[8] The general increase in Jewish identification, spurred largely by the creation of the State of Israel, organizations promoting the yeshivas, the high caliber of the schools themselves, especially in the cities, when compared to public schools, and the general prestige of attending a private school are also important factors in the growth of the day school movement.[9]

Only a minority of children in the day schools are observant (just how many is not known) or continue in religious high schools, and an even smaller number go on to advanced yeshivas. Nevertheless, it is the day school and the *mesivta* that provide the basic education for almost all of those who study at the *beis medrash* level. Without such a background, advanced talmudic study would be impossible for most young men.[10] Table 11-1 indicates the increase up to 1978.

The enrollment figures cited in the table include coeducational day and high schools, the vast majority of whose graduates do not continue in advanced yeshivas. Nevertheless, among those who do not are individuals who, having been imbued with a strong Jewish background, provide support for advanced yeshivas. Also, while our focus is on the Strictly Orthodox, it ought to be noted that the majority of those who identify themselves as Modern Orthodox have probably had a yeshiva high school education. Finally, there has always been a good deal of "crossing over" between schools characterized as "modern" and those that are "traditional." Parents may find a particular emphasis not to their liking at the elementary school level and compensate for it by sending their children to a different type of high school. In addition, factors such as tuition, friendship networks, and geographic location may impinge upon the true ideological leanings of the families.

Those yeshiva day schools that are oriented toward the approach favored by the advanced yeshivas provide intensive

Table 11-1

Year	Day School Enrollment (United States) Number of Schools	Enrollment
1945	69	10,000
1955	180	35,000
1965	323	63,500
1978	463	83,350

Year	High School Enrollment (United States) Number of Schools	Enrollment
1944	9	?
1964	83	10,200
1967	105	13,400
1978	150	16,800

Figures are as given in *Tempo*, Report No. 10, June 1979, p. 1, a publication of Torah Umesorah.

preparation of a sort reminiscent of the strictest European yeshivas. In 1977, for example, Pirchei Agudath Israel, the children's division of the Agudah, sponsored a contest to see how many Mishnas students could recite from memory. (The average Mishna is eight or nine lines long.) More than 1,200 boys competed: "The top finalist . . . knew 2,287 Mishnas by heart. Seven other youngsters memorized more than 1,000 . . . each."[11] Rabbi Nisson Wolpin, a former principal of Yeshiva Ohr Yisroel, a right-wing day school and *mesivta* and now editor of the *Jewish Observer*, explained the process by which this level of knowledge was achieved:

> First you buy talented teachers. Second, it's the long hours and the steady conditioning. As a result they experience success in this area at an early age and they're psychologically ready to go on to *mesivta* and *yeshiva gedola*.[12]

Thus, we see the crucial role of the day school in socializing the yeshiva *bochur* into the world of the Talmud.

The advanced yeshivas themselves played a crucial role in the development of the day school movement, for it was their leaders who anticipated both the need for and the importance of such education to provide a steady stream of students to the higher schools. The National Society for Hebrew Day Schools (Torah Umesorah),[13] which is involved in almost every aspect of day school education, is staffed primarily by graduates of advanced yeshivas, and is strongly influenced by a board of *rosh yeshivas* with respect to policy matters. In commenting upon its founding, Dr. Joseph Kaminetsky, its former director, said:

> When the lights of Torah went out in Europe, there arose a conviction mainly on the part of Rabbi Mendlowitz that they had to be put on here. He knew that starting more day schools would insure the growth of Torah in America. It could not, however, have been done without the spiritual help and support of Reb Aharon Kotler, Reb Reuvain Grozovsky, Reb Elya Meir Bloch, and others like them.[14]

Another related development was the establishment of the summer camps which dot the landscape in the Catskill Mountains and elsewhere. As we have noted, they provide continuity with yeshiva education, both by conducting summer classes and by reinforcing the values of family and school.[15]

Socioeconomic and Demographic Factors

Most of those who came here after the war were not well off, and the early years were difficult for them. Nevertheless, the immigrants found themselves in a society where economic advancement was possible, and many of them prospered. As a result, many parents who valued a yeshiva education for their children were now able to afford the costs.

With more parents able to pay tuition, and with generous donations from the wealthy,[16] the quality of the day schools gradually improved. By the mid-1960s those who had arrived in 1946 had sent a generation of children through elementary and high school, and enrollment began to increase noticeably at the *beis medrash* level. Economic prosperity meant that students could remain longer in the yeshiva while also pursuing a college degree. By 1970 many graduates had entered the professions and had begun to contribute their expertise as lawyers, professors, government officials, and business executives to help the yeshivas both articulate and satisfy their needs in a variety of areas. Others stayed on to study in *kollel,* an indication that the community was now wealthy enough to support such activities.

Of all the factors that could account for the strength of the yeshiva, those relating to the community's demographic character have the broadest implications for the Jewish community as a whole. Yeshiva alumni who responded to our questionnaire reported an average rate of 4.0 children per family compared to an average rate of 1.8 among Jews in general.[17]

Several reasons have been given to explain this phenomenon. First, having children is a biblical commandment. Also, improved economic conditions have made it possible for people to have more children. Finally, the Hasidim, who have always had large families, have influenced the yeshiva community in this area. Assimilation and intermarriage in the larger Jewish community also account for a significant rise in the proportion of Orthodox to other Jews. If these trends continue, the Orthodox community is likely to have increasing power with respect to policy making, organizational influence, and politics, particularly because Orthodox Jews are increasingly better educated and more prosperous.[18] A more powerful Orthodox community will obviously increase the influence and impact of the yeshiva upon Jews in general.

Political and Organizational Sophistication

As the educational and economic levels of the Orthodox community moved steadily upward, it became increasingly active in the political sphere. This was symbolized by the election, during the 1970s, of several New York State assemblymen who were openly Orthodox.[19] Actually, the community had become involved in the political process before then. In an interview with the writer, Rabbi Moshe Sherer, head of the Agudah, talked about the early stages of such activity:

> I remember the first time I was called upon to meet with President John Kennedy at the White House in the summer of 1963, on Tisha ba'Av. He had called together a small number of Jewish leaders, twelve or thirteen, to explain some vote the United States had cast at the U.N. that was not favorable to Israel. . . . Before I left for Washington I called Reb Aharon Kotler. . . . He was vacationing in Fleischmann's, New York. And I want you to know that he gave me an hour's lecture over the phone on how to talk to the President about the security needs of Israel, about tripartite guarantees, in an extremely knowledgeable manner. What I'm trying to say is that those who receive their outlook on life from the original sources, the essence of Torah, are somehow able to develop direction that shows us how to deal with our problems.[20]

According to Rabbi Sherer, one of the major contributions of the Agudah was

> to take the *rosh yeshivas* out of a corner to which others would like to restrict them, and plunge them into the outside world as policy makers. As a result, they have had tremendous influence over larger issues affecting the community. And we need the wisdom, based upon their untainted and broad knowledge, of the thousands of years of Jewish experience.[21]

Agudah was only one of numerous organizations that played a crucial role in this area. The National Jewish Commission on Law and Public Affairs (COLPA) has, from its inception, been an independent organization, serving the needs of all Orthodox Jews, be they Hasidic, Modern Orthodox, or Strictly Orthodox. Its membership consists primarily of young lawyers who volunteer their time to defend the rights of Orthodox Jews. Of the many causes in which COLPA has become involved, its greatest success has been in protecting the rights of Sabbath observers and in securing government aid for parochial schools. In the words of one of its founders, Dr. Marvin Schick, COLPA, because it represents "the entire spectrum of Orthodoxy... demonstrates the possibility of Orthodox unity."[22] As evidence, Schick notes that most of the volunteer attorneys are Modern Orthodox; yet the causes and groups for which they work are often those of Hasidic or Strictly Orthodox organizations.

Other important Orthodox groups in this area are Torah Umesorah, which is involved with Headstart programs, and the Board of Jewish Education, through which the yeshivas receive funds for school breakfasts and lunches and other support.

On a more subtle level, the yeshivas perceived the need to persuade the government that what was being taught in the yeshivas was educationally important and valid as well as a basic component of an ancient culture. Agudah, which has a close relationship with the advanced yeshivas, often spoke for them in this regard. As Rabbi Sherer explained:

> We felt the time had come for the U.S. Office of Education to realize that if they accredited Greek culture and all the other civilizations of the world, that Talmud and Bible were equally worthy of recognition because they represented, in their terms, a high quality education . . . we had to overcome the perception that studying in a yeshiva is some mumbo-jumbo over ancient tomes. It is the legitimate expression of our vast and relevant heritage. . . . But we had another goal too. We felt that if through these programs we could keep down the cost of tuition, then more parents would send their children to yeshivas. After all these parents are being doubly taxed—they pay for public schools and pay for private schools.[23]

Besides demonstrating adeptness at benefiting from state and federal funding, the Orthodox community began putting greater pressure on the Federation of Jewish Philanthropies to increase its support of education, an area that had not received priority until then.[24] The Federation proved responsive to a degree, perhaps because it recognized that groups committed to Jewish identity would ultimately strengthen the entire community. Indicative of this more positive attitude has been the increased involvement in recent years of Orthodox spokesmen in Federation. It can be added that the yeshiva community is politically quite conservative. The responses in the questionnaire to the question of political preference were: very liberal—3 percent, liberal—10 percent, middle of the road or moderate—34 percent, slightly conservative—39 percent, conservative—14 percent.

Willingness to Compromise in a Secular Society

At the onset of this project, it was hypothesized that the yeshiva might owe its ability to survive to its willingness to compromise with secular society. This was not the explanation offered by most members of the community, who argued vehemently that the yeshiva had succeeded in America because it had *not* compromised. A closer look suggests that the answer lies somewhere in between. The yeshiva *has* compromised, though its proponents might prefer the term "adjusted," but only in certain areas. It is by examining *where* the community draws the line that we begin to understand its survival.

In a study of Orthodox Jews in the Boro Park section of Brooklyn, sociologist Egon Mayer points out that most studies of American Jews have assumed that their ethnic identification is but a way-station on the road to assimilation, and that they desire most of all full acceptance by the larger society.[25] This assumption, he argues, cannot be applied to members of the Orthodox community because "they do not perceive the broader culture as dominant."[26] Having already established that the Strictly Orthodox have little meaningful contact with outsiders (see Chapter 10, pp. 277–278), it may be useful to look briefly at how and why such attitudes develop.

From the time the Strictly Orthodox Jew is a small child, there is a stress on the uniqueness of the community. "You are different and special," the youngster is told from the time he enters first grade. "You come from an ancient people to whom God gave the holiest book in the world, a work also recognized as such by other religions." As the child is introduced into the lives of Abraham, Isaac, and Jacob, he comes to associate the moral lessons derived from their behavior with the standards of the community to which he belongs. There is no attempt at ecumenicalism in the Strictly Orthodox yeshivas. The community believes that survival as a distinct entity necessitates more than education—it requires indoctrination, a goal which it unabashedly pursues. The recognition of this and the will to pursue it through intensive socialization of the young is an important factor in the hold that the community has on its members.

Such insularity is not due solely to internal reasons. It is also based on the degree of suspicion felt by members of the yeshiva community toward the outside world and their sense of vulnerability. Although Jews of all types encounter anti-Semitism, the Orthodox community probably experiences it to a greater degree and with greater intensity and, as a result, reacts more strongly to it. Moreover, as a group, the Orthodox were particularly hard hit by the Holocaust, and their community in America is made up primarily of survivors and their children. Asked what he felt were the implications of the Holocaust, Rabbi Yaakov Ruderman, head of Ner Israel Yeshiva, replied:

> People think the Holocaust made the world feel sympathy for the Jews but it really didn't result in sympathy. It just showed that it could be done. There is more anti-Semitism than ever before.[27]

A student at Breuer's Yeshiva echoed these comments:

> Sure it can happen again. And I don't think anyone would care. All you need is one person to rouse everybody. You're never safe from another Holocaust. Remember that Germany was very civilized and technologically advanced. Yet it happened there.

Such anxieties are heightened by the fact that those non-Jews with whom the yeshiva student has contact are often those who insult and revile him. Because of his dress, the yeshiva student, like his Hasidic counterpart, is often a target for ethnic slurs and even attacks. Virtually no yeshiva student has grown up without at least one such encounter.[28] As one student at Yeshiva Torah Vodaath put it:

> When I was in the Bronx as a kid, I used to be called names by the Puerto Ricans and the blacks. But even now, in New Jersey, there'll be middle-class kids who'll throw pennies at me on *shabbos* as I come home from *shul*.

Such experiences often have the effect of increasing group cohesiveness as well as decreasing concern for outsiders. As one young man, a student at the Mirrer Yeshiva, explained: "Why should I care about the Goyim? It's clear from everything they do that they don't care about us."

The yeshiva, or Strictly Orthodox community, retains a distinct consciousness of kind that separates it from the larger society in a most fundamental way, and this contributes to its survival. Still, there are other areas where the lines become somewhat blurred, where American culture has made inroads, and where compromise or adjustment has indeed occurred.

On a superficial level, the most obvious signs of compromise in the community are things such as kosher Chinese restaurants and pizza shops, kosher hamburger joints with a special place for ritually washing one's hands before eating bread, Hebrew versions of Scrabble, and Orthodox rock groups which set biblical passages to a modern beat. These are not factors that account for the survival of the yeshiva community as much as they are examples of how Orthodoxy in general has managed to adopt features of the larger society without violating religious laws. As Rabbi Nisson Wolpin stated:

> I think the pizza parlor introduces the kid to pizza that he would never know about, but it's not a preventative against buying non-kosher pizza. You might find kids in Long Island who hanker for a pizza and when you give them one they stay kosher but it doesn't do a thing for the yeshiva *bochur*.[29]

The approach of the Strictly Orthodox in these matters has been cautious. They will buy Jewish records, but of the all-male Pirchei Agudath Israel choir or the Gerer Hasidim, not the coed Yemenite Trio. They will go to resort hotels, but there must be separate swimming for men and women and entertainment that conforms to religious and moral standards. Even their reaching out to the uncommitted, which is a form of adjustment to developments outside the community, is pursued very carefully (see pp. 281–288).

On the other hand, life in America has brought about important changes that contrast sharply with the lifestyles common in earlier times. In Eastern Europe, the yeshiva *bochur* began full-time study at twelve or thirteen. Here he conforms to state law and studies secular subjects through high school, and only then will he begin studying Talmud seriously.[30] University attendance, almost unheard of in the Lithuanian yeshivas, is fairly common in this country. Similarly, many Strictly Orthodox women today have jobs that bring them into extensive contact with the outside world. A woman may, for example, be a research assistant or a typist in a law firm where she is the only Orthodox, if not Jewish, person working there.[31]

Though they may not readily admit it, the influences of the larger society on the Strictly Orthodox can be pervasive. The wives and daughters of many yeshiva graduates could certainly fit the following description of women in the Boro Park community, which shows the effects of mass media and culture upon their lives:

> If religious prescriptions regulate the modesty of women's clothing, middle-class values allow that no expense be spared to be as elegantly modest as possible. . .—a combination of Jewish modesty with the norms of American consumerism. . . . Here, as in the larger middle-class world, clothes are an important symbol of status.[32]

While not really an example of religious compromise, such behavior illustrates how the standards of the larger society find their way into the community. That the problem is regarded as serious is evidenced by the general criticisms of materialism that fill the pages of the *Jewish Observer* and the many speeches by community leaders inveighing against it. Typical is the following excerpt from an address by Rabbi Chaim Dov Keller, head of the Telshe Yeshiva in Chicago, at the 1974 convention of the Agudath Israel:

> Many of our people have suffered a warping of priorities, throwing themselves headlong into the pursuit of materialism. Unbelievable sums of money are spent for one night of a wedding celebration, while yeshivas pay their teachers coolie wages for lack of funds. Plush carpets and ornate furnishings have become status symbols among a people whose aristocracy was always measured in terms of Torah learning and *tzidkus* [righteousness]. The institution of *nadan* [giving a dowry] has undergone a renaissance, tending to blind suitors to the real merits (or lack of them) in girls to be considered as life-time partners. The daughters of the less affluent are overlooked by budding young scholars in

favor of the daughters of those who can plunk down 30 or 50 thousand dollars in advance.[33]

Several persons interviewed cited the effects of the Holocaust. One prominent leader in the yeshiva community cited the following example in support of this view:

> I was at a wedding of a man of modest means, a survivor of the death camps. The same was true of his wife. His daughter was getting married and he had to pay for the wedding. It was so lavish. When they were walking down the aisle I thought that the grandfather never would have thought that he would have a grandchild getting married like this. I thought that this fellow is saying: "I spit in Hitler's eye. Every bit of glitter means I'm getting back at them. He made me suffer and I'm showing him." There was vengeance in every bit of grandeur. I think the survivors have brought this over to some extent. Maybe it's not a nice thing to say but I grew up among Americans and we didn't have this.

Recent research on Holocaust survivors lends support to these statements. Many studies have cited the emphasis on material possessions and the feelings of insecurity responsible for it.

Another case in point is the divorce rate. Although there are no reliable figures available, all therapists, marriage counselors, rabbis, and school principals active in the yeshiva community with whom I spoke agreed that divorce was on the rise.[34] Some breakups are related to internal features of the community—that is, the lack of preparation for marriage in the yeshivas, marrying too young, and economic hardships. Most of those interviewed, however, blamed the influence of the larger society—the growing acceptance of divorce among Americans in general, its easier availability, the emphasis upon materialism, hedonism, and sexual gratification in the dominant society, and the effects of the women's liberation movement on a male-oriented society.[35]

Still, the Strictly Orthodox differ from their Modern Orthodox counterparts in a fundamental way that goes beyond the question of lifestyle. Whereas the Modern Orthodox tend to compromise wherever *possible*—that is, mixed dancing, watching certain TV programs, less fastidiousness in dietary observances—the Strictly Orthodox generally, but not always, compromise only where it is *necessary* or, at least, highly beneficial.

Thus, they will permit college, but only because it is necessary for employment. The Strictly Orthodox high school student who studies Talmud for only a half day is fully aware that this is only a step toward the ideal mode of study—full-time scholarly activity in the *beis medrash*. Moreover, he is taught that Torah is to be studied for its own sake, but that this does not apply to secular knowledge. In the same manner, a right-wing yeshiva graduate will justify his modern dress as necessary for his job. He will rationalize dating as a necessary evil in modern society but will rarely depict it as "fun." There are obvious inconsistencies and exceptions to these examples, but the point is that they represent different attitudes toward the outside world that ultimately affect the extent of secularization that occurs in the community.

A full determination of the influence of secularization on the yeshiva community will require much more research, but it is not insignificant.[36] It is important, however, to touch briefly on a recent turn to the right, away from compromise, that seems to be occurring in the general Orthodox community, and among younger elements in the yeshiva community in particular. Why this is happening is difficult to say but one possibility is that the now-maturing younger generation has been nurtured on the uncompromising philosophy exemplified by Rav Aharon Kotler. It is interesting that some of the most right-wing *rosh yeshivas* such as Rabbi Elya Svei of Philadelphia, Rabbi Yitzchok Feigelstock of Long Beach, New York, and Rabbi Chaim Epstein of Flatbush, Brooklyn, were all protégés of Rav Aharon. The older *rosh yeshivas* seem, by and large, to be more moderate.

Within the larger Orthodox community, the influence of the highly committed and visible Hasidim, especially the Satmarer, must be taken into account. Their lifestyles and strict adherence to the letter of the law have probably made others more aware of previously neglected areas in religion. In addition, the changing mores of society regarding sex, abortion, drugs, and so on, discussed earlier, may even have engendered a counterreaction among some of the more liberal Orthodox. This view was expressed as follows by one Modern Orthodox Jew:

> I'm sending my children to a *frum*, right-wing yeshiva even though I had a more liberal upbringing—you know, I went to Camp Hili [a well-known Modern Orthodox summer camp], coed swimming at the beaches in Far Rockaway, etc.—because, in today's society, with all its corrupting in-

fluences, you need a right-wing education just so your kids will wind up in the middle.

After more than thirty years of steady growth in America, it ought not to be surprising that the yeshiva is more assertive about the beliefs that it has always held. Of course, the rightward trend may only be a temporary phase. Nevertheless, for as long as it lasts, it will have strong repercussions within the Orthodox community.

Pre-Professional Training

Without belaboring the issue it is worth stressing that the yeshiva is functional for the Orthodox community. It transmits the tradition in a tradition-conscious community and it provides educators and rabbis to serve its needs. That it might, as discussed in Chapter 10, do a better job in these areas is incidental to the fact that it is the major source for preparation in them.

Lay leaders of the Orthodox community are aware that the community's well-being depends, in large measure, upon the quality of its spiritual leadership. They have therefore been willing to provide funds for the establishment and maintenance of advanced yeshivas to train rabbis and educators. The role played by the yeshiva in this area is therefore yet another reason for its survival.

The Need for a Social-Psychological Explanation

The long history of the yeshiva would seem to suggest that its historic ability to persist does not depend upon the often ephemeral shifts in various societies. Rather, one ought to look at the yeshiva's ability to withstand the pressures of assimilation in a community marked by unprecedented tolerance for Jews as yet another indication that it has an almost unique talent for resisting the dominant trends in both the Jewish and Gentile communities. Why this is so requires a consideration of the *social-psychological* factors that motivate individuals to attend the yeshiva. These need to be judged in tandem with the socio-economic and historical factors already mentioned.

As part of the effort to understand the yeshiva's ability to survive and grow, a number of *rosh yeshivas* were asked what they thought could account for it. The following response, given by Rabbi Hutner, was typical:

> They'll give you all sorts of reasons, but in reality it's a mystery just like the mystery of the Jews. How did the Jewish people survive? And this question about the yeshivas is a mystery within a mystery. And all the reasons are junk. It was the work of God. That it has lasted so long is to me a greater miracle than the crossing of the Red Sea. The Jew has a deep, mysterious connection to Torah that we don't fully understand although we know it's there. If you ask me, we have survived because Torah is true, because it is great and eternal.[37]

When pressed further, this *rosh yeshiva,* as well as others, obligingly provided sociological, psychological, and historical answers of the sort we have been discussing, but not before it was clearly understood that these were of considerably less importance in his eyes.

It can certainly be said even without presenting theological arguments that the Torah has kept the Jew's faith alive through the centuries by serving as a concrete embodiment and expression of his history and culture. It has played this role both when times were good for the Jews and when they were bad. Yet we must look further to see what personal appeal it has for members of the community. What psychological needs does the yeshiva fulfill for individuals who have been successfully socialized into a certain system of beliefs and values?

Intellectual Satisfaction and Spiritual Happiness

The primary activity in the yeshiva is intellectual study. As we saw in Chapter 4, the talmudic method is a highly complex one. Within the yeshiva, talmud is evaluated in a way that encourages the individual to develop his powers of reasoning to the utmost. It is reasonable to assume that it is therefore a highly attractive institution for those who derive pleasure from the challenge of developing and playing with ideas. The results of the questionnaire confirmed this. When asked what they liked best about the yeshiva experience, the process of study itself (along with *rebbe*-student relations) was the most frequently cited aspect. The following comments were representative of this view:

> There was the sheer pleasure of struggling with difficult concepts and then grasping and understanding them. There's no way you can match it with stuff you learn in college.
>
> A corporate vice president
> from New Jersey

> There was an air of excitement about learning *Gemora* that was created by the *rebbe*. Getting the point in an argument became the most important thing. It was a way of raising one's status purely by ability, not because you were born with a silver spoon in your mouth.
>
> A West Coast attorney

> I felt a very close historical connection to those who had written the *Gemora*. This was especially so when I was able to follow the arguments in the text and make a sharp point. These were my roots.
>
> A teacher in a day school

The Jewish community has always placed a high premium on intelligence and intellectual accomplishment. For the Orthodox Jew, however, respect for the intellect is accompanied by a realization of its limits in matters of faith. This creates a certain tension in the community, just as it does for believers of all faiths, who must balance their desire to comprehend life with an acceptance of their limitations in doing so. The Talmud, with its emphasis on the mind rather than on the emotional, provides a framework whereby individuals can engage in rational discourse and exchange of ideas without challenging the validity of the faith. Naturally, there are limits to their endeavors, inasmuch as they cannot challenge manifestly stated laws, but only their interpretation and application; still, they provide a great deal of satisfaction for the student. In short, much of the frustration that might arise from dogmatic acceptance finds its release in the freewheeling debates and exercises in logical thinking that characterize talmudic study. We might add that the excited debates, shouting, arguing, and general spirit of unrestrained

give-and-take are a source of deep, psychic gratification for people who live in a society that imposes restrictions on one's behavior in almost every area of life. For them the learning process is
an exercise in democracy, despite the relative authoritarianism of
the institution in which it takes place.

At the same time, the power of the Talmud in the purely
religious and aesthetic sense must not be underestimated. Those
who study it often see its brilliant expositions as proof of its
divine origin. As one *kollel* student at the Lakewood yeshiva
stated: "When you really know how to learn and begin ap-
preciating the beautiful logic of the *Gemora* you realize that only
with the help of God could such a brilliant work have been produced." Although they have been socialized into the faith long
before they reach the advanced yeshiva, the quest for God is for
many a lifelong pursuit and plays an important role even in the
life of those whose faith may be assumed to be unquestioning. Its
connection to the learning process is integral for it is believed that
constant study of the Talmud offers one the opportunity to better
understand and appreciate God. The yeshiva student is not likely
to express his doubts in matters of religion as freely as others but
he is prone to them. That this is a fact of yeshiva life may be inferred from the oft-quoted rabbinic maxim, "From doing
something without belief, belief eventually emerges." The
"something" is fulfilling a religious precept, be it talmudic study
or observing the Sabbath.

These considerations explain, in part, why intellectual study
in secular areas such as philosophy often lacks the appeal that it
might ordinarily have for the usually intelligent yeshiva student.
It does not satisfy the yearning for spiritual fulfillment and meaning in life that is an integral part of the Orthodox Jew's world
view. As Rabbi Feinstein put it: "The soul is satisfied with
things that are of the Torah."[38] Talmud, because of its perceived
divine origin, enables the individual to accomplish both objectives simultaneously. There is, quite simply, no other belief
system in contemporary society that offers its adherents a place
in an afterlife for honing and sharpening their intellectual
capabilities to the fullest extent possible.

This approach will not satisfy everyone. In stressing the intellect to such a degree the yeshiva, as a religious institution, carries within itself the seeds of discontent.[39] In what is a long process, the yeshiva *bochur* moves from a stage where he is taught the

content of the law to one where he seeks to apprehend its underlying logic. This creates a situation of "rising expectations" which, when not fully met, test the depth of belief that has been cultivated within the individual. Those who do not possess the requisite degree of faith may become disenchanted with the community. This tension between knowledge and belief may be the reason why many brilliant talmudic scholars have broken with Judaism to seek secular salvation in other forms of scholarship: philosophy, science, and the humanities. Others, afraid of their rationalistic doubts, may look for salvation in piety, completely emotional identification with God, and in purely ritualistic, yet joyous, practice. The Strictly Orthodox of the yeshiva world, however, maintain the tension between reason and belief at the highest level, and for the majority the system seems to work.

Infusing Daily Life with Religious Meaning

As we have indicated, many in the yeshiva are not intellectually gifted. For such individuals intellectual debate and constant study might not be enough, even if they believe that participating in such activities fulfills a divine commandment. Being constantly frustrated by not comprehending the class discussion or doing so only with great difficulty would seem to preclude a very long stay in the yeshiva. And yet we find that many mediocre or average students spend years in the institution. One possible explanation is that talmudic study can often be translated into concrete action.

When the student is able to show his father or his peers how to observe a certain ritual based on talmudic precepts, he solidifies the relationship between the theoretical and the practical, between ancient tomes and contemporary practice. This may involve knowing why one activity is permitted on the Sabbath while another seemingly similar one is prohibited.[40] It may find its expression in a discussion of what type of person ought to be given the greatest respect or to whom one is most obligated to give charity. The long-range effects of this become clear when one observes how the conversations of those who have attended yeshivas for a long period of time are liberally sprinkled with statements such as "You know, the *Gemora* says..." or "According to the *Gemora* you're really not supposed to . . . ,'' even when talking about everyday matters.

A Link in an Ancient Tradition

Belief in a common history gives a sense of rootedness to a people and is an important component of ethnic identity.[41] The fact that the yeshiva has existed so long further legitimates it in the minds of its students. Moreover, they are constantly reminded of its history, because the Talmud is itself a compilation of discussions that took place in yeshivas or academies. The yeshiva *bochur* knows that in every previous generation talmudic knowledge and those in possession of it were held in high esteem. In devoting himself to scholarly study of the tradition, he therefore thinks of himself as a member of an elite group whose responsibility it is to insure that what was given to the Jews on Mount Sinai will never die out. He is convinced that he was put on earth to fulfill a divine mission whose purpose was defined thousands of years ago. The significance of historical longevity is clear from the following remarks by Rabbi Weinberg, of Ner Yisroel Yeshiva:

> Look at the Jesus freaks, the Moonies, and all the other groups. They don't have any reality because they can't create an ongoing movement. They won't; it peters out. These are all fads that promise instant happiness which can't be. Our institutions have withstood the test of time. They've been proven to be of eternal value. This is despite the fact that it isn't easy to be in a yeshiva if one isn't serious. There's constant stress and conflict.[42]

In a remark typical of many respondents, a twenty-year-old student at Yeshiva Chofetz Chaim asserted: ''You know, I think the biggest thing that keeps me going in terms of faith is the knowledge that the Jews have been around for so long.'' The expression of such opinions suggests that some see the yeshiva as a rock of stability in a fast-changing world.[43] For such individuals, religious groups characterized by a willingness to accommodate themselves to American culture are not in the least attractive because they do not seem to stand for anything. They are more likely to be drawn to institutions that have strong leaders, firm commitment, and a clearly articulated philosophy.

Community Pressure

There are those who attend advanced yeshivas not out of genuine commitment but because it is considered the "thing to do" by friends, family, teachers, and so on. As discussed in Chapter 5 (see pp. 130–136), the socialization process within the Strictly Orthodox community encourages such a decision. A student graduating from a yeshiva high school may attend a *yeshiva gedola* simply because his friends are. Even if one is not especially talented in Talmud, going to a *yeshiva gedola* confers social respectability upon the individual. Moreover, though he may be bored with such study, the years spent in such an institution will probably increase his appeal in the Orthodox marriage market, as well as enhancing his status in the community as a whole. The yeshiva could not flourish as it has with a student body that attends for reasons of this sort alone, but an undetermined number of individuals enroll with such considerations in mind.

A Feeling of Belonging

For the individual brought up in the Orthodox community and sent to yeshivas all his life, the school is far more than a place where information is transmitted. It is a community of like-minded souls formed by a common culture and characterized by a similar outlook on life. Their presence in the institution is a collective statement of their positive feelings toward it. As we saw in Chapter 6, the yeshiva functions in many ways as a world unto itself, providing its members with a systematically ordered and clearly delineated way of life. The prayers, methods of study, and patterns of social interaction, and the very arranging of priorities combine to create a place where the young man can feel comfortable and secure.[44] Orthodoxy, with its almost infinite laws and customs, provides detailed and explicit guidelines for every area of life, and there are people for whom this is very appealing and comforting. Above all, yeshiva life gives them a sense of belonging. More than half of the respondents to the questionnaire mentioned the fellowship in the yeshiva or the community as a whole in their evaluation of what they most enjoyed about being there. From the many observations made in this regard, the following were representative of the general attitude:

> Living away from home, I found people with the same values. My personal relationships with faculty and friends gave me a basis for the lifestyle that I eventually adopted.
>
> A rabbi from Canada

> There was the easy camaraderie of being with one's own kind. I felt part of something special too because of the community's devotion to study.
>
> A psychologist from Brooklyn

> When I think back on the yeshiva days, I remember best the singing at the *Shabbos* table on Friday night, the warmth of the *rebbaim* [teachers], who were like a second family to me. It wasn't just studying. It was a complete way of life.
>
> A plastics manufacturer from New Jersey

Others told the same story, referring to "the *ruach* [spirit] of the place," "the close friends I made," or "the environment." These answers, taken together, indicate how important the social aspect of the yeshiva experience is for many students.

Becoming Psychologically Dependent

The above portrayal is, unfortunately, only one side of the same coin. The lifestyle that prevails in the yeshiva sometimes fosters a degree of dependence on the institution that results in a person's staying far longer than he ought to. According to one sociologist, "Religion often plays the role of institutionalizing immaturity and develops in its adherents dependence upon religious institutions and their leaders.[45] Of coure, the yeshiva wants its members to be loyal to its leaders; it does not, however, desire to see them enter the outside world unprepared to deal with its challenges. There are students in the yeshiva who appear afraid to face the larger society and assume the responsibilities of an adult. As one former student in a yeshiva said:

> It's a very secure place. You know where you stand and what you have to do. There's even a guy who puts away your *siddur* after you finish *davening*. And of course your

room is swept up and your meals are prepared. You don't
have to go out and make a living, find an apartment.

This dependency is noted in the literature on Christian seminaries too. As one writer observed:

[There is]...an excessive group dependence...a hazy
desire to be lost in numbers, a desire to feel accepted... and
to be saved the inevitable heartbreaking day when they [the
students] must stand alone, face to face with the reality of a
vocation.[46]

Interviews with psychiatrists and social workers in the community confirmed that this can sometimes become a serious problem.
One psychiatrist who had been treating yeshiva students with
problems for years asserted that such dependence was responsible for much of the passivity that he encountered among quite a
few of his patients, adding:

It's my impression that the yeshiva has a larger percentage
of passive types than the general population. On the other
hand, there are plenty of assertive people in the yeshiva but I
only deal with the problems.

There are several reasons why such types exist in the
yeshiva. First, those who enter advanced yeshivas have generally
led a sheltered life, shielded from contact with outsiders and from
different cultures in general. They have spent most of their lives
engaged in study, with less time to explore the world around
them than most youngsters their age. Because of this, the larger
society often seems strange and somewhat frightening. After all,
it is a world whose norms and values differ sharply from those
that predominate in the yeshiva. The environment of the yeshiva
also encourages passivity by demanding that students conform to
a rather rigid code of behavior. Finally, because of its strong
belief that persons ought not to be pressured into ending their
careers as students, the yeshiva finds it difficult to ask people to
leave, even when it knows that such a move might be in their best
interests. This makes matters more difficult, because, as one
therapist observed:

"When you allow people to stay too long because they can't
face the world, then they wind up breaking down much later
than the general population when they finally do get out,

and it's that much harder to treat them. You see, they've let
the problem build up.''

Whether people stay in the yeshiva because of personal
problems or, as is more common, because it seems to be an easy
life, provided that one is capable of studying Talmud, the same
conclusion presents itself: in some cases the yeshiva is attractive
for reasons that are not so much religious, but have more to do
with the psychological needs of the persons involved.

Summary and Conclusions

For those interested in understanding the conditions under
which religious institutions and perhaps religion itself can successfully operate in contemporary society, the centuries-old
yeshiva might serve as a model for which specific ideas can be
developed. Since the factors mentioned are so numerous and
varied, it may be useful to review them briefly.

The arrival in this country shortly after World War II of
large numbers of Orthodox Jews who regarded the yeshiva as an
integral part of their community provided much of the impetus
for the reestablishment of yeshivas here. Certain extraordinary
leaders gave both inspiration and direction to this community.
They were further aided by the arrival of whole scholarly communities which had survived the war and now served as models
for others, and by the immigration of numerous deeply religious
Hasidic sects determined not to compromise their beliefs in the
New Land. Finally, the fact that the immigrants came in large
numbers, almost as a group, heightened their solidarity and their
determination to preserve their culture.

At the same time there were various features of American
society during that period that made the rebuilding of the
yeshivas easier. After having promoted assimilation as a policy
toward immigrants, the country was now in the process of adopting the view known as "cultural pluralism," which encouraged
the expression and maintenance of ethnic identity. Sympathy for
those who had survived the Holocaust helped to create a
favorable climate for the new arrivals. They were aided in their
efforts to re-create their communities by various Jewish organizations, which gave them moral and economic support. The

fact that a small but established Orthodox community was already in place here meant that the immigrants could count on finding synagogues, schools, kosher food, and so on, thereby easing the adjustment to a new culture.

That the immigrants, recognizing the need to socialize children into the value system of the community at an early age, had the drive, determination, and foresight to establish hundreds of day schools and high schools was another crucial factor in the growth of the advanced yeshiva in America. As the schools grew and improved in quality, it became increasingly fashionable for even nonobservant Jews to send their children to them.

As time went on the Orthodox community prospered, and there was more money available to send children to yeshivas, support existing institutions, and build new ones. The natural increase in population made it both more powerful and more assertive. It began to make its influence felt in the political sphere primarily because of the efforts of Agudath Israel of America, which became the political arm of all the traditional advanced yeshivas. In addition, other Orthodox organizations as well as the yeshivas themselves began to take advantage of funding opportunities at the local, state, and federal levels. How the yeshiva responded to the dominant culture, especially the areas in which it compromised and those where it refused to do so, also help explain why the yeshiva survived. Generally, the yeshiva tended to compromise on the least important, external aspects of the larger society while holding on to the inner core of tradition and belief. Also important is the intensive indoctrination process that takes place in the yeshiva starting with the first grade.

The role of the yeshiva in transmitting the tradition and in training educators and rabbis is yet another reason for its continued existence. But to understand why it is attractive to so many individuals, social-psychological factors must be brought into the picture. Its appeal includes the intellectual and spiritual satisfaction it provides, the perceived linkage to an ancient and revered tradition, and the socialization process within the Orthodox community that makes it seem a desirable institution, as well as the feeling of belonging that the yeshiva gives to its members. The development, on the part of some, of psychological dependence on the institution, also accounts for its popularity.

The reasons that have been advanced to explain the yeshiva's survival do not necessarily answer the question of why

Orthodoxy has been able to maintain itself in modern society. As has been noted, the Orthodox community is made up of many subgroupings that range from almost fanatical observance to nominal affiliation. Much more investigation needs to be done before definitive conclusions about the community can be reached. Still, some of the observations with regard to the yeshiva suggest possibilities that ought to be examined. For example, the historical and social conditions that distinguished America during the period following World War II were as conducive to the survival of Orthodoxy as a whole as they were to the development of the yeshiva. The political sophistication that Orthodox organizations acquired resulted in a host of programs not limited to yeshivas but beneficial to Orthodox Jews in a variety of areas such as the establishment of senior citizens centers, day care centers and so on. In addition, the economic prosperity of the community and its growth in size had repercussions among its members in many areas besides the educational sphere. The successful expansion of the day school movement did much more than prepare people for advanced yeshivas, an option chosen only by a minority in any case. It raised the level of Jewish consciousness in the entire Orthodox community tremendously. Finally, the sense of kinship and security and the strong sense of order and purpose that comes from belonging to the yeshiva can be applied to the Orthodox community as a whole, whose members are united by a unique set of beliefs and practices reinforced on a daily basis.

When all is said and done, it must be recognized that the yeshiva and the Orthodox community are inextricably tied to one another. No Orthodox community can function efficiently without a vehicle for the transmission of its traditions, and in modern times this function has devolved from the home to the school to a greater degree than ever before. Given the centrality of education in the Jewish religion, it can be said that neither the yeshiva nor the Orthodox community could exist for long without the other.

For centuries people have been asking, Why have the Jews survived? Education, while perhaps not the complete answer, is certainly a major piece in the puzzle. Moreover, it is from the advanced yeshivas that the leaders and interpreters of the culture frequently emerge. It is they who, as members of an elite group, often set the standards for others to emulate and aspire to.

Whatever the fate of the Jewish community in the decades to come, the long and venerable history of the yeshiva and its ability to adapt within different cultural surroundings suggests that there will always be Jews who feel both obligated and honored to hold fast to their faith and to the ancient ways.

> Turn it [the Torah] and turn it again, for everything is in it, and contemplate it, and grow gray and old over it, and stir not from it, for you can have no better rule than this.
>
> Ethics of the Fathers (Pirkei Avot) 5:26

APPENDIX

How the Study Was Done

Participant Observation

The approaches used in the various phases of this study were both qualitative and quantitative. The first stage began in 1974 when I enrolled as a part-time student in a typical yeshiva studying Talmud and participating in its life over a two-year period. I was raised an Orthodox Jew and attended several advanced yeshivas, including Ner Israel Rabbinical College, Kamenitzer Mesivta of Boro Park, and Yeshiva University.[1] As a result I was familiar with the Talmud and spoke Hebrew and Yiddish fluently, which were invaluable in establishing contact and maintaining rapport with those in the yeshiva. The most significant practical outcome was that I was able, as a student in a class, to find an acceptable role and blend in more easily. As a rule, participant observation is most effective when the observer succeeds in drawing a minimal amount of attention to himself. The yeshiva, with its myriad of customs and religious laws, presents the uninformed outsider with serious problems in this area even if he knows something about Orthodoxy in general. For example, one does not wear a skullcap to pray in the yeshiva but a hat, most often black, of a certain size, and worn a certain way. On the Sabbath, conservative suits and white shirt are *de rigueur*. It is not enough to know the blessing one says upon being called up to the Torah; there is a certain accent on the words that

332

often prevails, a certain way to greet people (*"Gut Shabbos,"* never *"Shabbat Shalom"*), and countless other small details that are of great importance to insiders.

While I frequently pointed out that I was committed to doing an objective study of the yeshiva, members of the community seemed to feel that my Orthodox background would make me more sympathetic to their interests. In fact, awareness that I had gone to yeshiva probably made them less prone to present the yeshiva in only idyllic terms. Thus there were few attempts, as far as I could tell, to conceal their dislike for certain aspects of yeshiva life, critical views of various *rebbes,* and so on.

At the same time, certain factors increased social distance. The fact that I was twenty-eight when I began attending the yeshiva and that the students were in their late teens or early twenties, plus the fact that I was a university professor, meant that I could never really be considered "one of the boys." This did not, however, prevent students from seeking my advice on college-related matters, which helped to improve my relations with them.

Despite the fact that I am not today part of the "yeshiva community," as it has been described in these pages, my background may raise the question of bias among some readers. I do not think this is a valid issue; all sociologists as human beings are products of their environment and carry a variety of biases into the field. Is a sociologist who grew up as, say, a Conservative Jew any less biased? Would not a Christian sociologist bring certain personal feelings into the field too? The problem is not so much a matter of bias as of admitting one's prejudices. Once that step is taken, it becomes easier to cope with them. The social scientist who recognizes his limitations in this area stands a far better chance, in my view, of balancing different theoretical assumptions than the one who believes in the myth of value-free research.

My professional experience was highly useful. Prior to beginning this project, I had completed several studies using participant observation that were methodologically sensitive and difficult. These included a study of derelicts living on the Bowery, one where I actually stayed in a flophouse for an extended period of time, and a summer spent living in a rural Haitian mountain village where I had no contact with outsiders for almost two months.[2] I also lived, worked, and traveled with an urban black militant organization over a two-year period.[3] While the problems encountered in these projects and the populations studied were obviously very different, the challenges involved in winning over people, in integrating oneself into a community, and in being a careful observer were typical of those faced by sociologists in virtually every study requiring direct observation.

The yeshiva selected for the participant-observation phase of the study is a medium-sized institution located in New York City. It has a dormitory for out-of-town students, some of whom attend the high school that is also part of the yeshiva. Ideologically, it is somewhere between Beth Medrash Govoha of Lakewood and Yeshiva University's RIETS division. The majority of the students are enrolled in college, which they attend several evenings a week. The yeshiva requested anonymity but I do at least want to indicate that it is not the same school that was involved in the mail survey cited throughout the book.

One ought not to assume that institutions of this sort await researchers with open arms. As discussed in the book, they are, for the most part, closed societies that attempt to restrict contact with outsiders whenever possible. Although they recognize the value of good public relations, they do not perceive themselves as proselytizers out to persuade others that their way of life is best. While those who ran the yeshiva felt that a positive portrayal of their school might be beneficial, they were quite concerned about not being able to control how such a description would be presented. It was therefore necessary to exercise great caution whenever I spoke with them about doing a study.

I was first introduced to the *mashgiach* of the yeshiva by a personal friend who had been a student at the yeshiva many years ago. I explained that I was a professor, had gone to yeshiva in my youth, and was interested in studying Talmud during my spare time. This was not as unusual as it might seem. Most yeshivas have people who study in the *beis medrash* but are not really students. They are usually adults who have attended yeshivas in the past and who simply wish to study on an extracurricular basis. What was different, however, was my desire to be part of a class and the fact that I wished to attend in the morning hours as opposed to the evening session. The *mashgiach* "spoke with me in learning" for about forty-five minutes, meaning that we discussed a portion of the Talmud with which I was familiar. In this manner, he was able to determine what class I should be assigned to. In the course of our conversation, I mentioned that merely studying in the yeshiva might create problems with respect to my responsibilities to the college in terms of time. The problem might be solved, I indicated, if I could say I was writing something of a sociological nature about yeshivas, and if in fact I did such a study. The *mashgiach* was noncommittal on this point, hardly surprising, since he had just met me.

My motives in entering the yeshiva were mixed. I have always enjoyed studying Talmud because of the intellectual challenge it poses. I was also fascinated by the prospect of applying the tools of social science to an examination of the yeshiva as an institution and as part of an ancient culture. As a result, I felt that if doing research on the yeshiva proved too difficult, I would at least have had the benefit of studying there. Sensing this, Professor Irving Greenberg, then Chairman of City College's Judaic Studies Department, noted, in giving me permission to be released from a course for this purpose: "I don't know whether you're studying *Gemora* so you can write a book or whether you're writing a book so you can study *Gemora*—but I don't suppose it really matters." As indicated, he was correct on both counts.

From the yeshiva's perspective, there could be no doubt that study for its own sake should be the primary reason. I made no effort to discourage their thinking along these lines. Some even went so far as to take pity on me for having to "create" a project to justify Torah study while also admiring me for having been able to do so.

I entered the yeshiva in February 1974 as a daytime student. From 9:30 A.M. to 11:45 A.M. every day, except on the Sabbath, I studied in the *beis medrash* with a learning partner, and from 11:45 until about 1:30 P.M. I attended a lecture given by the *rebbe* of the class to which I had been assigned. Talmud study is a rather strenuous intellectual endeavor and is often interspersed with conversations about other matters simply to relax the mind. Although students generally make an effort to avoid such *batala,* or "wasting time," almost all engage in it to some degree. I learned a good deal during these conversations, brief as they were, about the attitudes of yeshiva students on a variety of matters. Although I had been a student in yeshivas of this sort in the past, more than ten years had elapsed since then. Surprisingly, perhaps, not much had changed. I remained in the yeshiva until

June 1974, returned to the library for some more reading and thinking and came back to the yeshiva in the same capacity in February 1975, staying there until June of that year.

Throughout, I did my best to adhere to Robert Ezra Park's by now famous sociological dictum of "Keep your eyes and ears open and your mouth shut." Each day, upon leaving the yeshiva, I either taped or wrote down my observations. As all researchers know, it is crucial that this be done immediately so that one's perception of events is not dimmed by the passage of time. I was aided in setting down my observations by the fact that students customarily take notes on talmudic discussions, both during class and in the *beis medrash*. On occasion, they could be seen engaged in this activity during their free time. Similarly, when I found I had some time to myself in the yeshiva, I would simply record my observations in a three-ring notebook without drawing the slightest bit of attention. To be sure, quite a few students knew I was probably going to write "something" about their yeshiva, but it is doubtful that they were conscious of it at all times and that it significantly affected their behavior. I was seen as a quasi-member both by virtue of my role as a student and because I was there so much of the time. I also benefited tremendously from tape recordings I made of class discussions. Recording classes is common practice in most yeshivas. It helps the student later in his review of the material, and it is not at all unusual to see three or four cassette recorders resting on or near the *rebbe*'s desk.

At first, I encountered some difficulty in adjusting to the schedule. Unlike the students, I had a family and was teaching two courses at the college. Moreover, it was a bit difficult to switch gears in the course of one day and go from a Talmud class to one where I talked about the Puerto Rican or black experience. Finally, I was a little rusty, and it took some time to acclimate myself to talmudic study on such an intense level. I vividly recall my pleasure when, after three weeks of sitting silently in class, I asked my first good *kashe* (question). After a while the questions came more often and I found myself treated like anyone in the class—reprimanded by the *rebbe,* a man in his early forties, whenever I was absent or did not know the *Gemora* and praised when I did. Nevertheless, I had the distinct impression, from comments made to me on several occasions, that those in the yeshiva derived a good deal of satisfaction from the fact that "a professor" wanted to come and study there. They seemed to regard it as a verification of their intellectual efforts.

Besides study in the yeshiva, I interacted with the students in a number of other contexts. I went to weddings and other celebrations whenever possible, ate lunch with them, and hung around the dormitory. I also invited them to my house on occasion. Some of the students confided in me, others did not, but virtually all provided me with insight into their values and beliefs about a host of topics, many of which have been incorporated into the text. All in all, I gathered several hundred pages of field notes and they proved invaluable in defining areas for further investigation.

Despite the yeshiva's generally positive reaction to the idea of writing about the life that went on there, I found the leaders to be somewhat apprehensive about the prospect of my doing formal interviews and examining documents about the yeshiva. This was clear from the following comments made to me by the *rosh yeshiva*'s assistant:

> Of course, if you write about what you see, we can't stop you and since we feel we have nothing to be ashamed of, that's okay. At the same time we might have different views than you do about what material should go in and how it should be presented. After all, everybody tries to whitewash things a little. Now a study detrimental to the yeshiva would be worse than no study at all, and we would want to have a hand in deciding what should go in.

I explained that to agree to prior censorship would compromise the study and raise serious questions about its validity, both for the publisher and for the reading public, and that I could only offer them anonymity. They were torn between the desire to let others know about the positive aspects of the yeshiva and their fear that critical things might be said about the institution. Rather than tell me no, they put off making a decision until I stopped asking them about it. In all fairness, it must be noted that the yeshiva would probably have felt far more comfortable had it been one of several schools studied in this manner. Indeed, when I subsequently expanded the study they were very cooperative and allowed me to speak for the record with those in the institution. In fact their reluctance to permit me to do a full-fledged study was a fortuitous development because it forced me to broaden the project in favor of one on advanced yeshivas in general, an idea I had been toying with anyway, rather than one institution. As a result, a much more varied and complete picture emerged of these schools.

In-Depth Interviews

By the time I began formally interviewing past and present members of the yeshiva community in 1976, I had already been a part of that general community for almost two years. Besides studying in the yeshiva, I had made numerous acquaintances (and renewed some old ones) through membership in a synagogue attended by many "yeshiva types." I also spent summer vacations in a Catskill Mountains bungalow colony populated by both Modern Orthodox and Strictly Orthodox Jews and made it a point to get together socially with such people. Finally, I read those newspapers and magazines—that is, the *Jewish Observer* and the *Morgen Journal*—that were popular in the community. All this gave me insight into who the real leaders of the community were, and this was an important factor in determining whom to interview.

A total of 179 in-depth interviews were conducted. Respondents came from 22 different yeshivas, including all the major institutions in the country. Those interviewed can be broken down into the following nine general categories: *rosh yeshivas,* yeshiva administrators, teachers or *rebbes,* present students, former students (including some no longer observant), *kollel* members and their wives, community leaders located in strategic positions and generally recognized as such by others, parents of students, and psychiatrists and therapists involved with the yeshiva community.

The primary goal in this phase of the research was to evaluate issues and problems facing the community in depth. Therefore, no effort was made to survey the population systematically. Nevertheless, since I wanted to be certain that those interviewed were representative of the general population, I drew up a number of categories and characteristics that I knew to be present in the community. Examples were: those who live in the dormitory and those who do not, older and younger students, observant and nonobservant, good and poor students, large and small yeshivas, those who came from observant as well as nonobservant homes, those born here and those who came from abroad, those who attended for many years and those whose stay in the yeshiva was short, and so on. By the time I had completed the interviewing, I was reasonably satisfied that all the important categories had been covered.

Respondents were selected in a number of ways. Those who were well known were contacted by phone or in person and asked if they were willing to be interviewed. A snowball approach was used with a large proportion of the students. In other words, I began by interviewing someone whom I met at a yeshiva or at a social occasion, or whom I knew from before. After the interview, I asked him to suggest other persons and when he did so they were contacted. Often, by the time I reached the third or fourth person I did not know him at all, even though I might have been quite friendly with the first person interviewed. On two occasions yeshivas that I visited selected people for me to interview. Although they promised to find students from a broad spectrum, I was skeptical, thinking that they would attempt to introduce me only to those who were likely to reflect positively on the yeshiva. The interviews indicated that either I was wrong or else they simply didn't know their students very well. A good number of them were openly critical of the institution itself. Later on, it occurred to me that the yeshiva's awareness of my intimate familiarity with the community probably prevented them from trying to give me a "snow job," if indeed they were predisposed to do so. Two yeshivas, Lakewood and the Talmudical Yeshiva of Philadelphia, graciously supplied me with lists of their entire student body and invited me to pick students at random, a suggestion which was followed.

In the case of the students, I concluded, after interviewing a number of them, that someone their own age might have better rapport with them. With this in mind, I had a nineteen-year-old student in a yeshiva interview a cross-section of students from various yeshivas. This was highly productive. Similarly, I felt that young women might do a better job of interviewing wives of yeshiva students, and found several who had attended seminary to speak with them. This too was very useful. I trained and supervised these individuals before sending them out into the field. For the most part, however, I tried to avoid having others do the interviewing, conducting all but 27 interviews myself.

This is, of course, very time-consuming, but of inestimable value when it comes to analyzing and evaluating the data. The introduction of other interviewers into the research process, while often unavoidable, is likely to deprive the principal investigator of certain basic information, for he must rely on someone else to re-create the interview setting, the inflections and nuances used by the respondents, and other features ascertainable only by direct observation. In this case, dealing as I was with people who were often somewhat suspicious of social science research and who were not accustomed to being interviewed, the use of student interviewers on an extensive basis would have been highly problematic.

The approaches employed in obtaining interviews varied according to individuals. I soon learned that the two most important criteria were persistence and flexibility. In one case I had to make more than twenty telephone calls and numerous personal visits before securing permission to interview a certain *rosh yeshiva*. Nevertheless, the experience taught me a valuable lesson. When in doubt, go to the top, for it was only when I sent the *rosh yeshiva* in question a certified registered letter explaining my purpose and the difficulty I was encountering in getting an appointment to see him that I succeeded in my efforts. He phoned me and invited me to speak with him at my convenience. Until then I had restricted my efforts to various persons who were supposedly close to him. In general, I found that those who were assistants to the *rosh yeshiva* followed a predictable pattern. They offered to arrange an interview and then procrastinated. This was probably because they wanted to appear powerful to me but were reluctant to accept responsibility for anything negative that might result from such an interview. Only in three or four cases were such individuals genuinely helpful. As a rule I found that when I phoned a *rosh yeshiva* directly, I had little difficulty in getting to see him. In one instance, when several calls resulted in ambiguous responses, I simply approached the *rosh yeshiva* in person without making an appointment in advance. He received me most cordially.

The reason for dwelling on this point at length is that, in an authoritarian structure such as the yeshiva, an interview with its leader is of tremendous value in obtaining the cooperation of others. Thus, a man who was hostile to my intentions said to me: ''Well, if Reb Shneur [Kotler] talked with you who am I to refuse?'' This kind of thing happened on many occasions. It was a useful tactic in general, not only with the *rosh yeshivas*. Many persons seemed afraid to speak out because they did not wish to be condemned by the yeshiva community. Assurances of anonymity and/or permission to see in advance what comments made by them would be quoted usually overcame such apprehensions. I discovered, as I went along, that many respondents, once having been reassured that their names would not be mentioned, saw me as a vehicle for transmitting deeply felt criticisms to others whom they felt would read the book. Such individuals often prefaced their comments with statements such as: ''I don't want my name mentioned, but this is a serious problem and someone's got to say it.'' Those in the yeshiva community have less social mobility than members of the larger society. Their belief system is such that they cannot live apart from it. Typical was the comment made by a day school principal as he voiced sharp criticism of yeshiva practices with regard to marriage: ''Please don't mention my name. I have several daughters and I want to be able to marry them off.'' Another man mentioned that a certain prominent figure in the yeshiva world had graduated from college many years ago, and added, half jestingly; ''Don't write that in your book. It's character assassination.''

Under such circumstances, one might wonder why respondents cooperated with me. They had, it would seem, much to lose and little to gain. While it might be convenient to pin the answer down to one or two possibilities, this was not, as far as I could tell, correct. The reasons varied greatly from person to person. In some cases I was not sure why they had agreed to speak with me but felt it would be impolitic to raise the issue. In other instances, perhaps all instances, developing personal rapport was a crucial determinant. Generally speaking, the following reasons were given either in response to my questions or as a result of other issues raised during the course of the interview: (1) A belief that the yeshiva had much to be proud of. (2) A conviction that I would portray the community fairly because of my own background. (3) The knowledge that I had written a popular book about yeshiva life that, while critical of certain aspects of the community, was generally sympathetic to it.[4] (4) A realization, especially on the part of community leaders, that if they failed to cooperate, the book would be written anyway. As one put it: "You could probably make a whole book just out of talking to yeshiva bums. At least this way you'll have the whole picture." (5) An opportunity to "get things off their chest," to be critical and make certain views known to community leaders that they would be afraid to be publicly identified with. This was true of both students and leaders in the yeshiva world, and particularly true of *rebbes* in yeshivas. (6) Resentment of what they felt were stereotyped views of Orthodoxy by mass media publications. (7) Personal acquaintance with me from my days as a youth in camp or school.

Asking the proper questions, while not cited by my respondents, was probably an important factor in their responsiveness and leads into the matter of how the interviews were conducted. Basically, they were partially structured. I had certain topics that I knew I wanted to cover but the questions themselves were most often spontaneous, arising out of the interview context and varying greatly with each respondent. Different questions were asked of different groupings. I would focus far more on organization and larger issues when speaking with the *rosh yeshivas* and more on daily life when talking to students. Certain areas were introduced in almost all the interviews. For example, I wanted to see if the students and those who ran the yeshiva perceived the institution's goals in the same manner and I wanted to determine how both groups viewed issues such as deviance, marriage, and secularism. A key element in conducting successful interviews was to stress the positive in the initial stages of the conversation. I frequently asked persons at the outset why they felt yeshivas had expanded so much in America or what they had most enjoyed about attending yeshiva. When dealing with sensitive matters I tried my best to phrase them positively. Thus, the question would be: In what ways could the yeshiva improve?, not What's wrong with the yeshiva? Naturally, if I was interviewing someone who had rebelled against Orthodoxy, the opposite approach was used.

Interviews varied in length from 30 minutes to 7 hours. Some were conducted in one sitting; others required several meetings. Locales included grocery stores, private homes, offices, automobiles, and dormitory rooms. In one instance, a very well-known *rosh yeshiva* found himself constantly interrupted by telephone calls and people approaching him personally as he sat in a Catskill Mountains hotel lobby. Suddenly he rose and motioned me to follow him outside. We walked across the lawn to a wooded area and I found myself in a small clearing with two chairs. "Sit down please. This is my hideout. Here we can talk."

Whenever possible, I taped the interviews. Without going into great detail, the researcher must determine, on a case-by-case basis, when to tape and when to take notes. Relying on an informant's preference is not always helpful. Frequently, a person will say he has no objection, only to become very nervous once the interview begins. Seven of the interviews were conducted in Yiddish and the quotes appearing in English in the book are actually translations. In all cases, these are major figures: Rabbi Moshe Feinstein, Rabbi Yitzchok Hutner, Rabbi Shneur Kotler, Rabbi Yaakov Kamenecki, Rabbi Yaakov Ruderman, Rabbi Shmuel Berenbaum, and Rabbi Shraga Moshe Kalmanowitz. Although I could have spoken with some of these leaders in English, they were far more comfortable in their native tongue. The quotes from interviews that appear throughout the book are word-for-word accounts with one qualification. In some cases the students interviewed used so many words foreign to those who know only English that I felt obliged to eliminate some of the less important expressions. But even this was kept to a minimum.

We have here, in the case of the *rosh yeshivas,* the views of men who are historically important figures in the Jewish community. They expressed their views on various topics which they have not, to my knowledge, discussed before in public. The transcripts and tapes of these interviews will be made available to qualified researchers in consultation with the *rosh yeshivas* themselves.

Survey of Yeshiva Alumni

The third approach was statistical. A detailed questionnaire was sent through the mails to 878 alumni of one of the larger advanced yeshivas in the United States. The school itself, referred to as "Beth David Yeshiva" (a fictitious name) in the text, is a representative institution, falling somewhere in the middle of an ideological continuum from left to right. It is fully accepted by the other right-wing yeshivas. Its *rosh yeshiva* is a major figure in the world of the Strictly Orthodox. Beth David does not permit its students to go to movies, date socially, and so on, and has a dormitory for out-of-town students.

Unlike Lakewood, which forbids college attendance and, unlike Yeshiva University, which incorporates it into its program, Beth David permits but does not specifically encourage college studies. Although most Beth David students attend college in the evening, restrictions are placed upon such attendance, and those who eschew college rank first in terms of status among both students and those in charge of the yeshiva. Finally, *more than half* of the respondents attended other yeshivas at the *beis medrash* level either before or after they came to Beth David. Thus, the sample consisted of individuals from numerous yeshivas.

The suggestion that I do a statistical study of yeshiva alumni was first broached by the institution in question. I had done a number of in-depth interviews with students and administrators of the school and had established good rapport with its executive director. In the course of my interview with him, he casually mentioned that it might be a good idea to survey the yeshiva's alumni, explaining that such information could be useful for the school in its long-range planning and its fund-raising efforts in particular. I had long been interested in doing such a survey and therefore welcomed the opportunity, cautioning the executive director that I would want to pursue the matter only if I were guaranteed complete freedom in my work. He assured me that the yeshiva would make no effort to control the study in any way. All that would be asked of me would be an agreement to make the results available to the school. Upon my informing them that this was acceptable to me, the yeshiva gave me a copy of the mailing list and I proceeded to make preparations for carrying out the project.

I was concerned that there might be some bias because the list was conceivably weighted in favor of those who had maintained contact with the yeshiva and that these individuals might differ significantly from those no longer on the list, especially in the area of religious observance. The yeshiva assured me that, to the best of its knowledge, the list included almost everyone who had been in the yeshiva for two or more years and quite a few who had been there for a shorter period of time.[5] Moreover, the school had a reputation for efficiency and highly capable administration, thus bolstering its contention that its records were accurate.

Despite these claims, I made an effort to ascertain the representativeness of the list. I asked five persons whom I knew and who had gone to the yeshiva at different times to examine it and let me know how many people they could think of who had attended for at least two years and who were not included. The results suggested that perhaps 10 percent or less of the names were missing. Furthermore, the size of the group and the response rate were sufficiently large, in my view, to insure representativeness. In addition, dates of attendance were more or less evenly distributed from the yeshiva's inception in 1933 up to 1977, with allowances made for changes in the size of the student body. Interestingly, I later discovered, as a result of follow-up telephone calls, that many on the list had been receiving mail from the yeshiva for many years but had never responded to any appeals or other requests.

It might seem reasonable to assume that those who were not so observant were less likely to respond to a questionnaire asking detailed questions about this subject despite guarantees of anonymity. While this is a possibility, it seemed to have been counterbalanced to an unknown degree by those who informed me that they would not answer the questionnaire because it was a waste of time for a truly religious person or that queries relating to religious behavior were "an insult to yeshiva graduates."

I designed a questionnaire in the spring of 1978 together with a colleague at City College's Sociology Department, Professor Philip Leonhard-Spark. The questionnaire was rather extensive, especially for one designed to be mailed, consisting of 78 items. While we were both somewhat apprehensive about how this would affect the response rate, we felt it important to cover as many areas as possible and decided to take our chances. The questions themselves included items concerning family background, education, income, political preference, religiosity, lifestyle, age, residence, and various attitudinal questions. Most of the questions were fixed-choice items. There was, however, one section of six questions that called for in-depth, open-ended responses.

In July 1978 the questionnaire was administered to 34 alumni from various yeshivas. This pretest sought to determine what problems existed with regard to the phrasing and content of the questions themselves and to estimate the response rate. In September 1978, we began sending out questionnaires to the target population. A cover letter accompanied the question-naires, informing the respondent that the study would be published in a book about yeshivas and that we were attempting to assess the long-range effects of the yeshiva exprience on their lives. Respondents were assured that their replies would be con-fidential and that the yeshiva would not see their questionnaires or learn of their identities. In fact, the self-addressed, stamped envelope accompanying the questionnaire was addressed to City College. Moreover, they were told that if they so requested in writing, they would receive a copy of the statistical results of the study. About twenty such requests were made and accom-modated. The executive director of Beth David Yeshiva also received a copy of the results.

The questionnaires were mailed out over a six-month period that ended in February 1979. Two weeks after a questionnaire had been sent, a follow-up postcard was mailed reiterating the re-quest. Finally, and perhaps most importantly, every respondent living in the New York City area with a listed phone number was called. The response rate was unusually high for a mailed survey with about 53 percent (464 out of 878 respondents) returning the questionnaire. This is especially significant when one considers the number of questions.[6] The estimated completion time for the average respondent was about 45 minutes. The pretest had in-dicated that phone calls were likely to affect the response rate significantly, but they also demonstrated that this was so only if I personally made the calls. This was because many of those phoned were suspicious of the motives for the research and talk-ing in their idiom—that is, using the appropriate Yiddish and Hebrew phrases—tended to reassure them. In all, I made 353 phone calls. While I would have preferred to have assigned the task to a research assistant, it was clear that one could not expect a person unknowledgeable in the ways of the community to allay the fears of people and to sense the many nuances and cues that often characterized such conversations. For example, those in the Strictly Orthodox community normally end their conversations with "*Kol tuv,*" meaning "May all be well." Yet a Modern Or-thodox person might be put off by such a parting phrase and decline to respond to the survey. At the same time it is important, if at all possible, not to present either oneself or the survey's purpose in such a way that might influence the responses.

This procedure paid off handsomely. It appears that telephone follow-ups literally doubled the response rate. Talking with people personally also tended to impress them with the seriousness of the project while also making them feel more important. Although I was often able to persuade reluctant respondents to cooperate, reluctance was not the only reason for their failure to return the survey. Sometimes they had simply lost it or forgotten about it, or they or someone else in their family had thrown it away because they "knew no one from City College" or had thought it was just another piece of junk mail.

Quite a few researchers familiar with the Orthodox community had predicted that the Strictly Orthodox, because of their suspicion of secular scholarship, would be unlikely to cooperate. Not only was this not so but the questions themselves were, as a rule, answered both thoroughly and carefully, especially the six in-depth queries.[7] When one asks a respondent what he thinks are the most important problems facing the Orthodox community, he can answer in one phrase or three pages. Many wrote pages of observations which they then attached to the questionnaire. Dozens wrote of their personal interest in the project and expressed satisfaction that someone had decided to focus on this topic. Many offered their advice and help. One possible explanation for this enthusiasm might be that people were being asked for the first time to talk about an experience that had played a major role in their lives. This feeling was reflected in many of their comments on the questionnaire. It seems that we had touched on a subject that others saw as both significant and neglected. As noted in the text, since more than half of the respondents had attended more than one yeshiva, the results cannot be seen as the opinions of graduates of one yeshiva alone.

Those with experience in quantitative research will have noticed that the statistical presentation has been rather simple. I plan, together with Professor Leonhard-Spark and perhaps others, to do a more rigorous evaluation of the data, using more sophisticated measures of statistical association and inference including multiple regression and factor analysis. In fact, such work is already well under way. This will, I hope, be published in scholarly journals. Given the large number of items and our desire to cross-correlate many of them, not to mention the enormous amount of work involved in categorizing and evaluating in-depth open-ended responses, it will be some time before the analysis of all the data is complete. Ultimately, it is hoped that such research will throw further light upon some of the more important questions raised in this work.

As indicated, the yeshiva community proved very cooperative on the whole. I was able to conduct the survey without any restrictions and almost everyone I approached for an interview consented, though some required a good deal of persuasion. This attitude was, however, not universal. Seven of those whom I contacted by phone with regard to the survey flatly refused to answer the questionnaire. One said: "These questions are an insult to yeshiva graduates. The nerve of you to ask whether a graduate would eat nonkosher food!" Another declined because "it takes away time from my learning," while a third said he was afraid the results might play into the hands of anti-Semites.

After the study was completed, a Strictly Orthodox professor who helps yeshivas in a number of areas called me and said: "I feel you have an obligation to show either me or someone else in the yeshiva world what you wrote. After all, we cooperated with you." "But you told me you personally were opposed to the study," I reminded him. "Then show it to someone else," he replied. He then named several persons involved in the administration of yeshivas. I politely but firmly declined his suggestion, explaining that I had already selected several readers prominent in yeshiva circles whom I felt would do a fine job. This did not satisfy him but he dropped the issue, apparently realizing that he could not compel me to follow his suggestions. This was the only pressure to which I was subjected. Ironically, it came from someone closely associated, by virtue of his profession, with the secular world.

Incidents of this sort are not unusual in research settings where sensitive communities are being studied. Each researcher must decide for himself how he will respond to them. The problem is actually far more difficult when they occur during the course of a project. Fortunately, this did not happen here.

Notes

Chapter 1: From Jacob's Tents to America's Cities (pp. 1–17)

1. *Midrash Rabbah, Bereishit (Genesis)*, 63:10. Based on the passage, "And Jacob was a quiet man, dwelling in tents" (*Genesis*, 25:27). Ever, who was affiliated with the school, was the grandson of Shem, the son of Noah. Midrash, in this context, refers to a form of rabbinic literature consisting of both sermons and exegesis. We may note that, while neither archeological or historical evidence points to a yeshiva in the days of the Patriarchs, the fact that observant Jews believe that such an institution functioned then and that the founding fathers, so to speak, of the religion, studied in them, has important ramifications for how Orthodox Jews today perceive their faith, the primacy of learning, and various other sociocultural and historical factors.

2. *Midrash Rabbah, Bereishit*, 95:2. Based on the passage: "And he sent Judah before him unto Joseph, to show the way before him unto Goshen" (*Genesis*, 46:28).

3. According to the talmudic sage Rabbi Hama ben Hanina, yeshivas existed during times of slavery in Egypt as well as the forty years of Israelite wanderings in the desert (*Yoma*, 28b). It is difficult to establish precisely what was meant by a yeshiva in those times—it may have simply been a few scholarly individuals meeting privately on an irregular basis. Whatever the case, it is clear that education as a goal was considered important through-

out the entire biblical period. It should be pointed out that the yeshiva has served numerous functions thoughout its history—as a house of study, court of law, and place where scholars meet.

4. A detailed account of life in the academy at Yavneh is provided by Judah Goldin, ''The Period of the Talmud,'' in Louis Finkelstein (ed.), *The Jews: Their History, Culture, and Religion,* vol. 1 (New York: Harper & Row, 1949), 146–152.

5. A great deal has been written about Hasidism and the reader has, therefore, much to choose from. On the life of the Baal Shem Tov, see Dan Amos and Jerome Mintz, *In Praise of the Baal Shem (Shivchei haBesht)* (Bloomington: Indiana University Press, 1970). A valuable introduction to different groups among the Hasidim has been written by Harry Rabinowicz, *A Guide to Hasidism* (New York: Yoseloff, 1960). See also Gershom Scholem, *Major Trends in Jewish Mysticism* (New York: Schocken, 1961), pp. 325–350; Jacob Minkin, *The Romance of Hasidism* (New York: Macmillan, 1935); and Wolf Zeev Rabinowitsch, *Lithuanian Hasidism* (New York: Schocken, 1971).

6. For biographical literature on the Vilna Gaon, see H.H. Ben-Sasson, ''Personality of Elijah, Gaon of Vilna and His Historical Influence,'' *Zion,* vol. 31 (1966), pp. 39–86, 197–216; S.J. Jazkan, *Rabbenu Eliyahu miVilna* (Warsaw: Sokolow, 1900).

7. Abraham Menes, ''Patterns of Jewish Scholarship in Eastern Europe,'' in Finkelstein, *The Jews: Their History, Culture, and Religion,* vol. 1, p. 396; and Martin Buber, *Tales of the Hasidim: Early Masters* (New York: Schocken, 1948), p. 107.

8. See Minkin, *The Romance of Hasidism,* pp. 178–229; S. Ettinger, ''The Internal Struggle in East European Jewry,'' in H.H. Ben-Sasson (ed.), *A History of the Jewish People* (Cambridge: Harvard University Press, 1976), pp. 772–774.

9. Jacob Katz, *Tradition and Crisis: Jewish Society at the End of the Middle Ages* (New York: Schocken, 1971), pp. 227–229.

10. Menes, ''Patterns of Jewish Scholarship,'' p. 397. One group that showed influences of both the Hasidim and *Misnagdim* was the *Habad* movement, founded in Lithuania and headed by Rabbi Shneur Zalman of Ladi. Known today as Lubavitcher Hasidim, their philosophy, while essentially Hasidic, stresses the importance of talmudic scholarship to a greater extent than most other Hasidic groups. For a description of Shneur Zalman's philosophy see Minkin, pp. 205–220.

11. See Gedalyahu Alon, ''The Lithuanian Yeshivas'' (translated by Sid Leiman), in Judah Goldin (ed.), *The Jewish Expression (New York: Bantam, 1970),* pp. 448–464. According to Alon, Slabodka

students said: "If you see a student devoting himself to the study of *Yoreh Deah,* or to the chapter of the talmudic treatise *Hullen,* beginning with the words 'These are considered *trefah,*' or to *Eben Ha-Ezer,* and if he prepares himself for ordination from the very start, you can be certain that he is neither gifted nor knowledgeable in Torah" (pp. 451–452).

12. Menes, "Patterns of Jewish Scholarship," p. 404.

13. Probably the best work on the Volozhin Yeshiva is M. Zinowitz, *Toldot Yeshivat Volozhin: Moraho, Chayeho, Talmideho, veToratah* (Tel-Aviv: MVR, 1972). Also important is Meir Berlin, *Fun Volozhin biz Yerusholayim,* 2, vols. (New York: Orion, 1933).

14. For those interested in capturing some of the flavor of the times and in understanding the analytic approach of Rabbi Chaim Soloveichik, the following two articles, written by a native of Brisk (Brest-Litovsk) who knew him, are useful: Chaim L. Balgley, "Growing Up in Brisk: Remembering Reb Chaim," *Jewish Observer,* September 1978, pp. 21–24; "The Brisker Legacy," *Jewish Observer,* June 1979, pp. 20–24.

15. Two excellent works on this period are Samuel K. Mirsky, *Mosdot Torah beAiropah beVinyanam ubeHurbanam* (New York: Histadrut haIvrit beAmerica, 1956); and Aaron Surasky, *Marbetzei Torah uMussar,* 4 vols. (New York: Sentry, 1977).

16. Intriguing accounts of life in the yeshiva and why people sometimes left appear in two little-noticed, well-written works: Solomon Simon, *In the Thicket* (Philadelphia: Jewish Publication Society, 1963); and Benjamin Gordon, *Between Two Worlds* (New York: Bookman, 1951).

17. Israel Efros (ed.), *Selected Poems of Hayyim Nahman Bialik* (New York: Bloch, 1965), p. 44.

18. Ibid., p. 49.

19. Rabbi Spektor headed a yeshiva in Kovno that trained young men for the rabbinate. He was a prolific writer of responsa as well as an activist who supported the idea of Jewish settlement in Palestine. See S.K. Mirsky, "Isaac Elhanan Spektor," in Leo Jung (ed.), *Guardians of Our Heritage, 1724–1953* (New York: Bloch, 1958), pp. 301–316.

20. The standard work in the field is Dov Katz, *Tenuat haMussar,* 5 vols. (Tel-Aviv: Bitan haSefer, Avraham Tzioni, 1952–1963). See also Louis Ginzberg, *Students, Scholars, and Saints* (Philadelphia: Jewish Publication Society, 1928), pp. 145–194. Despite its popularity among scholars, this work is not as precise or as extensive in its description of the philosophy of *mussar* as that of Katz.

21. Actually, the mentor of almost all the supervisors of that era, including Rabbi Finkel, was Rabbi Simcha Zissel Broyde of Chelm.

22. A number of articles have been written about this scholar, who made a deep impression upon hundreds of students. See Aaron Rothkoff, "The Saba from Slobodka," *Jewish Life,* November–December 1970, pp. 35–41; and M. Gerz, "The Old Man of Slobodka," in Lucy Dawidowicz (ed.), *The Golden Tradition* (Boston: Beacon Press, 1967), pp. 179–185.

23. Rabbi Yoseif Leib Bloch, as quoted in Tovia Lasdun and Leo Davids, "The Way of Telz," *Jewish Life,* October 1958, pp. 56–57. Telshe was a strict yeshiva with compulsory classroom attendance, reaching its height with a student body of close to 300 after the Volozhin Yeshiva was forced by the Russian government to close in 1892.

24. Actually, other factors such as internal strife also played a role in bringing about the closing of the yeshiva, including the founding of a secret society called "Nes Ziona," to which quite a few yeshiva *bochorim* belonged. See Menes, p. 404.

25. The core of Lubavitcher philosophy may be found in the *Tanya* by Shneur Zalman, a widely translated work available in English which first appeared in 1796.

26. For a profile of Reines, see Hayyim Reines, "Isaac Jacob Reines," in Leo Jung (ed.), *Jewish Leaders* (New York: Bloch, 1953), pp. 275–293. Among the leading scholars who taught at the yeshiva were Rabbi Solomon Polachek and Rabbi Meir Berlin, son of the famed "Netziv." Though Reines was respected by the other rabbis of the time for his scholarship, he became something of an outcast among the heads of the yeshivas and their followers because of his institution's inclusion of secular studies and his Zionistic beliefs. An exception to this was Rabbi Eliezer Gordon from the Telshe Yeshiva who, though he disagreed with Reines, invited him to the meeting of the Knesset Israel, an organization of rabbinic authorities founded in 1909 for the purpose of aiding Orthodox Jews throughout Eastern Europe. It was, incidentally, forced to disband by the Russian government soon afterward (see Aaron Rothkoff, "Chaim Ozer Grodzenski," *Jewish Life,* May–June 1967, p. 44). Another important yeshiva that used modern pedagogic methods and taught secular subjects was founded by Rabbi Chaim Tchernowitz in Odessa. Among its students was Chaim Nachman Bialik. (See Benjamin Hoffsmeyer, *"Rav Tzair" and the Yeshiva of Odessa,* Ph.D. dissertation, Yeshiva University, 1967.) Actually, secular studies were already part of the curriculum in the *mussar* yeshiva of Rabbi Simcha Zissel Broyde dur-

ing the nineteenth century. Located in Chelm, the school enabled students to learn the Russian language, history, geography, and arithmetic. Broyde felt it was crucial for people to realize that one could be a modern, yet observant, Jew. Among the important scholars who attended the yeshiva were Rabbi Note Hirsch Finkel, Rabbi Isser Zalman Meltzer, Rabbi Naftali Trop, and Rabbi Moshe Mordechai Epstein. See Eliezer Ebner, "Simha Zissel Broida (Ziff)," in Jung, *Guardians of Our Heritage,* pp. 319–335.

27. Altogether there were, in 1937 about 185,000 students in Jewish schools of all types throughout Poland. Included in this group were the students in the other major Orthodox group in the country, namely Mizrachi, whose enrollment in its schools came to 15,923. See Miriam Eisenstein, *Jewish Schools in Poland, 1919–1939* (New York: King's Crown Press, 1950), p. 96.

28. See Moses L. Burak, *The Hatam Sofer* (Toronto: Beth Jacob Congregation, 1967). The Hatam Sofer was a son-in-law of Rabbi Akiva Eger, noted talmudic commentator, who himself founded an important yeshiva in Posen, Germany.

29. The relationships between Hungarian and German Orthodoxy and that which prevailed in Lithuania and Poland is a fascinating subject that has never been fully researched. To do so here, however, would take us far afield from our focus on the predecessors of today's American yeshivas, most of whom are of Lithuanian origin.

30. Armin Friedman, *Major Aspects of Yeshiva Education in Hungary, 1848–1948,* Ph.D. dissertation, Yeshiva University, 1971. See also Abraham Fuchs, *Yeshivot Hungaria biGedulatam ubeHurbanam* (Jerusalem: Hed, 1979).

31. For biographical information, the following essays are useful: J.L. Kagan and H.B. Perlman, "Hayyim Ozer Grodzenski (1863–1940)," in Jung, *Jewish Leaders,* 435–455; Rothkoff, "Chaim Ozer Grodzenski," pp. 40–49; Chaim Shapiro, "Reb Chaim Ozer Grodzensky," *Jewish Observer,* June 1976, pp. 21–27.

32. See Chaim Shapiro, "My Years with Reb Elchonon: A Talmid Recalls His Years in Baranovitch," *Jewish Observer,* October 1973, pp. 12–17.

33. See Aaron Rothkoff, "Rav Isser Zalman Meltzer," *Jewish Life,* March–April 1971, pp. 51–57. Other important leaders in this period were Rabbi Yechiel Mordechai Gordon of Lomza, Rabbi Aharon Kotler of Kletsk, who later founded and headed the most influential yeshiva in America at Lakewood, New Jersey, Rabbi

Boruch Ber Leibowitz of Kamenitz, and Rabbi Shimon Shkop of Grodno.

34. Eisenstein, *Jewish Schools in Poland,* pp. 78–97.

35. For information regarding Agudath Israel's outlook and goals see *Agudist Essays,* London, 1944; and the *Jewish Observer* from 1963 to the present.

36. See Zvi Scharfstein, *Toldot haHinukh beYisrael beDorot haAharonim,* 3 vols. (Jerusalem: Reuben Mass, 1950–1962). For a brief essay about these years see H.M. Rabinowicz, "Yeshivoth in Poland in the Inter-War Years," *Jewish Life,* March–April 1964, pp. 53–59. An important yeshiva with Lithuanian antecedents was also founded in Gateshead, England, during this period. In 1929, Rabbi Nahum Landynski of the Radin Yeshiva became its first head. For more information see Arnold Levy, *The Story of Gateshead Yeshiva* (Somerset, England: Wessex Press, 1952).

37. Yeshivas in Israel, though similar to those in the U.S., are a separate topic not covered in this book.

Chapter 2: An Ancient Tradition in a New Land (pp. 18–51)

1. Gilbert Klaperman, *The Story of Yeshiva University* (New York: Macmillan, 1969), pp. 17–33.

2. Ibid., p. 49.

3. Irving Howe, *World of Our Fathers* (New York: Harcourt, Brace, Jovanovich, 1976), p. 106.

4. Hutchins Hapgood, *The Spirit of the Ghetto* (New York: Schocken, 1966), pp. 25–28.

5. Klaperman, *The Story of Yeshiva University,* p. 49.

6. Ibid., pp. 93–110.

7. Aaron Rothkoff, *Bernard Revel: Builder of American Jewish Orthodoxy* (Philadelphia: Jewish Publication Society, 1972), pp. 27–42.

8. Klaperman, *The Story of Yeshiva University,* p. 135.

9. Rothkoff, *Bernard Revel,* p. 139.

10. Ibid., p. 140.

11. Chaim Shapiro, "Rabbi Yerucham Levovitz," *Jewish Observer,* 1977, p. 22.

12. For a brief discussion of the college, see Saul Adelson, "Chicago's Hebrew Theological College," *Jewish Life,* December 1947, pp. 43–48.

13. Rabbi Feinstein's first real position upon arriving in America was as *rosh yeshiva* at the school after it had moved to Cleveland, Ohio. He was there for about six months in 1937 until the yeshiva folded. Rabbi Ruderman had left for Baltimore in 1933 with a group of people to found Ner Israel Rabbinical College. Dr. Belkin was persuaded to come to the Beis Medrash leRabbonim in 1929 but he stayed for only a few months. For most of this period in Cleveland, the *mashgiach* was Rabbi Sheftel Kramer.

14. Some of the more prominent students who attended the yeshiva were Rabbi Boruch Kaplan and rabbis Tzvi Eichenstein, Chaim Pinchus Scheinberg, and Alexander Linchner.

15. Interview, September 17, 1979.

16. For more on the Beis Medrash leRabbonim see Israel Shurin, "Rabbi Yehuda Heshel Levenberg," *Olomeinu,* January 1975, pp. 14–15. Also Isaac Ever, *Horav Yehuda Heschel Levenberg: Zayn Leben und Kamf* (Cleveland: Ivry, 1939). Although this book is biased in numerous respects, it is useful for certain figures and because of the list of yeshiva graduates that appears in the appendix. The following exchange, which occurred shortly before Rabbi Levenberg's death, was related to me by his son: "When the doctor came to see him, he said to my father: 'If every Jew would take a little part of your sickness, you would get well.' And so my father answered: 'Better I should suffer for *klal Yisroel* (the Jewish people) than that *klal Yisroel* should suffer for me.'" Interview with Rabbi Tzvi Levenberg, June 14, 1979.

17. See Hillel Seidman, *Shraga Feivel Mendlowitz* (Hebrew) (New York: Shengold, 1976); Alexander Gross and Joseph Kaminetsky, "Shraga Feivel Mendlowitz," in Leo Jung (ed.), *Men of the Spirit* (New York: Bloch, 1964), pp. 553–561; and Sylvia Fuchs, "And Now a Word from *Our* Fathers," *Jewish Observer,* January 1978, pp. 18–19. For general information regarding the yeshiva's earliest beginnings, see *Self Study of Yeshiva Torah Vodaath,* 1977, pp. 1–3; available at the office of the Association of Advanced Rabbinical and Talmudical schools in New York City. The association has in its possession "self studies" of about twenty major yeshivas. They were prepared by each institution for the association, which serves as an eligibility-granting organization for various forms of government funding. Since the studies are prepared by the yeshivas themselves, they tend to have a rather partisan flavor.

18. Interview with Rabbi Elias Karp, September 19, 1979.

19. For a history of the founding of Williamsburg, see George Kranzler, *Williamsburg: A Community in Transition* (New York: Feldheim, 1961). Especially interesting is the appendix, which deals with the development of the Zeirei Agudath Israel of

Williamsburg, an organization that counted many Torah Vodaath students among its members. In addition to tracing the growth of the community, this account accurately portrays the social and cultural milieu in which Orthodox Jews lived in those days.

20. Although compared to the total Jewish school-age population, enrollment was low, Torah Vodaath could claim 751 elementary and high school students by 1936, a scant ten years after its inception. Kranzler, *Williamsburg,* p. 141.

21. Interview with Mrs. Henoch Leibowitz, September 18, 1979. See also *Self Study of Rabbinical Seminary of America* (New York: Association of Advanced Rabbinical and Talmudical Schools, 1977), pp. 3–4.

22. One issue centered around the program of study. Rabbi Leibowitz wanted to institute a curriculum similar to that followed in Slabodka, with the primary emphasis on Talmud along with a certain amount of *mussar.* Rabbi Mendlowitz favored a broader curriculum designed for laymen (*baaleibatim*) that included Jewish history, Jewish philosophy, and *chassidus* (the study of Hasidic works). In fact, Rabbi Mendlowitz frequently gave classes on these topics as well as on the work of Rabbi Samson Raphael Hirsch, the German–Jewish Orthodox leader, none of which was welcome from Rabbi Leibowitz' standpoint. Others have noted that in giving *mussar* talks, as was the Lithuanian tradition, Rabbi Leibowitz was infringing on Rabbi Mendlowitz' area, since he too liked to give talks on ethics. There was also a dispute over whether Rabbi Leibowitz should teach only the highest class or, as he wished, also lecture to the younger students. Finally, there was animosity, some say envy, on the part of other *rebbes* at the yeshiva who resented Rabbi Leibowitz' status and popularity. In any event, Rabbi Mendlowitz won the power struggle, and it became clear that the *menahel* (principal) and not the *rosh yeshiva* ran Torah Vodaath. While many in the yeshiva world then were upset over the conflict, quite a few fine institutions, including the Chofetz Chaim Yeshiva, established by Rabbi Leibowitz, have been founded through the years as an outcome of disagreements between their leaders. As Lewis Coser has pointed out, conflict has many positive functions. It strengthens groups, maintains a balance of power, and serves, among other things, as a unifying force. (See Lewis Coser, *The Social Functions of Conflict* [Glencoe, Ill.: Free Press, 1956]).

23. Interview April 6, 1979.

24. Interview with Rabbi Paltiel Friend, September 19, 1979. Friend gives examinations to candidates for the rabbinate at the Rabbinical Seminary of America.

25. Interview, September 20, 1979. Charner is principal of the Dov Revel Yeshiva in Queens, New York.

26. Interview, September 19, 1979. Singer is rabbi of the Sefardishe Shul in Brooklyn, New York.

27. Marshall Sklare, *Conservative Judaism: An American Religious Movement* (New York: Schocken, 1972) (augmented edition).

28. Ibid., pp. 43–65.

29. Moshe Feinstein, *The Counsel of the Wicked* (New York: Vaad leHaromas Keren haTorah, 1978), p. 10 (pamphlet).

30. Interview, July 9, 1978.

31. Interview, December 14, 1978.

32. Moshe Davis, "Jewish Religious Life and Institutions in America (A Historical Study)," in Louis Finkelstein (ed.), *The Jews: Their History, Culture, and Religion,* vol. 1 (New York: Harper & Row, 1949), p. 561.

33. Interview, January 18, 1978.

34. Two people who played a major part in helping him organize the yeshiva were Rabbi Michoel Forschlager and Rabbi Avrohom Nachman Schwartz. See also *Self Study of Ner Israel Rabbinical College* (New York: Association of Advanced Rabbinical and Talmudical Schools, 1977), p. 1.

35. We need research on the geographical distribution of Orthodox Jews during this period and their motives for living where they did before we can provide a deep analysis of the role played by the yeshivas outside New York City.

36. See Sidney Lieberman, *A Historical Study on the Development of the Yeshiva High School Curriculum,* Ph.D. dissertation, Yeshiva University, 1958, p. 79; *Self Study: Yeshiva Rabbi Chaim Berlin* (New York: Association of Advanced Rabbinical and Talmudical Schools, 1977), pp. 1–3; M. Kimmel, "The History of Yeshivat Rabbi Chaim Berlin," *Sheviley haHinukh,* Fall 1948, pp. 51–54.

37. The selection process at Chaim Berlin mirrored the disparity of views then current among the board members of the yeshiva. One group reportedly favored Rabbi Hutner because he had attended a university, while the other favored Rabbi Joseph Arnest, who later taught at RIETS, because he had *not* been associated with a university.

38. Chaim Berlin produced many prominent leaders, including rabbis Yaakov Weinberg, Yaakov Perlow, Aharon Schechter, Dovid Cohen, Feivel Cohen, Meir Belsky, and Shlomo Freifeld, all of them well known in the Strictly Orthodox community.

39. Gross and Kaminetsky, "Shraga Feivel Mendlowitz", pp. 563–565.

40. Ibid., p. 564.

41. Interview, September 24, 1979. Schwartz is principal of Yeshiva Toras Emes in Brooklyn, New York.

42. Chaim Shapiro, "Escape from Europe: A Chronicle of Miracles," *Jewish Observer,* May 1973, pp. 20-24.

43. Rothkoff, *Bernard Revel,* pp. 208-214. Torah Vodaath, especially Rabbi Gedalia Schorr and Elimelech Tress of the Zeirei group, was also involved in these efforts.

44. Ibid., pp. 128-129; Klaperman, *The Story of Yeshiva University,* pp. 174-176.

45. See Aharon Lichtenstein, "Joseph Soloveitchik," in Simon Noveck (ed.), *Great Jewish Thinkers of the Twentieth Century* (Washington, D.C.: Bnai Brith Department of Adult Jewish Education, 1963), pp. 281-297; Joseph B. Soloveitchik, "The Lonely Man of Faith," *Tradition,* Summer 1965, pp. 5-67.

46. A good source for the early history of the Telshe Yeshiva is Judah A. Wohlgemuth, "Joseph Leib Bloch," in Leo Jung (ed.), *Guardians of Our Heritage (1724-1953)* (New York: Bloch, 1953), pp. 457-470. Also, Mordechai Gifter, "Yeshivat Telz," in Samuel K. Mirsky (ed.), *Mosdot Torah beAiropah beVinyanam ubeHurbanam* (New York: Histadrut haIvrit beAmerica, 1956), pp. 169-188; and Tovia Lasdun and Leo Davids, "The Way of Telz," *Jewish Life,* October 1958, pp. 55-60.

47. Dr. Revel had attended Telshe Yeshiva for a short while and had been in the class of Rabbi Yoseif Leib Bloch, then head of the school. Also, Rabbi Shimon Shkop, who had been at Telshe for eighteen years, taught at Yeshiva for a brief period during 1929. Rabbi Mordechai Gifter, presently head of the Telshe Yeshiva, had attended Y.U.'s Talmudical Academy before going to Europe in 1933 where he studied at Telshe. Upon his return to America, he taught briefly at Yeshiva as a substitute *rebbe* before becoming a pulpit rabbi. This is significant because Rabbi Gifter is prominently associated with a yeshiva considered quite conservative, even by the right wing in Orthodoxy, largely because it forbids college studies, even on a part-time basis. Speaking of experiences at Yeshiva University, Rabbi Gifter told me in an interview: "I was a student at Yeshiva and my love for Torah grew from there, from the rebbes there. But when I look back and see the effects of synthesis, it bothers me because it led to a search for beauty that is wrong . . . when a person goes there he's studying things *lishmo,* whereas when, as is the case with yeshivas like Chaim Berlin, he goes to college at night, he's only doing it to get a job. And there, when the yeshiva allows college, at least they know it for what it is." Interview, April 1, 1979.

48. This description of Telshe's philosophy is based on interviews with Rabbi Gifter, Rabbi Abba Zalka Gewirtz, Vice President of the school (September 29, 1979), and Rabbi Israel Meir Kirzner, a former student (December 2, 1977). A good general article on the yeshiva and its positions is Chaim Dov Keller, ''Reb Eliahu Meir Bloch,'' *Jewish Observer,* September 1977, pp. 6–13.

49. Interview, September 25, 1979. Relations between the ''Joint'' and the Vaad Hatzala were often strained and almost always complex. See Efraim Zuroff, ''Rescue Priority and Fund Raising as Issues During the Holocaust: A Case Study of the Relations Between the Vaad Hatzala and the Joint, 1939–1941,'' *American Jewish History,* March 1979, pp. 305–326. In the story related by Bunim, there was, of course, no violation of Jewish law because it is obligatory, to save lives, if possible, even if this means violation of the Sabbath.

50. He also gave private classes to advanced students from Torah Vodaath and Chofetz Chaim.

51. Many yeshivas place the burden of fund-raising primarily on the shoulders of the *rosh yeshivas,* a problem which several of them complained about in interviews.

52. This account is based on interviews with Reb Aharon's children, Rabbi Shneur Kotler, (August 2, 1977) and Sarah Kotler-Schwartzman (November 14, 1977).

53. Interview with Irving Bunim.

54. Private, written communication from Rabbi Nissan Waxman, January 16, 1980. Rabbi Waxman was a frequent visitor in Reb Aharon's home in Slutsk and knew him well. He had also studied in various European yeshivas, including those in Radin, Mir, and Slabodka.

55. See David Singer, ''The Yeshivah World,'' *Commentary,* October 1976, 70–73.

56. Interview, November 14, 1977. The position vis-a-vis compromise was staked out early by Rabbi Kotler. In 1943 Dr. Samuel Belkin became President of Yeshiva College and of the Rabbi Isaac Elchanan Theological Seminary. Like Dr. Revel and Rabbi Soloveitchik, he had an excellent background both in rabbinic and in secular studies, having studied in the yeshivas of Slonim, Mir, and Radin, and also receiving a Ph.D. from Brown University. Dr. Belkin made several efforts to attract Reb Aharon to Yeshiva, all without success. At one point, he offered to send some of the best students at RIETS to Lakewood to study and asked Rabbi Kotler if, as part of such an arrangement, he would be willing to give a class once a month at Yeshiva. But the college's position

was too far to the left philosophically for Reb Aharon and he politely but firmly declined the offer.

57. Ibid.

58. Interview August 2, 1977.

59. Shaul Kagan, "Reb Aharon Kotler: Ten Years After His Passing," *Jewish Observer,* May 1973, p. 12.

60. Ibid., p. 7.

61. Two very good studies of the Hasidim in America are Solomon Poll, *The Hasidic Community of Williamsburg* (New York: Free Press, 1962); Israel Rubin, *Satmar: An Island in the City* (New York: Quadrangle, 1972). With the exception of one community study (Egon Mayer, *From Suburb to Shtetl: The Jews of Boro Park* [Philadelphia: Temple University Press, 1979]), there has been no serious research on the historical and sociological development of the Orthodox in America since World War II. Their occupational and residential patterns have hardly been investigated; we know almost nothing about how they adjusted to life here, what cultural features of their previous lifestyles were retained, and which were cast aside, nor even how first-generation children felt about their European parents' accents. In the popular area there is only one work, William B. Helmreich, *Wake Up, Wake Up, to Do the Work of the Creator* (New York: Harper & Row, 1976). What is needed is a "World of Our Fathers" about this generation, both its Orthodox and non-Orthodox members.

62. Figures obtained from Torah Umesorah (The National Society for Hebrew Day Schools).

63. Partisans of the Rabbi Jacob Joseph Yeshiva argue that it, and not Yeshiva Etz Chaim, was the prototype of the day school in America. For a full discussion of this matter see Marvin Schick, "Rabbi Jacob Joseph School: The Oldest Yeshiva in America?", *RJJ Dinner Journal,* 1979; also Klaperman, *The Story of Yeshiva University,* pp. 124–130. As far as the later years are concerned it is important to emphasize that, although RJJ no longer exists as an advanced yeshiva, it produced hundreds of rabbis and community leaders in the late 1940s, the 1950s, and the 1960s, and was also an important feeder school for the Lakewood yeshiva, Beth Medrash Govoha.

64. See *Petition for American Hebrew Theological University,* pp. 1–10, prepared for The Regents of the University of the State of New York on March 30, 1946. In later correspondence, the school is sometimes called American Hebrew Junior College.

65. See *Petition,* p. 3.

66. At the time, Rabbi Leiman was also superintendent of all the

yeshiva high schools in New York City. Between 1933 and 1936, he was assistant to Rabbi Mendlowitz at Torah Vodaath.

67. See *Petition*, p. 3.
68. Interview, March 20, 1980.
69. See *Journal of Regents Meeting*, June 20, 1947, p. 573.

Chapter 3: The Yeshiva Today
(pp. 52–93)

1. There are no precise figures on the size of the Orthodox community and the figure cited here is based on estimates by professionals in the field. See also Charles S. Liebman, "Orthodoxy in American Jewish Life," in Morris Fine and Milton Himmelfarb (eds.), *American Jewish Yearbook,* vol. 66 (Philadelphia: Jewish Publication Society, 1965), p. 36. Also, Liebman, "Orthodox Judaism Today," *Midstream,* August–September 1979, p. 20.

2. Typical communities of this sort may be found in Woodmere, Plainview, Great Neck, West Hempstead, and North Bellmore, all in Long Island, N.Y., and in Scarsdale and New Rochelle, both in Westchester County, N.Y. Other typical communities are in Fairlawn, N.J., Atlanta, Ga., and St. Louis, Mo.

3. For an application of the church-sect typology as a way of distinguishing between Modern and Strictly Orthodox Jews see Liebman's article in the *American Jewish Yearbook,* pp. 22–97. Actually, Liebman refers to the yeshiva community as "traditional Jews," but, in this writer's view, the term is potentially confusing since many Jews who consider themselves somewhere between Orthodox and Conservative call themselves "traditional." "Strictly" is more accurate since the yeshiva-type Jew is, in fact, more strict in his observances than the Modern Orthodox Jew; e.g., he eats only *glatt* kosher meat (the most rigorous standard by which kosher meat is evaluated), his wife covers her hair all the time, he permits no mixed dancing, etc.

4. Hasidic students constitute a growing, yet still small minority in Lithuanian–style yeshivas, most notably at Beth Medrash Govoha, Beth Hatalmud, and Torah Vodaath. Nonetheless, they and the larger Hasidic community have probably influenced the Lithuanian institutions in a number of areas. Some examples are the attitudes toward mysticism and the philosophy of Hasidism, and the relationship to the *rebbe,* as the leaders of the various Hasidic sects are called. In turn, the Lithuanian idea of studying full time beyond one's teens instead of the Hasidic practice of leav-

ing the yeshiva to earn a livelihood and certain unique approaches to Talmud study have had an impact on the Hasidic style of learning in this country. The interrelationships between these two communities in this and other spheres are an important but separate topic beyond the scope of this book.

5. By contrast, in the nineteenth century, living conditions were poor even in the major yeshivas. Students in the Radin Yeshiva slept on hard benches in the *beis medrash* during the early years.

6. Factors such as physical facilities, while important, do not necessarily determine the success or failure of such institutions. A larger role is often played by such intangibles as esprit de corps and charismatic leadership, both of which are, in some measure, responsible for making Chofetz Chaim one of the more successful yeshivas in the country. Indicative of its success is the fact that the yeshiva has not only graduated hundreds of Hebrew day school teachers, communal leaders, and pulpit rabbis over the years but has also founded branches in other parts of the United States and one in Israel.

7. See Chapter 4, pp. 110–112.

8. The yeshivas have, in fact, used the method of studying aloud for centuries, viewing it as the most effective method for insuring that the material will be remembered. Indeed, the Talmud speaks about a disciple of Rabbi Eliezer who studied in a low voice. Three years later, according to the Talmud, he forgot what he had learned (*Erubin* 54a).

9. Samuel C. Heilman, *Synagogue Life: A Study in Symbolic Interaction* (Chicago: University of Chicago Press, 1976), pp. 141–149. Heilman presents a detailed account of conversations occurring at various points during the service.

10. See William B. Helmreich, *Wake Up, Wake Up, to Do the Work of the Creator* (New York: Harper & Row, 1976), pp. 145–146, for an account of a typical prayer service in a yeshiva.

11. For an account of some benefits of group living in a yeshiva see William Shaffir, *Life in a Religious Community: The Lubavitcher Hasidim of Montreal* (Montreal and Toronto: Holt, Rinehart & Winston of Canada, 1974), pp. 140–142.

12. This is taken from one of the "Self Studies" described in Chapter 2, note 17.

13. Catholic and Protestant seminaries display quite a few similarities in their hierarchical structures. See Walter Wagoner, *The Seminary* (New York: Sheed & Ward, 1966).

14. Chaim Shapiro, "Reb Chaim Ozer Grodzensky," *Jewish Observer,* June 1976, pp. 22–23.

15. Chaim Dov Keller, "When the Sun Set at Midday: An Appreciation of Rabbi Raphoel Boruch Sorotzkin," *Jewish Observer*, April 1979, p. 12. For an excellent description of the informal criteria employed by the community to identify such leadership, see Emanuel Feldman, "Trends in the American Yeshivot: A Rejoinder," *Tradition*, Spring 1969, pp. 61–62. Feldman notes: "What sets a *Gadol* apart is something unique: his perception, his ability to penetrate beneath the surface, his capacity for the intuitive flash of insight which discovers reality, not as it appears to be but as it is: reality in the light of Torah" (p. 61).

16. Moshe Feinstein, as quoted in "Yelamdeinu Rabbeinu: Enlighten Us O Teachers," *Jewish Observer*, December 1977, p. 22.

17. Interview, December 1, 1977.

18. Some observers of the yeshiva scene have charged that the Moetzes Gedolei Torah do not, in fact, make any decisions of a nonreligious nature, allowing lay and professional leaders to speak for them instead. Since their meetings are closed to outsiders, it is difficult to ascertain just how involved they are. While they no doubt respect both the views and political acumen of Rabbi Moshe Sherer, head of the Agudah, the *rosh yeshivas* are by no means cloistered individuals. They travel, generally keep abreast of world events, and maintain contact with a variety of interest groups.

19. The many responsibilities of the *rosh yeshiva* have some parallels among the religious leaders of other groups, especially in terms of the total commitment required of the leader toward his followers. See Kaspar D. Naegle, "Clergymen, Teachers and Psychiatrists: A Study in Roles and Socialization," *Canadian Journal of Economics and Political Science*, vol. 12, no. 1 (1956), pp. 46–62.

20. The problems of change, bureaucratization, and institutionalization that occur in religious organizations are treated in Thomas F. O'Dea, "Sociological Dilemmas: Five Paradoxes of Institutionalization," in Edward Tiryakin (ed.), *Sociological Theory, Values, and Sociocultural Change* (New York: Free Press, 1963), pp. 71–89.

21. Examples of *rosh yeshivas* who dominate their schools are Rabbi Shneur Kotler at Lakewood and Rabbi Henoch Leibowitz at Chofetz Chaim. There is a widespread perception that Torah Vodaath is controlled by the *baalei batim*, though this is denied by administrators there. The Rabbi Jacob Joseph Yeshiva, now defunct as an advanced yeshiva, is said to have brought about its own downfall because of excessive politicking by both the *rosh yeshivas* and the board.

22. For a discussion of power and its relationship to organizational ef-

ficiency see Paul Harrison, *Authority and Power in the Free Church Tradition: A Social Case Study of the American Baptist Convention* (Princeton: Princeton University Press, 1959), pp. 5–13; and David L. Sills, *The Volunteers* (Glencoe, Ill.: Free Press, 1957).

23. On this tradition as it existed in Lithuania see Chaim Shapiro, "Rabbi Yerucham Levovitz," *Jewish Observer,* June 1977, pp. 18–23; and Aaron Rothkoff, "The Saba from Slabodka," *Jewish Life,* November–December 1970, pp. 34–42.

24. An excellent article describing the degree to which students can be influenced by a *mashgiach* is Gershon Weiss, "A European Mashgiach in an American Yeshiva," *Jewish Observer,* March 1975, pp. 10–13.

25. Although, as noted earlier, some *rebbes* might have attained their position because they were related to those who ran the yeshiva or "knew someone," there are limits to how far an individual can go because of connections, especially at the higher levels. *Rebbes* teaching advanced students are constantly challenged both in and out of the classroom and could not survive for long in such an intensely intellectual setting were they incompetent. What can be said is that, if all else is equal, a person with an "in" might get a job ahead of someone else.

26. *Kollel* is fully discussed in Chapter 9.

27. Contributions were also made by nonobservant Jews during the nineteenth century in Europe. Baroness Clara Hirsch, for example, gave generously to the Mirrer Yeshiva. See Joseph D. Epstein, "Yeshivat Mir," in S. K. Mirsky (ed.), *Mosdot Torah beAiropah beVinyanam ubeHurbanam* (New York: Histadrut haIvrit beAmerica, 1956) p. 93.

28. See Chaim Shapiro, "My Years with Reb Elchonon: A Talmid Recalls His Years in Baranovich, "*Jewish Observer,* October 1973, p. 14.

29. See Jack Nusan Porter and Shlomo Sender Porter, "The Last of the Big Time Collectors," *Genesis* 2, vol. 8, no. 6 (1977), p. 3, for a poignant description of Kowalsky and other *meshullachim.* Collectors were frequent guests in the Porter home in Milwaukee.

30. Some respondents expressed concern that government support might ultimately reduce the degree of control yeshivas currently enjoy over internal matters. For a discussion of a similar case see Amitai Etzioni, "The Organizational Structure of 'Closed' Educational Institutions in Israel," *Harvard Educational Review,* vol. 27, no. 2 (1957), pp. 107–125.

31. Creating such a setting is not always easy. At the yeshiva I attended it became necessary to cancel plans to rent a site when it

was discovered that the boys would be obliged to share the lake with a girls' camp.

Chapter 4: In the Path of the Lord: Teachings of the Faith (pp. 94–125)

1. *Makkoth,* 23b.
2. The actual procedure varies. In some yeshivas a bell rings and in others students simply rely on an alarm clock. For a description of a typical day in the yeshiva in terms of its effects on the individual, see William B. Helmreich, *Wake Up, Wake Up to Do the Work of the Creator* (New York: Harper & Row, 1976), pp. 143–163.
3. Ibid., pp. 171–173.
4. The reader interested in an extended discussion of this theme should look at Stafford Poole, *Seminary in Crisis* (New York: Herder, 1965).
5. Perhaps the best of such introductions is Adin Steinsaltz, *The Essential Talmud* (New York: Basic Books, 1967). A brief but nonetheless excellent description of talmudic methodology appears in Harry A. Wolfson, *Cresca's Critique of Aristotle* (Cambridge: Harvard University Press, 1929), pp. 24–28.
6. There are, in fact, many societies in which great importance is placed on knowledge that has no practical application. See Florian Znaniecki, *The Social Role of the Man of Knowledge* (New York: Harper & Row, Torchbooks ed., 1968), pp. 92–94.
7. *Avot,* 4b.
8. Interview, June 25, 1979.
9. The institutions named here might disagree with these characterizations. The point, however, is that they are perceived in this manner by many students.
10. Interview, September 13, 1978.
11. Interview, January 26, 1978.
12. Ibid.
13. See Chapter 1, pp. 9–11.
14. Helmreich, *Wake Up,* pp. 171–173.
15. Katherine Hulme, *The Nun's Story* (Boston: Little, Brown, 1956).
16. Interview, January 24, 1978.
17. Erving Goffman, *Asylums* (New York: Anchor, 1968), p. 108.
18. Samuel Heilman, *Synagogue Life* (Chicago: University of Chicago Press, 1973) pp. 74–80.

19. Helmreich, *Wake Up,* pp. 191–194.

20. For a concise and instructive statement about the various functions fulfilled by prayer, see Leonard B. Gewirtz, *The Authentic Jew and His Judaism* (New York: Bloch, 1961), pp. 87–94.

Chapter 5: Yeshiva Students: Who are They and Why Do They Go? (pp. 126–138)

1. See Marc Silver, "Giving up the Assimilated Life: A First Hand Report on American Jews at a Jerusalem Yeshiva," *Baltimore Jewish Times,* January 20, 1978, pp. 32–43. Also Mordechai Beck, *Learning to Learn: A Guide to the New Yeshivot in Israel,* 2nd ed. (Jerusalem: Israel Economist & World Union of Jewish Students, 1977).

2. Interview, June 25, 1979.

3. See especially Silver, "Giving Up the Assimilated Life."

4. It is difficult to ascertain what "myself" means to different persons, but it may indicate that the graduating eighth-grader was given some latitude in making a choice. We do not, however, know what role persons with whom he may have had contact, books he read, etc., had in the decision.

5. This is consistent with Mayer's findings in his study of Boro Park. See Egon Mayer, *From Suburb to Shtetl: The Jews of Boro Park* (Philadelphia: Temple University Press, 1979), pp. 86–88.

6. The percentage of parents who were strictly observant (kept the Sabbath laws and maintained a kosher home) also remained fairly constant.

7. See Chapter 2, p. 32.

8. Some research has been done on the importance of religious figures on the choice of a religious life by those with whom they have contact. See Joseph Fichter, *Religion as an Occupation* (Notre Dame, Ind.: University of Notre Dame Press, 1961); and Keith Bridston and Dwight Culver, *Pre-Seminary Education* (Minneapolis: Augsburg, 1965). The latter study concluded that both the pastor and the mother are crucial in the decision-making process.

9. This refers to Rabbi Joseph Breuer, who, until his death in 1980, was head of the German-Jewish Orthodox community in upper Manhattan. The school is located there and draws most of its financial support from the community.

10. Interview, January 26, 1978.

Chapter 6: A Self-Enclosed World: Life in the Yeshiva (pp. 139–179)

1. Sociologists use the term "total institution" to describe a community that bars or discourages contact with the outside world. Examples are convents, prisons, and mental institutions. The yeshiva shares some, but by no means all, of the characteristics that typify such institutions. See Erving Goffman, *Asylums* (New York: Anchor, 1961), pp. 3–124; and Helen R. F. Ebaugh, *Out of the Cloister* (Austin: University of Texas Press, 1977). Also Samuel Sampson, *Crisis in the Cloister: A Sociological Analysis of Social Relationships and Change in a Novitiate* (Norwood, N.J.: Ablex, 1979).

2. For a physical description of a relatively isolated yeshiva, see Thomas Blass, *Social Structure and Social Organization in a Rabbinical Seminary,* unpublished paper prepared for Professor J. Gumperz at Bernard Revel Graduate School, Yeshiva University, 1967, p. 2.

3. Interview, April 1, 1979.

4. The same motives exist among founders of Christian seminaries. See Stafford Poole, *Seminary in Crisis* (New York: Herder, 1965).

5. See Clifton D. Bryant, *Khaki Collar Crime* (New York: Free Press, 1979), pp. 153–156; and S. J. G. Spencer, "Homosexuality Among Oxford Undergraduates," *Journal of Mental Science,* vol. 105 (1959), pp. 393–405.

6. The development of such friendships is not specifically discouraged in the yeshiva. Within the learning structure, the importance of the *chavrusa* provides further legitimacy for the development of close ties between individuals that often go beyond the learning relationship. In another study, Lucinda San Giovanni, *Ex-Nuns: A Study of Emergent Role Passage* (Norwood, N.J.: Ablex, 1978), the author notes how "one respondent stated she wished I had not raised the question (of lesbianism) because 'many people think we're lesbians, all of us living so close together like that' " (p. 74). A good number of persons, almost all of them outsiders, asked me whether I would write about homosexual behavior in yeshivas without even bothering to inquire if it was a common feature of yeshiva life.

7. The idea of sublimation is firmly rooted in talmudic literature. When, for example, the sage Ben Azzai was asked why he did not marry, he replied that he felt no need to because he had great love for the study of Torah (*Yebamoth,* 63b).

8. The extent to which mental illness is viewed as a stigma among Orthodox Jews is dealt with in Meir Wikler, "The Torah View of

Mental Illness: Sin or Sickness?'', *Journal of Jewish Communal Service,* July 1977, pp. 339–344.

9. For a parallel case see ''Such, Such were the Joys,'' in Sonia Orwell and Ian Angus (eds.), *The Collected Essays, Journalism, and Letters of George Orwell,* vol. 4, *In Front of Your Nose, 1945–1950* (New York: Harcourt, Brace & World, 1968), p. 352. Goffman, *Asylums,* p. 87 talks about the need for prison inmates ''to self-direct themselves in a manageable way.''

10. The entire issue of social control is fully discussed in Chapter 8.

11. Interview, February 9, 1979.

12. Goffman, *Asylums,* p. 21.

13. See Samuel Heilman, *Synagogue Life* (Chicago: University of Chicago Press, 1976), pp. 229–233. Also Lawrence Kaplan, ''The Ambiguous American Jew,'' *Judaism,* Fall 1979, pp. 439–448.

14. Goffman, *Asylums,* p. 22.

15. The sociological term for the various roles ordinarily played by one human being in society is ''role-set.'' See Robert K. Merton, ''The Role-Set: Problems in Sociological Theory,'' *British Journal of Sociology,* vol. 8 (1956), pp. 106–118.

16. Goffman, *Asylums,* p. 72.

17. Ibid., p. 85.

18. Interview, June 11, 1979.

19. A brief discussion about Rabbi Soloveitchik appears in Chapter 2, pp. 37–38 and in Chapter 9, pp. 231–232.

20. See Morris Lasson, ''Alienation Among Yeshiva Youth,'' *Jewish Observer,* July 1970, pp. 12–15.

21. Subsequent events indicate that Barry is still searching. He has taken EST training seminars and has gone through other programs of a similar nature. That he rebelled at a relatively late age presented him with problems over and above the act of rebellion itself. See Matilda W. Riley, Marilyn Johnson, and Anne Foner. *Aging and Society,* vol. 3 (New York: Russell Sage, 1972), pp. 413–414.

22. See William B. Helmreich, *Wake Up, Wake Up, to Do the Work of the Creator* (New York: Harper & Row, 1976), pp. 163–164, 170, 205.

23. Sometimes such students will continue their studies at the *beis medrash* level because of parental pressure that they are unwilling to challenge.

24. See Menachem Z. Greenfield, ''The Rebbe–Talmid Relationship,'' *Jewish Observer,* June 1979, p. 10. Although this article focuses on the high school *rebbe,* the insights are equally valid.

25. Back in the 1950s, before advanced yeshivas swung so much to the right, many yeshivas had high school–level basketball teams that competed against each other. There was a league of schools, including Chaim Berlin, Kamenitzer Mesivta of Boro Park, Mesivta Tifereth Jerusalem, and Rabbi Jacob Joseph School. As the yeshivas became more conservative in their outlook, such activities were discontinued.

26. For a useful framework within which to assess the importance of such actions, see Herbert Blumer, *Symbolic Interaction: Perspective and Action* (Englewood Cliffs, N.J.: Prentice-Hall, 1969), pp. 1–60.

27. Going to the beach is forbidden because women's bathing attire is considered immodest. Except for a vacation, a weekend or even a day in the country is considered impossible since the students have no free days. Dancing and dating (except in explicit search for a marriage partner) are taboo. Movies are prohibited or, at best, frowned upon, as is popular music.

28. Joseph Elias, "Dealing with Churban Europe," *Jewish Observer,* October 1977, p. 18n.

29. The liberal position of this yeshiva regarding secular studies and its general attitude toward the larger society were, in part, shaped by the historical circumstances of the nineteenth-century German–Jewish community in Europe. This philosophy, known as "*Torah im Derech Eretz* [literally, "the sum of Jewish and social knowledge,"]," is far too complex to be treated here. Those interested in a detailed exposition of its essential elements can find it in Mordechai Breuer, *The "Torah-im-Derech Eretz" of Rabbi Samson Raphael Hirsch* (New York: Feldheim, 1970). Breuer clears up many misconceptions that have developed on this topic, including the notion that Rabbi Hirsch did not intend to propagate his system in Lithuania and Poland but wanted it to apply only to the German Orthodox community. In fact, he hoped it would spread to all Jewish communities "where there was a conflict between Torah education and the spirit of the time" (p. 47). Interestingly, a former *rosh yeshiva* of the school was Rabbi Yaakov Perlow. Regarded as one of the outstanding figures in the yeshiva world today, he is a man with unique credentials. He studied in Lithuanian-style yeshivas, namely Chaim Berlin and Lakewood, is a Hasidic *rebbe* (the Novominsker dynasty), and graduated from Brooklyn College with honors. Under his guidance, the German–Jewish yeshiva moved into closer alignment with the Lithuanian-style yeshivas of this country.

30. A student at Lakewood mentioned to me that he found the televi-

sion program *Happy Days* quite funny. Surprised that he watched television, I asked where he had seen it. "Oh—Chany [his wife] and I were watching it in a hotel lobby once."

31. Joseph Bensman and Bernard Rosenberg, *Mass, Class, and Bureaucracy: An Introduction to Sociology* (New York: Praeger, 1976), p. 344. For a good discussion on the effects of mass media see especially pp. 333–383.

32. Joseph Heller, *Good as Gold* (New York: Simon & Schuster, 1979), p. 447.

33. See Emile Durkheim, *The Elementary Forms of the Religious Life* (London: Allen & Unwin, 1915); and Mircea Eliade, *Birth and Rebirth,* trans. by Willard Trask (New York: Harper & Row, 1958).

Chapter 7: Making It in the Yeshiva (pp. 180–193)

1. Many of the basic concepts concerning status and role were developed by Ralph Linton in *The Study of Man* (New York: Appleton-Century-Crofts, 1936).

2. See Erving Goffman, *The Presentation of Self in Everyday Life* (New York: Doubleday, 1959).

3. An example of this at one yeshiva was the adoption by the students of ending many common, everyday words with the suffix "ex." Thus, "not too bright" became "nex tex brex." See also Howard S. Becker, *Outsiders: Studies in the Sociology of Deviance* (Glencoe, Ill.: Free Press, 1963), p. 100.

4. In Samuel C. Heilman, *Synagogue Life* (Chicago: University of Chicago Press, 1973), pp. 214–215, there is a brief description of this phenomenon in a Modern Orthodox synagogue that contrasts sharply with acceptable norms in the yeshiva: "One man, who appears enraptured during even the most simple of group songs, has become the object of open ridicule among the members . . . . ('The guy's off his rocker; I mean he gets a little carried away,' one member puts it. Others agree)" (p. 214).

5. See Andrzej Malewski, "The Degree of Status Incongruence and Its Effects," in Reinhard Bendix and Seymour Martin Lipset (eds.), *Class, Status, and Power: Social Stratification in Comparative Perspective* (New York: Free Press, 1966), pp. 303–308.

6. See Mark Zborowski and Elizabeth Herzog, *Life Is With People:*

The Culture of the Shtetl (New York: Schocken ed., 1962). In this classic work, the authors identify these three factors as the key elements in achieving social status within the Orthodox community of Eastern Europe. They assert, correctly, I believe, that family background is usually a combination of money and learning (p. 74). In the intellectual environment of the yeshiva, a descendant from a long line of talmudists is considered to have a better family backgound than one from a family known primarily for its wealth. In the larger Orthodox community, however, the two have more nearly equal status.

7. Thomas Blass, *Social Structure and Social Organization in a Rabbinical Seminary,* unpublished paper done at Bernard Revel Graduate School, Yeshiva University, 1967, p. 10.

8. Robert K. Merton, *Social Theory and Social Structure,* rev. ed. (New York: Free Press, 1957), pp. 116–117.

9. Interview, February 9, 1979.

10. Ibid.

11. Ibid.

12. Interview, March 12, 1978.

13. Interview, March 12, 1979.

Chapter 8: "Out on the Next Bus." Deviance in the Yeshiva (pp. 194–218)

1. Emile Durkheim, *The Rules of Sociological Method* (New York: Free Press, 1950), trans. by Sarah Solovnay and John H. Mueller pp. 68–69.

2. Much has been written about the relative nature of deviance. See, for example, Howard Becker, *Outsiders: Studies in the Sociology of Deviance* (New York: Free Press, 1963). There is disagreement among sociologists as to where to draw the line between deviance and nonconformity.

3. For a full treatment of the attitudes toward sex by members of the Strictly Orthodox community, see Shraga Silverstein, *The Antidote: Human Sexuality in a Torah Perspective* (New York: Feldheim, 1979).

4. See Thomas Blass, *Social Structure and Social Organization in a Rabbinical Seminary,* unpublished paper, Bernard Revel Graduate School, Yeshiva University, January 1967, p. 8. Blass describes

how, while he was a student at the seminary, a student caught stealing was expelled.

5. The labeling process is fully discussed in Edwin Lemert, *Social Pathology* (New York: McGraw-Hill, 1951). In some cases contact with others who are generally deviant by yeshiva standards may result in the student learning forms of behavior to which he might not otherwise have been exposed. This theory, known as "differential association," is developed in Edwin Sutherland, *Principles of Criminology* (Philadelphia: Lippincott, 1939).

6. Albert Cohen, *Delinquent Boys: The Culture of the Gang* (New York: Free Press, 1955).

7. Interview, January 26, 1978.

8. See Samuel C. Heilman, *Synagogue Life* (Chicago: University of Chicago Press, 1973), pp. 151–192, for an insightful analysis of how such pressure can affect individual behavior.

9. See Harold Garfinkel, "Conditions of Successful Degradation Ceremonies," *American Journal of Sociology*, vol. 61 (1956), pp. 420–424.

10. Uri Sondhelm, "Why Not Wednesday?", *Jewish Observer*, September 1975, p. 9.

11. Interview, January 18, 1978.

12. Mordechai Gifter, "Yeshivat Telz," in S. K. Mirsky (ed.), *Mosdot Torah beAiropah beVinyanam ubeChurbanam* (New York: Histadrut haIvrit beAmerica, 1956), p. 174.

13. Interview, January 26, 1978.

14. Durkheim points out that Socrates' death at the hands of the Athenians who opposed his moral and ethical positions, actually prepared the way for a new definition of morality in Athenian society. See Durkheim, *The Rules of Sociological Method*, pp. 65–75.

15. See Emile Durkheim, *The Division of Labor in Society*, trans. by George Simpson (New York: Free Press, 1964), pp. 102–103; and Lewis A. Coser, "Some Functions of Deviant Behavior and Normative Flexibility," *American Journal of Sociology*, vol. 69 (1962), pp. 172–181.

16. Sondhelm, "Why Not Wednesday?", pp. 9–12.

17. Interview, June 11, 1979.

18. See Kai Erikson, *Wayward Puritans* (New York: Wiley, 1966), for a landmark case study of how deviance is a natural component of virtually every society.

Chapter 9: Preparing for Life Outside the Yeshiva (pp. 219–265)

1. For a good discussion of on-the-job problems see Gershon Kranzler, "Challenge and Commitment," *Jewish Observer,* April 1978, pp. 3–6.

2. Undoubtedly, the majority of Orthodox students who do not attend college are from Hasidic families where norms against it are far stronger than among the Strictly Orthodox.

3. Rabbi Bernard Weinberger has put the matter succinctly: "(The *rosh yeshivas*) have accorded college *de facto* recognition and have adamantly refused to grant it *de jure* recognition." In "The Yeshiva Bochur and College: A New Look at an Old Problem," *Jewish Observer,* March 1966, p. 7.

4. For the original talmudic and biblical sources for proscriptions against secular learning and the positions of prominent Torah scholars who opposed it, see Boruch Ber Leibowitz, *Birchat Shmuel,* vol. 1 (New York, 1947), pp. 38–42; and Elchonon Wasserman, *Kovetz Heorot* (New York, 1952), pp. 146–148.

5. Interview, April 30, 1978.

6. Interview, January 18, 1978.

7. Interview, August 2, 1977.

8. Interview, April 6, 1979.

9. Interview, April 1, 1979.

10. For more on the attitudes toward the sciences, see *Proceedings of the Association of Orthodox Jewish Scientists,* vol. 1 (New York, 1966), pp. 106–112.

11. For a discussion of role conflict see Robert K. Merton, *Social Theory and Social Structure,* rev. ed. (New York: Free Press, 1957), pp. 116–117.

12. See Irving Levitz, "Crisis in Orthodoxy: The Ethical Paradox," *Jewish Life,* Fall–Winter 1977–1978, pp. 23–28.

13. Accounting and law are probably the most popular professions for yeshiva graduates.

14. Bernard Fryshman, "On Butchers, Bakers, and Candlestick Makers," *Jewish Observer,* September 1976, p. 17. Also Egon Mayer, *From Suburb to Shtetl: The Jews of Boro Park* (Philadelphia: Temple University Press, 1979), pp. 26–27.

15. Simon Raskin, "A Third Alternative: The Orthodox Worker-Scholar," *Jewish Observer,* June 1969, p. 17.

16. Some of the animosity between the two camps is rooted in events that transpired decades ago. For background material in this area see Aaron Rothkoff, *Bernard Revel: Builder of American Jewish Orthodoxy* (Philadelphia: Jewish Publication Society, 1972).

17. Norman Lamm, "Modern Orthodoxy's Identity Crisis," *Jewish Life*, May–June 1969, p. 7.

18. Although Dr. Belkin might have envisioned the idea of secular studies being evaluated from a religious perspective, no serious effort was ever made to integrate the two within the framework of classroom instruction. No doubt, certain individuals, such as Rabbi Joseph B. Soloveitchik, have discussed secular philosophical concepts together with Jewish ideas, but in truth he is one of very few of those teaching at Yeshiva University who is thoroughly trained in both areas. In reality, students were expected to become proficient in both spheres with the hope that they would make good use of their knowledge of each in later life. Certain elements of this idealized version of integrated knowledge are present in the Hirschian idea of *"Torah im Derech Eretz"* (see Chapter 6, footnote 29) and the true origins of both probably lie in the ninth-century community of Moslem Spain. In theory, both Yeshiva University and Breuer's Yeshiva believe that the study of Torah comes first but, in practice, Yeshiva University is the more liberal of the two.

19. One well-known leader in the Strictly Orthodox community said to me: "A major problem is the differing levels of observance and priorities. Look at how many Y.U. grads are in synagogues without *mechitzas* [partition found in Orthodox synagogues that separates men from women]." While there are a fair amount of Y.U. graduates officiating in such synagogues, there are also graduates of right-wing yeshivas who fit this description. Conversely, many Y.U. rabbis could easily be characterized as Strictly Orthodox.

20. During his early years as head of RIETS, Rabbi Soloveitchik played a role in the Agudath Israel organization.

21. The pages of *Commentator,* Yeshiva's undergraduate newspaper, *Inside Yeshiva University,* published by the Public Relations Department, and many other publications of the school, are good sources for an understanding of Yeshiva's position on Israel. The general Modern Orthodox position, to which Yeshiva subscribes, and, in fact, helps formulate, is perhaps best explained in Eliezer Berkovitz, *Faith After the Holocaust* (New York: KTAV, 1973). For a better understanding of the Strictly Orthodox community's ambiguity toward Israel, one heightened by the quasi-religious

nature of the Begin government, the following articles are useful: Nisson Wolpin, "Zionism: A Dream and Its Failure," *Jewish Observer,* January–February 1976, pp. 3–8; "Withdrawal from Administered Territories?" *Jewish Observer,* 1974, pp. 7–8; Yitzchak Hutner, "Holocaust," *Jewish Observer,* October 1977, pp. 4–9; Ralph Pelcovitz, "A Response to the Yom Kippur War, in Retrospect," *Jewish Observer,* January 1975, pp. 11–15.

22. "Lamm Warns Intolerants: Error Based on Truth Is Not Heresy," *Jewish Week–American Examiner,* July 1–14, 1979, p. 4.

23. Interview, June 21, 1979. Rather than placating militant right-wingers, such changes may be a catalyst for new demands. See Marvin Schick, "The New Style of American Orthodox Jewry," *Jewish Life,* January–February 1967, pp. 29–36.

24. Interview July 9, 1978.

25. Data from the Yeshiva College admissions office reveal some interesting patterns. Of those who attend the school, between 5 and 10 percent come from the right-wing yeshivas (based on 1978 figures,) evidence that Yeshiva University holds no great attraction for the products of these institutions. Of course, it must be considered that anyone from these yeshivas who even *thinks* of going to Y.U. is likely to be subjected to peer pressure and attempts at dissuasion on the part of *rebbes* and the *rosh yeshiva.* An analysis of the figures indicated that the years 1969 and 1970 saw the largest numbers of students from the right-wing yeshivas and that the number dropped drastically between 1971 and 1974. Since 1975, however, the numbers have risen, though not to their earlier levels. This may indicate that as Yeshiva moves rightward, it is becoming a bit more appealing to such youths. Nevertheless, the numbers, ranging from 12 to 38 students, are too small to permit anything more than very tentative statements.

26. "Lamm Warns Intolerants," p. 7.

27. Ibid.

28. There are many Modern Orthodox Jews who will explain their more liberal interpretations of *halacha* by saying: "I'm not *that* religious." This argument is, however, almost never made at the official leadership levels. For an article critical of Modern Orthodoxy, see Shlomo Riskin, "Where Modern Orthodoxy Is At—And Where It Is Going," *Jewish Life,* Spring 1976, pp. 27–31.

29. See David Shapiro, "Secular Studies and Judaism," *Tradition,* Summer 1966, pp. 15–39.

30. Interview, January 13, 1980.

31. Ibid.

32. Press release (of unknown origin), January 23, 1979. Signed "Bnei Torah of Boro Park." It is significant that no major figure in the yeshiva community signed the document.

33. Interview, January 13, 1980. Another example of opposition to secular studies even when there are no problems of heretical teachings or an "immoral" atmosphere is the story of the Institute for Professional Enrichment (IPE). Established in the mid-1970s by Torah Umesorah with the support of leading *rosh yeshivas*, IPE provided yeshiva students (and Orthodox women) with the opportunity to earn B.A. and M.A. degrees through intensive study limited to Sundays. The program essentially operated in conjunction with Adelphi University and it was in a convenient Manhattan location. It was a quick and smashing success; but several younger *rosh yeshivas* opposed Torah Umesorah's involvement in IPE. First, they made a rule excluding yeshiva students below the age of twenty-two. Then they forced Torah Umesorah to disassociate itself from the program. IPE now operates as an independent program.

34. Interview with Dr. Joseph Kaminetsky, National Director Emeritus, Torah Umesorah, September 18, 1977.

35. Interview, January 24, 1978. There are some *rebbes* in the New York area capable of making ends meet through teaching alone. This is, however, mostly in schools that give the *rebbe* full employment by having him teach Hebrew subjects to one class in the morning hours and to another in the afternoon. However, not only is this the exception in New York, but even after, say, eleven years on the job, a top-flight teacher can expect to earn no more than about $22,000. Yeshiva principals do better. According to one survey more than half earn over $15,000 annually, with many earning more than $25,000. See Wallace Greene, "Summary of NCYP [National Conference of Yeshiva Principals] Survey: 23rd Annual Torah Umesorah Principal's Conference," *Yeshiva Educator's Notebook*, November 1978, p. 7. The survey included many principals from New York City.

36. Interview, March 22, 1979.

37. Interview, April 1, 1979.

38. See *Encyclopedia Judaica* (Jerusalem: Keter, 1972), p. 1639.

39. See Yaakov Jacobs, "The Bankruptcy of Jewish Education," *Jewish Observer*, April 1966, pp. 3–5; and Morris Lasson, "Yeshiva Teaching—Vocation or Avocation, *Jewish Observer*, October 1969, pp. 9–11. Among the *rosh yeshivas* who observed that part of the problem was overqualification in talmudic knowledge were Rabbi Aharon Schechter, head of Yeshiva Chaim Berlin (interview,

April 13, 1978) and Rabbi Elya Svei, head of the Talmudical Yeshiva of Philadelphia (interview, January 24, 1978). Both stressed the need for greater idealism on the part of the *bochorim*.

40. Another program that provides real training, while also socializing the young man into the importance of Jewish education, is the SEED (Summer Educational Environmental Development) program, sponsored by Torah Umesorah, which brings yeshiva students into communities to lay the foundation for permanent programs of study and new yeshivas. See Moshe Turk, ''Bringing Torah to the Valley,'' *Jewish Observer,* October 1977, pp. 21–25.

41. There are, nonetheless, many exceptions to this rule. Among them are Rabbi Emanuel Feldman from Ner Israel Yeshiva who heads a very large congregation in Atlanta, Ga., Rabbi Simcha Krauss, head of the Young Israel of Hillcrest in Queens, New York City, and Rabbi Sholom Gold, leader of the Young Israel of West Hempstead, on Long Island, N.Y. The point is, however, that those who enter the rabbinate constitute a very small proportion of right-wing yeshiva alumni. Furthermore, those who come from the right-wing yeshivas usually graduated prior to 1965.

42. See the ''Self Studies'' of the yeshivas, available at the Association of Advanced Rabbinical and Talmudic Schools, for descriptions of the placement process.

43. See Charles S. Liebman, ''The Training of American Rabbis,'' in Morris Fine and Milton Himmelfarb (eds.), *American Jewish Yearbook* (Philadelphia: Jewish Publication Society, 1968), pp. 3–112; and Murray Polner, *Rabbi: The American Experience* (New York: Holt, Rinehart, & Winston, 1977), pp. 115–147.

44. Interview, April 1, 1979.

45. Emanuel Feldman, ''Trends in the American Yeshivot: A Rejoinder,'' *Tradition,* Spring 1968, p. 59.

46. Interview, December 14, 1978. For an interesting parallel position by a Modern Orthodox Jew on the need to attract others to Judaism through the role of rabbi, see Dov Fisch, ''Ye Shall Be Accountants and Yea, Even Doctors,'' *Hamevaser,* May 17, 1979, p. 12.

47. Nosson Scherman, ''The Rabbi and the Rosh Yeshiva: A Look at Their Respective Roles,'' *Jewish Observer,* June 1964, pp. 15–16.

48. The Chofetz Chaim Yeshiva already offers a program including such training for prospective pulpit rabbis. In sociological terms, such developments may be seen as part of a pattern by which the community begins to take on the characteristics of a denomination rather than a sect.

49. Mayer, *From Suburb to Shtetl,* p. 103.

50. Some have questioned the authenticity of such letters (they are not signed). Regardless, the attitudes they portray exist in the community.

51. The *Jewish Press,* in this writer's opinion, with a weekly circulation estimated at between 100,000 and 150,000, many of them Orthodox Jews, will become within twenty years or so an important historical source for historians of the American Jewish community. This, if it comes to pass, would be ironic, since it is often derided and lampooned by members of the Jewish community, including the Orthodox who are among its most avid readers. Its columns, advertisements, and letters to the editor are a gold mine for the student of Jewish culture, despite the charges by some that the paper is intellectually unappealing and tasteless.

52. Meir Wikler, "Preparation for Marriage: A Prevention for Divorce," *Jewish Observer,* January 1979, p. 11.

53. Interview, March 12, 1979.

54. I am indebted to Rabbi Dov Lesser for providing me with information on *kollels* in general.

55. Some students admitted to *kollel* are not married but this is unusual.

56. For a comprehensive discussion of this subject see Nisson Wolpin, "The Community Kollel: Reaching Out with Torah," *Jewish Observer,* October 1979, pp. 19–26.

57. Interview with Rabbi Dov Lesser, June 27, 1979.

58. The *kollel* wives were, with three exceptions, interviewed by trained young women who had themselves attended yeshivas.

59. See H. D. Wolpin, "Kollel U.S.A.: A New Look Inside a New-Old Torah Institution," *Jewish Observer,* December 1965, pp. 9–11.

60. Interview, March 13, 1978.

61. Interview with Yaakov Salomon, March 12, 1979. Also Leonard Topp (psychologist), March 12, 1978.

Chapter 10: Is the Yeshiva Successful in Reaching Its Goals? (pp. 266–299)

1. *Bulletin of Beth Medrash Govoha,* 1977–1978, p. 14.

2. Many in the community seem to feel that the American yeshivas have produced almost no truly outstanding scholars. Whether or not this is true, such a judgment appears a bit premature. Three

decades is hardly enough time for a transplanted institution as complex as the yeshiva to fully mature. Moreover, it is entirely possible that those who are today viewed as merely "good scholars" will, as so often happens with such evaluations, be seen as "great" twenty years from now.

3. Interview, December 28, 1977.

4. Interview, May 16, 1979.

5. This idea has attracted attention beyond the community. See Ari Goldman, "At Yeshiva, Study for Study's Sake," *New York Times,* Sunday, April 30, 1978, Section 12, p. 5. Etzioni has observed that all educational institutions "contribute to the preservation of the cultural heritage by transferring it from generation to generation, mainly through teaching." Amitai Etzioni, *A Comparative Analysis of Complex Organizations* (Glencoe, Ill.: Free Press, 1961), p. 73.

6. Respondents were not asked how much time they spent on Bible study because such study is far easier and is engaged in by many Jews who do not have even a yeshiva background. Hence, it would not be indicative of a strong impact by the yeshiva on their lives.

7. One might give such a class to one's fellow congregants in a synagogue on Sabbath afternoon as part of the congregation's activities. A group of businessmen, lawyers, and accountants who work in the same part of town might attend a class led by a knowledgeable layman during their lunch hour. See Kenneth A. Briggs, "When May a Businessman Study Talmud?", *New York Times,* May 11, 1978, p. B1.

8. Quite a few yeshivas have programs where alumni return to the yeshiva in later life for a week or two to engage in full-time study. Known as *yarchei kallah,* these retreats are usually held in the summer. The term means "months of the great assembly" and it refers to the talmudic period when large numbers of people gathered in the Babylonian academies to review various tractates that had been studied during the course of a year. Today people come with their families, and there are generally a day care center and special activities for the wives. Most of the time is spent engaged in study, though there is time for recreation too. Only a small proportion of yeshiva alumni participate in such programs, but for those who do it is a way of retaining one's ties with the school and keeping alive the spirit often remembered with fondness when talking about "the old days."

9. A study of the Yeshiva of Flatbush High School also showed positive correlations between Jewish study and religious obser-

vance, on the one hand, and level of religious education, on the other. See Joseph Heimowitz, *A Study of the Graduates of the Yeshiva of Flatbush High School,* Ph.D. dissertation, Yeshiva University, 1979. See also Harold Himmelfarb, *The Impact of Religious Schooling: The Effects of Jewish Education upon Adult Religious Involvement,* Ph.D. dissertation, University of Chicago, 1974.

10. Interview, July 2, 1980. In recent years several hospitals have begun special programs for Orthodox interns and residents that make it unnecessary for them to work on the Sabbath.

11. Interview, April 30, 1978.

12. For a parallel case among Christians see Peter Berger, "Some Sociological Comments on Theological Education," *Perspective,* Summer 1968, no page available.

13. The head of one well-known elementary–high school yeshiva commented to me: "Whenever there's a high school job I have literally hundreds of applicants, but for the elementary school I have to conduct a nationwide talent search." Several principals noted that the availability of highly qualified women who, regarding teaching as a second job (the husband was the primary wage earner), were willing to accept the low salaries, had kept the caliber of the staff at a high level.

14. A study by Liebman of Yeshiva University graduates indicated that those entering the rabbinate were probably more to the left ideologically than those who did not. See Charles S. Liebman, "The Training of American Rabbis," in Morris Fine and Milton Himmelfarb (eds.), *American Jewish Yearbook* (Philadelphia: Jewish Publication Society, 1968), pp. 69–70.

15. Interview, August 2, 1977.

16. "30,000 at Knessia Gedola Sessions: Hear Call for New Torah Role in Judaism," *Jewish Press,* January 18, 1980, p. 22. Similar calls have been issued in previous years by various leading *rosh yeshivas.*

17. Interview, December 24, 1978.

18. Interview, December 13, 1979.

19. Interview, April 1, 1979.

20. Interview, February 12, 1979.

21. Interview, April 6, 1979.

22. William Shaffir, *Life in a Religious Community: The Lubavitcher Hasidim in Montreal* (Toronto and Montreal: Holt, Rinehart, and Winston of Canada, 1974).

23. Interview, August 2, 1977.

24. For a general discussion of the historical antecedents of this rela-

tionship, see Chaim Raphael, "The Litvak Connection and Hasidic Chic," *Commentary,* May 1976, pp. 48–53.

25. Others have criticized the yeshivas for their unwillingness to teach their students how to communicate with the general Jewish community. See David Singer, "The Yeshivah World," *Commentary,* October 1976, p. 73.

26. This is part of the Release Time Program, one in which the Lubavitcher Hasidim play a major role.

27. See Pinchas Stolper, "Youth's Positive Revolt," *Jewish Life,* February–March 1969, pp. 10–21.

28. This may create the problem of appearing elitist to the larger Jewish community.

29. See Mayer Schiller, *The Road Back: A Discovery of Judaism Without Embellishments* (New York: Feldheim, 1978). Also, the entire issue of the June 1980 *Jewish Observer* is devoted to articles about the *baal teshuva.*

30. Singer "The Yeshivah World," discusses this failing.

31. Beth David Yeshiva is somewhat unique in this respect because the person responsible for this topic was considered to be exceptionally gifted in this area throughout the yeshiva world and, in fact, many respondents mentioned his impact on their lives.

32. Finding such individuals is not easy because they do not appear on any lists and are often reluctant to talk about their experiences. Still, using a "snowball" approach of having informants identify others it was possible to learn something about them. By rebels and malcontents, we mean those who no longer are Orthodox in practice and in terms of commitment. The number of such persons would be far higher if one included those who left after elementary school or high school. In fact, in looking for those who had rejected Orthodoxy, I was frequently led to people who, it was claimed, had left the yeshiva. As things turned out, most of these had never gone to yeshiva at the advanced level. This distinction is important since those who leave *yeshiva gedolas* have been in the system much longer.

33. For an understanding of some of the problems that arise when individuals attempt to reconstruct their pasts, see Peter Berger, *Invitation to Sociology* (New York: Anchor, 1963), pp. 54–65; and Barney Glaser and Anselm Strauss, *Status Passage* (Chicago: Aldine, 1971).

34. Yisroel Belsky, "What Can a Yeshiva Bochur Do?", *Jewish Observer,* June 1973, p. 14. See also Singer, "The Yeshivah World," pp. 72–73. Singer points out that the standards in

American yeshivas are lower than was the case in Lithuania because they have, for a variety of reasons, become less particular about whom they admit. Yet, he argues, the yeshivas have refused to recognize that they can no longer cater to an elite whose members study Talmud day and night to the exclusion of anything else.

Chapter 11: Why Has the Yeshiva Survived? (pp. 300-331)

1. Marshall Sklare and Joseph Greenblum, *Jewish Identity on the Suburban Frontier* (New York: Basic Books, 1967), p. 89-96.
2. Interview, December 24, 1978.
3. Irving Howe, *World of Our Fathers* (New York: Harcourt, Brace, Jovanovich, 1976), p. 61.
4. Interview, May 16, 1979.
5. Interview, April 25, 1978.
6. For fuller descriptions of efforts in this direction and the social milieu in which they operated, see Milton Gordon, *Assimilation in American Life* (New York: Oxford University Press, 1964).
7. The sense of loss is beautifully described in Alfred Kazin, *A Walker in the City* (New York: Harcourt, Brace, and World, 1951).
8. The reader desiring an introduction to this subject might choose from among the following books and articles: Alvin Schiff, *The Jewish Day School in America* (New York: Jewish Education Committee Press, 1966); Joseph Kaminetsky and Murray Friedman (eds.), *Hebrew Day School Education: An Overview* (New York: Torah Umesorah, 1970); David Singer, "The Growth of the Day School Movement," *Commentary*, August 1973, pp. 53-57; Nisson Wolpin, "The American Hebrew Day School Movement Comes of Age: A Report and Analysis," *Jewish Observer*, October 1976, pp. 3-10; "The Jewish Day School: A Symposium," *Tradition*, Summer 1972, pp. 95-130; Milton Himmelfarb, "Reflections on the Day School," *Commentary*, July 1960, pp. 29-36. Actually, Schiff dates the era of great expansion as beginning in 1940, well before the European influx (p. 48). However, a closer look at the statistics he presents indicates that it began in 1944-45. Between 1940-41 and 1944-45, a period of four years, enrollment increased by only 1,300 students, an average of 352 students a year. Starting in 1944-45, the yearly rate was at least 2,000 and, in most cases, 3,000 children per year, a reflection, it would seem, of immigration patterns.

9. See Schiff, *The Jewish Day School,* pp. 78–83. Singer ("The Growth of the Day School Movement," p. 54). points out that the prestige factor is most likely to apply in suburban areas where high-quality, nonsectarian private schools are not as common as in the cities themselves.

10. Most research on the high schools has focused on more liberal, coed yeshivas that send few graduates to advanced yeshivas. See, for example, Joseph Heimowitz, *A Study of the Graduates of the Yeshiva of Flatbush High School,* Ph.D. dissertation, Yeshiva University, 1979. A fine work, it does not, unfortunately, have data on students attending yeshivas at the *beis medrash* level. Of more limited scope but still useful as background material is Sidney Lieberman, *A Historical Study on the Development of the Yeshiva High School Curriculum,* Ph.D. dissertation, Yeshiva University, 1958.

11. As reported in the *Jewish Observer,* April 1977, p. 42.

12. Interview, March 16, 1978.

13. Other organizations that have made contributions in the development of day school education include the United Lubavitcher Yeshivoth, and the National Council for Torah Education.

14. Interview, September 18, 1977.

15. See Chapter 3, pp. 91–93. For a description of life in an Orthodox summer camp see William B. Helmreich, *Wake Up, Wake Up, to Do the Work of the Creator* (New York: Harper & Row, 1976), pp. 120–138.

16. The donors were often rewarded by having such institutions, or at least a building, named after them. Interestingly, quite a few benefactors of right-wing yeshivas were themselves Modern Orthodox or even nonobservant.

17. The 4.0 rate is adjusted according to marital status, length of marriage, and age. Among the Modern Orthodox, the rate in one study was 2.2. See Gina Geselewitz, "A Modern Orthodox Synagogue Looks at Itself: Members Take Sociologist's Test," *Jewish News–New Jersey,* February 15, 1979, pp. 1,30. See also Bertram A. Leff, *The Modern Orthodox Jew: Acculturation and Identification,* M.A. Thesis, Adelphi University, 1974. The national Jewish average, according to the latest figures, is estimated at 1.8. See Sidney Goldstein, "Jewish Fertility in Contemporary America," in Paul Ritterband (ed.), *Modern Jewish Fertility* (Leiden: Brill, 1981).

18. For evidence of the large number of Orthodox Jews who are in the professions and their middle-class socioeconomic status, see Egon Mayer, *From Suburb to Shtetl: The Jews of Boro Park* (Philadelphia: Temple University Press, 1979), pp. 53–54.

19. Among them are Samuel Hirsch, Sheldon Silver, and Howard Lasher. One of the first to call attention to the emergence of the Orthodox as an ethnic pressure group was Marvin Schick in "The New Style of American Orthodox Jewry," *Jewish Life,* January–February 1967, pp. 29–36.

20. Interview, December 14, 1978.

21. Interview, December 14, 1978. As noted earlier, some have questioned how independently the *rosh yeshivas* act and how much they rely on Rabbi Sherer's judgment. While it is to be expected that Rabbi Sherer's views carry great weight, both because of his reputation for astuteness and because of his extensive experience in community matters, quite a few of the *rosh yeshivas* are strong-willed individuals with very definite views of their own.

22. Private written communication on March 9, 1980. Also, an excellent article on COLPA and the need for political involvement by the Orthodox if they are to achieve their aims is Marvin Schick, "The National Jewish Commission on Law and Public Affairs: An Analytical Report," in Marvin Schick (ed.), *Government Aid to Parochial Schools: How Far?* (New York: Commission on Law and Public Affairs, 1968), pp. 4–17.

23. Interview, December 14, 1978.

24. See Singer, "The Growth of the Day School Movement," p. 56; Marshall Sklare, *America's Jews* (New York: Random House, 1971), p. 172; Nisson Wolpin, "Who's Saving American Jewry?", *Jewish Observer,* December 1977, pp. 3–7. It has also been suggested that Federation leaders and the nonobservant Jewish community, in general, have gradually come to view the Orthodox with admiration because their observance level indicates both self-sacrifice and commitment. See Charles S. Liebman, "Orthodox Judaism Today," *Midstream,* August–September 1979, p. 22. Also Marshall Sklare, *Conservative Judaism: An American Religious Movement,* augmented ed. (New York: Schocken, 1972), pp. 261–267.

25. See Mayer, *From Suburb to Shtetl.* Judith R. Kramer and Seymour Leventman, *Children of the Gilded Ghetto* (New Haven: Yale University Press, 1961); and Sidney Goldstein and Calvin Goldscheider, *Jewish Americans: Three Generations in a Jewish Community* (Englewood Cliffs, N.J: Prentice-Hall, 1968).

26. Mayer, *From Suburb to Shtetl,* p. 18.

27. Interview, January 18, 1978.

28. See, for example, Walter Waggoner, "Vandals Attack Jewish Seminary and Injure Four," *New York Times,* June 28, 1979, p. B3.

29. Interview, March 16, 1978. As Mayer observes, Orthodox Jews, and this includes the Strictly Orthodox, adapt features of modern society to their own needs, often making religious observance easier. Examples are serving coffee after a meat meal and substituting a nondairy creamer for milk, using a preset electric timer on the Sabbath so that lights go on and off whenever one so desires, etc. These are not, however, real compromises in either the letter or spirit of the law (see Mayer, *From Suburb to Shtetl*, pp. 154-155). Something like college attendance is far more serious in its implications for it is much more of a gray area.

30. As Professor Marvin Schick has noted (interview, June 11, 1979), this contrasts sharply with the situation in Israel. There, students begin intensive study in high school. (They are not required, as is the case in the United States, to take secular studies.) This may account for the seemingly higher standards in many yeshivas in that country.

31. See Mayer, *From Suburb to Shtetl*, pp. 100-101, for a discussion of how the desire to work among Orthodox women is not only based on economic necessity but on status aspirations as well.

32. Ibid., pp. 73-74.

33. "The Lonely Jew in a World of Upheaval," *Jewish Observer*, January 1975, p. 10. See also Yaakov Perlow, "Our Generation: Churban Plus One," *Jewish Observer*, June 1976, p. 10. Agudah has also been attacked by those to the right of it and accused, among other things, of being too liberal. For example, the Neturei Karta, a group of ultra-Orthodox Jews best known for their opposition to Israel, have repeatedly lashed out at the Agudah for giving in to secular influences. See *Jewish Guardian*, November 1979, pp. 3, 13-15.

34. For a discussion of some of the difficulties in ascertaining the divorce rate, see the exchange of letters between professors Egon Mayer and Chaim I. Waxman in the *Jewish Week-Herald Examiner*, July 1, 1979, p. 38, and July 15, 1979, p. 22.

35. The problem is not limited to the Strictly Orthodox. It is also one that concerns the Hasidic and Modern Orthodox communities. For more on this subject see Ruth Koenigsberg, "Panel Discusses Rise in Orthodox Divorce," *Neshama*, February 1979, pp. 1, 4-6; Meir Wikler, "Preparation for Marriage: A Prevention for Divorce," *Jewish Observer*, January 1979, pp. 9-13; Nisson Wolpin, "RCA: Friend of the Family?", *Jewish Observer*, March 1978, pp. 35-37. What is needed is a full-scale empirical study of the question that would determine, among other things, which of

the factors for divorce given in the text are most relevant to each of the three major groupings within the Orthodox community.

36. For an excellent analysis of how and why secularization influences religion, see Peter L. Berger, *The Sacred Canopy: Elements of a Sociological Theory of Religion* (New York: Anchor ed., 1969); and Andrew Greeley, *Unsecular Man* (New York: Delta Books ed., 1974).

37. Interview, July 9, 1978.

38. Interview, December 24, 1978. The "problem of meaning" was first developed in sociology by Max Weber, who focused on it extensively in his writings on the major world religions. Other sociologists drew on Weber's insights and formulated their own interpretations in this area. See, for example, Thomas Luckmann, *The Invisible Religion* (New York: Macmillan, 1967); Talcott Parsons, "Sociology and Social Psychology," in Hoxie N. Fairchild (ed.), *Religious Perspectives in College Teaching* (New York: Ronald Press, 1952), pp. 286–337.

39. The relationships and conflicts between religion and intellectual knowledge are incisively discussed in an essay by Weber titled "Religious Rejections of the World and Their Direction," in H. H. Gerth and C. Wright Mills (trans. and eds.), *From Max Weber: Essays in Sociology* (New York: Oxford University Press, 1958), pp. 350–357.

40. See Bronislaw Malinowski, *Magic, Science, and Religion* (Glencoe, Ill.: Free Press, 1954); and A. R. Radcliffe-Brown, *Taboo* (Cambridge: Cambridge University Press, 1938).

41. See Max Weber, *Economy and Society,* vol. 1 (New York: Bedminster Press, 1968), pp. 387–393.

42. Interview, January 17, 1978.

43. Writing more than two decades ago, Will Herberg stated in *Protestant–Catholic–Jew* rev. ed. (New York: Anchor Books, 1960) p. 61: "The turn to the private life, reflecting the attempt to find meaning and security in what is basic and unchanging, rather than in the fluctuating fortunes of social and political activity, is one of the major factors in the upswing of religion among the American people today." This seems as true today as it was then. See also Berger, *The Sacred Canopy*, pp. 22–28, and Collette Dowling, "The Nun's Story," *Sunday New York Times Magazine,* November 28, 1976, p. 34.

44. The major work on the integrative functions of religion has been done, of course, by Emile Durkheim, in his classic work, *The Elementary Forms of the Religious Life* (London: Allen & Unwin, 1915).

45. Thomas F. O'Dea, *The Sociology of Religion* (Englewood Cliffs, N.J.: Prentice-Hall, 1966), p. 101.

46. Stafford Poole, *Seminary in Crisis* (New York: Herder, 1965), p. 70.

Appendix: How the Study Was Done (pp. 332–348)

1. At Kamenitz I was actually in the high school, at Ner Israel I was, at various times, in both the *beis medrash* and high school for religious studies and in the high school for secular studies, while at Yeshiva University I was, for a time, in the RIETS division. Attending what were, essentially, three different types of institutions broadened my perspective considerably.

2. William B. Helmreich, "Bowery City, U.S.A.," *Yeshiva College Journal of Sociology,* 1966, pp. 9–14; and *Observations on Haiti,* unpublished paper, November 1969.

3. William B. Helmreich, *The Black Crusaders: A Case Study of a Black Militant Organization* (New York: Harper & Row, 1973).

4. William B. Helmreich, *Wake Up, Wake Up, to Do the Work of the Creator* (New York: Harper & Row, 1976).

5. In fact, the average number of years attended among those responding was 3.2. No comparative figures were available for those who did not respond. What is most significant about this figure is that it indicates a period of attendance of sufficient length for the yeshiva to have had an opportunity to make an impact on the student.

6. For an interesting discussion of this entire subject see Thomas A. Heberlein and Robert Baumgartner, "Factors Affecting Response Rates to Mailed Questionnaires," *American Sociological Review,* vol. 43 (1978), pp. 447–462.

7. See Egon Mayer, *From Suburb to Shtetl: The Jews of Boro Park* (Philadelphia: Temple University Press, 1979), p. 161.

Glossary

THIS GLOSSARY PRIMARILY DEFINES words that *frequently* appear throughout the text. An attempt has been made to strike a balance between spelling which scholars are accustomed to and that which lay persons are used to seeing. Since the ways in which a community expresses itself are an integral part of it, I have tried, except where it is especially jarring, to spell words as they *commonly* appear in the publications and literature of the yeshiva world. For words having a guttural sound, as in *"Bach,"* I have chosen *ch* except for the Bibliography, where the more common *kh* has been retained. This makes matters easier for scholars unfamiliar with yeshiva usage. Names of persons and institutions are spelled according to how they are used in the community—that is, "Chofetz Chaim" and not "Hafez Hayyim." I have dropped the *h* at the end of words such as "yeshiva" or "Mishna" because they do not affect the pronunciation. Ashkenazic and Sephardic spelling vary according to common usage too. While I confess to a great degree of arbitrariness in the rules I have established, they have at least been applied consistently. Readers should be aware that certain terms such as *rosh yeshiva* or *beis medrash* have the more grammatically precise *ha* dropped because I tried to remain faithful to colloquial usage— that is, *rosh (ha)yeshiva.* I have sometimes capitalized "Yeshiva" when identifying schools even if that is not the official name of the yeshiva—Chaim Berlin Yeshiva instead of Yeshiva Rabbi

Chaim Berlin. Often, the schools themselves are inconsistent. Finally, I have relied on popular usages of plurals such as *rebbes* (not *rebbaim*), *rosh yeshivas* (not *roshei hayeshiva*), and so on.

am haaretz—in contemporary usage it refers to one unknowledgeable in Jewish law and is often used pejoratively.

amoraim—scholars who lived in the period between the Mishna's completion (about 200 C.E.) until the completion of the Talmud (about 400 C.E.).

apikorsus (*apikorus,* n.)—religious heresy.

baal habayis (*baalei batim,* pl.)—lay member of the community.

baal teshuva—one who "returns" to the faith.

bar mitzvah—confirmation.

bechina—examination.

beis medrash—house of study; the large hall in which talmudic study takes place within the yeshiva.

ben Torah (*b'nai Torah,* pl.)—literally, "son of the Torah," it denotes a young man who both studies Torah and who lives his life according to its precepts.

bochur (*bochorim,* pl.)—yeshiva student.

chachomim—sages.

chap—1. grasp 2. stump or stymie.

chasene—wedding.

chavrusa—study partner.

cheder—Hebrew elementary school.

chinuch—Jewish education.

chunyock—a pejorative term referring to a person who acts extremely religious in a cloying, perhaps overbearing, way.

daas Torah—the idea that certain great men, by virtue of their total immersion in the Torah, are best able to discern the truth and define it in relation to material life and its challenges, especially regarding problems facing the community.

derech—approach.

din—law.

frum—observant or religious.

gadol (*gedolim,* pl.)—giant in Torah scholarship, character, and personality and a leader of the "Torah community."

gaon—title given to heads of the talmudic academies in Sura and Pumbedita between 589 and 1040. It is also sometimes used as a synonym for *gadol*—that is, Vilna Gaon.

Gemora—analysis and interpretation of the Mishna. Sometimes, however, it is used loosely to refer to the entire Talmud.

glatt kosher—the most rigorous standard by which kosher food is evaluated.

halacha (*halachic,* adj.)—Jewish law.

Hashem—God.

hashkofoh—belief and value system (in a religious-spiritual sense).

Hasidism—an eighteenth-century religious movement emphasizing the value of spiritualism, prayer, and faith.

kashe—question.

kashrus—pertaining to food that is kosher (religiously permissible).

kavana—sincerity and emotion.

Kiddush Hashem—for the sanctification of God's name.

kiruv rechokim—bringing nonobservant Jews closer to the faith.

knas—a fine, or special penalty.

kollel—postgraduate institution for talmudic study.

kovod—honor.

leining—moving ahead in the talmudic text on one's own or with a learning partner.

loshon hora—gossip.

masechta—tractate or volume of the Talmud.

mashgiach—supervisor of a yeshiva.

mensch—a person who has made something of himself.

meshullach—fund-raiser.

mesivta—generally refers to a yeshiva high school for boys.

middos—ethical behavior or good deeds.

minyan—a quorum for prayer.

Mishna—interpretation of biblical law that, along with the *Gemora,* makes up the Talmud.

Misnagdim—a term describing those who opposed the Hasidim. *Misnagdim* were and are further differentiated by their greater emphasis upon talmudic study and by specific prayer rites.

mitzva—a religious commandment or good deed.

mussar—exhortations toward higher levels of ethical and moral behavior.

parnoseh—a livelihood.

rebbe (*rebbes* or *rebbaim,* pl.)—teacher in a yeshiva (also means leader of a Hasidic sect).

rosh yeshiva—head of a yeshiva.

sefer (*seforim,* pl.)—religious books.

semicha—rabbinical ordination.

Shabbos—Sabbath.

shadchan—matchmaker.

shema—a prayer expressing the Jew's faith in God that is recited several times a day by observant Jews.

shidduch—a marital match.

shiur—a Talmud class.

shmuess—a talk, that is, *mussar shmuess* (*mussar shmuessim,* pl.).

shtender—lightweight wooden lectern.

shtick—a certain way of doing things or interacting with people. It can mean acting in a whimsical manner or playing pranks on people. It is sometimes used pejoratively to describe an individual who behaves in a manner that seems arbitrary and even, perhaps, idiosyncratic. It can also refer to illegal or quasi-legal activities.

succah—branch-covered hut in which meals are eaten on the holiday of Succoth.

taaveh—temptation.

tachlis—for a specific purpose or with a goal in mind.

talis—prayer shawl.

talmid—(*talmidim,* pl.)—student.

talmid chochom—scholar.

Talmud—the 63-volume work that discusses and elaborates upon the Bible.

Talmud Torah—afternoon Hebrew school.

tannaim—scholars of the first two centuries C.E. who interpreted biblical law and who wrote the Mishna.

Torah—The Scriptures plus both Written and Oral Law, according to Pharisaic Judaism.

Torah lishmo—the study of Torah for a higher spiritual purpose (also referred to literally as "study for its own sake").

tzaddik—a saintly man (can also mean a Hasidic *rebbe*).

yarmulke—skullcap.

yeitzer horo—evil inclination or temptation.

yeshiva gedola—advanced yeshiva.

yichus—status derived from one's ancestry.

Selected Bibliography

THIS LISTING INCLUDES BOTH scholarly and popular sources, some of which are of high quality, and others that have been selected simply because they fill a gap in the literature. It is meant to be representative, not exhaustive, and will hopefully serve as a guide for both the researcher and the interested layman. Some works that do not focus primarily on yeshivas have been listed because it was felt that they have an important bearing on the institution.

ABRAHAMS, ISRAEL, *Jewish Life in the Middle Ages.* New York: Atheneum, 1969, pp. 340–372.

ADELSON, SAUL, "Chicago's Hebrew Theological College." *Jewish Life,* December 1947, pp. 43–48.

———, "From Volozhin to Jerusalem: An Appreciation of Rabbi Meir Bar Ilan (Berlin)." *Jewish Life,* June 1949, pp. 14–20.

AGUS, IRVING A., "Rabbinic Scholarship in Northern Europe," in Cecil Roth (ed.), *The World History of the Jewish People,* vol. 2, *The Dark Ages: 711–1096.* New Brunswick: Rutgers University Press, 1966, pp. 189–209.

———, "Rashi and his School," in Cecil Roth (ed.), *The World History of the Jewish People,* vol. 2, *The Dark Ages, 711–1096.* New Brunswick: Rutgers University Press, 1966, pp. 210–248.

ALON, GEDALYOHU, "The Lithuanian Yeshivas," trans. by Sid Z.

Leiman, in Judah Goldin (ed.), *The Jewish Expression*. New York: Bantam, 1970, pp. 448–464.

ASAF, SIMCHA, *Mekorot leToldot haHinukh beYisrael.*, vols. 1–4. Tel-Aviv and Jerusalem: Dvir, 1925–1942.

——, *Tekufat haGeonim véSafrutah*. Jerusalem: Mossad haRav Kook, 1955.

ASHTOR, ELIYAHU, *The History of the Jews in Moslem Spain*, vols. 1, 2. Philadelphia: Jewish Publication Society, 1973.

Association of Advanced Rabbinical and Talmudic Schools, New York. Contains various self-studies prepared by major contemporary advanced yeshivas. Organization founded in 1971.

BABAD, A. M., "Gateshead." *Jewish Life*, March–April 1953, pp. 27–33.

BAER, YITZCHAK, *A History of the Jews in Christian Spain*, vols. 1, 2. Philadelphia: Jewish Publication Society, 1961–1966.

BALGLEY, CHAIM LEIB, "Growing Up in Brisk. Remembering Reb Chaim Zatzal." *Jewish Observer*, September 1978, pp. 21–24.

——, "The Brisker Legacy." *Jewish Observer*, June 1979, pp. 20–24.

BECK, MORDECHAI, *Learning to Learn: A Guide to the New Yeshivot in Israel*, 2nd ed. Jerusalem: Israel Economist and World Union of Jewish Students, 1977.

BELSKY, YISROEL, "Our Alienated Brethren: What Can a Yeshiva Bochur Do?" *Jewish Observer*, June 1973, pp. 12–16.

BENEDICT, B. Z., "leToldotah shel Merkaz haTorah beProvence." *Tarbiz*, vol. 12 (1951), pp. 85–109.

BEN-SASSON, HAIM, "Lithuania—the Structure and Trends of Its Culture." *Encyclopedia Judaica Yearbook*, 1974, pp. 137–147.

BERKOVITZ, ELIEZER, "A Contemporary Rabbinical School for Orthodox Jewry." *Tradition*, Fall 1971, pp. 56–64.

BERKOWER, LARY R., "Emotional Problems of Yeshiva Students." *Tradition*, Fall 1974, pp. 80–89.

BERLIN, M., *Fun Volozhin biz Yerusholayim*, vols. 1, 2. New York: Orion Press, 1933.

BETTLEHEIM, S., "Geschichte der Pressburger Jeschiba," in H. Gold (ed.), *Die Juden und die Judengemeinde Bratislava in Vergangenheit und Gegenwart*. Brunn: Judischer Buchverlag., 1932, pp. 61–71.

BLASS, THOMAS, *Social Structure and Social Organization in a Rabbinical Seminary*, unpublished paper done for Professor J. Gumperz at Bernard Revel Graduate School, Yeshiva University, January 1967.

BREUER, MORDECHAI, *haYeshiva haAshkenazit beShlavei Yemai haBeinayim*, Ph.D. dissertation, Hebrew University, 1967.

BRICKMAN, WILLIAM W., "Samuel K. Mirsky's Contribution to Jewish Educational Historiography," in Gersion Appel (ed.), *Samuel K. Mirsky Memorial Volume: Studies in Jewish Law, Philosophy and Literature.* Jerusalem: Sura Institute for Research and New York: Yeshiva University Press, 1970, pp. 271-281.

BRIGGS, KENNETH A., "When May a Businessman Study Talmud?" *New York Times,* May 11, 1978, p. B1.

BURAK, MOSES L., *The Hatam Sofer.* Toronto: Beth Jacob Congregation, 1967.

CHARNA, S. J., *leToldot haHinukh beYisrael,* vol. 3. Jerusalem: Reuben Mass, 1939.

DAVIS, AVROHOM, "Fund Saving for Yeshivos." *Jewish Observer,* May 1967, p. 4.

———, "New Outposts of Torah." *Jewish Observer,* October 1968, pp. 14-15.

DRALITSCH, S., *Die Grundung der Judischebabylonischen Hochschulen Sura und Pumbadita und ihre Ersten Rektoren.* Vienna: Union, 1926.

DRAZIN, NATHAN, *History of Jewish Education from 515 B.C.E. to 220 C.E.* Baltimore: Johns Hopkins Press, 1940.

DUSHKIN, ALEXANDER, *Jewish Education in New York City.* New York: Bureau of Jewish Education, 1918.

EBNER, ELIEZER, "Simha Zissel Broida (Ziff)," in Leo Jung (ed.), *Guardians of Our Heritage.* New York: Bloch, 1958, pp. 319-335.

EGOZI, AKIBA, "Beit Medrash Govoha beLakewood." *Shevilei haHinukh,* Winter 1962, p. 120.

EISENSTEIN, MIRIAM, *Jewish Schools in Poland, 1919-1939.* New York: King's Crown Press, 1950.

EVER, ISAAC, *hoRav Yehuda Heschel Levenberg: Zein Leben und Kamf.* Cleveland: Ivry, 1939.

FASMAN, OSCAR Z., "Trends in the American Yeshiva Today." *Tradition,* Fall 1967, pp. 48-64.

FEITMAN, YAAKOV, "The Ohr Sameach—Fifty Years Since His Passing." *Jewish Observer,* September 1976, p. 3-9.

FELDMAN, EMANUEL, "The American Yeshiva *Bochur*." *Jewish Parent,* April 1959, p. 12.

———, "Trends in the American Yeshivot: A Rejoinder." *Tradition,* Spring 1968, pp. 56-64.

FINKELSTEIN, R., "The Rabbi and the Ben Torah." *Jewish Observer,* October 1967, pp. 14-15.

FISCH, DOV, "Ye Shall Be Accountants and Yea, Even Doctors." *Hamevaser,* May 17, 1979, p. 12.

FISHMAN, ISIDORE, *The History of Jewish Education in Central Europe: From the End of the Sixteenth Century to the End of the Eighteenth Century.* London: Goldston, 1944.

FRIEDMAN, ARMIN, *Major Aspects of Yeshiva Education in Hungary, 1848-1948,* Ph.D. dissertation, Yeshiva University, 1971.

FRIEDMAN, M. Y., "The Ben Torah's Dilemma: The Problem of the Divided Selfs." *Jewish Observer,* October 1973, pp. 3-7.

FRYSHMAN, BERNARD, "On Butchers, Bakers, and Candlestick Makers." *Jewish Observer,* September 1976, pp. 13-18.

FUCHS, SYLVIA, "And Now a Word from *Our* Fathers." *Jewish Observer,* January 1978, pp. 16-19.

GARTNER, LLOYD P., *Jewish Education in the United States: A Documentary History.* New York: Teachers College Press, 1969.

GERZ, M., "The Old Man of Slobodka" (trans.), in Lucy Dawidowicz (ed.), *The Golden Tradition: Jewish Life and Thought in Eastern Europe.* Boston: Beacon Press, 1967, pp. 179-185.

GINZBERG, LOUIS, *Students, Scholars, and Saints.* Philadelphia: Jewish Publication Society, 1928.

GOLDBERG, HILLEL, "The Last Mashgiach of Slobodka." *Jewish Observer,* June 1976, pp. 11-12.

GOLDIN, JUDAH, "The Period of the Talmud (135 B.C.E.-1035 C.E.)," in Louis Finkelstein (ed.), *The Jews: Their History, Culture, and Religion.* New York: Harper & Row, 1949, pp. 115-215.

GOLDMAN, ARI, "At Yeshiva, Study for Study's Sake." *New York Times,* Sunday Section 12, April 30, 1978, p. 5.

GOLDMAN, ISRAEL M., *Lifelong Learning Among Jews.* New York: Ktav, 1975.

GORDON, BENJAMIN, *Between Two Worlds.* New York: Bookman, 1952.

GRADE, CHAIM, *The Yeshiva,* vols. 1, 2. New York: Menorah ed., 1979.

GREENBERG, MENACHEM, "The Yeshiva World's Outlook on Torah and Secular Studies." *Jewish Observer,* December 1969, pp. 11-14.

GREENBERG, SIMON, "Jewish Educational Institutions," in Louis Finkelstein (ed.), *The Jews: Their History, Culture, and Religion,* vol. 2. New York: Harper & Row, 1949, pp. 1234-1253.

GREENFIELD, MENACHEM, "The Rebbe-Talmid Relationship." *Jewish Observer,* June 1979, pp. 8-11.

GROSS, ALEXANDER, AND JOSEPH KAMINETSKY, "Shraga Feivel Mendlowitz," in Leo Jung (ed.), *Men of the Spirit.* New York: Bloch, 1964, pp. 553-561.

GROSSMAN, DAVID, "Machon Yerushalayim: Kollel Manpower at Work." *Jewish Observer,* February 1979, pp. 22-24.

GRUNSFELD, J., "Neue Geschichte der Jeschiba," in H. Gold (ed.), *Die Juden und die Judengemeinde Bratislava in Vergangenheit und Gegenwart.* Brunn: Judischer Buchverlag, 1932, pp. 67–70.

GUEDEMANN, MORITZ, *Geschichte des Erziehungswesens und der Kultur der abendländischen Juden wahrend des Mittelalters,* 3 vols. Vienna: Holder, 1888.

HELMREICH, WILLIAM B., *Wake Up, Wake Up to Do the Work of the Creator.* New York: Harper & Row, 1976.

HERZMAN, CHUNA, "From Mir to Shanghai." *Jewish Observer,* January 1967, pp. 10–13.

HIRSCHBERG, H. Z., *A History of the Jews of North Africa,* vol. 1. Leiden: Brill, 1974, pp. 298–361.

HOENIG, SIDNEY, *The Great Sanhedrin.* Philadelphia: Dropsie College, 1953.

HOFFSMEYER, BENJAMIN, *Rabbi Chaim Tchernowitz: "Rav Tzair" and the Yeshiva of Odessa,* Ph.D. dissertation (Hebrew), Yeshiva University, 1967.

HOLLANDER, C. T., "The Telsher Yeshiva." *Jewish Parent,* March 1957, pp. 12–13;25.

HORODETSKI, S. A., *Lekorot haRabbanut.* Warsaw: Tushiya, 1914.

"Hundert Yohr Telzer Yeshiva." *Dos Yiddishe Vort,* December 1975: 17–28.

JAZKAN, S. J., *Rabbenu Eliyahu miVilnah,* Warsaw: Sokolow, 1900.

KAGAN, J. L., AND H. B. PERLMAN, "Hayyim Ozer Grodzenski (1863–1940)," in Leo Jung (ed.), *Jewish Leaders (1750–1940).* New York: Bloch, 1953, pp. 435–455.

KAMENETSKY, YAAKOV, "Filling the Void: Reflections on the Passing of a Gadol." *Jewish Observer,* October 1976, pp. 15–19.

KAPLAN, ARYEH, "The Partnership: Variations on the Yissachar-Zevulun Theme." *Jewish Observer,* January 1978, pp. 23–26.

———, "Who Shall Render the Decisions?: Meeting the Needs." *Jewish Observer,* June 1978, pp. 8–11.

KATZBURG, N., "Yeshivat Pressburg: Kavim liDemutah," *Sinai,* vol. 12, nos. 5, 6 (1949), pp. 352–358.

KATZ, DOV, *Tenuat haMussar,* 5 vols. Tel-Aviv: Bitan haSefer, Abraham Tzioni, 1952–1963.

KELLER, CHAIM DOV, "Is the Ben Torah Meeting His Obligations to the American Jewish Society?" *Jewish Observer,* May 1967, pp. 3–6.

———, "Reb Eliahu Meir Bloch." *Jewish Observer,* September 1977, pp. 6–13.

————, "When the Sun Set at Midday: An Appreciation of Rabbi Raphoel Boruch Sorotzkin." *Jewish Observer,* April 1979, pp. 11-16.

KIMMEL, M., "The History of Yeshivat Rabbi Chaim Berlin." *Sheviley haHinukh,* Fall 1948, pp. 51-54.

KIRZNER, ISRAEL M., "The Utilitarian View of the Yeshiva: A Complaint." *Jewish Observer,* September 1965, pp. 12-14.

KLAPERMAN, GILBERT, *The Story of Yeshiva University.* New York: Macmillan, 1969.

KLUGMAN, ELIYAHU M., "A Tribute to Rabbi Chaim Leib Shmulevitz." *Jewish Observer,* February 1979, pp. 9-17.

KOSSOWSKY, M., "HaYeshiva b'Yeshiva," in Simon Bernstein and Gershon A. Churgin (eds.), *Sefer Yovel leKovod Shmuel Kalman Mirsky.* New York: Vaad haYovel, 1958, pp. 313-327.

KRANZLER, DAVID, *Japanese, Nazis, and Jews: The Refugee Community of Shanghai, 1938-1945.* New York: Yeshiva University Press, 1976.

KRANZLER, GERSHON, "Challenge and Commitment." *Jewish Observer,* April 1978, pp. 3-6.

LASDUN, TUVIA, AND LEO DAVIDS, "The Way of Telz." *Jewish Life,* October 1958, pp. 55-60.

LASSON, MOSHE, "Yeshiva Teaching—Vocation or—Avocation?" *Jewish Observer,* October 1969, pp. 9-11.

————, "Alienation Among Yeshiva Youth." *Jewish Observer,* September 1970, pp. 12-15.

LEIMAN, SHNAYER Z., "The Campus Problem and Jewish Education." *Jewish Life,* March–April 1968, pp. 22-28.

LEVIN, LEO, "Can a College Education Supplement the Yeshiva Program? *Jewish Parent,* October 1959, p. 12.

LEVY, ARNOLD, *The Story of Gateshead Yeshiva.* Somerset, Eng.: Wessex Press, 1952.

LEWIS, THEODORE, "Reminiscences of Mir Yeshiva." *Jewish Life,* February 1949, pp. 6-12.

LIBER, MAURICE, *Rashi,* trans. by Adele Szold. New York: Hermon Press, 1970.

LIEBMAN, CHARLES S., "Orthodoxy in American Jewish Life," in M. Fine and M. Himmelfarb (eds.), *American Jewish Yearbook,* vol. 66. Philadelphia: Jewish Publication Society, 1965, pp. 21-97.

————, "The Training of American Rabbis," in M. Fine and M. Himmelfarb (eds.), *American Jewish Yearbook,* vol. 69. Philadelphia: Jewish Publication Society, 1968, pp. 3-112.

LUBINSKY, MENACHEM, "Orthodox Vocational Guidance: Is There a Need?" *Jewish Observer,* June 1976, pp. 28–31.

MALLER, JULIUS B., "The Role of Education in Jewish History," in L. Finkelstein (ed.), *The Jews: Their History, Culture, and Religion,* vol. 2. New York: Harper & Row, 1949, pp. 1234–1253.

MANTEL, HUGO, *Studies in the History of the Sanhedrin.* Cambridge: Harvard University Press, 1961.

MARCUS, S., *Die Paedagogik des Israelitischen Volkes,* 2 vols. Vienna: Bruder Winter, 1877.

MAYER, EGON, *From Suburb to Shtetl: The Jews of Boro Park.* Philadelphia: Temple University Press, 1979, esp. pp. 111–134.

MENES, ABRAHAM, "Patterns of Jewish Scholarship in Eastern Europe," in Louis Finkelstein (ed.), *The Jews: Their History, Culture, and Religion,* vol. 1. New York: Harper & Row, 1949, pp. 376–426.

———, "Yeshivas in Russia," in J. Frunkin, G. Aronson, and A. Goldenweiser (eds.), *Russian Jewry (1860–1917),* 2 vols. New York: Yosseloff, 1966–1969, pp. 382–407.

MIRSKY, SAMUEL K. (ed.), *Mosdot Torah beAiropah beVinyanam ubeHurbanam.* New York: Histadrut haIvrit beAmerica, 1956.

———, "Isaac Elhanan Spector," in Leo Jung (ed.), *Guardians of Our Heritage, 1724–1953.* New York: Bloch, 1958, pp. 301–316.

———, "Types of Lectures in the Babylonian Academies," in Joseph L. Blau et al. (eds.), *Essays on Jewish Life and Thought.* New York: Columbia University Press, 1959, pp. 375–402.

MYKOFF, DAVID, "Are We Preparing Torah Communicators?: Salesman or Sage—Who Will They Listen To?" *Jewish Observer,* February 1968, pp. 3–4.

NARDI, N., *Zionism and Education in Palestine.* New York: Teachers College Press, Columbia University, 1934.

NEUSNER, JACOB, *A History of the Jews in Babylonia,* 5 vols. Leiden: Brill, 1965–1970.

———, *There We Sat Down.* New York: Abingdon, 1972.

NEWMAN, ARYEH, "Rabbi Jacob Reines—Torah Statesman and Educational Trailblazer." *Jewish Life,* January–February 1966, pp. 20–25.

PAM, AVROHOM, "The Yeshiva Graduate's Obligation." *Jewish Observer,* June 1979, pp. 3–4.

PELCOVITZ, RALPH, "The Rabbi and the Rosh Yeshiva." *Jewish Observer,* October 1967, pp. 12–14.

PERR, YECHIEL J., "The Yeshiva World and Orthodoxy: Self Protection or Encounter?" *Jewish Observer,* 1970, pp. 22–23.

PORTER, JACK NUSAN AND SHLOMO SENDER PORTER, "The Last of the Big Time Collectors." *Genesis 2,* vol. 8, no. 6 (1977), p. 3.

RABINOWICZ, H. M., "Yeshivoth in Poland in the Inter-War Years." *Jewish Life,* March–April 1964, pp. 53–59.

REINES, CHAIM W., "Public Support of Rabbis, Scholars, and Students in the Jewish Past." *YIVO Annual of Jewish Social Science,* vol. 3 (1952), pp. 84–109.

——, "Isaac Jacob Reines," in Leo Jung (ed.), *Jewish Leaders.* New York: Bloch, 1953, pp. 275–293.

ROKEACH, M., "The Kollel: American Phase." *Jewish Life,* May–June 1963, pp. 13–21.

ROSENBAUM, BEINISH, "The Novominsker Rebbe as Seen Through the Eyes of a Talmid." *Jewish Observer,* December 1976, pp. 13–14.

ROTHKOFF, AARON, "Rabbi Shimon Shkop." *Jewish Life,* November–December 1966, pp. 31–36.

——, "Chaim Ozer Grodzenski." *Jewish Life,* May–June 1967, pp. 40–49.

——, "The 'Meitsheter Illui,'" *Jewish Life,* November–December 1967, pp. 29–35.

——, "The Last Rabbi of Kovno." *Jewish Life,* March–April 1968, pp. 35–40.

——, "The 'Saba' from Slobodka." *Jewish Life,* November–December 1970, pp. 34–42.

——, "Rav Isser Zalman Meltzer." *Jewish Life,* March–April 1971, pp. 51–57.

——, *Bernard Revel: Builder of American Jewish Orthodoxy.* Philadelphia: Jewish Publication Society, 1972.

SACHS, ABRAHAM S., *Worlds That Passed.* Philadelphia: Jewish Publication Society, 1928.

SAMUEL, J. A., "Yeshiva or College." *Jewish Parent,* April 1959, p. 12.

SCHARFSTEIN, ZVI, *Toldot haHinukh beYisrael beDorot haAharonim,* 2 vols. Jerusalem: Reuben Mass, 1950–1962.

SCHEINMAN, A., "Growing into Marriage." *Jewish Observer,* January 1979, pp. 13–16.

SCHERMAN, NOSSON, "The Rabbi and the Rosh Yeshiva: A Look at Their Respective Roles in American Jewish Life." *Jewish Observer,* June 1964, pp. 14–16.

———, "One Hundred Years Since the Chofetz Chaim." *Jewish Observer,* January 1972, pp. 3–8.

———, "An Appreciation of Rabbi Gedalia Schorr: An American-Bred Torah Giant." *Jewish Observer,* October 1979, pp. 8–17.

SCHICK, MARVIN, "Yeshiva Graduates: Their Emergent Role." *Jewish Observer,* January 1964, pp. 7–8, 20.

SCHOSTAK, ZEV, "The Yeshiva of Tomorrow." *Jewish Observer,* June 1979, p. 5–7.

SCHWARTZ, ELKANAH, "Two Lecterns." *Jewish Observer,* February 1964, pp. 12–13.

———, "The Gap and the Revolution." *Jewish Life,* July–August 1967, pp. 40–52.

———, "My Student, My Teacher." *Jewish Observer,* May 1972, pp. 22–24.

SEIDMAN, HILLEL, *Shraga Feivel Mendlowitz* (Hebrew). New York: Shengold, 1976.

SHAPIRO, CHAIM, "Reb Yisroel Yaakov: The Mashgiach of Baranovich." *Jewish Observer,* June 1970, pp. 15–18.

———, "A Rosh Yeshiva in Baranovich: Reb Dovid Rapoport." *Jewish Observer,* January 1973, pp. 19–24.

———, "Escape from Europe: A Chronicle of Miracles." *Jewish Observer,* May 1973, pp. 20–24.

———, "My Years with Reb Elchonon: A Talmid Recalls His Years in Baranovitch." *Jewish Observer,* October 1973, pp. 12–17.

———, "Lomza: A Yeshiva Grew in Poland." *Jewish Observer,* March 1974, pp. 13–16.

———, "Torah Pioneers." *Jewish Observer,* June 1974, pp. 17–21.

———, "The Prince of Roshei Yeshiva: Rabbi Yechiel Mordechai Gordon." *Jewish Observer,* January–February 1976, pp. 15–19.

———, "Reb Chaim Ozer Grodzensky." *Jewish Observer,* June 1976, pp. 21–27.

———, "The World of Novardok. "*Jewish Observer,* February–March, 1977, pp. 31–37.

———, "Rabbi Yerucham Levovitz." *Jewish Observer,* June 1977, pp. 18–23.

———, "Reb Pesach Pruskin: Rav and Rosh Yeshiva of Kubrin." *Jewish Observer,* June 1978, pp. 18–21.

———, "Tiktin, Poland." *Jewish Observer,* December 1978, pp. 17–24.

SHAPIRO, DAVID S. "Secular Studies and Judaism." *Tradition,* Summer 1966, pp. 15–39.

SHENKER, SAUL, "Released Time: What's It Worth? *Jewish Observer,* March 1975, pp. 14–16.

SHIMOFF, EPHRAIM, *Rabbi Isaac Elhanan Spektor.* New York: Sura Institute and Yeshiva University, 1959.

SHURIN, ISRAEL, "Rabbi Yehuda Heschel Levenberg." *Olomeinu,* January 1975, pp. 14–15.

SILVER, MARC, "Giving Up the Assimilated Life: A First Hand Report on American Jews at a Jerusalem Yeshiva." *Baltimore Jewish Times,* January 20, 1978, pp. 32–43.

SIMON, SOLOMON, *In the Thicket.* Philadelphia: Jewish Publication Society, 1963.

SINGER, DAVID, "The Yeshivah World." *Commentary,* October 1976, pp. 70–73.

SOBEL, BERNARD, *The M'lochim: A Study of a Religious Community,* Master's thesis, New School for Social Research, 1956.

SONDHELM, URI, "Why Not Wednesday?" *Jewish Observer,* September 1975, pp. 9–12.

STEINBERG, MILTON, *As a Driven Leaf.* New York: Behrman House, 1939.

SURASKY, AHARON, *Marbeitzei Torah uMussar.* New York: Sentry Press, 1977.

TURK, MOSHE, "Bringing Torah to the Valley." *Jewish Observer,* October 1977, pp. 21–25.

TWERSKI, AARON, "In Flight from Confrontation." *Jewish Observer,* February–March 1977, pp. 7–10.

TWERSKY, ISIDORE, *Rabad of Posquieres.* Cambridge: Harvard University Press, 1962.

———, "Aspects of the Social and Cultural History of Provencal Jewry," in H. H. Ben-Sasson and S. Ettinger (eds.), *Jewish Society Through the Ages.* New York: Schocken, 1971, pp. 185–207.

URBACH, E. E., "The Talmudic Sage—Character and Authority," in H. H. Ben-Sasson and S. Ettinger (eds.), *Jewish Society Through the Ages.* New York: Schocken, 1971, pp. 116–147.

UZIEL, BEN ZION, "Al haYeshivot beYisrael." *Sura,* 1953–1954, pp. 304–318.

VISHNITZER, M., "haOmer leToldot haYeshiva beAiropah haMizrachit biShnot 1919–1939." *Talpioth,* no. 5 (1950), pp. 157–175.

WASSERMAN, SIMCHA, "Postscripts: Our Responsibility to the Baal Teshuva." *Jewish Observer,* February 1979, pp. 18–21.

WAXMAN, MEYER, "The Gaon of Vilna." *Jewish Life,* October 1948, pp. 17–24.

WEIN, BEREL, "The American Rabbinate: Is being a Rabbi Really 'No Job for a Jewish Boy'?" *Jewish Observer,* March 1964, pp. 11–13.

———, "The American Rabbinate—Revisited." *Jewish Observer,* April 1965, pp. 11–12.

WEINBERG, NOACH, "The Teshuva Phenomenon: II. 'It's Time to Go Professional." *Jewish Observer,* June 1977, pp. 14–17.

WEISBROD, M., "From 'The Diary of a Judaic Studies Student." *Jewish Observer,* March–April 1972, pp. 23–25.

WEISS, GERSHON, "A European Mashgiach in an American Yeshiva." *Jewish Observer,* March 1975, pp. 10–13.

WEISS, I. H., *Dor Dor veDorshav,* 4 vols. Warsaw: Romm, 1904.

WIKLER, MEIR, "Preparation for Marriage: A Prevention for Divorce." *Jewish Observer,* January 1979, pp. 9–13.

WILLIS, ELLEN, "Next Year in Jerusalem." *Rolling Stone,* April 21, 1977, p. 64,.

WOLBE, SHLOMO, "The Yeshiva Today: The Significance of This Institution Throughout Our History—and in Our Days." *Jewish Observer,* May 1970, pp. 8–10, 23.

WOLPIN, H. D., "KOLLEL U.S.A.: A New Look Inside a New-Old Torah Institution." *Jewish Observer,* December 1965, pp. 9–11.

WOLPIN, NISSON, "The Community Kollel: Reaching Out with Torah." *Jewish Observer,* October 1979, pp. 19–26.

ZIMMELS, H. J., "Scholars and Scholarship in Byzantium and Italy," in Cecil Roth (ed.), *The World History of the Jewish People,* vol. 2, *The Dark Ages, 711–1096.* New Brunswick, N.J.: Rutgers University Press, 1966, pp. 189–209.

ZINOWITZ, M., *Toldot, Yeshivat Volozhin: Moraho, Hayeho, Talmideho, veToratha.* Tel-Aviv: MVR, 1972.

ZUROFF, EFRAIM, "Rescue Priority and Fund Rasing as Issues During the Holocaust: A Case Study of the Relations Between the Vaad Hatzala and the Joint, 1939–1941." *American Jewish History,* March 1979, pp. 305–326.

Index